Defining Digital Humanities

For
Anthony, Edward and Fergusson,
Clara and Joey,
and
Wonne and Senne

Defining Digital Humanities
A Reader

Edited by

MELISSA TERRAS

JULIANNE NYHAN

EDWARD VANHOUTTE

Routledge
Taylor & Francis Group

LONDON AND NEW YORK

First published 2013 by Ashgate Publishing

Published 2016 by Routledge
2 Park Square, Milton Park, Abingdon, Oxon OX14 4RN
711 Third Avenue, New York, NY 10017, USA

Routledge is an imprint of the Taylor & Francis Group, an informa business

British Library Cataloguing in Publication Data
A catalogue record for this book is available from the British Library

The Library of Congress has cataloged the printed edition as follows:
Defining digital humanities : a reader / [edited] by Melissa Terras, Julianne Nyhan, and Edward Vanhoutte.
    pages cm
  Includes bibliographical references and index.
  ISBN 978-1-4094-6962-9 (hardback) – ISBN 978-1-4094-6963-6 (pbk)
  1. Humanities–Data processing.
  2. Humanities–Research–Data processing. 3. Information storage and retrieval systems–Humanities. 4. Humanities–Electronic information resources.
  I. Terras, Melissa M. II. Nyhan, Julianne. III. Vanhoutte, Edward.

  AZ105.D44 2013
  001.30285–dc23

                                                                    2013020285

ISBN 9781409469629 (hbk)
ISBN 9781409469636 (pbk)

Contents

SECTION III: FROM THE BLOGOSPHERE

SECTION IV: VOICES FROM THE COMMUNITY

SECTION V: FURTHER MATERIALS

Acknowledgements

The editors and publishers wish to thank the following for permission to use copyright and previously published material.

The Alliance of Digital Humanities Organizations and the authors for the articles: Julia Flanders (2009), 'The Productive Unease of 21st-century Digital Scholarship', *Digital Humanities Quarterly*, 3 (3). Wendell Piez (2008), 'Something Called Digital Humanities', *Digital Humanities Quarterly*, 2 (1). Paul S. Rosenbloom (2012), 'Toward a Conceptual Framework for the Digital Humanities', *Digital Humanities Quarterly*, 6 (2). Patrick Svensson (2009), 'Humanities Computing as Digital Humanities', *Digital Humanities Quarterly*, 3 (3).

Chris Forster for the blog post: 'I'm Chris, Where Am I Wrong?'

Fred Gibbs for the article: 'Digital Humanities Definitions by Type'.

Mentis for the article: John Unsworth (2002), 'What is Humanities Computing and What is Not?', *Jahrbuch für Computerphilologie*, 4.

Lincoln Mullen for the blog post: 'Digital Humanities is a Spectrum, or "We're All Digital Humanists Now"'.

Bethany Nowviskie for the blog post: 'ADHO, On Love and Money'.

Oxford Journals and the authors for the articles: Willard McCarty (2006), 'Tree, Turf, Centre, Archipelago – or Wild Acre? Metaphors and Stories for Humanities Computing', *Literary and Linguistic Computing*, 21 (1). Melissa Terras (2006), 'Disciplined: Using Educational Studies to Analyse "Humanities Computing"', *Literary and Linguistic Computing*, 21 (2).

Stephen Ramsay for the blog posts: 'Who's In and Who's Out' and 'On Building'.

Geoffrey Rockwell for the article: (1999), 'Is Humanities Computing an Academic Discipline?' originally published at http://www.iath.virginia.

edu/hcs/rockwell.html and for the blog post 'Inclusion in the Digital Humanities'.

Mark Sample for the blog post: 'The Digital Humanities is not about Building, it's about Sharing'.

Melissa Terras for the blog post: 'Peering Inside the Big Tent'.

TEXT Technology and the author for the article: Jerome J. McGann (2005), 'Information Technology and the Troubled Humanities', *TEXT Technology*, 14 (2).

The Modern Language Association of America for the article: Matthew Kirschenbaum (2010), 'What is Digital Humanities and What's it Doing in English Departments', *ADE Bulletin*, 150.

Notes on Contributors

Julia Flanders is the Director of the Brown University Women Writers Project and co-founder and editor-in-chief of *Digital Humanities Quarterly*. Her research focuses on text encoding, digital scholarly editing, and the politics of digital scholarship.

Chris Forster is Assistant Professor of Twentieth-Century British Literature at Syracuse University. His current research focuses on modernist literature and the history of obscenity. He also has interests extending into digital humanities. He sometimes blogs about such matters at cforster.com.

Fred Gibbs is Director of Digital Scholarship at the Roy Rosenzweig Center for History and New Media, and Assistant Professor in the History and Art History Department at George Mason University. He explores the application of new digital technologies and methodologies to historical research, and how to employ theories of new media in service of transforming scholarly publishing.

Matthew G. Kirschenbaum is Associate Professor in the Department of English at the University of Maryland and Associate Director of the Maryland Institute for Technology in the Humanities (MITH). He is a 2011 Guggenheim Fellow and a member of the teaching faculty at the Rare Book School. His current book project is entitled *Track-Changes: A Literary History of Word Processing*, and is under contract to Harvard University Press. See http://www.mkirschenbaum.net or follow him on Twitter as @mkirschenbaum for more.

Willard McCarty is Professor of Humanities Computing, King's College London; Professor, University of Western Sydney; Fellow of the Royal Anthropological Institute; Editor of the on-line seminar *Humanist* and of the British Journal *Interdisciplinary Science Reviews*. In 2005 he received the Canadian Award for Outstanding Achievement, Computing in the Arts and Humanities, in 2006 the Richard W. Lyman Award and in 2013 the Roberto Busa Award. His current book project, *Machines of Demanding Grace*, argues for the human as a central concern of the digital humanities. See www.mccarty.org.uk.

Jerome McGann is the John Stewart Bryan University Professor, University of Virginia. He was co-founder of IATH (Institute for Advanced Technology in the Humanities) and the founding director of NINES (Networked Infrastructure for Nineteenth-century Electronic Scholarship). His book *Radiant Textuality. Literature after the Worldwide Web* was awarded the MLA's 2002 James Russell Lowell Prize. He is the editor of the online *Complete Writings and Pictures of Dante Gabriel Rossetti. A Hypermedia Research Archive* (1992–2008) and *Online Humanities Scholarship. The Shape of Things to Come* (2010). A new book, *Memory Now. Philology in a New Key* is in press and he has begun to collaborate on a new online project, *The American World of James Fenimore Cooper.*

Lincoln Mullen is a PhD candidate in the Department of History at Brandeis University, and a historian of American religion. He is writing a dissertation on converts between religion in the nineteenth-century United States. He is also the web editor of *The Journal of Southern Religion*, an open-access scholarly journal.

Bethany Nowviskie is Director of the Scholars' Lab and Department of Digital Research and Scholarship at the University of Virginia Library, where she also serves as associate director of the Scholarly Communication Institute. Nowviskie is President of the Association for Computers and the Humanities and a long-time digital humanities practitioner, focusing on textual materiality, humanities interpretation, and academic labour. Her projects include Neatline, NINES/Collex, the Rossetti Archive, #Alt-Academy, Digital Humanities Questions and Answers, Juxta, the Ivanhoe Game, and Temporal Modelling. See http://nowviskie.org and follow on Twitter @nowviskie.

Julianne Nyhan is lecturer in Digital Information Studies in the Department of Information Studies, University College London. Her research interests include the history of computing in the humanities and most aspects of digital humanities with special emphasis on meta-markup languages and digital lexicography. Most recently she has co-edited *Digital Humanities in Practice* (Facet 2012 http://www.facetpublishing.co.uk/title.php?id=7661). Among other things, she is a member of AHRC's Peer Review College, a member of the European Science Foundation's expert working group on Research Infrastructures in the Humanities and European Liaison manager in the UCL Centre for Digital Humanities. She is at work on an Oral History of Computing in the Humanities. Read her blog at http://archelogos.hypotheses.org/ and follow her on Twitter @juliannenyhan.

Wendell Piez is a designer and builder of electronic publishing systems, a leading practitioner of XSLT, and has developed XML tag sets and applications for both documentary publishing (such as journals and conference proceedings) and for more highly structured information processing systems. Piez has a PhD in English, and has worked at the Center for Electronic Texts in the Humanities (Rutgers and Princeton Universities) and Mulberry Technologies Inc. Since 2008 he has served as adjunct faculty at the Graduate School for Library and Information Science (GSLIS) at the University of Illinois. Piez has published widely and is co-founder and General Editor of *Digital Humanities Quarterly*. See http://www.wendellpiez.com.

Stephen Ramsay is Susan J. Rosowski University Associate Professor of English and a Fellow at the Center for Digital Research in the Humanities at the University of Nebraska-Lincoln. He is the author of *Reading Machines: Toward an Algorithmic Criticism* (University of Illinois Press, 2011).

Geoffrey Martin Rockwell is a Professor of Philosophy and Humanities Computing at the University of Alberta, Canada. He has published and presented papers in the area of philosophical dialogue, textual visualization and analysis, humanities computing, instructional technology, computer games and multimedia including a book, *Defining Dialogue: From Socrates to the Internet*. He is currently the Interim Director of the Kule Institute for Advanced Studies and a network investigator in the GRAND Network of Centres of Excellence that is studying gaming, animation and new media. He is collaborating with Stéfan Sinclair on Voyant, a suite of text analysis tools at http://voyant-tools.org and *Hermeneutica*, a book/ website about text analysis.

Paul S. Rosenbloom is Professor of Computer Science at the University of Southern California and a project leader at USC's Institute for Creative Technologies. He was a key member of USC's Information Sciences Institute for two decades, leading new directions activities over the second decade, and finishing his time there as Deputy Director. Earlier he was on the faculty at Carnegie Mellon University (where he also received his PhD) and Stanford University (where he also received his BS). His research concentrates on cognitive architectures – models of the fixed structure underlying minds, whether natural or artificial – and on understanding the nature, structure and stature of computing as a scientific domain. He is the author of *On Computing: The Fourth Great Scientific Domain* (MIT Press, 2012).

Mark L. Sample is associate professor of English at George Mason University, where he teaches and researches contemporary literature and new media. Mark is also an affiliated faculty member with Mason's Honors College, its Cultural Studies programme, and the Center for History and New Media. Mark's most recent project is *10 PRINT CHR$(205.5+RND(1)); : GOTO 10*, a collaboratively written book about creative computing and the Commodore 64, which was published by MIT Press in November 2012. See http://www.samplereality.com or follow him on Twitter as @samplereality.

Patrik Svensson is a Professor in the Humanities and Information Technology, and director of HUMlab at Umeå University, Sweden. As the director of HUMlab, Svensson is deeply engaged in facilitating cross-sectional meetings and innovation, in the future of the humanities and the university, and in the intersection of the humanities, culture and information technology. Svensson's research interests span information technology and learning, research infrastructure, screen cultures, and the digital humanities as an emerging field.

Melissa Terras is Director of University College London Centre for Digital Humanities and Professor of Digital Humanities in UCL's Department of Information Studies. With a background in Classical Art History, English Literature, and Computing Science, her doctorate (Engineering, University of Oxford) examined how to use advanced information engineering technologies to interpret and read Roman texts. Publications include *Image to Interpretation: Intelligent Systems to Aid Historians in the Reading of the Vindolanda Texts* (2006, Oxford University Press), *Digital Images for the Information Professional* (2008, Ashgate) and *Digital Humanities in Practice* (2012, Facet). She is the co-founder and General Editor of *Digital Humanities Quarterly* journal, the secretary of The European Association of Digital Humanities, and on the board of the Alliance of Digital Humanities Organizations. Her research focuses on the use of computational techniques to enable research in the Arts and Humanities that would otherwise be impossible. You can generally find her on Twitter @melissaterras.

John Unsworth is Vice-Provost for Library and Technology Services and Chief Information Officer at Brandeis University. From 2003 to 2012 he was Dean of the Graduate School of Library and Information Science (GSLIS) at the University of Illinois, Urbana-Champaign. In addition to being a Professor in GSLIS, at Illinois he also held appointments in the department of English and on the Library faculty; also, from 2008 to 2011, he served as Director of the Illinois Informatics Institute. From 1993 to 2003, he served as the first Director of the Institute for Advanced Technology in the Humanities, and a faculty member in the English Department, at the University of Virginia. For his work at IATH, he received the 2005 Richard W. Lyman Award from the National Humanities Center. His first faculty appointment was in English, at North Carolina State University, from 1989 to 1993. He attended Princeton University and Amherst College as an undergraduate, graduating from Amherst in 1981. He received a Master's degree in English from Boston University in 1982 and a PhD in English from the University of Virginia in 1988. In 1990, at NCSU, he co-founded the first peer-reviewed electronic journal in the humanities, *Postmodern Culture* (now published by Johns Hopkins University Press, as part of Project Muse). He also organised, incorporated and chaired the Text Encoding Initiative Consortium, co-chaired the Modern Language Association's Committee on Scholarly Editions, and served as President of the Association for Computers and the Humanities and later as chair of the steering committee for the Alliance of Digital Humanities Organizations, as well as serving on many other editorial and advisory boards. More information is available at http://www3.isrl.uiuc.edu/~unsworth.

Edward Vanhoutte is currently Director of Research and Publications in the Royal Academy of Dutch Language and Literature – KANTL (Gent, Belgium), Editor-in-Chief of *LLC: The Journal of Digital Scholarship in the Humanities*, and a Research Associate of the University College of London Centre for Digital Humanities (UCLDH). He is the editor of ten (digital) scholarly editions, the co-editor of the *DALF Guidelines for the Description and Encoding of Modern Correspondence Material*, and the co-author of *TEI by Example*, http://www.teibyexample.org. His research interests include textual scholarship, (digital) scholarly editing, genetic editing, text encoding and the markup of modern manuscript material next to his overall interest in the history of the field now called the Digital Humanities. He publishes, lectures and blogs widely on these subjects. See http://www.edwardvanhoutte.org or follow him on Twitter @evanhoutte.

Introduction

Julianne Nyhan and Melissa Terras
University College London, UK

Edward Vanhoutte
Royal Academy of Dutch Language & Literature, Belgium
University College London, UK

Searchinge out a holiday gifte for yower academic frendes? Thei maye enjoye a definicioun of the digital humanities.
(Chaucer Doth Tweet (@LeVostreGC), 8 December 2012
https://twitter.com/LeVostreGC/status/277501777182613504)

Much has been written about how digital humanities might be defined but, for those new to the discipline, where does one start in tackling this issue? The aim of this volume is to bring together, in one teaching-focused text, core historical and contemporary reading on the act of defining 'digital humanities' to demonstrate aspects of the history of the field, to indicate the range of opinions that exist and to encourage others to articulate what it is we think we do when we do digital humanities.

Why would one define an academic field? From one perspective such definitions have an obvious practical and utilitarian purpose: we must be able to define and describe what it is that we are doing not only to colleagues and students but to university management, funding agencies and the general public. Nevertheless, we should not view such work from this practical perspective alone. The ways that digital humanities are being (and have been) defined can reveal much about the implicit assumptions that we as a community hold. So too the act of defining can reveal much about the identities that we are in the process of forging for ourselves, how we view ourselves in relation to other disciplines and the internal tensions that exist within the digital humanities community as a whole. In short the ever growing literature on defining digital humanities can offer us an important insight into the dynamics of disciplinary formation. A condensed selection of this literature is presented in this volume, which features the most popular items listed as set reading within Digital Humanities courses, as ascertained from a content analysis of the syllabi of a range of courses around the world.[1] There is core material, of course, that does not appear in this volume due to harsh editorial choices that had to be made, or copyright and licensing issues. As well as the core material presented here, we therefore give a list of suggested further reading: we hope that any student or practitioner in digital humanities who becomes conversant with this literature will understand the many facets to the question: how do you define the digital humanities?

Defining the remit and scope of our discipline seems to be a central concern to many in the field. Aspects of this literature (which could not in all cases be included in this volume) will now be presented and some pertinent themes pointed to. For convenience the term 'digital humanities' will be used throughout, even though, as will be made clear (particularly in Chapter 6, written for this volume), many other terms were used to refer to this field before 2005.

Nomenclature and Boundaries

Over the past years, the field that we now refer to as digital humanities has been known by many terms: humanities computing, humanist informatics, literary and linguistic computing and digital resources in the humanities, to name but a few. Most recently it has predominantly been known as digital humanities, though other variations such as eHumanities are occasionally to be found in literature emanating from continental Europe (see, for example, Neuroth et al., 2009 though agreement on the synonymy of these terms is not universal. Matthew G. Kirschenbaum has noted that 'the rapid and remarkable rise of digital humanities as a term can be traced to a set of surprisingly specific circumstances' (Kirschenbaum, 2010, p. 2). These he identifies as the 2005 publication of Blackwell's *Companion to Digital Humanities,* the name that was chosen at the end of 2005 for the organisation that arose out of the amalgamation of the Association for Computers in the Humanities and the Association for Literary and Linguistic Computing (that is, the Alliance of Digital Humanities Organizations, ADHO) and the 2006 launch of the National Endowment for the Humanities (NEH) digital humanities programme (Kirschenbaum, 2010, p. 3). Though digital humanities has had its 'own' journals since *Computers and the Humanities* was first published in 1966, it is clear that one important effect of the rise of the term 'digital humanities' is in the practicality of enabling scholars to self-identify as digital humanities scholars. The importance of this seemingly obvious advantage is reflected

---

[1]   Syllabi of different courses in Digital Humanities have been collected by Lisa Spiro and are available at http://www.zotero.org/groups/digital_humanities_education.

in Willard McCarty's discussion of the difficulties of compiling a comprehensive bibliography of the field. Discussing the bibliographies that were published in *Literary and Linguistic Computing Journal* (LLC) from 1986 until 1994 he observed that by 1994:

> finding and gathering relevant publications exhaustively had become impractical: too many of them, in too many disciplines, appearing in minor, as well as major places in many languages. The assimilation of computing into the older disciplines meant that, increasingly, much of the relevant work, when mentioned at all, had become subsumed in articles and books whose titles might give no clue. (McCarty, 2003a, p. 1226)

Indeed, it seems likely that the increasing currency of the term digital humanities will play an important role in helping to consolidate the community. Nevertheless, scholars such as Svensson (2009), Unsworth (2010), Terras (2011) and Rockwell (2011) have reflected on the issues of inclusion and exclusion in digital humanities, while Galina and Priana (2011) have examined the internationalisation of the community from the perspective of South America. According to Rockwell, 'We are a point of disciplinary evolution that calls for reflection, grace, and a renewed commitment to inclusion. Above all we need to critically review our history and our narrative of exclusion and inclusion lest it blind us to needs of the next generation' (Rockwell, 2011).

What DH is and is not

Judging by the 1966 foreword to *Computers and the Humanities* (the field's first journal) at that time digital humanities was not considered as being distinct from traditional humanities:

> We define humanities as broadly as possible. Our interests include literature of all times and countries, music, the visual arts, folklore, the non-mathematical aspects of linguistics, and all phases of the social sciences that stress the humane. When, for example, the archaeologist is concerned with fine arts of the past, when the sociologist studies the non-material facets of culture, when the linguist analyzes poetry, we may define their intentions as humanistic; if they employ computers, we wish to encourage them and to learn from them. (Prospect, 1966, p. 1)

A number of the writings that were published between 1980 and 2000 focused on defining the field in terms of how it might be taught. For example, between 1996 and 2000 a consortium of European universities participated in a project called Advanced Computing in the Humanities (ACO*HUM). The book that resulted from the network explores how digital humanities might be taught, thus implicitly exploring what it was then considered to be:

> Computer technology has mediated in the development of formal methods in humanities scholarship. Such methods are often much more powerful than traditional research with pencil and paper. They include, for instance, parsing techniques in computational linguistics, the calculus for expressive timing in music, the use of exploratory statistics in formal stylistics, visual search in art history, and data mining in history. Although scientific progress is in the first place due to better methods, rather than solely due to better computers, new advanced methods strongly rely on computers for their validation and effective use. Put in a different way, if you are going to compare two texts, you can do it with traditional pencil and paper; but if you are going to compare fifty texts with each other, you need sound computational methods. (de Smedt et al., 1999, chapter 1)

Terras (2006, p. 230–1) has given a comprehensive overview of relevant literature from this educational perspective. A persistent theme has been the question of the interrelatedness of the traditional and digital humanities. On the one hand, many scholars have emphasised the many ways that digital humanities furthers, or at least allows us to reconnect with, age-old concerns of the humanities. Katz (2005, p. 108) has written that, 'For the humanist perhaps nothing is more important than the capacity to organise and search large bodies of information'. Turkel has reflected on how the seemingly age-old distinction between thinking and doing in the humanities is not as old as some like to think:

> Just because the separation between thinking and making is long-standing and well-entrenched doesn't make it a good idea. At various times in the past, humanists have been deeply involved in making stuff: Archimedes, the Banu Musa brothers, da Vinci, Vaucanson, the Lunar Men, Bauhaus, W. Grey Walter, Gordon Mumma. The list could easily be multiplied into every time and place. (Turkel, 2008, par. 5)

Recently Moulin et al. (2011) have argued that, as unlikely as it may seem, it was the humanities that brought the earliest research infrastructures into being (p. 3).

Setting boundary lines between digital humanities, what it is and is not has also concerned many. In 2002, for example, Unsworth reflected that the mere use of the computer in humanities research does not make that research digital humanities:

One of the many things you can do with computers is something that I would call humanities computing, in which the computer is used as tool for modelling humanities data and our understanding of it, and that activity is entirely distinct from using the computer when it models the typewriter, or the telephone, or the phonograph, or any of the many other things it can be. (Unsworth, 2002)

This is a point that is echoed by both Orlandi (2002) and de Smedt (2002), choosing the evocative analogy that

The telescope was invented in 1608 and was initially thought useful in war. Galileo obtained one, improved it a little, and used it to challenge existing ideas about the Solar System. Although a magnificent new technology in itself, the telescope was hardly a scientific tool until Galileo used it to create new knowledge. (de Smedt, 2002, p. 99)

Orlandi (2002), while not denying the potential of the computer to fundamentally change humanities, argued that 'part of the humanities was "computed" well before computers were used'. Willard McCarty, one of the most prolific contributors to the questions of what digital humanities is, meanwhile stated, 'I celebrate computing as one of our most potent speculative instruments, for its enabling of competent hands to force us all to rethink what we trusted that we knew' (2009; see also McCarty, 1998, 1999, 2002a, 2002b, 2003a, 2003b, 2004, 2006 and 2008; McCarty and Kirschenbaum, 2003a; and McCarty and Short, 2002).

Since 2009, when William Pannapacker described digital humanities as 'the next big thing' in the *Chronicle of Higher Education*, a number of articles, blog posts (and even a *Downfall* detournement[2]) have been appearing, with increased alacrity, exploring and defining what digital humanities is and is not.

Alvarado (2011) argues that the term digital humanities is 'a social category, not an ontological one'. At the time of writing a common theme is whether one must programme or not in order to be a digital humanist. At one end of the spectrum is Stephen Ramsay, who wrote, 'If you are not making anything, you are not ... a digital humanist' (Ramsay, 2011a, further sketched out in his blog post featured in this volume). At the other end is Marc Sample (2011) who argues that, 'The digital humanities is not about building, it's about sharing'. Another important theme is the perceived lack of theory in digital humanities, which has been explored by, among others, Liu (2011) and Rockwell (2011).

---

[2]   http://www.criticalcommons.org/Members/ccManager/clips/5-ccdownfall.mov/view.

Answering the question 'What is digital humanities?' continues to be a rich source of intellectual debate for scholars. In addition to the blog posts and articles discussed above the question has also been explored over the past three years as part of the 'Day in the life of the Digital Humanities' community publication project that brought together digital humanists from around the world to document their activities on that day.[3] Gibbs (2011) has proposed a categorisation of these definitions in a useful post that reveals the many differing interpretations that are current. Indeed, at the current time, not only does a comprehensive definition appear to be impossible to formulate, when the breadth of work that is covered by a number of recent and forthcoming companions is considered (e.g. Crawford, 2009; Deegan and Sutherland, 2009; Greengrass and Hughes, 2008; Schreibman and Siemens, 2008; Schreibman et al., 2004; Siemens and Moorman, 2006; Sutherland, 1997; also see the Further Reading section in this volume), it might ultimately prove unproductive, by fossilising an emerging field and constraining new, boundary-pushing work. Terras (2006, p. 242) has asked whether a definition of the field is essential and reflected that such an absence may offer its practitioners additional freedom when deciding their research and career paths. This seems to hold true in Sinclair and Gouglas and their discussion of the establishment of the Humanities Computing MA programme at the University of Alberta. In the context of designing the MA, they choose not to ask what humanities computing is, but rather 'what do we want humanities computing to be?' (2002, p. 168). McCarty has argued for the fundamental importance of the self-reflection that appears so prominently in the literature of the field, and comments: 'What is humanities computing? This, for the humanities, is a question not to be answered but continually to be explored and refined' (2003a, p. 1233).

It is with this in mind that we wished to publish *Defining Digital Humanities: a Reader*. By capturing a selection of the various journal articles and blog postings, many of which respond to one another, we can provide in one volume the core necessary readings of our discipline and, in doing so, provide a set text for students beginning to engage in this field, and a volume for others to refer to in order to discuss how we wended to the place we are at today, where everyone defines digital humanities, but there is not a definition we all adhere to. We have chosen the contents of this volume based on their popularity within the discipline, the core themes that they highlight, and the relationships between the different pieces. As well as reprinting key articles and blog posts (some of which are re-edited and updated for this volume), we provide an introduction from the editors

---

[3]   http://tapor.ualberta.ca/taporwiki/index.php/Day_in_the_Life_of_the_Digital_Humanities.

to place and explain the importance of journal articles, and an addendum from most authors, to provide a contemporary review of their piece. We also provide a new chapter by Edward Vanhoutte, explaining the historical shift from humanities computing to digital humanities, a selected further reading list, and a list of questions to aid a discussion about this topic in class. We will expand, maintain, and explore our reading list and point to other media which tackle the definition of digital humanities, including posters, images, manifestos and book cover art, at the companion website to the volume.[4]

We do not try to define digital humanities ourselves: our editorial perspective is to highlight the range of discussions that attempt to scope out the limits and purview of the discipline. We hope that this volume is of interest both to those new to the discipline and established scholars in the field, to frame the debate on how best to define digital humanities.

Bibliography

Aarseth, E.J. (1997). 'The Field of Humanistic Informatics and its Relation to the Humanities', *Human IT*, 4 (97), pp. 7–13.

Alvarado, R. (2011). 'The Digital Humanities Situation', *The Transducer*, 11 May (accessed 12 May 2011).

Crawford, T. (2009). *Modern Methods for Musicology: Prospects, Proposals and Realities*, UK: Ashgate.

Deegan, M. and Sutherland, K. (2009). *Text Editing, Print, and the Digital World*, UK: Ashgate.

de Smedt, K. (2002). 'Some Reflections on Studies in Humanities Computing', *Literary and Linguistic Computing*, 17 (1), pp. 89–101.

de Smedt, K. et al. (1999). *Computing in Humanities Education: A European Perspective*, SOCRATES/ERASMUS thematic network project on Advanced Computing in the Humanities (ACO*HUM), Bergen: University of Bergen.

Galina, Isabel and Ernesto Priani (2011) 'Is There Anybody out There? Discovering New DH Practitioners in other Countries'. Digital Humanities 2011: Conference Abstracts. p.135–137

Gibbs, F.W. (2011) 'Digital Humanities Definitions by Type' (accessed 19 September 2011).

Greengrass, M. and Hughes, L. (2008). *Virtual Representations of the Past*, UK: Ashgate.

---

[4] http://blogs.ucl.ac.uk/definingdh and on Twitter @DefiningDH.

Hockey, S. (2004). 'The History of Humanities Computing', in S. Schreibman, R. Siemens and J. Unsworth (eds), *A Companion to Digital Humanities*, Malden: Blackwell, pp. 3–19.

Katz, S.N., 2005. *Why technology matters: the humanities in the twenty-first century. Interdisciplinary Science Reviews*, 30(2), pp.105–118.

Kirschenbaum, M.G. (2010). 'What is Digital Humanities and What's it Doing in English Departments?' *ADE Bulletin*, 150, pp. 1–7 (online pagination, accessed 9 May 2011).

Liu, A. (2011). 'Where is Cultural Criticism in the Digital Humanities', Paper delivered at MLA Conference, Los Angeles.

McCarty, W. (1998). '*What Is Humanities Computing? Toward a Definition of the Field*', Liverpool, 20 February 1998, Reed College (Portland, Oregon, US) and Stanford University (Palo Alto, California, US), March 1998 and Würzburg (Germany), July 1998.

McCarty, W. (1999). 'Humanities Computing as Interdiscipline', part of the 'Is Humanities Computing an Academic Discipline?' series, University of Virginia: IATH.

McCarty, W. (2002a). 'Humanities Computing: Essential Problems, Experimental Practice', *Literary and Linguistic Computing*, 17 (1), pp. 103–25.

McCarty, W. (2002b). 'New Splashings in the Old Pond: The Cohesibility of Humanities Computing', in G. Braungart, K. Eibl and F. Jannidis (eds), *Jahrbuch für Computerphilologie*, 4, Paderborn: Mentis Verlag, pp. 9–18.

McCarty, W. (2003a). 'Humanities Computing', in *Encyclopedia of Library and Information Science*, New York: Marcel Dekker, pp. 1224–35.

McCarty, W. (2003b). '"Knowing true things by what their mockeries be": Modelling in the Humanities', *Computing in the Humanities Working Papers*, A.24, jointly published with *TEXT Technology*, 12 (1).

McCarty, W. (2004). 'As It Almost Was: Historiography of Recent Things', *Literary and Linguistic Computing*, 19 (2), pp. 161–80.

McCarty, W. (2006). 'Tree, Turf, Centre, Archipelago – or Wild Acre? Metaphors and Stories for Humanities Computing', *Literary and Linguistic Computing*, 21 (1), pp. 1–13.

McCarty, W. (2008). 'What's Going On?', *Literary and Linguistic Computing*, 23 (3), pp. 253–61.

McCarty, W., 2010. Inaugural lecture: Attending from and to the machine. King's College London.

McCarty, W. and Kirschenbaum, M. (2003). 'Institutional Models for Humanities Computing', *Literary and Linguistic Computing*, 18 (4), pp. 465–89.

McCarty, W. and Short, H. (2002). 'A Roadmap for Humanities Computing', http://www.allc.org/reports/map.

McGann, J. (2005). 'Culture and Technology: The Way We Live Now, What Is To Be Done?', *Interdisciplinary Science Reviews*, 30 (2), pp. 179–88.

Moulin, C., Nyhan, J. and Ciula, A. (2011). *ESF Science Policy Briefing 43: Research Infrastructures in the Humanities*. European Science Foundation.

Neuroth, H., Jannidis, F., Rapp, A. and Lohmeier, F. (2009). 'Virtuelle Forschungsumgebungen für e-Humanities. Maßssnahmen zur optimalen Unterstützung von Forschungsprozessen in den Geistes-wissenschaften', *BIBLIOTHEK Forschung und Praxis*, 33 (2), pp. 161–69.

Orlandi, T. (2002). 'Is Humanities Computing a Discipline?' in G. Braungart, K. Eibl and F. Jannidis (eds), *Jahrbuch für Computerphilologie*, 4, Paderborn: Mentis Verlag, pp. 51–8.

Pannapacker, W. (2009). 'The MLA and the Digital Humanities', *Chronicle of Higher Education*, 28 December.

'Prospect' (1966). *Computers and the Humanities: a newsletter*. I(1) p. 1–2.

Ramsay, S. (2011a). 'Who's In and Who's Out' (accessed 22 November 2011) further sketched out in http://lenz.unl.edu/papers/2011/01/11/on-building.html.

Ramsay, S. (2011b). 'On Building' (accessed 22 November 2011).

Rockwell, G. (2011). 'Inclusion in the Digital Humanities', *philosophi.ca* (accessed 20 January 2011).

Sample, M. (2011). 'The Digital Humanities is not about Building, it's about Sharing', *Sample Reality*, 25 May (accessed 19 September 2011).

Schreibman, S. and Siemens, R. (2008). '*A Companion to Digital Literary Studies*', Oxford: Blackwell.

Schreibman, S., Siemens, R. and Unsworth, J. (eds) (2004). *A Companion to Digital Humanities*, Malden: Blackwell.

Short, H. (2006), 'The Role of Humanities Computing: Experiences and Challenges', *Literary and Linguistic Computing*, 21 (1), pp. 15–27.

Siemens, R. and Moorman, D. (2006). *Mind Technologies. Humanities Computing and the Canadian Academic Community*, Calgary: University of Calgary Press.

Sinclair, S. and Gouglas, W. (2002). 'A Theory into Practice: A Case Study of the Humanities Computing Master of Arts Programme at the University of Alberta', *Arts and Humanities in Higher Education*, 1 (2), pp. 167–83.

Sutherland, K. (ed.) (1997). *Electronic Text: Investigations in Method and Theory*, Oxford. Clarendon Press, pp. 107–26.

Svensson, P. (2009). 'Humanities Computing as Digital Humanities', *Digital Humanities Quarterly*, 3 (3) (accessed 9 February 2010).

Terras, M. (2006). 'Disciplined: Using Educational Studies to Analyse "Humanities Computing"', *Literary and Linguistic Computing*, 21 (2), pp. 229–46.

Terras, M. (2011). 'Peering Inside the Big Tent: Digital Humanities and the Crisis of Inclusion', *Melissa Terras' Blog*, 26 July (accessed 19 September 2011).

Turkel, W.J. (2008). 'A Few Arguments for Humanistic Fabrication' [Webblog entry 21 November] *Digital History Hacks: Methodology for the Infinite Archive* (2005–08) (accessed 20 August 2010).

Unsworth, J. (1997). 'Documenting the Reinvention of Text. The Importance of Failure', *The Journal of Electronic Publishing*, 3 (2).

Unsworth, J. (2000). *Scholarly Primitives: What methods do humanities researchers have in common, and how might our tools reflect this?*, Paper read at the symposium on 'Humanities Computing; formal methods, experimental practice', London: King's College, 13 May.

Unsworth, J. (2002). 'What is Humanities Computing, and What is it Not?', in G. Braungart, K. Eibl and F. Jannidis (eds) *Jahrbuch für Computerphilologie*, 4, Paderborn: Mentis Verlag, pp. 71–84.

Unsworth, J. (2010). 'The State of Digital Humanities', Lecture at the Digital Humanities Summer Institute.

SECTION I
Humanities Computing

CHAPTER 1

Is Humanities Computing an Academic Discipline?

Geoffrey Rockwell
University of Alberta

Geoffrey Rockwell (1999). Originally published online after being presented at "Is Humanities Computing an Academic Discipline?", An Interdisciplinary Seminar Series, November 12, 1999, Institute for Advanced Technology in the Humanities, University of Virginia.

Note from the Editors:
During the late 1990s, a signi cant theme in the 'What is Humanities Computing' literature was whether the eld could be de ned and categorised as an academic discipline. Rockwell presented this paper, published in 1999, to a seminar held on this topic in the Institute for Advanced Technology in the Humanities at the University of Virginia (other papers presented at this seminar by leading gures in humanities computing remain available[1]). In it he argues that the ontological questions of what the discipline 'is' may never be satisfactorily settled; therefore, he argues for the importance and value of considering this question from an administrative and institutional perspective. In order to do this he discusses at length his experience of setting up a 'Combined Honours in Multimedia and Another Subject' programme at McMaster University. He also explains the decision to use the term multimedia as opposed to that of humanities computing to describe the programme. In essence, the term multimedia could be used to communicate to prospective students and colleagues (especially those of the senior, administrative and budget-approving persuasion) what the programme would entail and the traditions it would draw on. However, the term humanities computing was, he argued 'a liability and confusion'.

---

[1]   See http//www.iath.virginia.edu/hcs/papers.html.

> I wish either my father or my mother, or indeed both of them, as they were in duty both equally bound to it, had minded what they were about when the begot me.
>
> (Sterne, *Tristram Shandy*, p. 35)

I propose in this paper to tackle the question of whether humanities computing is an academic discipline from an administrative and instructional perspective by recasting is thus, "Who should humanities computing benefit and how should it be administered and taught to benefit them?" I would have you think concretely about the child you will beget by concentrating less on the issue of what humanities computing is than on questions about its administrative and instructional details. I have two reasons for begging your indulgence as I digress from the original question. The first is that woven into the purpose of this seminar *are* questions about the administrative and instructional potential of humanities computing. To ask if humanities computing is an academic discipline is anticipated by the question of whether it can be administered and taught as other disciplines are in the academy. This precedence can be seen, for example, in the purpose page for this seminar where the author sets up a hierarchy of questions proceeding from the instructional question to the ontological.

> This seems a good time to ask whether we should be offering such a degree— but before we can answer that question, we need to have a clear idea of what the field is, and whether it is, in fact, a field of scholarly inquiry. (http://www. iath.virginia.edu/hcs/purpose.html, accessed on October 27, 1999)

While I sympathize with the view that we need to know what humanities computing is before we can ask whether it can be taught, I can't help suspecting that the ontological question will never be answered to your satisfaction, especially in a seminar which could be argued is an administrative form designed more for appreciating questions than answering them. Rather, the ontological question could become the subject of the teachable discipline. Therefore at some point you will have to confront the administrative question and confront it without the certainty of knowing what humanities computing is.

My second reason for digressing, and I should warn you that this paper will be nothing but digressions, is that what little I have to offer after the excellent presentations you have already heard lies in the area of administrative and instructional experience, namely the experience of setting up a Combined Honours in Multimedia and Another Subject program at McMaster University. Thus these digressions will attempt to abstract from the experience of those of us who conceived and carried this program to term in a fashion that will eventually lead to an answer to the question you should have asked.

The Place of Administration

In a well known passage in Plato's *Phaedrus* Socrates discusses the invention of writing by telling a story that has come down from the forefathers about the invention of writing: Theuth, an Egyptian god, brought his inventions including writing before the king Thamus who made it his business to evaluate the inventions before passing them on to the Egyptians. Theuth is excited about writing; it "will make the people of Egypt wiser and improve their memories; my discovery provides a recipe for memory and wisdom." Thamus like any good philosopher king is not so enthusiastic. He first distinguishes the role of the god as inventor from his role as legislator. Theuth is so enamored with his offspring writing that he can't see whether it will really profit or harm the citizens. Thamus answers Theuth's enthusiasm thus,

> O man full of arts, to one it is given to create the things of art, and to another to judge what measure of harm and of profit they have for those that shall employ them. ... And it is no true wisdom that you offer your disciples, but only its semblance, for by telling them of many things without teaching them you will make them seem to know much, while for the most part they know nothing, and as men filled, not with wisdom, but with the conceit of wisdom, they will be a burden to their fellows. (Plato, *Phaedrus*, 274e–275b)

This story of Socrates' has become an important text in the current discussion about the place of technologies of information in society. Neil Postman in *Technopoly* turns to it in his first chapter to remind us of the importance of technological criticism and judgment. I have my own reading of this story.

One of the first points I would make about Socrates' myth of writing is that it is presented as a short dialogue between Theuth (often known as Thoth) and Thamus. (Phaedrus actually questions Socrates about the place of such stories in their dialogue, but that is another story.) Your seminar might likewise end up being such a formative dialogue if it is open to questions around the administration and instruction of technology. What story will be told about this symposium?

Second, Socrates' story connects the ontological issue of what a thing is, in our case humanities computing, with the administrative question of whether it will be of benefit or not to others. Socrates does this dramatically by distinguishing characters and introducing the role of the administrator Thamus who asks about the implementation of the invention. He wants to know what good the technology will do, and I would argue a discipline is an administrative technology. That is my challenge to you; you aren't really asking only what humanities computing is, but you are also asking what it would be like at UVA and who would it serve, however distasteful such administrative questions are. (Our distaste for administration in academia is another issue.) Bring them out into the open; play another role for a moment.

Third, Socrates distinguishes between a technology that helps tell about wisdom from the teaching of wisdom. (Much of the *Phaedrus* can be read as a demonstration by Socrates of this difference.) He provides us thus with a clue as to what would constitute an administratively appropriate implementation—one that does not fill us with the conceit of wisdom, but one which is pedagogically appropriate. Which is why I have recast the question, to ask what might be taught.

Fourth, Socrates' criticism of writing could very well be updated to sound like current criticism of computers in the humanities, namely that they are not devices (or methods) for acquiring deeper wisdom about texts but a recipe for forgetting about books. To put it more generally, any new technology, especially those that are supposed to assist us with the study of other things, can also hide that which they are meant to reveal. This is a danger we are all struggling with in humanities computing—to what extent does it hide or distract us from that which it was supposed to compute. This danger reveals itself in the different tacks we take to the administration of humanities computing. Willard McCarty is trying to keep it connected to the humanities by advocating interdisciplinarity. Others, myself included, are trying to identify a new subject area which humanities computing can reveal through humanistic inquiry. McCarty wants to bring computing methods to traditional objects of study, I want to argue for bringing the culture of the humanities to new objects, those that surround us on CD-ROMs and the WWW.

Let me summarize this section with a collection of questions I will attempt to answer in the rest of the paper. Who is humanities computing for? How can it be administered to benefit others? How can it teach rather than tell? What should be taught and to whom? How can we create a community that will continue to ask about computing in the humanities? How can we create a community of research? I propose to answer these questions by wandering off along the path of humanities computing at McMaster.

A Brief History of Humanities Computing at McMaster

In 1986 the Humanities Computing Centre was founded out of the existing Language Labs. Dr. Samuel Cioran, who was the Assistant to the Dean for Computing and director of the Language Labs at the time, began moving the courses from traditional audio instructional technology to computer-based instruction by developing a series of language modules built around the mcBOOKmaster authoring system. He also took the Faculty of Humanities out of a system of central computer labs when they were unwilling to upgrade their computers with CD-ROMs and sound cards. He negotiated an arrangement with the central Computing and Information Services whereby the Faculty took over the computer labs for humanities students and merged them with the Language Labs to create a hybrid set of labs and media classrooms that could serve our purposes better. This arrangement still exists so that, while our labs are partially funded by the central administration, we manage them and adapt them to our purposes. I cannot stress how important it has been to have in place a set of labs and staff under the academic control of the Faculty and therefore responsive to our instructional needs. Reading Susan Hockey's description of the problems she faced putting on a single course I am thankful for Dr. Cioran's foresight. To put it bluntly, you need labs under the academic control of the discipline if you are going to mount courses on a regular basis and especially if you are going to mount a program with any multimedia courses. Do not count on resources that do not answer to the needs of the unit. I know of too many humanities computing courses that stumble along fighting for time in labs and appropriate configurations of tools to believe a program can be mounted with good intentions.

When I was hired to replace Dr. Cioran in 1994 I was asked to introduce courses in Humanities Computing almost as an afterthought. The first course, "Introduction to Humanities Computing," was taught in the winter term of 1995. Three courses were introduced at that time, including "Introduction to Multimedia in the Humanities" and a course on electronic texts and computational linguistics. These courses were to be courses for all humanities students to provide them with suitable introductions to information technology in an academic context. In 1998 as a result of donations and internal competitions two new faculty members were hired and we introduced six new courses in multimedia and communication. In effect, the creation of a Humanities Computing Centre and the introduction of courses in the area was due to a series of administrative decisions that had little to do with questions about the existence of any such discipline. The Faculty got their labs (and hence a Centre) partly because multimedia language titles could not be developed for central labs that at the time were aimed at computer science and statistics students. Courses were introduced because faculty were brought on board to help administer the facilities and because funding was available only for positions connected to technology. I am, of course, exaggerating, but my point is that humanities computing at McMaster (and I imagine at many other places) evolved along faculty lines and out of existing administrative structures. If we didn't have faculties of humanities would we have humanities computing? That is not to say that one should be ashamed of such lineage, rather it is a series of often inconsequential administrative decisions combined with stubborn personalities which can put one in a position to make bold initiatives. Has it been any different at Virginia?

In the summer of 1998 we were alerted that the Province of Ontario had created the Access to Opportunities Program (ATOP) to encourage the expansion of programs that prepare students for careers in the advanced technology sector, specifically Computer Engineering, Software Engineering, and Computer Science. We held discussions with the Ministry of Education officer responsible for the program in order to determine if a proposal for a program based in the Humanities would be acceptable and were encouraged to submit a draft of the proposal in August to get clearance for the submission of a full proposal. Once we received clearance in late August we had to put together a full proposal with courses and get it through the relevant committees so that it could be approved by the University and submitted in December of 1998. The program was subsequently approved for funding and started in 1999 with a target enrollment of 30 students a year for a steady state of approximately 110 students over four years.[2] The demand we have experienced for the first year courses has been such that we are planning to expand the program to accommodate 50 students a year for a steady state of just under 200 students.

In a province where base budget funding to universities has been declining ATOP was one of the first opportunities to compete for an increase in ongoing funds, which explains the support we got from the administration in designing a program so quickly and moving it through committees. This is not only true of Ontario, governments and administrations are increasingly targeting new funding instead of providing across the board increases. We are constantly told that one cannot simply argue for funds to do the same (old) things and that therefore when framing any funding request we need to be a) innovative, b) interdisciplinary, c) inter-institutional where it is appropriate, and d) relevant to the information age economy. This puts the humanities in the unfortunate position where it can only get funds to try new things, sometimes at the expense of excellence already established in traditional areas. We are forced either to dig in our heels and fight the trend or to try to pour our well aged wine into digital bottles. This is an unfortunate state of affairs if you believe (as I do) in the excellence of a humanities education even without computing. It puts those of us in Humanities Computing who can propose new programs in the position of proposing

---

[2]   See http://www.humanities.mcmaster.ca/~macmedia for details.

things in the face of a lack of appreciation for exactly the programs we came from and respect. We struggle with our colleagues who think we have sold out to business and we struggle with the danger that what we do may hide the traditions we were taught to love. Administratively and concretely we have to struggle to make sure new programs do not come at the expense of existing ones but enhance them creatively. Whatever else we do we should bring new resources in, not steal from the already strained departments.

While in a perfect world one could plan new programs carefully, the reality of most funding opportunities is that they open unexpectedly and disappear quickly. If you want to create something new without stealing from existing programs you need to be able to move quickly. To be more precise, you need to have most of the work done in anticipation of support and then you have to listen, lobby, and wait until the right opportunity arises. If you have developed a preliminary consensus about the administrative structure and developed a tentative program you can then start circulating it for discussion and try to attract the funding needed. In our case we had in place a lab structure, we had done a substantial amount of work designing courses, we had hired faculty and were even preparing a Certificate proposal when the opportunity for a full program arose so it was not a great leap to design the full program. This gets back to administration and Socrates. Don't just ask whether Humanities Computing is a discipline, ask what the discipline and a program would look like? What will it cost? What sorts of resources will be needed and who will provide them? What would you have taught? What will your students look like? You should not be afraid of the concrete or the administrative, it is an application of the ontological. Which is why I will turn now to the particular program we designed and our reasons for not mounting a humanities computing program.

The Name of the Discipline

The ATOP proposal guidelines that we had to follow were typical of the administrative questions new programs face today in Ontario. We were asked to show that there was student demand, to show that there was a societal need, to secure industry and community support, to show that the program was in the area of computing and to show that we had the resources to implement the proposed program. We started with a name, Multimedia. Why Multimedia and not Humanities Computing? The following are some of the reasons we had for choosing to propose a Multimedia program.

- The name of a program should communicate clearly to prospective students and other stakeholders. Humanities Computing is meaningless to people outside its traditions and the program was unlikely to be approved with such an awkward name. Multimedia has the virtue that it is the name of the object of creation and study for the program. Multimedia, if one is generous about the media subsumed, includes in our case the study of electronic texts too, which are often what humanities computing courses turn out to be.

- We wanted to design a program that would enhance all the humanities including the creative, fine, and performing arts. Too often humanities computing is focused exclusively on textual computing and is therefore only of interest to students in textual disciplines like English, Linguistics, and Comparative Literature. If one is serious about connecting with all the disciplines generally contained within the humanities one needs to address the needs not only of the critical disciplines but also the creative ones where students are not only asked to discuss media, but are taught to create it. Thus the challenge is to develop a program that combines the critical with instruction in the creative and performing aspects of computer-based media. Multimedia is the best title we could find for such a program.

- Further, our experience is that what students want is to learn to participate fully in the field of information technology. They don't want to just read and write about new media, they want to build it so that they can choose careers other than further graduate studies. They want to be artists, musicians, designers, and writers not just teachers. The courses that are invariably the most popular (alas) are those that weave concrete creative skills into academic contexts not the electronic text courses (that I teach.) The demand is in multimedia not electronic text encoding and text-analysis methodologies.

- The information we could find about societal need pointed to a need, especially in Canada, for multimedia designers not humanities computing specialists. Most of what others have argued is central to humanities computing, namely methods and presentation of information, is taught adequately by Information Science programs. What is not taught in universities in Ontario is multimedia creation, communication and criticism. No doubt programs in media studies and communications will ramp up to handle new media and meet this need, but we felt there was a place for a program connected to the arts and humanities.

What is Multimedia?

Having chosen a name and taken the position that we wanted the program to connect to the arts and therefore include design courses, we set about to try to define multimedia not humanities computing. (To be honest none of what follows was put on paper before this seminar, but I am trying to make it sound like a rational process.) Here are some definitions I have found for multimedia.

> A *multimedia* computer system is one that is capable of input or output of more than one medium. Typically, the term is applied to systems that support more than one physical output medium, such as a computer display, video, and audio. Occasionally, *multimedia* is used to refer to the combination of text and images on a computer display terminal. Although text and images are in fact distinct carriers of information, hence media, this usage of *multimedia* is not preferred. After all, newspapers with text and images are not considered to be multimedia publications!
>
> The term *medium* can also refer to an input device such as a keyboard, mouse, microphone, camera, or other sensor. Regarding computer input, *multimedia* then refers to the capability of using multiple input devices to interact with a computer system. (Blattner and Dannenberg, 1992, p. xxiii)

Blattner and Dannenberg also make the observation that "Multimedia systems strive to take the best advantage of human senses in order to facilitate communication" (Blattner and Dannenberg, 1992, p. xix). The Encyclopædia Britannica Online defines Interactive Multimedia thus:

> any computer-delivered electronic system that allows the user to control, combine, and manipulate different types of media, such as text, sound, video, computer graphics, and animation. Interactive multimedia integrate computer, memory storage, digital (binary) data, telephone, television, and other information technologies. Their most common applications include training programs, video games, electronic encyclopedias, and travel guides. Interactive multimedia shift the user's role from observer to participant and are considered the next generation of electronic information systems.

In the book *Multimedia Demystified* it is defined in this fashion:

> In its most basic definition, multimedia can be thought of as applications that bring together multiple types of media. text, illustrations, photos, sounds, voice, animations, and video. A combination of three or more of these with some measure of user interactivity is usually thought of as multimedia computing. (Haykin, 1994, p. 3)

One of the interesting features of these definitions is what they are defining. The first defines a "multimedia system", the second "interactive multimedia" while the third defines multimedia applications. I have settled on the following definition that combines many of the features in the others with a focus on multimedia as a genre of artistic work.

> A multimedia work is a computer-based rhetorical artifact in which multiple media are integrated into an interactive artistic whole.

Let me go through the parts of the definition.

Computer-Based: The word multimedia has been used synonymously with "mixed-media" to refer to works of art that combine traditional artistic media like paint, found objects, metal, and so on. Only since the 1980s has it come to mean exclusively those works that are computer-based, which is the way I take it. In this definition I am therefore excluding mixed-media works if they were not created to be accessed through a computer. This also excludes works that might have been created on a computer like a desktop publishing file, but were intended to be accessed through print. A multimedia work proper is one that is viewed or browsed on the computer. Thus the computer in this view of what humanities computing should deal with is not just a tool for study of other objects, it is the delivery vehicle for content. This raises interesting questions about the limitations and possibilities afforded by the computer as form which I take to be one of the theoretical issues in multimedia.

Rhetorical: A multimedia work is one designed to convince, delight, or instruct. It is not a work designed for administrative purposes or solely for communicating information. Nor is it a solely technological artifact from the perspective of the multimedia student. Technical questions about bandwidth and compression algorithms are for computer scientists and engineers. Multimedia is about the computer as a rhetorical performance.

Artifact: A multimedia work is a work of human creation or art. I am not defining what multimedia is in general or what a multimedia computer is, but focusing on multimedia works.

Multiple Media: Central to all definitions of multimedia is the idea that multimedia combines types of information that have traditionally been considered distinct because they had different means of production and distribution. This combination or convergence is made possible by the computer that through digitization stores all information, whatever its original form, as binary digital data. Thus the computer allows the combination of media because they are on the computer all stored in the same fashion and accessible to the same procedures. In particular, multimedia works can bring together media that are incompatible in other formats like audio (which is time-dependent) and text (which is not). The possibilities for design when one can combine media and the problems of interpretation of works that do so are the central problems of the field. I believe these problems subsume those traditionally articulated for humanities computing.

Integration ... Artistic Whole: A multimedia work is not just a collection of different types of media concatenated into a collection. By this definition the integration of media is the result of deliberate artistic imagination aimed at producing a work that has integrity. My hard drive has multiple media encoded on it, but it is not a multimedia work because those different media were not consciously integrated into a single work for rhetorical purposes. That said, one of the interesting features hypertext theorists find in hypermedia is a blurring of the boundaries of the artistic work. My colleagues are trying to get me to back down on this point and agree that we do not expect unity in a multimedia work, that hypertextual links outside the work are an important difference to multimedia. What do you think?

Interactive: One of the new media integrated into a multimedia work is the interactivity or the programming that provides for the viewer's experience. Some level of interactivity is assumed in any computer-based work, but by this definition interactivity becomes part of the palette of media being woven into a whole. The type of interactivity is thus important to the artistic performance. We might go further and say that interactivity is the dominant media that integrates the others and that the computer is what bears interactive possibilities to the creative arts. Multimedia is therefore about computing in that it is about the possibilities for interactive integration and performance.

Implementation of a Multimedia Program

This defining choice and the trajectory set by the administrative guidelines that constrained us led to a particular implementation of a humanities computing program in the form of a multimedia program. This implementation has the following advantages from an administrative point of view.

- We were able to create a program that connected to the various disciplines within the humanities by having elective courses that dealt with particular media in digital form. Thus we have courses on "Writing in the Electronic Age", "Electronic Texts and Their Study", "Technical Writing" to connect with the textual disciplines. We have courses on "Introduction to MIDI and Computer Music" for music majors. We have courses on computer graphics and animation for art students. With the umbrella of multimedia we could argue the case for teaching courses on different media including text thus weaving the traditional text-oriented tradition of humanities computing into a more comprehensive whole.

- While the elective courses dealt with the intersections with particular media and their disciplines, the core courses dealt with the integration of media into multimedia. Thus we steered between a program that was simply a service program for other programs and one that was isolated unto itself with its own methods. The core courses provide a unity to the program which would be lacking in a program made up of service courses with a few methods courses tacked on. The multimedia work as an object of study and creation provides a focus to the program that can be explained and demonstrated.
- We designed the program to be a Combined Honours program that had to be taken with another program as a double major. The program thus avoids hiding the humanities by being designed so that it can only be taken if in conjunction with another.
- The program is of interest to prospective students and can be explained to senior administrators, something I could never do with humanities computing. To put it crudely it can be sold to the stakeholders outside the unit which in a fiscally stressful environment is a prerequisite to the creation of any program. I do not believe this is at the expense of what should be done, because I do not think there is anything that we cannot do under the banner of multimedia which humanities computing could do. By contrast humanities computing as a name is a liability and a confusion.
- The program, despite its new media flavor, could still be reasonably placed in the existing administrative structure by becoming a program within the School of Art, Drama and Music. This placed the program in a congenial setting within a unit already committed to interdisciplinary programs, creative and performing arts, and capable of dealing with faculty positions that are not assessed solely in terms of paper publications. The last feature of the School was especially important if we were going to be able to attract people doing things in humanities computing other than writing about it.

As we brought the Multimedia program proposal through the various committees we were asked a number of questions which I suspect any program in this area has to face. Most of these questions came from our colleagues, especially those in administrative positions who understood the dangers of new programs. In fact humanists were the most skeptical of the program, which is a sign of health, I believe. I have summarized them here along with the answers that were offered.

What evidence do you have that this is a discipline? Are there similar programs elsewhere? Are there journals in the area? Are there books that one can point to as original research in the area?

It is interesting that they did not ask if it was a discipline, but we were asked to provide evidence that others thought it was a discipline. In order to answer this we gathered a number of different types of evidence that multimedia was a viable discipline. We prepared a dossier of WWW sites of similar programs and courses elsewhere. Harold Short and others at King's College London were particularly helpful with information about their "Humanities with Applied Computing" BA minor which like ours is meant to be combined with a traditional discipline. We also compiled a list of sample books in the discipline, journals, conferences, and graduate programs to which students apply.

Should a program with a strong technical component be in the humanities? Should university programs have technical components?

Questions about the place of technical instruction in the humanities were the most difficult to answer. On the one hand we pointed out that in art, drama, and language courses techniques are taught. A printmaking course, for example, is partly about the craft of printmaking. Language classes teach practical language skills which only with practice lead to critical application. On the other hand we designed the program and each course so that the technical skills were always taught in a communicative context. This manifests itself at different levels. First, the program, like the King's program, is a Combined Honours program which means it has to be combined with another program. As I have mentioned above, central to the design of the program was the idea that it was not to be a stand-alone degree, but one which would enhance traditional humanities degrees and hence students could not escape untutored in criticism or theory. Second, the courses were all designed so that they would have readings and critical assignments that complemented the technical skills acquired. Mastery of a technique is not sufficient in any course; student assignments ask that students apply techniques to communicative, creative, and critical problems. Thus it is not enough to be able to create a WWW site for a course; building the site is like being able to type a paper, it is the threshold of participation. The WWW site, like a paper, is assessed in terms of the issues dealt with in the course as a creative contribution. Third, we made sure there were courses in the program that would focus on philosophical, critical, and communicative aspects of multimedia independent of technology. Finally we made sure that none of the courses were about a particular and therefore time-dependent technology. There is no course on Macromedia Director as you would find in a college program. There is a course on Advanced Multimedia where students currently learn Director this year, but the technical skills taught will change as the industry changes.

My colleague Andrew Mactavish in a paper we coauthored for the 1999 ACH/ALLC at UVA went further and asked *What are the assumptions about technology, technical skill, and intellectual skill that underlie the anxieties expressed in objections to our program?* In that paper, which I will not digress too far to summarize, he raises the possibility that such objections are based on an unexamined and essentialist view "which supports the division of technical skill and intellectually enriched knowledge, gets played out in a host of symbolic social divisions, including those that structure and intersect with education, class, and culture" (Mactavish, Rockwell, and Buckley, 1999, p. 11). Needless to say, we did not accuse our colleagues in public of such anxieties, but the very place of technical skill in the humanities which the introduction of such a program raises needs to be worked out further.

Why isn't this a stream in computer science? Why don't we leave this to the community colleges?

The question of which type of institution or which department is best suited to teach multimedia and humanities computing gets to the heart of the Socratic legislative question. In Canada there is a hierarchy of institutions and degrees from college certificates that generally take a year to complete to honours BAs that take four years. Generally speaking technical skills like carpentry and graphic design are taught in community colleges while universities offer bachelor degrees that focus more on the [academic aspects].

Aren't students likely to start coming who already have the technical expertise in multimedia? Do we therefore need to have a program that teaches skills that will soon be universally taught in high school?

This is like asking if we should ditch our English program if students came to university able to write. Regardless of their technical skill level the university should be a place where they can study multimedia further and in an academic fashion. I also doubt we will see this mythical student who knows everything there is to know about computing.

Are we just doing this to get money and recruit students?

No, it should not be done simply because it can be funded. It should be done because we are interested in creating a community that studies multimedia.

What evidence is there that this program would be successful? How can we be sure students would enroll in such a program instead of just taking a course or two?

To answer this question we gathered statistics not only from existing courses but also from other programs in related fields.

What would students do with such a degree? Are there graduate programs that they could apply to?

As I mentioned above we gathered lists of possible careers and graduate programs that such a program would prepare a student for. The ATOP guidelines also forced us to get letters of support from industry, in our case multimedia design firms and computer firms. These letters, while solicited, provided the perspective of people in the position to hire graduates. The short answer is that the multimedia content industry is expected to need more and more technically skilled and articulate designers, writers, animators, and artists.

What are the hidden costs to such a program? Will this program compete with others in the humanities and steal students from traditional programs?

Essential to taking this program through various, often antagonistic, bodies was a clear accounting of the costs so that humanists could see that its concrete implementation would not draw on their resources. The spreadsheet in this case spoke better than the word. To imagine the concrete financial consequences of a particular implementation of a new discipline should not be left to the last moment, but should be part of initial planning even when funding opportunities don't exist. I have often found that if I can put a price to an activity it is much easier to find the opportunity than if I leave it a vague academic wish. As for competition, the program was designed to be combined with others not to replace them in a fashion that would attract students that otherwise would not consider the humanities.

Competencies

While answering questions in committees is one of the administrative challenges to designing a healthy program it is important to keep in mind who the program is for and how it will meet your objectives. At the suggestion of the Instructional Development Centre we also embarked on a more comprehensive diagnostic process which was one of the most useful things we did in terms of the final outcome. What we did first was to try to describe in concrete terms what our students would be able to do once they graduated. What would they know and how would that manifest itself? What aptitudes and attitudes might they have? What would they be able to discuss? We were encouraged to describe the outcomes in details like, "Students should enjoy reading computer magazines in the bookstore like *Wired*." We decided to abstract our expectations into a spreadsheet of competencies charted against courses. Competency was chosen as the term to cover both skills and knowledge. We boiled down what we wanted students to know into a series of competencies and then looked at our courses to see if these competencies were properly introduced, properly developed, and then reinforced. The competencies are of three types:

- Core Technical Competencies like the ability to code HTML
- Core Intellectual Competencies like the knowledge of and ability to discuss the history of multimedia
- Other Competencies like the ability to work in groups.

When you take the time to ask whether your combination of courses called a program actually does what you want it to do you discover courses that are overloaded, competencies that are not taught or not reinforced, and you discover things that are missing. You can link out to a slow loading HTML version of the spreadsheet at http://www.iath.virginia.edu/hcs/mmcomp.html.

Conclusions

I can finally now, in the concluding section of this paper, survey all these digressions and plot a course back to your problem. I therefore place a Table of Digressions here rather than where it should be in a well-formed paper.

Is humanities computing an academic discipline?
It is if it can be taught and administered as a discipline within the academy. No discipline can exist in theory. The theory of the discipline should be one of the questions discussed by practitioners within an appropriate administrative and instructional context.

Is humanities computing a teachable discipline?
That depends on who you think your audience is and what you think you can teach them. The problem is what would benefit students in the humanities and how to best implement such instruction.

Who do you think will benefit from instruction in computing within the humanities?

Students who want to participate in the creation and criticism of multimedia. Students who want to be the artists, designers, writers, and critics of computer-based multimedia works.

How can we be of benefit to them?

By introducing teaching them the creative skills within the context of the traditions of interpretation of the humanities. By teaching them to apply the critical and theoretical learning that comes with a humanities education to new media and its culture.

Why should we worry about the administration of humanities computing?

Because the health of a discipline lies in the administrative details. A discipline exists in implementations for which reason you have to ask what implementation would foster a healthy community of inquiry at your institution.

OK, how should humanities computing be administered?

It should be funded appropriately without endangering the disciplines with which it connects. It should be integrated appropriately into the administrative structure of the humanities. It should be taught. It should have spaces at its disposal where students, faculty, and staff can pursue their studies and gather.

Is it a field of scholarly inquiry?

It is if the structures are put in place to encourage people to inquire into it, but that inquiry should be more than the activities associated with textual disciplines. Inquiry in the humanities should include performance, artistic creation, and musical interpretation. Administrative structures in a field where the object of study is evolving before our eyes should encourage the creation of multimedia, not just its criticism. Scholarly inquiry should not be only about computing, it should be in computing.

There is another story of the creation of technology which is probably more appropriate to this age and that is Mary Shelley's story of Frankenstein and his daemon. Let me take you back to the "dreary night of November," not unlike this coming evening, when Frankenstein animates his creation.

> With an anxiety that almost amounted to agony, I collected the instruments of life around me, that I might infuse a spark of being into the lifeless thing that

lay at my feet. It was already one in the morning; the rain pattered dismally against the panes, and my candle was nearly burnt out, when by the glimmer of the half-extinguished light, I saw the dull yellow eye of the creature open; it breathed hard, and convulsive motion agitated its limbs.

How can I describe my emotions at this catastrophe, or how delineate the wretch whom with such infinite pains and care I had endeavored to form? ... Unable to endure the aspect of the being I had created, I rushed out of the room. (Shelley, *Frankenstein*, p. 52)

Frankenstein at the moment of creation is appalled by his child. I am not the first to comment that for Mary Shelley it is not so much the creation of artificial life that is the animating sin of this story as the abandonment of one's creation. When Frankenstein's wretch finally has a chance to talk to him he says, "Yet you, my creator, detest and spurn me, thy creature, to whom thou art bound by ties only dissoluble by the annihilation of one of us" (Shelley, *Frankenstein*, p. 101). Socrates in his unrealistic Platonic way would have us be philosopher-midwives who judge the health of the children of our thought and abandon those found wanting. Mary Shelley confronts us with a technologist who does just that and is haunted by his abandoned creation. In her story the question is not what do we make, but how do we respond and care for our inventions. Computing is here in the humanities, the problem is what to do with it once we have overcome our anxieties. Our students want to participate in the discovery of raising this invention to an unforeseeable maturity. We can ignore the call to play with computing and leave it to its own horrific devices or we can pay attention to it and care for it in the ways we care for other artifacts, through study, through artistic interpretation, through dialogue, and through teaching. I ask you who are reconceiving humanities computing with a view to giving birth to a discipline and program, will you take responsibility for this creation or will you judge it a catastrophe and abandon it? Will you ever know what it is before you care for it?

Bibliography

Blattner, M.M. and Dannenberg, R.B. (eds) (1992). *Multimedia Interface Design*, New York: ACM Press.

Campbell, B. (1994). *The Information Highway: Avenues for Expanding Canada's Economy, Employment and Productivity*, Ottawa: Information Technology Industry and Industry Canada.

Centre for Educational Research and Innovation (1995). *Knowledge Bases for Education Policies*, Maastricht, The Netherlands: Organisation for Economic Co-operation and Development.

Encyclopædia Britannica Online, http://search.eb.com/bol/topic?eu=
1461&sctn=1 (accessed 25 October 1999).

Foray, D. and Lundvall, B-A. (1996). "The Knowledge-Based Economy:
From the Economics of Knowledge to the Learning Economy,"
Employment and Growth in the Knowledge-based Economy, Paris:
Organisation for Economic Co-operation and Development, pp.
11–34.

Gera, S. and Massé, P. (1996). *Employment Performance in the Knowledge-
Based Economy*, Ottawa: Industry Canada, Human Resources
Development Canada.

Haykin, R. (ed.) (1994). *Multimedia Demystified*, New York: Random
House.

Immen, W. (1998). "High-tech Talent on Fast Track," *The Globe and
Mail*, 14 July, A10.

Information Highway Advisory Council (1996). *Building the Information
Society: Moving Canada into the 21st Century*, Ottawa: Information
Highway Advisory Council.

Information Highway Advisory Council (1997). *Preparing Canada for a
Digital World*, Ottawa: Information Highway Advisory Council.

Learning and Training Working Group (1995). *Making It Happen:
Final Report of the Learning and Training Working Group*, Ottawa:
Information Highway Advisory Council.

Lee, F. and Has, H. (1996). "A Quantitative Assessment of High-
Knowledge Industries versus Low-Knowledge Industries," in P. Howitt
(ed.) *The Implications of Knowledge-Based Growth for Micro-
Economic Policies*, Calgary: University of Calgary Press, pp. 39–82.

Mactavish, A., Rockwell, G. and Buckley, J. (1999). "Whisperings in the
Hall: Building a Place for Multimedia Studies in the Humanities,"
presented at the ACH-ALLC 1999 conference in Virginia.

Newell, E. (1996). "Business and Education Partnership must Tackle
Dilemma of both Work and Worker Shortages," *Canadian Speeches*,
10 (5), pp. 23–9.

NORTEL (1998). *The Supply of High-Technology Professionals: An Issue
for Ontario's and Canada's Future*, Brampton: NORTEL.

Ontario College Application Services, *CommuniCAAT 1998–99; Your
Guide to Ontario's Colleges*, Guelph, Ontario.

Organisation for Economic Co-operation and Development (1989).
Information Technology and New Growth Opportunities, Paris:
OECD.

Organisation for Economic Co-operation and Development (1996).
Information Infrastructure Policies in OECD Countries, Paris: OECD.

Plato (1989). *The Collected Dialogues of Plato*, E. Hamilton and H.
Cairns (eds), Princeton: Princeton University Press.

Postman, N. (1993). *Technopoly: The Surrender of Culture to Technology*, New York: Vintage Books.

SECOR (1997). *The Multimedia Industry in Canada: An Analysis of Development Options*.

Senn, J. (1995). *Information Technology in Business: Principles, Practices, and Opportunities*, Englewood Cliffs: Prentice Hall.

Shelley, M. (1995). *Frankenstein; or, the Modern Prometheus*, New York: Washington Square Press.

Sterne, L. (1985). *The Life and Opinions of Tristram Shandy*, London: Penguin.

Woodall, P. (1996). "The World Economy: The Hitchhiker's Guide to Cybernomics," *The Economist*, September 28, pp. 1–46.

Note from the author:

This essay was written for a seminar on the question of disciplinarity at the University of Virginia (UVA) that was run in November 1999 a millennium ago before we started calling the field the "digital humanities".[3] In this essay I was addressing the folk associated with the UVA's Institute for Advanced Technology in the Humanities (IATH) who were taking the first steps in developing a humanities computing degree. As it turns out they did develop a proposal for a Master's degree in Digital Humanities, though that degree program was never implemented. Something happened between all the years of work developing the program and its implementation, and that is an administrative story, though not for this volume.

At the time we were still fascinated by the ontological question as to what the discipline was, if it was indeed a discipline. I was on the side of disciplinarity and opposed to Willard McCarty's view that humanities computing was an interdisciplinary methods commons,[4] but what I really wanted to do was to shift the discussion to another form of creative work, namely the administrative work of creating a degree that those before me were embarking on. The act of developing degree programs was one way of administratively answering the question of disciplinarity through building. If you can create a program then the digital humanities becomes a discipline in the sense of being able to reproduce itself through the preparation of students (disciples.)

A second move I made was to claim a student focus for the paper. Who is this discipline for? How will we take care of it over time? Few students

---

[3] See the website at http://www.iath.virginia.edu/hcs. On the site are a number of other interventions on this question by people like Susan Hockey, Willard McCarty, Lou Burnard, Espen Aarseth and Stuart Moulthrop.

[4] This was worked out in detail in Willard McCarty (2005), *Humanities Computing*, New York: Palgrave.

understand or care what the humanities are. They want to learn to think about and participate in the creation of new media works which is why terms like "humanities computing" and now "digital humanities" don't capture the breadth of what we can do in a discipline. I was arguing for a long-term engagement with students as partners that goes beyond the different names for this emerging field like information studies, media studies, cultural informatics, software studies, interactive arts, game design, and multimedia. The opportunities are so rich I no longer think there will be one digital humanities, instead digital practices will flourish both in existing fields and in fluid new ones. Perhaps McCarty was right—perhaps humanities computing is only the thread that brings together the humanists in these emerging disciplines. Personally I prefer to include the arts and call this thread the "digital arts," but that's another story.

Geoffrey Rockwell, November 2012

CHAPTER 2

What is Humanities Computing and What is Not?

John Unsworth
Brandeis University

John Unsworth (2002). Originally published in *Jahrbuch für Computerphilologie*, 4, pp. 71–84, http://computerphilologie.uni-muenchen. de/jg02/unsworth.html.

Note from the Editors:

Implicit in this article is the reminder that the most widely used model of computation, the Universal Turing machine, can, by definition, simulate any other machine. Here Unsworth identifies that a key implication of using the computer or 'all-purpose modeling machine' is that it can be very difficult to establish (for both ourselves and onlookers) firm boundaries between the various tasks that we might do with it (for example, to choose modern-day examples, carry out research into social networks or publicise research on social networks). Hence, this article explores what humanities computing is and what it is not. It is distinguished by the fact that it can be described as being even more relevant and important today than when it was first published in 2002 because it provides a unique perspective on the perennial question of whether the digital humanities is 'just' the humanities done digitally and whether the computer is merely a tool. Both this text and Unsworth's observation that 'one of the many things you can do with computers is something that I would call humanities computing, in which the computer is used as a tool for modeling humanities data and our understanding of it, and that activity is entirely distinct from using the computer when it models the typewriter, or the telephone, or the phonograph, or any of the many other things it can be' are fundamental to this debate.

We are the mimics. Clouds are pedagogues.

(Wallace Stevens, *Notes Toward a Supreme Fiction*[1])

Any intelligent entity that wishes to reason about its world encounters an important, inescapable fact: reasoning is a process that goes on internally, while most things it wishes to reason about exist only externally.

(Davis et al., 1993)[2]

Abstract

I'll give the short answer to the question "what is humanities computing?" up front: it is foreshadowed by my two epigraphs. Humanities computing is a practice of representation, a form of modeling or, as Wallace Stevens has it, mimicry. It is also (as Davis and his co-authors put it) a way of reasoning and a set of ontological commitments, and its representational practice is shaped by the need for efficient computation on the one hand, and for human communication on the other. We'll come back to these ideas but, before we do, let's stop for a moment to consider why one would ask a question such as "what is humanities computing?"

First, I think the question arises because it is important to distinguish a tool from the various uses that can be made of it, if for no other reason than to evaluate the effectiveness of the tool for different purposes. A hammer is very good nail-driver, not such a good screwdriver, a fairly effective weapon, and a lousy musical instrument. Because the computer is – much more than the hammer – a general-purpose machine (in fact, a general-purpose modeling machine) it tends to blur distinctions among the different activities it enables. Are we word-processing or doing email? Are we doing research or shopping? Are we entertaining ourselves or working? It's all data: isn't it all just data processing? Sure it is, and no it isn't. The goals, rhetoric, consequences, benefits, of the various things we do with computers are not the same, in spite of the hegemony of Windows and the Web. All our activities may look the same, and they may all take place in the same interface, the same 'discourse universe' of icons, menus, and behaviors, but they're not all equally valuable, they don't all work on the same assumptions – they're not, in fact, interchangeable. To put a more narrowly academic focus on all this, I would hazard a guess that everyone reading this uses a word-processor and email as basic tools of the

---

[1]   *The Collected Poems of Wallace Stevens*, New York: Alfred A. Knopf, 1951, p. 384.

[2]   Randall Davis, Howard Shrobe and Peter Szolovits (1993). "What is a Knowledge Representation?" in *AI Magazine*, 14 (1), pp. 17–33; see http://www.medg.lcs.mit.edu/ftp/psz/k-rep.html (accessed October 31, 2002).

profession, and I expect that many readers are also in the humanities. Even so, you do not all do humanities computing – nor should you, for heaven's sake – any more than you should all be medievalists, or modernists, or linguists.

So, one of the many things you can do with computers is something that I would call humanities computing, in which the computer is used as a tool for modeling humanities data and our understanding of it, and that activity is entirely distinct from using the computer when it models the typewriter, or the telephone, or the phonograph, or any of the many other things it can be.

The second reason one might ask the question "what is humanities computing" is in order to distinguish between exemplars of that activity and charlatans (c.f. Tito Orlandi) or pretenders to it. Charlatans are, in Professor Orlandi's view, people who present as "humanities computing" some body of work that is not that. It may be computer-based (for example, it may be published on the Web), and it may present very engaging content, but if it doesn't have a way to be wrong, if one can't say whether it does or doesn't work, whether it is or isn't internally consistent and logically coherent, then it's something other than humanities computing. The problem with charlatanism is that it undersells the market by providing a quick-and-dirty simulacrum of something that, done right, is expensive, time-consuming, and difficult. Put another way, charlatans trade intellectual self-consistency and internal logical coherence (in what probably ought to be a massive and complicated act of representation) for surface effects, immediate production, and canned conclusions. When one does this, one is competing unfairly with projects that are more thorough and thoughtful, both in their approach to the problem of representation and in their planning and testing of technical and intellectual infrastructure.

The bad news here is that all humanities computing projects today are involved in some degree of charlatanism, even the best of them. But degree matters, and one way in which that degree can be measured is by the interactivity offered to users who wish to frame their own research questions. If there is none offered, and no interactivity, then the project is probably pure charlatanism. If it offers some (say, keyword searching), then it can be taken a bit more seriously. If it offers structured searching, a bit more so. If it offers combinatorial queries, more so. If it allows you to change parameters and values in order to produce new models, it starts to look very much like something that must be built on a thoroughgoing representation. If it lets you introduce new algorithms for calculating the outcomes of changed parameters and values, then it is extremely well designed indeed. And so on. This evaluative scale is not, as it seems to be, based on functional characteristics: it uses those functional characteristics as an index to the infrastructure that is required to support certain kinds of functionality. On this scale of relative charlatanism, no perfectly exemplary project exists, as far as I know. But you see the principle implied by this scale – the more room a resource offers for the exercise of independent imagination and curiosity, the more substantially well thought-out, well designed, and well produced a resource it must be.

Finally, and most candidly, one asks the question "what is humanities computing" in order to justify, on the basis of distinctions like those I have just drawn, new and continuing investments of personal, professional, institutional, and cultural resources. This investment could take the form of a funded project, or a new undergraduate or graduate degree, or a new center or institute. At this level, the activity that is humanities computing competes with other intellectual pursuits – history, literary study, religious study, etc. – for the hearts, minds, and purses of the university, and external funding agencies, even though, in practice, the particulars of humanities computing may well – and will likely – call upon and fall into one of its competitors' traditional disciplinary areas of expertise. So, as Willard McCarty has often noted, we have a problem distinguishing between computing in the service of a research agenda framed by the traditional parameters of the humanities, and, on the other hand, the much rarer, more peculiar case where the humanities research agenda itself is framed and formed by what we can do with computers.

So, given that humanities computing isn't general-purpose academic computing – isn't word-processing, email, web-browsing – what is it, and how do you know when you're doing it, or when you might need to learn how to do it? At the opening of this discussion, I said that

> [h]umanities computing is a practice of representation, a form of modeling or ... mimicry. It is ... a way of reasoning and a set of ontological commitments, and its representational practice is shaped by the need for efficient computation on the one hand, and for human communication on the other.

I've long believed this, but the terms of these assertions are drawn from Davis, Shrobe, and Szolovits, "What is a Knowledge Representation?" in a 1993 issue of *AI Magazine*. As I unpack these terms, one at a time, I will begin by expanding my quotation of Davis et al. a little bit, stopping on each of six points to look at some examples from the realm of humanities computing, and concluding with some observations about why all of this matters.

I. Humanities Computing as Model or Mimicry

Davis et al. use the term "surrogate" instead of "mimicry" or "model". Here's what they say about surrogates:

The first question about any surrogate is its intended identity: what is it a surrogate for? There must be some form of correspondence specified between the surrogate and its intended referent in the world; the correspondence is the semantics for the representation.

The second question is fidelity: how close is the surrogate to the real thing? What attributes of the original does it capture and make explicit, and which does it omit? Perfect fidelity is in general impossible, both in practice and in principle. It is impossible in principle because any thing other than the thing itself is necessarily different from the thing itself (in location if nothing else). Put the other way around, the only completely accurate representation of an object is the object itself. All other representations are inaccurate; they inevitably contain simplifying assumptions and possibly artifacts.[3]

I.1 Example

A *catalogue record (vs. full-text representation)*. The catalogue record is obviously not the thing it refers to: it is, nonetheless, a certain kind of surrogate, and it captures and makes explicit certain attributes of the original object – title, author, publication date, number of pages, topical reference. It obviously omits others – the full text of the book, for example. Now, other types of surrogates would capture those features (a full-text transcription, for example) but would leave out still other aspects (illustrations, cover art, binding). You can go on pushing that as far as you like, or until you come up with a surrogate that is only distinguished from the original by not occupying the same space, but the point is all of these surrogates along the way are "inaccurate; they inevitably contain simplifying assumptions and possibly artifacts"[4] – meaning new features introduced by the process of creating the representation. Humanities computing, as a practice of knowledge representation, grapples with this realization that its representations are surrogates in a very self-conscious way, more self-conscious, I would say, than we generally are in the humanities when we 'represent' the objects of our attention in essays, books, and lectures.

---

[3] Ibid.
[4] Ibid.

II. Humanities Computing as a Way of Reasoning

Actually, what Davis et al. say is that any knowledge representation is a "fragmentary theory of intelligent reasoning"[5] and any knowledge representation begins with:

> some insight indicating how people reason intelligently, or ... some belief about what it means to reason intelligently at all ... A representation's theory of intelligent reasoning is often implicit, but can be made more evident by examining its three components: (i) the representation's fundamental conception of intelligent inference; (ii) the set of inferences the representation sanctions; and (iii) the set of inferences it recommends. Where the sanctioned inferences indicate what can be inferred at all, the recommended inferences are concerned with what should be inferred. (Guidance is needed because the set of sanctioned inferences is typically far too large to be used indiscriminately.) Where the ontology we examined earlier tells us how to see, the recommended inferences suggest how to reason. These components can also be seen as the representation's answers to three corresponding fundamental questions: (i) What does it mean to reason intelligently? (ii) What can we infer from what we know? and (iii) What ought we to infer from what we know? Answers to these questions are at the heart of a representation's spirit and mindset; knowing its position on these issues tells us a great deal about it.[6]

Later on, the authors quote a foundational paper by Marvin Minsky, setting forth the frame theory. Minsky explains:

> Whenever one encounters a new situation (or makes a substantial change in one's viewpoint), he selects from memory a structure called a frame; a remembered framework to be adapted to fit reality by changing details as necessary. A frame ... [represents] a stereotyped situation, like being in a certain kind of living room, or going to a child's birthday party.[7]

And they go on to point out how reasoning and representation are intertwined – how we think by way of representations.

II.1 Examples

A concordance. (i) the concordance's fundamental conception of intelligent inference? It assumes that verbal patterns in a text are a key to the meaning of that text. (ii) the set of inferences the concordance sanctions? It would

---

[5]   Ibid.
[6]   Ibid.
[7]   Ibid.

support certain kinds of stylistic analysis, because it can report the frequency with which certain words are used in a text, or the frequency with which words of a certain length are used in a text, and it would support the inference that some words are not important, assuming it can use a stop-list and, if it incorporated a lemmatiser, it would support the notion that word-stems are more important than actual word forms, but (iii) the set of inferences it recommends? Most concordancing software makes sorting by frequency and examination of keywords in context much easier than other functions (or forms of inference).

A relational database. Think about how a relational database establishes the grounds of rational inference by establishing fields in records in tables, and think about how it sanctions any sort of question having to do with any combination of the elements in its tables, but actually recommends certain kinds of queries by establishing relationships between elements of different tables.

III. Humanities Computing as a Set of Ontological Commitments

On the matter of ontological commitments, Davis et al. say:

> [S]electing a representation means making a set of ontological commitments. The commitments are in effect a strong pair of glasses that determine what we can see, bringing some part of the world into sharp focus, at the expense of blurring other parts. These commitments and their focusing/blurring effect are not an incidental side effect of a representation choice; they are of the essence: a KR is a set of ontological commitments. It is unavoidably so because of the inevitable imperfections of representations. It is usefully so because judicious selection of commitments provides the opportunity to focus attention on aspects of the world we believe to be relevant.[8]

III.1 Examples

OHCO (Renear, Mylonas, and Durand, "Refining our Notion of What Text Really Is" from 1993 – the same year as the Davis et al. article, though to be fair it draws on an earlier piece, S.J. DeRose, D.G. Durand, E. Mylonas, and A.H. Renear (1990), "What is Text, Really?"). This view of text says that text is an Ordered Hierarchy of Content Objects, which means, for example, that content objects nest – paragraphs occur within chapters, chapters in volumes, and so on. It also means that a language

---

[8]   Ibid.

that captures ordered hierarchical relationships and allows content to be carried within its expression of those relationships can capture what matters about text. Hence SGML. But, as Jerry McGann and others have pointed out, this view of text misses certain textual ontologies – metaphor, for example – because they are not hierarchical, or more accurately, they violate hierarchy. Davis et al. would say that's not a sign of a flaw in SGML (or XML, which shares the same requirement for nesting) or in the OHCO thesis, but a sign that both are true knowledge representations – they bring certain things into focus and blur others, allowing us to pay particular attention to particular aspects of what's out there.

Deborah Parker's Dante Project. For a much simpler example, consider Deborah Parker's SGML edition of Dante's Inferno.[9] In this edition, Parker has marked up (in the TEI DTD) all of the cantos, stanzas, and lines in Dante's poem, and then all of the proper names and epithets, distinguishing mythical, historical, biblical, and literary sources, different types of animals, different types of people, regularizing forms of proper names, etc. All of this implies that the form of the poem is important as a kind of substrate for references to proper names and that, by paying attention to the categories in which named things participate, we can learn something important about this poem.

IV. Humanities Computing as Shaped by the Need for Efficient Computation

Davis et al. explain:

> From a purely mechanistic view, reasoning in machines (and somewhat more debatably, in people) is a computational process. Simply put, to use a representation we must compute with it. As a result, questions about computational efficiency are inevitably central to the notion of representation.[10]

And later, they point out that different modes of representation have different efficiencies:

> Traditional semantic nets facilitate bi-directional propagation by the simple expedient of providing an appropriate set of links, while rule-based systems facilitate plausible inferences by supplying indices from goals to rules whose

---

[9]   http://www.iath.virginia.edu/dante (accessed October 31, 2002).
[10] Davis et al, "What is a Knowledge Representation?"

conclusion matches (for backward chaining) and from facts to rules whose premise matches (forward chaining).[11]

IV.1 Examples

Markup and computation. The reason for requiring that elements nest properly within a specified hierarchy is to enable efficient computation. In fact, the SGML grammar in its original form was really too flexible to be efficient, which is why certain features permitted in the grammar (like overlapping or concurrent hierarchies) were never implemented in software. XML simplifies out of SGML some of its other expressive possibilities – possibilities that made SGML difficult to write software for – and, as a result, suddenly we have lots more software for XML than we ever had for SGML. On the other hand, none of this software is any good at computing things that can't be expressed in neatly nesting hierarchies.

Latent semantic indexing. Compare the characteristics of the concordance, and its efficiencies, with those of latent semantic indexing. Like the concordance,

> LSI relies on the constituent terms of a document to suggest the document's semantic content. However, the LSI model views the terms in a document as somewhat unreliable indicators of the concepts contained in the document. It assumes that the variability of word choice partially obscures the semantic structure of the document. By reducing the dimensionality of the term-document space, the underlying, semantic relationships between documents are revealed, and much of the 'noise' (differences in word usage, terms that do not help distinguish documents, etc.) is eliminated. LSI statistically analyses the patterns of word usage across the entire document collection, placing documents with similar word usage patterns near each other in the term-document space, and allowing semantically-related documents to be near each other even though they may not share terms (Letsche and Berry, "Large-Scale Information Retrieval With Latent Semantic Indexing"[12]).

If you really believed that the occurrence of a particular word was the important thing, then you'd want to be working with the efficiencies of the concordance – but if, on the other hand, you believed that meaning was more important than the word chosen to express it, you'd want to be working with the efficiencies of latent semantic indexing.

---

[11]   Ibid.
[12]   See http://www.medg.lcs.mit.edu/ftp/psz/k-rep.html (accessed October 31, 2002).

V. Humanities Computing as Shaped by the Need for Human Communication

Davis et al. conclude that any efficiency stands opposed in some way to the fullness of expression, and that

> [e]ither end of this spectrum seems problematic: we ignore computational considerations at our peril, but we can also be overly concerned with them, producing representations that are fast but inadequate for real use.[13]

Of course, there is something about the brute facticity of the computer that makes its results – especially when they are fast – seem definitive, so much so that we may overlook the inadequacy of a representation that seems to work well computationally. But eventually, we are likely to recognize inadequacy, and we are more likely to do so if we have not only to use these representations, but also to produce them. On this final point, Davis et al. go on to say:

> Knowledge representations are also the means by which we express things about the world, the medium of expression and communication in which we tell the machine (and perhaps one another) about the world. ... a medium of expression and communication for use by us. That in turn presents two important sets of questions. One set is familiar: How well does the representation function as a medium of expression? How general is it? How precise? Does it provide expressive adequacy? etc. An important question less often discussed is, How well does it function as a medium of communication? That is, how easy is it for us to "talk" or think in that language? What kinds of things are easily said in the language and what kinds of things are so difficult as to be pragmatically impossible? Note that the questions here are of the form "how easy is it?" rather than "can we?" This is a language we must use, so things that are possible in principle are useful but insufficient; the real question is one of pragmatic utility. If the representation makes things possible but not easy, then as real users we may never know whether we have misunderstood the representation and just do not know how to use it, or it truly cannot express some things we would like to say. A representation is the language in which we communicate, hence we must be able to speak it without heroic effort.[14]

V.1 Example

The difficulty of using markup languages. Ever since we started using markup languages like SGML, one has heard expressed the fear that

---

[13]   Davis et al., "What is a Knowledge Representation?"
[14]   Ibid.

humanists would never be able to speak it "without heroic effort". To be fair, good (and with XML, readily available) software removes some of the complexity – for example, by offering you only the elements that can legally be used in a particular point in the hierarchy. But still, you have to be able to grasp the purpose and intent of the DTD in order to use it sensibly, you have to understand the principles of stylesheets, and so on. It would probably be accurate, at this moment in the evolution of humanities computing, to say that markup languages are still problematic as a medium of communication. Experts can 'talk' or 'think' in these languages, but most of us cannot, and there are many examples out there, in discussions on TEI-L (the TEI users list) for example, where the question at issue is exactly whether one has misunderstood the TEI or whether it really cannot express some of the things we would like to say about literary and linguistic texts.

VI. Humanities Computing and Formal Expression

There is also one other feature of knowledge representations that Davis and his co-authors don't mention, because their discussion takes it for granted. That feature is the formal language in which any such representation must be expressed. This formal language can be any one that is

> composed of primitive symbols acted on by certain rules of formation (statements concerning the symbols, functions, and sentences allowable in the system) and developed by inference from a set of axioms. The system thus consists of any number of formulas built up through finite combinations of the primitive symbols—combinations that are formed from the axioms in accordance with the stated rules.[15]

For our purposes, what is important about the requirement of formal expression is that it puts humanities computing, or rather the computing humanist, in the position of having to do two things that mostly, in the humanities, we don't do: provide unambiguous expressions of ideas, and provide them according to stated rules. In short, once we begin to express our understanding of, say, a literary text in a language such as XML, a formal grammar that requires us to state the rules according to which we will deploy that grammar in a text or texts, then we find that our representation of the text is subject to verification – for internal consistency, and especially for consistency with the rules we have stated.

---

[15]   Ibid.

Conclusions

Having said what I think humanities computing is, it remains to say what it is good for, or why it matters. Why do we need to worry about whether we can express what we know about the humanities in formal language, in terms that are tractable to computation, in utterances that are internally coherent and consistent with a declared set of rules? Why indeed, when we know that to do this inevitably involves some loss of expressive power, some tradeoff at the expense of nuance, meaning, and significance? My answer? Navigation and exchange.

We are by now well into a phase of civilization when the terrain to be mapped, explored, and annexed is information space, and what's mapped is not continents, regions, or acres but disciplines, ontologies, and concepts. We need representations in order to navigate this new world, and those representations need to be computable, because the computer mediates our access to this world, and those representations need to be produced at first-hand, by someone who knows the terrain. If, where the humanities should be represented, we in the humanities scrawl, or allow others to scrawl, "Here be dragons," then we will have failed. We should not refuse to engage in representation simply because we feel no representation can do justice to all that we know or feel about our territory. That's too fastidious. We ought to understand that maps are always schematic and simplified, but those qualities are what make them useful.

In some form, the semantic web is our future, and it will require formal representations of the human record. Those representations – ontologies, schemas, knowledge representations, call them what you will – should be produced by people trained in the humanities. Producing them is a discipline that requires training in the humanities, but also in elements of mathematics, logic, engineering, and computer science. Up to now, most of the people who have this mix of skills have been self-made, but as we become serious about making the known world computable, we will need to train such people deliberately. There is a great deal of work for such people to do – not all of it technical, by any means. Much of this map-making will be social work, consensus-building, compromise. But even that will need to be done by people who know how consensus can be enabled and embodied in a computational medium.

Consensus-based ontologies (in history, music, archaeology, architecture, literature, etc.) will be necessary, in a computational medium, if we hope to be able to travel across the borders of particular collections, institutions, languages, nations, in order to exchange ideas. Those ontologies will in turn exist in a network of topics, a web of 'trading zones', to use a term that Willard McCarty has used to explain humanities computing, having borrowed that term from a book that itself borrows concepts of anthropology to explain the practice of physics. And as that genealogy of that metaphor suggests, come tomorrow we will require the rigor of computational methods in the discipline of the humanities not in spite of, but because of, the way that human understanding and human creativity violate containment, exceed representation, and muddle distinctions.

Bibliography

Davis, R., Shrobe, R.H. and Szolovits, P. (1993). "What is a Knowledge Representation?" *AI Magazine*, 14 (1), pp. 17–33, http://www.medg. lcs.mit.edu/ftp/psz/k-rep.html (accessed October 31, 2002).

DeRose, S.J., Durand, D.G., Mylonas, E. and Renear, A.H. (1990). "What is Text, Really?" *Journal of Computing in Higher Education*, 1 (2), pp. 3–26.

"Is Humanities Computing an Academic Discipline?" An Interdisciplinary Seminar at the University of Virginia (1999–2000), http://www.iath. virginia.edu/hcs (accessed October 31, 2002).

Letsche, T.A. and Berry, M.W. (1997). "Large-Scale Information Retrieval with Latent Semantic Indexing," *Information Sciences – Applications*, 100, pp. 105–37, http://www.cs.utk.edu/~berry/lsi++/index.html (accessed October 31, 2002).

McCarty, W. (n.d.). "We Would Know How We Know What We Know. Responding to the Computational Transformation of the Humanities," http://www.kcl.ac.uk/humanities/cch/wlm/essays/know/know.html (accessed October 31, 2002).

McCarty, W. and Kirschenbaum, M. (n.d.). "Institutional Models for Humanities Computing," http://www.kcl.ac.uk/humanities/cch/allc/ archive/hcim/hcim-021009.htm (accessed October 31, 2002).

Orlandi, T. (n.d.). "The Scholarly Environment of Humanities Computing. A Reaction to Willard McCarty's talk on The Computational Transformation of the Humanities," http://RmCisadu.let.uniroma1. it/~orlandi/mccarty1.html (accessed October 31, 2002).

Renear, A., Mylonas, E. and Durand, D. (n.d.). "Refining our Notion of What Text Really Is. The Problem of Overlapping Hierarchies," http://www.stg.brown.edu/resources/stg/monographs/ohco.htm (accessed October 31, 2002).

TEI-L (n.d.). http://listserv.brown.edu/archives/tei-l.html (accessed October 31, 2002).

The Text Encoding Initiative Consortium (n.d.). http://www.tei-c.org (accessed October 21, 2002).

Note from the author:

What was Humanities Computing?
The history of the term "humanities computing" has been discussed elsewhere (Willard McCarty, *Humanities Computing*, New York: Palgrave 2005), as has the shift from "humanities computing" to "digital humanities" (Patrick Svensson, "Humanities Computing as Digital Humanities" in *Digital Humanities Quarterly*, 3 (3), 2009): what I observe, looking back at my essay on "What is Humanities Computing and What is Not?" is that the essay seems nervous about its own question. It seems important to establish that "humanities computing" is not just an instrumental term, with the focus on using the computer, but an intellectual activity in its own right. Or maybe not exactly in its own right: as an intellectual activity, it appears to require validation in terms of another field of inquiry (artificial intelligence). But even after having provided that validation, the essay still needs to ask:

> Why do we need to worry about whether we can express what we know about the humanities in formal language, in terms that are tractable to computation, in utterances that are internally coherent and consistent with a declared set of rules? Why indeed, when we know that to do this inevitably involves some loss of expressive power, some tradeoff at the expense of nuance, meaning, and significance?

My answer, at the time, was "navigation and exchange," by which I meant the semantic web, though I didn't know I meant that, because the term wouldn't be coined until 2001 (by Tim Berners-Lee). Computable humanities was important, I argued, because "we are by now well into a phase of civilization when the terrain to be mapped, explored, and annexed is information space, and what's mapped is not continents, regions, or acres but disciplines, ontologies, and concepts." But really, the mapping I describe in this essay is craftwork, mostly markup, done by hand. To be honest, looking back at this piece, the weak link in my argument has to do with the need to make ideas "computationally tractable". I liked the idea of having a computational framework that required one to articulate ideas explicitly and consistently, but I didn't actually provide a lot of examples of the value of computation itself, or of analytical operations that require computation. Perhaps that's because it wasn't until 2003 that I started tinkering with text mining, and it wasn't until 2004 that Google Books came along, rapidly digitizing huge swaths of the textual record of world cultures, and inaugurating the era of big data in the humanities.

John Unsworth, November 2012

CHAPTER 3

Information Technology and the Troubled Humanities

Jerome McGann
University of Virginia

Jerome McGann (2005). Originally published in *Text Technology*, 14 (2) (2005), pp. 105–21.

Note from the Editors:
This article has a Janus-like intellectual vision. On the one hand McGann argues that digital technology must be integrated into every possible facet of scholarship; on the other he persuasively argues for the enduring quintessentiality of textual and bibliographical work. Why? Because technology is transforming the library, 'the chief locus of our cultural memory as well as our central symbol of that memory's life and importance'. Among the 'what is DH?' body of work there is no shortage of literature that expounds the remarkable breakthroughs that computing is likely to bring to the Humanities and the revolutionary developments that are, all too often it seems, just around the corner. This article is especially noteworthy in that it provides a foil to such extreme positions. In it McGann takes a balanced and wide-ranging, albeit dramatic, look at the implications of such changes for the humanities. These range from the positive one of the almost instant access for scholars to some resources that were otherwise locked away in libraries to the more negative ones such as the publishing and tenure crisis that still exists today.

Abstract

Where will Information Technology leave humanities education five, ten, twenty … years from now. This essay addresses that question in the context of several current "crises" facing humanities scholarship and education. These crises have followed from the displacement of traditional philological work from the center of the literary and cultural studies' curriculum—in particular editorial theory and method, history of the language, and bibliographical studies. The coming of digital technology to the humanities has revealed the historical necessity of recovering these basic disciplinary skills.

KEYWORDS: Humanities computing, Theory of textuality, Scholarly publishing, Theory and method of interpretation, Research libraries.

1.

Let me begin with Henry Adams, whose urbane pessimism gets summarized in this late passage from his famous autobiography:

> He saw his education complete, and was sorry he ever began it. As a matter of taste, he greatly preferred his eighteenth-century education when God was a father and nature a mother, and all was for the best in a scientific universe. He repudiated all share in the world as it was to be and yet he could not detect where his responsibility began or ended.

(Henry Adams, The Education of Henry Adams, chapter 31 (1907)).

An education ought to make one ready for life, but Adams' education has turned out a kind of black comedy. His humanistic training has left him unprepared for the dynamo of the twentieth century. So he joins the coming race as an observer, a scholar—what he calls an "historian". But "all that the historian won was a vehement wish to escape."

Today, as we pass through a similar historical moment, a moment even more wrenching for a humanist than Adams' moment, *The Education* seems especially pertinent. We don't want to guide our passage through this moment with tabloid reports like *The Gutenberg Elegies*, which supply us with a cartoon set of alternatives (Birkerts, 1994). Information technology comprises an axis of evil that Birkerts advises us to "refuse". We can no more "refuse" this digital environment than we can "refuse" the empire the US, for better and for worse, has become. We may well feel "a violent wish to escape" both of these unfolding—and closely enfolded—histories, but we do better to recall that as we are characters in these events, we bear a responsibility toward them.

And there precisely we find Henry Adams waiting for us, caught between two worlds. Not between a dead world and a world powerless to be born, however, but between two living worlds, one relatively young, the other ancient. He neither abandons the one nor refuses the other. The positive revelation of his great book tells us that we all always inhabit such a condition. At certain historical moments, that universal experience seems especially clear, and certain figures come forward to render an honest accounting.

His book also tells a cautionary tale, which is the second gift it passes on to us. If the dynamo and the Virgin each have their humanities in Adams' view, he represents himself as the Nowhere Man. Not that he takes no action, but that he restricts his action to honest reporting. As a consequence, both Virgin and dynamo emerge from his book as mysterious forces—in fact, as those "images" which so preoccupy and immobilize him throughout his book.

"Where will information technology leave humanities education five/ten/twenty ... n years from now?" The question implicitly asks for something more than an honest report. Reading Adams helps me remember to be wary of making forecasts. But he also reminds me that I do have hopes, as well as a few convictions about how we should look at those futures we imagine lying ahead of us.

So let me begin with a conviction: that we have to carry out what Marxist scholars used to call "the praxis of theory"—or as the poet better said, we must learn by going where we have to go. Involved here are two hard sayings that can no longer be fudged or tabled. First, integrating digital technology into our scholarship will have to be pursued on as broad a scale as possible. Circumstances are such that this work can no longer be safely postponed. Second, we have to restore textual and bibliographical work to the center of what we do.

"What are you saying? Learn UNIX, hypermedia design, one or more programming languages, or textual markup and its discontents? Learn bibliography and the sociology of texts, ancient and modern textual theory, history of the book?" Yes, that is exactly what I am saying. And of course you ask why. At this point I give only one reason, though by itself—if we draw out its implications—the reason will more than suffice: because information technology is even now transforming the fundamental character of the library. The library, the chief locus of our cultural memory as well as our central symbol of that memory's life and importance. That transformation is already altering the geography of scholarship, criticism, and educational method throughout the humanities and it forecasts even more dramatic changes ahead, as I shall indicate later. Moreover, the shifting plates are already registering on the seismographs.

Let's begin at that point, with the signals coming from current, well-known events. First of all, some happy signs of the times. Already the library's reference rooms are well along to virtually complete virtualization, and it's difficult to believe any scholar regrets this. The transformation reflects the relative ease with which expository and informational materials translate into digital forms. To have immediately available to you those resources, wherever you might choose to set up your computer and go online, is a clear gain, and for older persons, an amazement. Such things can turn the soberest scholar into a digital groupie. Young persons tend to take such marvels for granted.

And it's also the case that some remarkable scholars have been acute to see the educational opportunities that information technology makes possible for the humanities. The list is distinguished and extensive. But of course it's also the case that, compared with the distinguished and extensive body of paper-based scholarship, this list of IT projects is minuscule.

Now for some tales from the dark side.

Late in the nineteenth century Matthew Arnold looked to France as a model for a salutary "influence of academies" on culture in general. Twenty-five years ago Arnold's academic inheritors appeared to be living the realization of his hope. But then came the crash. Humanities scholarship and education has been a holy mess for some time. Looking at the way we live now in the academy, one can hardly not recall Trollope's dark portrayal of The Way We Live Now. What's going on? Where are the snows of yesteryear?

Something like those very questions drove the editor of *Critical Inquiry*, W.J.T. Mitchell, to summon the journal's board of editors to a symposium in April 2003 "to discuss the future of the journal and of the interdisciplinary fields of criticism and theory" (2004, p. 324). Some of the most distinguished North American academics gathered in Chicago to assess the bad eminence that higher education in the humanities has gained—specifically, to ponder "The Future of Criticism" and in particular of Critical Theory. I missed the Friday night public forum and pep-rally for the symposium but made it for the key event, the day-long Saturday discussions. From these I went home shocked and more than a little dismayed by what I learned.

Most of us registered, one way or another, the malaise that has grown widespread in the humanities in America, and I wasn't particularly disheartened that we were all uncertain about how best to deal with the problems we talked about. Something else was troubling, however: the degree of ignorance about information technology and its critical relevance to humanities education and scholarship. I've spent almost twenty years studying this subject in the only way you have a chance of doing something useful. That is, by hands-on collaborative interdisciplinary work. By designing and building the materials and applications tools that alone can teach how best to make and use these things. You don't learn a language by talking about it or reading books. You learn it by speaking it and writing it. There's no other way. Anything less is just, well, theoretical.

So far as information technology concerns traditional humanities, the issues are more clearly understood in the United Kingdom and Europe than they are in the United States. Moreover, if you want to engage serious, practical conversation about humanities education and digital culture, America's most famous humanities research institutions—with few exceptions—are not the places to go.

The *CI* meeting explained why. We're illiterate. Besides myself, no one on the *CI* board can use any of the languages we need to understand how to operate with our proliferating digital technologies— not even elementary markup languages. Most had never heard of TEI and no one I talked with was aware of the impact it was already exerting on humanities scholarship and education. The library, especially the research library, is a cornerstone if not the very foundation of modern humanities. It is undergoing right now a complete digital transformation. In the coming decades—the process has already begun—the entirety of our cultural inheritance will be transformed and re-edited in digital forms. Do we understand what that means, what problems it brings, how they might be addressed? Theoretical as well as very practical discussions about these matters have been going on for years and decisions are taken every day. Yet digital illiteracy puts many of us on the margin of conversations and actions that affect the center of our cultural interests (as citizens) and our professional interests (as scholars and educators).

This situation has to change, and in the last part of this essay I will briefly describe a project called NINES that would if successful help the change along. The project is practical in four ways: it addresses some of the most basic needs and self-interests of the working humanities scholar; it focuses on a limited, controllable region of the humanities (nineteenth-century literary and cultural studies in Britain and America); it involves a collaboration between three key institutional entities (the research library, the individual scholar, and the professional organizations that help us to integrate and organize our work); and it has been designed for adaptation and scalability to other disciplinary areas.

What seems to me *im*practical is to continue framing the crisis in humanities scholarship and education in the theological terms of "critical theory" and "cultural studies". The public glances at goings-on like the *Critical Inquiry* symposium with ironic amusement. To the reporters from New York and Boston who covered the symposium, it recalled nothing so much as Chaucer's Parliament of Foules, as we know from the stories they filed. And every year, as we also know, the MLA's annual meeting provides the media with comic relief.

But our tight little island's problems are by no means trivial, nor are they removed from the larger social scene. We have obligations as we are educators, obligations that society expects us to meet because of our special humanist vocation.

Remember that Marxian distinction between the base and the superstructure? Remember it. Our ideological conflicts today are deeply imbedded—commercially, economically, institutionally. Because this is the case, we have useful, practical things we can and should be *doing*. But before those doings become possible, we shall first have to stop the cant pervading so much of our discourse. An especially dismal aspect of our professional writing today is its ineffectual angelism, which is widespread.

This problem is not simply a matter of prose styles, or their failure. Our publications ride high on jargons of moral, social, and political engagement. In truth, these styles largely measure the extremity of our intramural focus and social *dis*engagement. To be "transgressive" in a Routledge book or a *Critical Inquiry* essay—that word "transgressive" has grown legions—is simply dispiriting. Jargons of impiety and critique—our current rhetorics of displacement—define the treason of the intellectuals, the signs of a transgression that has no referent, not even an intramural one. Writing for tenure committees and an overhearing professoriat, we mistake shop talk for scholarship and criticism. The worst of it, for the humanities scholar anyhow, is the abuse we inflict on the language we are missioned to preserve and protect.

To begin with such a practical self-criticism would make a real difference in the way we do our work. But humanities scholars face another set of problems and obligations—perhaps even more serious, certainly much less tractable. To expose them clearly let me revisit the way we live now from a slightly different perspective. Let us set our inner standing-point at the level of the base this time, not the superstructure.

Next to *Critical Inquiry*'s apprehensions about the state of Critical Theory we should reflect on Stephen Greenblatt's pragmatic worry about "The Crisis in Tenure and Publishing". In a special letter to the members of the Modern Language Association in May 2002, Greenblatt—then MLA president—pointed to dire academic publishing conditions. He called the problem, correctly, a "systemic" one. A network of relations has bound together for a long time the work of scholarship, academic appointment, and paper-based—in particular, university press—publishing. This network has been breaking up, or down, for many years, and the pace of its unraveling only accelerates.

The problem is that most university presses are running at increasingly sharp deficits. This trend will not be reversed, as everyone inside the university publishing network knows. We produce larger and larger amounts of scholarship and pass it to a delivery system with diminishing capacities to sustain its publication. As an editor of a monograph series, the Virginia Victorian Studies, I have seen how this pressure alters what a university press is prepared to undertake. The notorious stigma that has grown up recently against "single-author studies" is only one sign of the difficulty. In a grotesque inversion of our most basic goals, near-term economics, not long-term scholarship, has become a serious factor shaping and guiding humanities research for some time. Just try to find a publisher for primary documentary materials, or for any basic research that doesn't come labeled for immediate consumption: "Sell this by such and such a date"—before it spoils.

But that is to speak only of book publication. We should be aware that a parallel problem, every bit as acute, exists for periodical publication, where a similar dysfunction can be observed. In each of these cases the university library has become almost the only reliable purchaser of scholarly books and periodicals; and every year, as we know, library funds for such materials get cut further.

The problem has been revisited in the most recent issue of *Profession* (2004), the "journal of opinion about and for the modern language profession". But while the four essays in this "Publishing and Tenure Crises Forum" describe the problem quite well, their hopes and proposals, I'm sorry to say, fail to address the "systemic"—the institutional and economic—issues. To imagine that funding infusions from ACLS, NEH, and Mellon will stem this tide is to imagine that sandbags will hold back a tsunami.

Understand, we're not talking here about "the death of the book". As we know, book publishing is alive and well and shows no signs of crisis. The problem is that scholarly communication operates in a highly restricted and specialized market. General publishing, by contrast, is open, with a diverse and dynamically changing audience to which publishers can both appeal and respond. The academic market is largely closed. We are the persons who, all but alone, produce and consume in this market. The academic market used to be somewhat more broadly distributed, but in the past twenty-five years it has drastically shrunk back upon itself. At the same time, the number of producers—of those who, by *systematic* and professional demand, are *required* to produce—has grown enormously. When we then add to the equation the drastic collapse in consumer demand in this market, we are not surprised at the telling numbers. In 1990 a university press would typically print 1000–1500 copies of an academic book. Today the number is 200–250 and dropping every year.

Many realize that online scholarly publication is the natural and inevitable response to this crisis of scholarly and educational communication. How to bring about the transition to online publication is the $64,000 question. And it's not the technology that makes the problem so difficult, as the examples of online journal publication, JSTORE (http://www.jstor.org) and Project Muse (http://muse.jhu.edu), demonstrate. The Jordan will not be crossed until scholars and educators are prepared not simply to search and access archived materials online— which is increasingly done—but to publish and to peer-review online—to carry out the major part of our productive educational work in digital forms.

The institutional resistance to such a major change in scholarly work behaviors is widespread, deep, and entirely understandable. It is not in the short-term (immediate) interest of scholars or their institutions to make a transition to digital work. The upfront costs are high, the learning curve is steep. Most telling of all, the design of the in-place paper-based system has the sophistication and clear strengths that come from hundreds of years of practical use. With rare exceptions, established scholars have the least practical involvement with information technology. This too is understandable. The known scholar can still, usually, get his or her work published in the usual paper-based ways precisely because they are known, if diminished, quantities.

The consequences of this situation are apparent. For traditional paper-based work, it is "the crisis in humanities". For humanists who work with information technology, it is another form of that crisis. Digital scholarship—even the best of it—is all more or less atomized, growing like so many Topsies. Worse, these creatures are idiosyncratically designed and so can't easily talk to each other. They also typically get born into poverty— even the best-funded ones. Ensuring their maintenance, development, and survival is a daunting challenge. Worst of all, the work regularly passes without much practical institutional notice. The annual MLA bibliography still does not cite online works, no matter how distinguished. Accepted professional standards do not control the work in objective ways. Most of it comes into being without oversight or peer-review.

"What is to be done?" Lenin's famous question is very much to the point here, for our scholarship is facing a future that is at once certain and uncertain. It is going to be cast and maintained and disseminated in digital forms. We may not now approve of this but it is nonetheless inevitable. We may not now know how to do this but we will learn. Because we have no choice.

2.

Before getting to the choice I want to talk about, I have to tell one more academic story. This tale stretches back a bit.

For as long as I've been an educator—since the mid-1960s—a system of apartheid has been in place in literary and cultural studies. On one hand we have editing, bibliography, and archival work, on the other theory and interpretation. I don't have to tell you which of these two classes of work has been regarded as menial if somehow necessary. And like any system of apartheid, both groups were corrupted by it. As Don McKenzie once remarked, material culture is never more grossly perceived than it is by theoreticians, whose ideas tend to remove them from base contacts with the physical objects that code and comprise material culture. But of course, as he went on to remark, the gross theoretician met his match in the myopic scholar, who gets lost in the forest by trancing on the bark of the trees.

To this day at my own university—an institution known for its commitment to serious work in textual and bibliographical studies—most of our advanced graduate students could not talk sensibly, least of all seriously or interestingly, on problems of editing and textuality and why those problems are fundamental to every kind of critical work in literary and cultural studies. I no longer ask our students in their Ph.D. exams to talk about the editions they read and use, why they choose this one rather than another, what difference it would or might make. It goes without saying that these are bright and hardworking young people. Nonetheless, the institutional tradition they have inherited largely set those matters at the margin of attention, and never more unfortunately so than in the last quarter of the twentieth century. Until that time the American research program in English studies regularly made history of the language, editing, and bibliographical studies a requirement of work. I know from my own, painful experience that these requirements were often taught in killingly mindless ways. Many therefore decided that these basic disciplines had little to teach us about literature, art, and culture—either of the past or the present. As we all know, in the US these requirements were universally dropped or eviscerated between about 1965 and 1990. (In England and Europe the situation is very different. Highly developed philological traditions permeate their scholarship.)

When I have described our recent educational history in these terms, I have been suspected of fellow-traveling with a cadre of moralizers and promoting an instrumentalist approach to education. But remember, William Bennett, Denish DeSousa, and Lynn Cheney are not enemies of theory or interpretation, they are simply strict constructionists in a field where Cornell West, Catherine Simpson, and Stanley Fish look for broader intellectual opportunities. Seeing the educational history of the past fifteen or twenty years in terms of the celebrated struggles between these groups has obscured our view of an educational emergency now grown acute with the proliferation of digital technology.

I earlier said I shouldn't be forecasting events. But here I am prepared to make a prophecy.

In the next fifty years the entirety of our inherited archive of cultural works will have to be re-edited within a network of digital storage, access, and dissemination. This system, which is already under development, is transnational and transcultural.

Let's say this prophecy is true. Now ask yourself these questions: "Who is carrying out this work, who will do it, who should do it?" These turn to sobering queries when we reflect on the recent history of higher education in the United States. Just when we will be needing young people well-trained in the histories of textual transmission and the theory and practice of scholarly method and editing, our universities are seriously unprepared to educate such persons. Electronic scholarship and editing necessarily draw their primary models from long-standing philological practices in language study, textual scholarship, and bibliography. As we know, these three core disciplines preserve but a ghostly presence in most of our Ph.D. programs.

Designing and executing editorial and archival projects in digital forms are now taking place and will proliferate. Departments of literary study have perhaps the greatest stake in these momentous events, and yet they are—in the United States—probably the least involved. The work is mostly being carried out by librarians and systems engineers. Many, perhaps most, of these people are smart, hardworking, and literate. Their digital skills and scholarship are often outstanding. Few know anything about theory of texts, and they too, like we literary and cultural types, have labored for years in intellectually underfunded conditions. It has been decades since library schools in this country required or even offered courses in the history of the book. Does it shock you to learn that? We aren't shocked at our own instituted ignorance of history of the language or bibliography.

Restoring intimate relations between literarians and librarians, a pressing current need, has thus been hampered from institutional developments on both sides. Insofar as departments of literature participate in the work and conversations of digitized librarians, it happens through that small band of angels who continue to pursue serious editorial and bibliographical work: scholarly editors and bibliographers.

Ok, then, what's the problem? Our traditional departments have managed to keep around a few old-fashioned editorial and bibliographical types. Let's send them out to help with the technical jobs and hope that their—(that's our)—brains aren't completely fried by beetle-browed and positivist habits. Once upon a time even they (that's we) were involved with the readerly text, right?

Those contacts might perhaps prove barely sufficient were it not for another recent upheaval in the world of higher education. For it happens that between about 1965 and 1985 textual scholars began to rethink some of the most basic ideas and methods of their discipline. I chose those dates because Ernest Honigman published *The Stability of Shakespeare's Text* in 1965, and in 1985 D.F. McKenzie delivered his famous inaugural Panizzi Lectures, *Bibliography and the Sociology of Texts* (published

1986). So disconnected had the general scholarly community grown from its foundational subfield of textual and bibliographical studies, however, that this historic moment passed it by with little notice. The "genetic" and "social" editing theories and methods that emerged in those years signaled a major shift in literary and cultural scholarship. Because this change overlapped with the more public emergence of what would be called Literary Theory—perhaps "underlapped" is the better word—it drew scant attention to itself in that more visible orbit of literary and cultural studies. And after that came the dismal "Culture Wars".

A forthcoming publication measures the change that overtook textual scholarship at the end of the last century. In 1982 Harold Jenkins published his celebrated edition of *Hamlet* in the Arden Shakespeare series. A lifetime's work, the book epitomized a traditional so-called eclectic approach whereby Jenkins educed a single text of the play out of a careful study of the three chief documentary witnesses. Soon a new Arden Shakespeare *Hamlet*, edited by Ann Thompson and Neil Taylor, will replace Jenkins' remarkable work. The new Arden *Hamlet* will not publish a single conflated text, it will present all three witnesses—F1 (1623), Q1 (1603), and Q2 (1604–5)—each in their special integrity (or lack thereof).

In May 2002 *The New Yorker* reported this event in a substantial piece by Ron Rosenbaum. The article gives a good general introduction to an upheaval in textual studies that had been going on for almost forty years, and that had been at white heat for twenty. Because the world of scholarship moves in a kind of slow motion, such belated awareness would not normally be cause for much notice. But at this particular historical moment, when information storage and transmission and methods of knowledge representation are calling for immediate practical attention, Rosenbaum's piece seems most interesting for what it does *not* talk about. Force of circumstance today calls us to develop scholarly editions in digital forms. The people who used to do this work in paper forms—people like Jenkins and Thompson—are involved in serious controversies over how it should be done. The theory and practice of traditional textual scholarship is in a lively, not to say volatile, state of self-reflection. Scholarly editing today cannot be undertaken in *any* medium without a disciplined engagement with editorial theory and method. Scholars who think to use information technology resources, as now we must, therefore face a double difficulty. We must learn to use digital tools whose capacities are still being explored in fundamental ways even by technicians. We must also approach all the traditional questions of scholarly editing as if a transformed world stood all before us, and where to choose was fraught with uncertainty.

3.

That, ladies and gentlemen, is the context which envelops my main subject, NINES (or 9S: Networked Infrastructure for Nineteenth-century Electronic Scholarship). It is a three-year undertaking initiated in 2003 by myself and a group of scholars to establish an online environment for publishing peer-reviewed research in nineteenth-century British and American studies. Although the resource will have significant pedagogical and classroom components, it is primarily an institutional mechanism for digitally-organized research and scholarship.

NINES is conceived partly as a professional facilitator and partly as an advocacy group to protect the interests of scholars and educators. It is, as they say, results-oriented. It will liaise with interested publishing venues on behalf and in the interests of scholars and educators and the work we produce. A coordinated group of editorial boards oversees the work, which will include various kinds of content: traditional texts and documents— editions, critical works of all kinds—as well as "born-digital" studies that relate to all aspects of nineteenth-century culture. NINES is a model and working example for scholarship that takes advantage of digital resources and internet transmission. It provides scholars with access to a uniformly coded textual environment and a suite of computerized analytic and interpretive tools. A key goal of NINES is to expose the rich hermeneutic potential of the electronic medium—beyond the dazzle of digital imaging and the early breakthrough of hypertext.

Most important, NINES is not just a committee of concerned educators who mean to discuss the problems and opportunities presented by digital technology. NINES is a practical undertaking and it is already underway. Here is its three-year initial plan:

To establish the editorial mechanisms for soliciting, peer-reviewing, aggregating, and finally publishing born-digital scholarship and criticism in nineteenth-century British and American studies. The effort necessarily involves re-examining how traditional scholarly standards and best practices can be migrated and adapted to a digital environment.

To begin modeling a technical and institutional framework that integrates our inherited archive of paper-based materials—primary as well as secondary—with emerging forms of digital scholarship and criticism.

To develop a suite of user-friendly procedures and easily-accessible tools and applications that will help scholars and students produce interesting work in digital form. Digital technology offers remarkable new possibilities for studying, analyzing, and interpreting our cultural inheritance in ways—both individual and collaborative—that have not been possible previously.

To run a series of summer fellowships for scholars who are working on IT projects in nineteenth-century studies. The first workshop of twelve scholars ran for a week in the summer of 2005 at University of Virginia. Organized within a robust technical and scholarly environment, the workshop was designed to help the participants develop and explore their projects in the company of other scholars doing similar projects.

That is the general administrative design model of NINES. Under its auspices we are developing software conceived specifically for scholars and educators working in the humanities, and in particular in literary and cultural studies. Creating such applications is one of the most pressing needs we now have. Unless IT can provide humanists with tools and methods that overgo what we already have with book technology, why would we take any interest in it (IT)?

(These tools use the special capacities of computerized systems to augment the traditional interpretive activities of the humanist scholar.)

1. A text-comparison tool called JUXTA for comparing and collating textual similarities and differences in a given set of equivalent documents. Since the critical re-editing of our inherited corpus will necessarily occupy a central focus of coming humanities scholarship, a tool of this kind is fundamental. Aside from Peter Robinson's COLLATE, no such tool exists, and COLLATE has not been widely used because it has significant limitations. JUXTA is entirely cross-platform and will be able to execute three basic collation and text-comparison operations: (a) collation by line or work string of poetical works (with the collation able to choose any witness as the basic reference point); (b) collation of prose documents by word string (of different sizes); (c) mining a dataset to locate and output equivalent word strings, with the output organized through a computerized analysis by degree of semantic, syntactic, or phonetic equivalence.

2. An online collaborative playspace called IVANHOE for organizing interpretive investigations of traditional humanities materials of any kind. Applicable for either classroom or research use, IVANHOE's design has a double (dialectical) function: to promote the critical investigation of textual and graphical works, and to expose those investigations themselves to critical reflection and study. IVANHOE 1.0 was released in December 2004 and is currently being used in four classes, graduate and undergraduate, at University of Virginia.

3. COLLEX. In collaboration with a project to redesign *The Rossetti Archive*, NINES is developing a data model and set of tools called COLLEX that allows users of digital resources to assemble and share virtual "collections" and to present annotated "exhibits" and

rearrangements of online materials. These critical rearrangements can of course bring together materials that are variously diverse—materially, formally, historically. COLLEX is an interface for exploring complex bodies of diverse cultural materials in order to expose new networks of relations.

4. The 'Patacritical Demon'. This is a tool for tracking and visualizing acts of critical reflection and interpretation as they are being applied in real-time to specific works, and in particular to imaginative works like poems or stories. It is a device for addressing the following problem: How does one formalize "exceptional" and highly subjective activities like acts of interpretation and at the same time preserve their subjective status. The Demon derives its name, incidentally, from Alfred Jarry's proposal for a science that he called Pataphysics, that is, "a science of exceptions" (or "the science of imaginary solutions").[1]

Like IVANHOE and JUXTA, the Patacritical Demon outputs XML coded data. Consequently, the work done with all three of these interpretive tools can be integrated with the rest of the NINES-environment materials.

Oh yes, one other thing. Whatever happens with NINES—whether that institutional event takes hold or not—these critical tools will be built. They will also be freely distributed to anyone who wants them.

Conclusion

I'm a book scholar, about as traditional as you get. My work, including my theoretical work, is historicist and even philological and my orientation is decidedly humanist. "Glory to man in the highest, for man is the master of things." That witty and impish line from Swinburne is very much to my taste. Men (and women) are indeed called to the mastery of things. Of things precisely. Of people and of life events we are and always will be participants and students, never masters. Drawing that distinction—between things and people, between mastery and learning—is what it means to be—as Swinburne was—a humanist.

Today we have to try to master some new *things*. We have to learn how to make them and how to use them. To pursue that goal commits us to a demanding, and therefore humbling, adventure in knowledge. We will do this by becoming students again—a role that, as educators and humanists,

---

[1] See Jarry's *Exploits and Opinions of Dr. Faustroll, Pataphysician*, trans. and annotated by Simon Watson Taylor, Introduction by Roger Shattuck (Exact Change: Boston, 1996), especially Book II.

I think we're especially good at. For some of us, this will be a road not taken. Fair enough. But whether we choose to or not, we should all be clear about the slow train that's coming and that won't be sidetracked. "The publishing and tenure crisis" is one certain sign of what's happening. So is the digital transformation of our research archives, the seat of our cultural memory.

NINES is a proposal to engage with these problems in specific and practical ways. It takes a relatively short rather than a long view— because in matters that concern us, we are always humanists, even in the short run. We know that our longest views, our totalizing conceptions, are finally only heuristic and hypothetical. But that humanist understanding is exactly why, as Shelley observed, we mustn't "let I dare not wait upon I would." We have to get going now, we can't wait to see if there's more to learn. Of course there's more to learn, that's why we must fare forth. How else will we learn what we need to know. We have to set the stage for our certain failures if we're to have any chance of measuring our measured successes. We will, as the poet observed, "learn by going where we have to go".

One last point is worth our reflection. Capitalist entrepreneurs are already actively trying to gain control over as much information as they can. Perhaps never before has knowledge been so clearly perceived as a fungible thing, as a commodity to be bought and sold. Humanities scholarship has a calculable market price, and the market will work to buy low and sell high, as the dreadful examples of Elsevier and Kluwer have recently revealed to the science community.[2]

And don't imagine that our cultural heritage—what Shelley called our poetry—is safe from commercial exploitation by agents that view our work—what they call "the content" we create—as a marketable commodity. Perhaps the chief virtue of a project like NINES is to supply scholars with an institutional mechanism for preserving and protecting what we do.

I don't know if we will be successful in our primary objective: leveraging NINES to assemble and publish an initial body of peer-reviewed online scholarship and criticism that can initiate an ongoing venue for such work. Several models are imaginable that would use libraries or traditional scholarly presses as the publishing vehicles, or some combination of the two. Whether or not the agents needed to make any of these models work

---

[2]   The charges levied by this pair of traditional publishers of scientific journals grew so outrageus that a serious reaction has set in, and scientists are now developing their own online publishing venues: see Biomed Central, the Public Library of Science, and HighWire. NINES has taken some of its inspiration from these ventures. But scientists and humanists have very different requirements with respect to the inherited cultural archive. The preservation and transmission of that archive—ideally, the entirety of that archive—is perhaps the central mission of the humanist. The case is far different for the scientist qua scientist.

will decide to do so is unclear. The agents—that's to say, ourselves. The matter won't become clear, one way or the other, until we undertake to design and implement a model. NINES—or anything like it—can only exist in practice, not in theory.

Works Cited

Adams, H. (1907). *The Education of Henry Adams*, chapter 31.

Birkerts, S. (1994). *The Gutenberg Elegies. The Fate of Reading in an Electronic Age*, London: Faber and Faber.

Drucker, J. and Rockwell, G. (eds) (2003). *Text Technology* (Special Issue devoted to the IVANHOE gamespace), 12 (2).

Greenblatt, S. (2002). "A Letter to MLA Members", reprinted in *The Chronicle of Higher Education* (July 2), http://chronicle.com/jobs/2002/07/ 2002070202c.htm.

Honigman, E. (1965). *The Stability of Shakespeare's Text*.

McGann, J. (ed.) (1994). *The Complete Writings and Pictures of Dante Gabriel Rossetti. A Hypermedia Research Archive*, http://www.iath.virginia.edu/ rossetti.

McKenzie, D.F. (1985). *Bibliography and the Sociology of Texts* (published 1986).

Mitchell, W.J.T. (ed.) (2004). "The Future of Criticism—A Critical Inquiry Symposium," *Critical Inquiry* 30 (2) (winter), pp. 324–479.

NINES (Networked Infrastructure for Nineteenth-century Electronic Scholarship) http://nines.org.

Profession (2004). "Publishing and Tenure Crises Forum", New York: MLA.

Rosenbaum, R. (2002). "Onward and Upward With The Arts: Shakespeare In Rewrite", *The New Yorker*.

Thompson, E.P. (1978). *The Poverty of Theory*, New York: Monthly Review Press.

Unsworth, J. (2003). "The Crisis in Scholarly Publishing in the Humanities," *ARL*, 228 (June), pp. 1–4, http://www.arl.org/newsltr/228/crisis.html.

Note from the author:
When I began exploring the educational and scholarly potential of digital resources in 1992 my thoughts (and work) focused on issues of theory, method, and technical practice. Ten years later my attention began shifting toward the social and institutional networks that are needed to sustain any kind of research and educational work. That shift is registered in this essay, originally a lecture, "Information Technology and the Troubled Humanities". Today the institutional issues – particularly the curricular issues – remain the

most di cult and the most imperative. I would therefore add the following speci c addendum: that "we now have a pressing need to integrate online humanities scholarship into the programmatic heart of the university."[3] The rst generation of digital humanities work very much *needed* to work outside the orbit of the departments and their traditional programs and curricula. But the situation we are now facing is di erent. Traditional programs are graduating Ph.D. students with no programmatic training in the tools and resources that have already become a regular part of their scholarly and educational lives. Nor is this only an issue for the graduate programs. If our humanities curricula and students are to be taken seriously in a globally digitized world, our undergraduate and graduate programs of study will have to be critically re-examined and redesigned. They need to be shaped for work in a world where our cultural resources are being globally reorganized within digital internetworks.

Jerome McGann, November 2012

---

[3]   "On Creating a Usable Future", *Profession* (2011).

CHAPTER 4

Disciplined: Using Educational Studies to Analyse 'Humanities Computing'

Melissa Terras
University College London

Melissa Terras (2006). Originally published in *Literary and Linguistic Computing*, 21 (2), pp. 229–46.

Note from the Editors:

When this article was published in 2006 a number of articles that sought to define Humanities Computing had already been published, many of which focused on the development and detail of curricula and teaching programmes. This article took a new approach. It investigated how Education theory defined the concept of a discipline in order to investigate whether such an approach could be transferrable to the analysis and definition of Humanities Computing.

In doing so it captured a snapshot of the state of the art at that time. Though Humanities Computing had many of the hallmarks of a discipline it fell down when it came to the issue of institutionalisation as few academic Humanities Computing departments existed then. Notwithstanding this, the field did have an identifiable interdisciplinary and transnational community and an analysis of ACH/ALLC conference abstracts from 1996 to 2005 (with the exclusion of 2003 which was not available) revealed that they were primarily concerned with studying text.

Abstract

Humanities Computing is an emergent field. The activities described as 'Humanities Computing' continue to expand in number and sophistication, yet no concrete definition of the field exists, and there are few academic departments that specialize in this area. Most introspection regarding the role, meaning, and focus of 'Humanities Computing' has come from a practical and pragmatic perspective from scholars and educators within the field itself. This article provides an alternative, externalized, viewpoint of the focus of Humanities Computing, by analysing the discipline through its community, research, curriculum, teaching programmes, and the message they deliver, either consciously or unconsciously, about the scope of the discipline. It engages with Educational theory to provide a means to analyse, measure, and define the field, and focuses specifically on the ACH/ALLC 2005 Conference to identify and analyse those who are involved with the humanities computing community.

1 Introduction

Humanities Computing is a relatively new, and small, field of academic activity. Although the community is growing, with an expansion of tools, techniques, and activities which identify themselves as 'Humanities Computing' (or its various pseudonyms),[1] no definition of the subject exists, and very few academic institutions have a dedicated Humanities Computing department. This article looks towards Education theory to ascertain what a discipline is, and to see how this can be used to define the status of Humanities Computing. This article also reports on an analysis of the Humanities Computing curriculum and community, from an educational, and curriculum, studies perspective. As a novel and alternative approach to answering the perennial question 'What is Humanities Computing?', this research yields useful insights. As Kelly (1999, p. 19) notes, 'A study of curriculum, while not offering us spurious answers to questions of values, will ... draw our attention to important questions that need to be asked about policies and practices and help us achieve the kind of clarity which will enable us to see underlying ideologies more clearly'. Is Humanities Computing a discipline at all? Does it exist as an academic field?

The article is presented in sections. Section 2 introduces the type of activities associated with Humanities Computing, and describes the problems associated with trying to ascertain its status. The methodology used to analyse Humanities Computing in this enquiry is then sketched. Section 3 asks: what is an academic discipline? A definition of disciplinarity is propagated from Educational theory, and Humanities Computing is assessed from this perspective. Section 4 looks at the curriculum and issues of the 'hidden curriculum'. Teaching programmes are contrasted

---

[1] It should be noted that 'Humanities Computing' can also be referred to as Digital Humanities, Digital Resources for the Humanities, Digital Resources in the Humanities, Cultural and Heritage Informatics, Humanities Computer Science, and Literary and Linguistic Computing. Throughout this article, 'Humanities Computing' is used for consistency.

and compared with the research agenda, and aspects about the identity of Humanities Computing are raised. Section 5 attempts to ascertain who constitutes the Humanities Computing community through analysis of available data. Section 6 concludes the research, highlighting issues raised and identifying future work that could be carried out to develop this research further.

2 What is Humanities Computing?

Academic activity associated with Humanities Computing typically revolves around specific applications, such as the development and analysis of large textual corpora, the construction of digital editions of works of literature, the creation of digital artefacts through the process of digitization, the use of 'Virtual Reality' for reconstruction of architectural models, etc. New techniques and technologies are continually being developed and applied to Humanities data. Let us not discuss here the history of Humanities Computing, as it has been covered elsewhere by Fraser (1996), Schreibman et al. (2004), and Vanhoutte (forthcoming and Chapter 6 in this volume).

However, defining Humanities Computing as an academic field is problematic. There are few established academic departments in the field. A lot of work in Humanities Computing is project-based, usually resulting in a product for other academics to utilize, and there is concern whether this is an academic endeavour. Humanities Computing 'units' or 'centres' often provide technical support facilities for Humanities Divisions in universities, meaning that Humanities Computing is often viewed as a support to 'proper' academic research. There are also few teaching programmes in existence, perhaps because it is hard to define a skills set to pass on which would individually define the discipline, rather than just providing technical 'training' on specific computer technologies.

This can create problems for those in the field. Firstly, there is the question of academic kudos: if you are in a discipline which is not worthy of an academic department, is your research that meaningful or useful? There is often a bias from more traditional Humanities scholars that work with computing is not 'proper' research. Secondly, there are funding implications for research. Research councils tend to ask the academic to identify which traditional discipline they belong to: Humanities Computing is not a 'panel' within itself. Scholars using Humanities Computing are often 'too technical' to be eligible for funding from the Humanities sector, and 'not technical enough' to secure funding through Engineering and Computing Science channels. This situation may be changing as computers and Internet technologies become more pervasive and embedded in everyday, and academic, life, but an interdisciplinary scholar is often battling different cultures and regimes to succeed in either, or both, disciplines. Finally, if the subject cannot define a set of core theories and techniques to be taught, is it really a subject at all? Is a research community enough to define a 'discipline', or does this merely reflect a community of like-minded scholars who meet occasionally to swap battle scars?

These problems have been fairly exhaustively detailed by papers from many of the luminaries in the Humanities Computing field. However, these papers have generally focused on the content of specific teaching programmes and the development of a curriculum. There was an entire conference devoted to 'The Humanities Computing Curriculum: The Computing Curriculum in the Arts and Humanities' (Siemens, 2001) at Malaspina University College, Nanaimo, British Columbia, Canada. Most papers necessarily described the practical aspects of setting up Humanities Computing programmes and courses and defining an overview of their content. For example, Gilfillan and Musick (2001) outlined the practicalities involved in promoting the use of computing in Humanities-based teaching and research at the University of Oregon, and Hockey (2001) examined the role of computing in the humanities curriculum at both postgraduate and undergraduate levels. There was a seminar series which was undertaken to define and generate a syllabus for a graduate course in knowledge representation for humanists at the University of Virginia, which resulted in a comprehensive syllabus for a Master's Degree in Digital Humanities (Drucker et al., 2002), although this course was never actually established due to funding cuts (sending a disappointing message to the wider academic community). Various papers from this seminar detail the problems in belonging to a discipline-less discipline (Burnard, 1999; Hockey, 1999; McCarty, 1999a; McGann, 1999; Moulthrop, 1999; Nerbonne, 1999). More generally, the Advanced Computing in the Humanities (ACO*HUM) project produced a study on how Computing was or is, and could be used in Humanities subjects (de Smedt et al., 1999). These studies all serve to illustrate how important defining the curriculum is to Humanities Computing, and how, as a nascent subject, much is still being done to define the teaching programme, and the field although their focus is mostly (and necessarily) a practical approach to how teaching programmes can be implemented and integrated into academic departments and scholarly frameworks.

Additionally, some of the papers were concerned with ascertaining whether Humanities Computing is an academic endeavour or merely a support subject. Various other papers exist that question the role and focus of Humanities Computing (Aarseth, 1997; de Smedt, 2002; Orlandi, n.d.; Warwick, 2004). Most work has been done by Willard McCarty, Senior Lecturer in the Centre for Computing and the Humanities at King's College London (McCarty, 1998, 1999a, 1999b, 2002, 2003, 2005a, 2005b;

McCarty and Short, 2002; McCarty et al., 1997) and John Unsworth, Dean and Professor of the Graduate School of Library and Information Science, University of Illinois, Urbana-Champaign (Unsworth, 1993, 1996, 2000, 2002, 2003, 2004).

However, these papers are written by academics within the field, describing their own experiences of teaching, learning, and research with very little thought given to educational theory—only one of these papers, Burnard (1999) mentions in passing 'educational theory from the 1960s' without providing any reference. The aim of this article is to apply the definitions and measures from education to the Humanities Computing community, to ascertain whether it exists as an academic subject.

There has been much discussion within education as to what actually makes a discipline, or what defines the work of a group of academic individuals as a bona fide 'subject'. Academic culture can define a 'tribe' of scholars, whilst the span of disciplinary knowledge can be described as the 'territory' of the discipline (Becher and Trowler, 2001). 'Fields gradually develop distinctive methodological approaches, conceptual and theoretical frameworks and their own sets of internal schisms' (Becher and Trowler, 2001, p. 14). What are the methodological approaches of Humanities Computing? Is there a culture which binds the scholars together? Or, is the Humanities Computing community merely that—a community of practice, which shares theories of meaning and power, collectivity and subjectivity (Wenger, 1998) but is little more than a support network for academic scholars who use outlier methods in their own individual fields? Additionally, the notion of the hidden curriculum is also of relevance. What thoughts are we projecting in our teaching programmes and research as to the scope and relevance of Humanities Computing?

This research is an ambitious attempt to provide an overview of an academic field. A literature review was carried out, both in Humanities Computing, and in Education, to understand notions of disciplinarity and the hidden curriculum. Secondly, a series of interviews with ten scholars in Humanities Computing was undertaken: six from the United Kingdom, two from the USA, one from Canada and one from Belgium. Comments and opinions from scholars are integrated throughout this article. Thirdly, four teaching programmes were compared and contrasted to see the focus of their teaching, and which notions of Humanities Computing were being projected onto students. Subject focus was compared and contrasted with available research materials to see whether the teaching covered the same scope as the research: this is quantifiable through textual analysis of available conference abstracts. Fourthly, a database was constructed of the Humanities Computing community, taking as its basis presenters at the main conference in the field: the annual Association of Computing in the Humanities and the Association of Literary and Linguistic Computing

Joint International Conference (ACH/ALLC). In 2005, this conference was held at the University of Victoria, British Columbia, Canada, June 15–18.[2] An analysis of who attended provides an overview of who is part of the Humanities Computing community, how it functions, and what this projects onto the discipline as a whole.

3 Disciplines, Disciplinarity, and Humanities Computing

Being part of a discipline gives a scholar a sense of belonging, identity, and kudos. But the idea of what constitutes a discipline is muddy, and often hinges around the bricks and mortar proof of a university department's existence:

> [A Discipline] can be enacted and negotiated in various ways: the international; invisible college; individuals exchanging preprints and reprints, conferences, workshops ... But the most concrete and permanent enactment is the department; this is where a discipline becomes an institutional subject. The match between discipline and subject is always imperfect; this can cause practical difficulties when, for example, the (discipline-based) categories of research selectively do not fit the way the subject is ordered in a particular department. (Evans, 1995, pp. 253–4)

This notion of institutionalizing the subject would seem to give gravitas: if you can point at an academic department, the discipline exists. However, this definition of a 'discipline' is problematic, as many have specialisms and subspecialisms, which may or may not be represented in every university department, and every 'discipline' is different in character and scope from the next:

> most embrace a wide range of subspecialisms, some with one set of features and the other with different sets. There is no single method of enquiry, no standard verification procedure, no definitive set of concepts that uniquely characterises each particular discipline. (Becher and Trowler, 2001, p. 65)

Additionally, a 'discipline' is not an immutable topic of research or body of individuals: 'For nothing is more certain in the lives of the disciplines, whatever the field, whatever the institutional setting, than that they are forever changing' (Monroe, 2002, p. 2).

The discipline gains kudos from becoming permanently established in the university subject roll call, but does not having this institutional

---

[2]   http://web.uvic.ca/hrd/achallc2005.

branding preclude a body of research and teaching from actually being a discipline? Most 'new' academic subjects have had to gradually be accepted into the university pantheon, with much discussion along the way regarding whether they actually are disciplines in the first place. For example, there is continuing debate in the field of education as to whether it is really a discipline or not (Hughes, 1971; Kymlicka; 1992; Scheffler, 1963; Viñao, 2002). It would seem like asking 'is this a discipline?', akin to asking 'is this art?': it is, if the person involved in the activity thinks it is.

> That said, although it is difficult to provide a definition of what a discipline may be, there are characteristics which are associated with disciplinary practice. Disciplines have identities and cultural attributes. They have measurable communities, which have public outputs, and can be measured by the number and types of departments in universities, the change and increase in types of HE courses, the proliferation of disciplinary associations, the explosion in the number of journals and articles published, and the multiplication of recognised research topics and clusters. (Becher and Trowler, 2001, p. 14)

Disciplines have identifiable idols in their subject (Clark, 1980), heroes and mythology (Taylor, 1976) and sometimes artefacts peculiar to the subject domain, or ethnographic similarities in workspaces (Becher and Trowler, 2001), meaning that the community is defined and reinforced by being formally accepted as a university subject, but also instituting a publication record and means of output, and, more implicitly, by 'the nurturance of myth, the identification of unifying symbols, the canonisation of exemplars, and the formation of guilds' (Dill, 1992).

It is, therefore, possible to ascertain if Humanities Computing is a discipline by taking an overview of the activities of the field utilizing these measures.

3.1 Is Humanities Computing a Discipline?

Opinion was split between the interviewed scholars in Humanities Computing as to whether it was a discipline. Some felt very strongly that it was, others strongly denied it, defining a discipline as a 'core set of skills' or 'lingua franca' which could not be identified in the case of Humanities Computing. Two ascertained that it did not really matter: 'I don't know what it is. I don't know if it is. Actually, I doubt whether we need it to be.' Most identified that there was a definable community, but that they were bound together by the fact that they were traditional Humanities experts who happened to use new technologies to research in their field. If technology is all there is in common, this does not make a discipline, as an academic commented:

Hey, you write with a ballpoint pen, and I write with a ballpoint pen ... Let's make us the Blue Pen Club! It is what we write with the pen that is important, not the technology.

However, there are a number of activities solely associated with the Humanities Computing community. It is now over thirty years since the Association of Literary and Linguistic Computing (ALLC)[3] was founded (in 1973), and almost twenty years since the first issue of the journal *Literary and Linguistic Computing* (published by Oxford University Press) was issued in 1986.[4] The Association of Computers and the Humanities (ACH)[5] was founded in the early 1990s. The Humanist electronic discussion list, which describes itself as 'an international electronic seminar on the application of computers to the Humanities', has been in operation since 1987:[6] more than 10 million words on the subject have been posted during that time. There has been a yearly conference (held by ALLC) since 1970, becoming an international conference (jointly held between ALLC and ACH)[7] since 1989. Other more local conferences emerge: Digital Resources in the Humanities,[8] a predominantly UK-based yearly conference, was first held in 1996. McCarty and Kirschenbaum (2003, regularly updated) attempt to keep a register of conferences, associations, journals, and teaching programmes in Humanities Computing: they currently list seven printed and eleven electronic journals devoted to Humanities Computing, thirteen professional societies, six specific online portals, and three dedicated discussion groups. Clearly, something is going on that can be classed as 'Humanities Computing'.

Histories of and companions to the discipline have begun to emerge (Fraser, 1996; Schreibman et al., 2004; Vanhoutte, forthcoming and Chapter 6 in this volume), from research, scholarly, and institutional perspectives (Warwick, 2004). When asked who the academic 'heroes' of Humanities Computing were, most experts came up with the same names: Professors Roberto Busa, Susan Hockey, Roy Wisbey and John Unsworth. Others mentioned (Professors Mark Greengrass, Alan Bowman, Manfred Thaler, Lisa Jardine, and Ray Siemens) were all active members in the field, and the head of often ambitious and very successful initiatives in the discipline.

---

[3]   http://www.allc.org.

[4]   The Association of Literary and Linguistic Computing published its journal twice yearly from 1980 to 1985, when this was merged with the ALLC bulletin to become *Literary and Linguistic Computing* (1986).

[5]   http://www.ach.org.

[6]   http://www.princeton.edu/~mccarty/humanist.

[7]   http://www.kcl.ac.uk/humanities/cch/allc/refdocs/conf.htm.

[8]   http://www.drh.org.uk.

As for artefacts and workspace: most of the experts; workspaces were characterized by having one (or more) powerful computers, contrasted with shelves of books on traditional Humanities subjects such as English Literature, with the odd technical manual about the Internet or eXtensible Markup Language (XML)[9] thrown in. There was usually some large artwork on the wall (perhaps stressing how they are routed in the 'creativity' of the Humanities, not Computer Science, which has a bad name for being 'geeky' although it is also a creative discipline). There are also identifiable artefacts from Humanities Computing: the mug from DRH;98, the rucksack from ACH/ALLC 2003.

There are undoubtedly cliques of scholars in the community, unofficial discussion groups, friendships, scholarly support networks, mentoring programmes, and many other relationships associated with academic communities and disciplines active within Humanities Computing. The amount of activity would suggest that there was an identity associated with the Humanities Computing community, as well as issues of shared practice, and that the amount of academic activity detailed above does classify this as a discipline, rather than just a 'community of practice' (Wenger, 2002, p. 150).

However, where the argument falls down for Humanities Computing as a discipline is in its institutionalization, or lack of it. McCarty and Kirschenbaum (2003) provide 'a structured list of departments, centres, institutes and other institutional forms that variously instantiate humanities computing' (although this is slightly out of date). Only ten institutions worldwide are listed that provide academic teaching programmes in the field. These are generally at the postgraduate level, with only a minor in Humanities Computing being available at the undergraduate level at two institutions: the 'major' degree is always a traditional Humanities subject. Additionally, the majority of these programmes are provided not through 'departments' but through 'Centres' or 'Institutes', such as the Centre for Computing in the Humanities at King's College London,[10] or the Humanities Advanced Technology and Information Institute[11] at the University of Glasgow. As computing becomes more pervasive, Information Technology skills are becoming more important to all scholars, and these centres usually also provide general IT skills training to Humanities scholars. This makes it hard to differentiate between general training in computing applications, and bona fide 'academic' study. 'Humanities Computing' has yet to be institutionalized as an academic subject.

---

[9]   http://www.w3.org/XML.

[10] http://www.kcl.ac.uk/humanities/cch.

[11] http://www.hatii.arts.gla.ac.uk.

There was a feeling amongst some of those interviewed that 'the lady doth protest too much' regarding the perennial 'is-Humanities-Computing-a-discipline' question. Surely, if it was, it would have become established by now? But given the above evidence, it would seem to be established as a discipline. The question is why it is not an established university subject. This may be because there is not a definable skills set or focus that can be passed on to the next generation of scholars. Additionally, the subject is reliant on technologies which continually change, requiring learning of specific applications and the application of knowledge and action rather than the traditional Humanities focus on development of the 'self' (Barnett et al., 2001, p. 439). Also, there is an inherent understanding that the domain will always exist as applied to traditional Humanities scholarship, as it uses computational techniques to undertake Humanities research. It does not exist 'in itself' away from the Humanities, and will always depend on the traditional disciplines to provide questions that need to be answered. Experts variably described this as 'symbiosis' (giving a positive view of the intertwining of computer technologies with the Humanities) or the negative 'parasitic': 'It's like mistletoe. It cannot exist on its own.' The Humanities Computing scholar was often described as a 'magpie' who had to visit other domains to gather shiny pieces of knowledge for use at home, or a 'chameleon' who has to jump from one mode of disciplinary thinking and culture to another. McCarty (2005b) describes Humanities Computing as an 'archipelago' of subjects that we visit. We are like a 'Jack of all trades: master of none'. Finally, to be able to understand how computing technologies can benefit the Humanities there needs to be an understanding of how the Humanities function. Therefore, most scholars need traditional Humanities training or qualification before they can use Humanities Computing: it is essentially a research environment, and that befits teaching at a postgraduate level better than undergraduate level.

Humanities Computing would seem to display many traits that are associated with being a discipline, apart from being institutionalized as a 'proper' academic subject. This raises problems, as detailed in Section 2, regarding kudos and funding. However, although there are only a small number of teaching programmes available, this would suggest that there is something to be taught, and this is analysed in Section 4.

4 Curriculum, Hidden Curriculum, and Humanities Computing

The syllabus and curriculum of Humanities Computing has never really been decided (as demonstrated by the discussion papers listed in Section 2). However, some teaching programmes do exist. This section gives a brief overview of some programmes and compares and contrasts their content, comparing this to the research agenda of Humanities Computing through analysis of conference abstracts in the field. Issues of the 'hidden curriculum' are then discussed, illuminating what message Humanities Computing is giving out through its teaching programmes and institutional representation.

Four university courses were looked at to compare and contrast their content and implementation. These were:

1. The MA in Applied Computing in the Humanities[12] in the Centre for Computing in the Humanities, at King's College London. This is a one-year Master's degree.
2. 'Humanities Computing: Electronic Text',[13] a one-term, one module course at Master's level in the English Department of the University of Antwerp.
3. 'Digital Resources in the Humanities',[14] a one-term, one module course at Master's level in the School of Library, Archive, and Information Studies, University College London.
4. 'Digital Humanities'[15] a one-term, one module course at Master's level in the Graduate School of Library and Information Studies, University of Illinois at Urbana-Champaign.

4.1 The Syllabus and Curriculum

From an educational and curriculum studies perspective, the term 'curriculum' applies not only to the content of a particular subject of study, but refers to the total programme of an educational institution: being 'the overall rationale for any educational programme, including those more subtle features of curriculum change and development and especially those underlying elements [explanation and justification] ... which are the most crucial element in Curriculum studies' (Kelly, 1999, p. 3). Syllabus here is taken to mean the course content.

The courses listed above have a remarkably similar focus, mostly taking as their syllabus the techniques used to produce, manipulate, and deliver electronic text. Some, such as Antwerp, focus exclusively on this, whilst others, such as UCL, have this as the focus but introduce some other computational application to the Humanities in the course of teaching, such as digitization and outlier methods such as Virtual Reality. Illinois is more discursive than the others, with more written elements

---

12 http://www.kcl.ac.uk/humanities/cch/ma/4.html.
13 http://www.kantl.be/ctb/vanhoutte/teach/hc2005.htm.
14 http://www.ucl.ac.uk/slais/melissa-terras/drh.htm.
15 http://www3.isrl.uiuc.edu/unsworth/LIS590DH-S04.html.

and less technical work, and of course the one-year course at King's is more extensive than the others, and can go into more depth about various tools and techniques. There is a significant amount of group work, which is relatively rare in the Humanities. Courses are relatively small and have much direct contact with the tutors, with practical sessions as well as lectures and tutorial sessions. Assessment is by practical project, or takehome exam, in which the students are expected to demonstrate that they can implement the technologies whilst understanding the theory behind them. But the focus of these courses is digital text, and the theory, tools, and technologies which can be used for markup and analysis. The reading lists are remarkably similar, and the projects which the students have to do involve practical project work where they create an electronic text using the techniques taught in the session (all of the courses teach eXtensible Markup Language (XML),[16] and the form of XML espoused by the Text Encoding Initiative (TEI):[17] major technical developments by the Humanities Computing research community).

There is good reason for this, as it would seem that it is the thrust of academic research within the discipline. This can be shown by a simple analysis of conference abstracts published for ACH/ALLC, which were obtained in electronic format, and run through a commonly used text analysis program, Concordance,[18] to show which are the most commonly used words in these papers (Figure 4.1).

All available conference abstracts from ACH/ALLC were mined,[19] from 1996 to 2005, with the exclusion of 2003 which was not available. This resulted in a corpus of 1,026,503 words, which, when analysed, demonstrated that 'text' is indeed the focus of Humanities Computing research.

Further analysis (not shown here) demonstrates that this is consistently the case across all years of the conference. Humanities Computing research is predominantly about text: it follows that the teaching programmes should concentrate on this aspect. This also demonstrates that the teaching and research agendas are similar—this is perhaps debatable in other subjects, and could be the focus of further research. It would seem then, that the rationale for the courses is to pass on the theory and techniques used in the Humanities Computing research community.

---

[16] http://www.w3.org/XML.
[17] http://www.tei-c.org.
[18] http://www.concordancesoftware.co.uk.
[19] They were downloaded from the relevant web pages using a utility called PageSucker, http:// www.pagesucker.com/, and concatenated using a Python script, for analysis with Concordance.

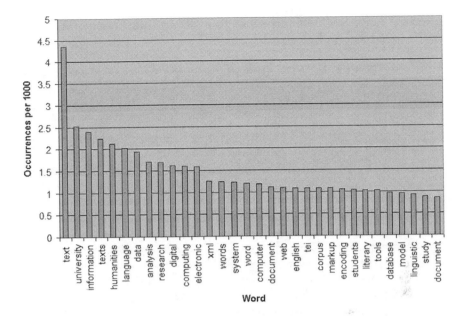

Figure 4.1   The most commonly used words in abstracts of the Association
for Computing and the Humanities and Association of
Literary and Linguistic Computing Joint Conference

Notes: Words are shown in occurrences per 1000, excluding words like 'the' and 'a'
(using the Glasgow Stop Words List, available at http://www.dcs.gla.ac.uk/idom/
ir_resources/ linguistic_utils/stop_words). 'Text' is by far the most commonly used
word, statistically occurring in every single abstract. Other key words demonstrate
that Humanities Computing is about the computational analysis of data, especially
language, words, and documents.

4.2 The Hidden Curriculum

The term 'Hidden Curriculum', coined by Philip Jackson (1968), refers to
the fact that education is a socialization process, and that cultural norms,
socially accepted practices and acceptable types and levels of knowledge are
passed on to students through the way the teaching process is constructed.
Investigation into the hidden curriculum can be used to understand more
fully how the educational process works at different institutional levels (see
Snyder, 1973; Tobias, 1997; and Margolis, 2001 for further discussion).

Academics in Humanities Computing were asked about the aspects of
teaching and research which could pass on implicit messages about the
subject to either the student, or to the wider academic community. It was
difficult to gather statistics about the courses regarding usual aspects of
hidden curriculum research: gender, social background, ethnicity, etc. as

the courses were new, of different sizes, and in very different organizations. Various other issues were raised.

1. In teaching specific technologies, specifically regarding text processing and manipulation, the field was not seen to be engaging in the full spectrum of technology development, but a narrow focus. Because the field was so insular, and did not engage with Computer Science, it was shielding itself away from further developments.

2. All of these courses are taught in Humanities faculties: only one course exists which teaches people in a Computing Science Department.[20] Scholars were seen to need Humanities training before they could be 'trusted' to undertake computational analysis of Humanities data, and this precluded students with a background in technical subjects such as computing or engineering being 'allowed' to join the field at Master's level—when actually they could have a lot to contribute.

3. Links between traditional Humanities departments could not be guaranteed as there was scepticism about the value of some courses. Where links were made, these were generally because of a few keen individuals in the institution.

4. The fact that courses are taught (or research is done) in 'centres' or 'institutes' for the most part, rather than 'departments', suggests to both students and other academics that this is not a proper subject. This has an effect on recruitment for courses. The closure of a research institute by a major Oxford University (see Burnard (2001)), and the funding of the creation but not implementation of an MA degree (Virginia, see Drucker et al., 2002) has also done a lot of damage to the growth of the 'subject' because of the way these actions have been perceived in the wider community. Humanities Computing was seen as a 'help desk' rather than as a research field in its own right.

5. The Humanities Computing community is small and friendly, and it was seen that graduate students could rapidly become part of this community and have the opportunity to engage with leaders in the field from quite early in their study of the subject. However, it was relatively insular.

6. The use of small group and practical project work was very different from traditional Humanities disciplines and required a different skill set from the average Humanities graduate student. Students have to

---

[20] The MSc in IT and the Humanities at the University of Glasgow, recently changed to the name MSc in Information Management and Preservation, which is jointly taught between the Humanities Advanced Technology Institute and the Department of Computer Science, http:// www.hatii.arts.gla.ac.uk/imp/index.htm.

be technically very adept, and also have an access to technology to be able to undertake the courses.

7. It can be very difficult to ascertain funding to undertake graduate research in Humanities Computing, although this may be changing as computing becomes more pervasive throughout all disciplines.

Although there is a similar curriculum and syllabus throughout available courses, which relates very closely to the research agenda of Humanities Computing, there are various issues that need to be addressed in the way that the discipline projects its values onto students, and to the wider academic world. Although the community is warm and welcoming, Humanities Computing needs to engage more with both Computer Science and Humanities disciplines, rather than being an insular community. Issues of curriculum and the hidden curriculum require much more attention and analysis in the future if Humanities Computing is to expand and become institutionalized as an academic subject.

5 Who is Part of the Humanities Computing Community?

It has been suggested in Section 2 that academic fields can be 'measured' by their number of publications, associations, conferences, etc. In Section 4, it was suggested that the Humanities Computing community was small and insular, and it has also been suggested that academics active in research in Humanities Computing generally are employed to research in traditional disciplines. This section aims to ratify these claims by briefly attempting to measure the Humanities Computing community.

5.1 Membership of Associations, Journals, and Discussion Groups

The major associations in Humanities Computing are the Association of Literary and Linguistic Computing[21] (which is based in Europe) and the Association for Computing and the Humanities[22] (based in the USA). Subscribers can be members of both, but as the membership is tied to paid subscription to the journal *Literary and Linguistic Computing*[23] and as it is necessary to choose one or the other or pay extra to be a member of both, most subscribers belong to one organization only. Statistics for membership

---

[21] http://www.kcl.ac.uk/humanities/cch/allc.
[22] http://www.ach.org.
[23] http://llc.oxfordjournals.org.

Table 4.1   Membership of various initiatives in Humanities Computing

Name	Membership
ALLC	100 (approx.)
ACH	100 (approx.)
Humanist Discussion list	1375 subscribers
TEI _L Discussion list	533 subscribers

of these, and also the main free discussion lists in the subject (Humanist[24] and the Text Encoding Initiative List[25]) were collected (Table 4.1).

There are between 100 and 200 scholars who are willing to pay for yearly subscription to the field journal (members can subscribe once but can be members of both the organizations), and over 1,300 interested parties in the field who will sign up for free, almost daily, postings and discussions about the discipline. Over 500 engage in almost daily discussions about the application of textual markup in the Humanities. Although the community is relatively small, it is not inconsequential. But who are these people?

5.2 Analysis of ACH/ALLC 2005 Conference Abstracts

One way to measure who partakes in the Humanities Computing community, given that is has such a diverse spread, is to analyse conference proceedings, attendance lists, and abstracts. The biggest conference in Humanities Computing is ACH/ALLC (see Section 2). Attendance lists were not available for any of the annual conferences, and only a selection of full papers will ever be published. However, the 1,000-word abstracts selected for presentation from those submitted were made available[26] by the Program Committee for analysis.

A database was constructed, from abstracts and personal webpages, of all the presenters attending ACH/ALLC 2005, with their name, paper title, department and institution affiliation, and job title stored for each presenter. Not everyone who undertakes teaching or research in Humanities Computing presented at (or attended) this conference but, as the single large conference in the field, it should provide an overview of activity, affiliation, and structure of Humanities Computing.[27]

---

[24]   http://www.princeton.edu/mccarty/humanist.

[25]   http://listserv.brown.edu/archives/tei-l.html.

[26]   Thanks must go to Alejandro Bia (Chair of the ACH/ALLC Program Committee, Universidad de Alicante, Spain) for access to these files prior to official release.

[27]   Of course, these statistics are of no use without comparison with other conferences. Conference size and attendance varies greatly between subject

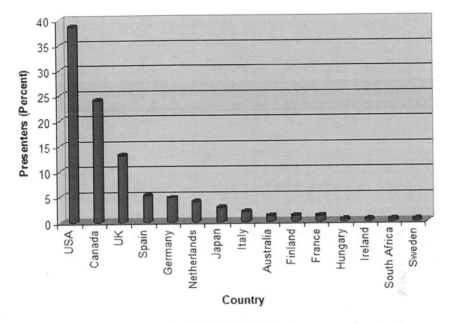

Figure 4.2   Presenters at ACH/ALLC 2005 by country of institution

Note: It can be clearly seen that the conference is dominated by those from the USA and Canada.

A total of 250 individuals were presentation authors at ACH/ALLC, which consisted of 122 sessions: eight full sessions, thirteen panel sessions, and 101 individual papers (indicating that there are, on average, more than two presenters associated with each paper: perhaps a rarity in Humanities scholarship?) A few scholars presented more than one paper.

---

and 'importance' of host association. Take these two examples as extremes: (1) Siggraph 2004, the 31st annual conference and exhibition on computer graphics and interactive techniques, consisted of 83 papers, 225 exhibitors, and seven panel sessions. 27,825 professionals from nearly 90 countries attended the conference in Los Angeles, 8–12 August 2004. See http://www.siggraph.org/s2004; (2) Computers and History of Art (CHArt) 2004 consisted of 15 papers, with 15 presenters from 6 different countries. Approximately 100 people attended the two-day conference on 11–12 November, University of London. See http://www.chart.ac.uk/chart2004-abstracts/index.html. ACH/ALLC is a medium-sized conference which represents a specific subject matter. Attendance at ACH/ALLC 2005 was approximately 300 scholars (including presenters). The percentage of attendees who were present is much higher in this medium-size conference than a conference like Siggraph: perhaps meaning that presenting at ACH/ALLC has less academic kudos than presenting at a larger conference, even though it is the leading conference in its field.

The 250 presenters came from fifteen countries (see Figure 4.2 where they are logged by country of the institution they were affiliated to).

The domination by the USA and Canada is not altogether surprising, considering the location of the conference. When the conference is held in Paris in 2006,[28] there will probably be more presenters submitting papers from Europe. Nevertheless, 77% of those presenting are from countries where English is the native tongue. Only five abstracts were accepted in other languages: French, German, and Spanish. This may construct barriers to non-native English speakers adopting the techniques developed by scholars in the discipline.

Additionally, the scholars are all from western countries (the one presenter from Africa being from its richest and most 'Western' country). Humanities Computing relies on access to computational technologies which would exclude scholars from poorer institutions from participating. Also noticeable in their absence are China and India, which have both experienced massive technological growth and expansion of Internet usage in recent years.[29]

The presenters at the conference come from 102 different academic institutions,[30] with four scholars coming from the industry. The host institution, the University of Victoria, fields the most presenters (although it has a very strong Humanities Computing Centre). This attendance is matched by the University of Illinois at Urbana-Champaign, which has a large and strong library school. Most institutions represented are fairly large, well-known and respected universities (Figure 4.3).

In a few institutions, Humanities Computing is more prevalent, but there still remains a large number of lone, or almost lone, scholars in the field: twenty institutions fielded two scholars, fifty-two fielded a lone scholar (although a large number of these work or present with scholars from other institutions).

The scope of the Humanities Computing community can also be judged by the host department each presenter is affiliated to[31] (Table 4.2).

---

[28] http://www.allc-ach2006.colloques.paris-sorbonne.fr.

[29] Internet World Stats, http://www.internetworldstats.com/stats3.htm, demonstrates that Asia has experienced a 164% growth in Internet usage since 2000, with the rest of the world experiencing 137% growth. The European Union experienced 131% growth during this period.

[30] The International Association of Universities holds records of almost 9,200 academic institutions: http://www.unesco.org/iau/onlinedatabases/list.html. This would indicate that only 1.1% of academic institutions have a scholar attending ACH/ALLC. http://www.unesco.org/iau/onlinedatabases/list.html.

[31] A degree of abstraction had to be used to pigeonhole the departments because of different naming conventions: for example, centres in Humanities Computing were variously named: Centre for Computing and the Humanities, Centre for Technology and the Arts, Computing for Humanities, Institute for Technological Research in Humanities, Arts

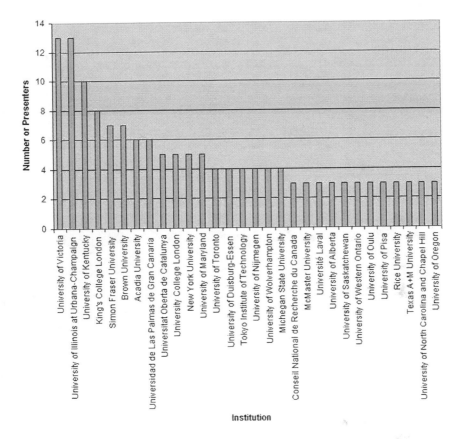

Figure 4.3   Most represented institutions

Note: Any institution fielding less than three scholars is not shown.

The most represented academic discipline is Library and Information Studies. This subject has made extensive use of technology for the organization, storage, and retrieval of data. English follows, as literary and linguistic textual analysis and manipulation are common applications in the field (hence the name 'Literary and Linguistic Computing'). Reassuringly, a large proportion of scholars are linked to Humanities Computing centres, showing that their presence is central to the field. A distinction has been made between library schools and university libraries (as a place for

Informatics, Humanities Computing, Humanities Computing and Media Centre, Humanities Computing Centre, Institute for Technology in the Humanities, Research Computing (Faculty of Arts), and the Institute for Technology and Liberal Education, with only one 'Department of Computing in the Humanities' (at the University of Groningen, Netherlands).

Table 4.2   Official departmental affiliation of presenters

Academic Department	Number of Presenters
School of Library and Information Studies	37
English	32
Humanities Computing Centre	24
Library	24
Linguistics	20
Computing Science	17
Digital Project	13
Education	8
Literature	8
Classics	7
History	7
Computational Linguistics	5
Information Services	5
French	4
Italian	4
German Linguistics	3
Humanities	3
Philology	3
Phonetics	3
Social Sciences	3
Dutch Linguistics and Literary Studies	2
Management Sciences	2
Slavic Languages and Literatures	2
Archaeology	1
Art and Design	1
Cognitive Science	1
Communications	1
Economics and Business	1
Multimedia	1
Philosophy	1
Public Policy	1
Retired	1
Sociology	1
Spanish	1
Women and Gender Studies	1

training of librarians versus the university facility), but staff from university libraries are also well represented, indicating the take-up of technologies in this area. Linguistics is also strongly represented. Interestingly, however, seventeen scholars are computer scientists, indicating that Humanities Computing is of interest to not only the Humanities scholar, but also those involved in Computer Science. Digital projects are specific projects which use Humanities Computing techniques to construct digital resources (for example Matrix,[32] the Centre for Humane Arts, Letters and Social Services online, which develops online teaching tools). Various other arts and social science disciplines are also part of the Humanities Computing community, indicating that the techniques, theory, and applications discussed at this meeting are of broad interest in the Humanities themselves.

In addition to tracking the academic affiliation of presenters, their job titles were noted (Table 4.3). Again, this required some degree of abstraction, and it is also possible that lecturers could be grouped further: a 'Lecturer' can be seen as being akin to being an Assistant Professor, for example. Additionally, five presenters' job titles could not be ascertained. The type of job undertaken with the number of presenters is shown subsequently: most represented job first. The resulting spread of academic positions demonstrates that those involved in Humanities Computing cover the whole spectrum of academic posts: there is a high number of professors, associate and assistant professors, lecturers, researchers and graduate students, as well as support staff, directors of projects, Web developers, post-docs, and independent consultants. Although it is hard to make any statistical judgement on this without comparing it to other disciplines, the fact that this wide range of posts is represented would suggest that Humanities Computing functions as an academic field where promotion and development is possible. It is not only a service to be provided to Humanities scholars, but a discipline in its own right. That said, many of the academic professors earned their chair from more traditional disciplines, such as English or Linguistics, without the use of computing, and their interest in computing may have come after significant academic success had already been achieved.

This analysis has shown that, although there are very few academic departments called 'Humanities Computing', there is a community of scholars who partake in the discipline and who cover a broad range of traditional academic disciplines. These scholars are involved at every level from undergraduate student to Professor. Humanities Computing is international—if international is limited to developed, Western countries, that is. Nevertheless, the fact that such a community clearly exists would suggest that there is enough academic activity being undertaken to identify

---

[32] http://matrix.msu.edu/projects.php.

Table 4.3   Official posts of presenters

Job Type	Number of Presenters
Associate Professor	41
Graduate Student	40
Professor	35
Researcher	33
Lecturer	20
Director	13
Librarian	12
Programmer/Developer	8
Post Doctoral Fellow	7
Associate Director	4
Computing Officer	3
Humanities Computing Specialist	3
Research Development	3
Senior Analyst	3
Senior Lecturer	3
Undergraduate Student	3
Consultant	2
Manager	2
Research Assistant	2
Teacher	2
Web Architect	2
Archivist	1
Assistant Curator	1
Assistant Dean	1
Reader	1

this as a separate field in its own right, confirming the 'disciplinary' status. Further analysis of the abstracts from ACH/ALLC 2005 would include citation and publication analysis, which could provide further information regarding the operation of the field and how it interacts with others. Additionally, it would be useful to compare these results to previous ACH/ALLC conferences, to see any potential changes in the community, and to compare and contrast the Humanities Computing community with those from other disciplines.

6 Conclusion

This article has taken an externalized viewpoint, from Educational theory, to demonstrate that Humanities Computing consists of a diverse community from various subjects in the Humanities whose activities constitute those associated with an academic discipline. Although few teaching programmes exist, Humanities Computing has not yet been accepted as a subject by the majority of institutions, and this can cause problems to scholars undertaking research in this area. This enquiry has raised points about the acceptance of Humanities Computing by both academics and students, whilst demonstrating that there is an identifiable community operating in the field of computing and the arts, from various traditional academic subjects, at all academic level from the student to the professor.

Further studies need to be carried out to further analyse and define the Humanities Computing discipline, field, and community. A citation analysis could be carried out to see which texts are cited by scholars in the field: are they Computing Science texts, or pure Humanities texts? Which journals are most popular? Which are the seminal texts in Humanities Computing that emerge from this analysis? Who would be the most cited author(s)? Continuing this analysis, it would then be useful to return to individual scholars in Humanities Computing and analyse where they publish their articles: what is the publication scope of Humanities Computing? How could this be measured, and what could it tell us about the field? Do Humanities Computing scholars publish in 'traditional' Humanities single-subject journals, or is there a cross-over with Computing Science? Looking at publication records would show the impact factor that Humanities Computing scholarship has in the wider academic field, and so could illuminate some of the boundaries that the discipline operates within.

Further analysis of the curriculum and hidden curriculum is needed across the teaching programmes, with comparison to be made looking at the differences between pure Computing Science and Humanities Computing, and also more traditional Humanities academic subjects and Humanities Computing. Students from various courses could be interviewed so that more detailed information could be ascertained about the different issues present between different academic subjects. There is room for also engaging more with curricular theory, on issues of the hidden curriculum and how we can intrinsically promote and expand Humanities Computing through our teaching programmes and methods.

By turning to a different discipline, Education, to understand its views on issues of disciplinarity, curriculum, and identity, it has been possible to measure and analyse the Humanities Computing community and academic activity in a novel and illuminating way, highlighting areas of concern, and confirming that we do, indeed, seem to function as an academic discipline. What this research has not done is to provide an over-arching definition of the 'subject': it has demonstrated that Humanities Computing exists as an academic discipline, without having to be accepted into the university subject pantheon. Although this creates problems with funding and academic kudos, it can also be seen as an indication of the strength of the discipline: the community exists, and functions, and has found a way to continue disseminating its knowledge and encouraging others into the community without the institutionalization of the subject.

This gives the discipline and the scholars within it additional freedom: if they are not defined, or their activities are not prescribed, then they are free to develop their own research and career paths, which may not fit into the normal mode of operation for academic subjects, but could allow the subject to remain fluid and undefined. Is it such a bad thing if a definition of the subject does not exist?:

> who, for example, ever learnt anything of significance of learning or loving by defining these concepts? Reflecting on and writing about learning should preserve or create an openness, which is a fundamental part of the practice of learning, rather than the closure of categorization, which has more to do with oppression and control. (Rowland, 2000, p. 82)

There may be a time when every academic institution worldwide may have some element of Humanities Computing research and teaching present within it. Alternatively, given that computing is becoming more pervasive, perhaps the Humanities Computing scholar will just be accepted back into the individual discipline they are applying the techniques to: the safe haven of a community of Humanities scholars who happen to use computational techniques may no longer be needed. The techniques and tools of Humanities Computing will then become absorbed back into the support function of information systems and services in academic institutions.

The field may only flourish as an academic subject if it becomes less insular and interacts both with Computer Science and those Humanities scholars who are less willing to accept computing as part of their research tools. Research and teaching methods peculiar to Humanities Computing have to be promoted and developed as useful adjuncts to usual training for Humanities students. The community must continue to develop, but extend its remit to be more inclusive, international, and interdisciplinary: in the cross-faculty sense, encouraging work between the sciences and the arts. Humanities Computing is an emergent discipline which may or may not flourish into an emergent academic subject if the community does not work to extend its focus, scope, and relevance.

Acknowledgements

The author would like to thank the following academics involved in Humanities Computing for their aid in researching this work (in no particular order): Edward Vanhoutte, Lou Burnard, Dr Willard McCarty, Professor Seamus Ross, Professor Susan Hockey, Dr Claire Warwick, Dr Mike Fraser, Dr Stan Ruecker, Professor John Unsworth and Dr Wendell Piez. The author also thanks Alejandro Bia for providing abstracts from ACH/ALLC 2005 ahead of public release and Andrew Ostler who provided technical advice on data mining.

References

Aarseth, E. (1997). 'The Field of Humanistic Informatics and its Relation to the Humanities', *Human IT*, 4 (97), pp. 7–13, http://www.hf.uib.no/hi/espen/HI.html.

Barnett, R., Parry, R. and Coate, K. (2001). 'Conceptualising Curriculum Change', *Teaching in Higher Education*, 6 (4), pp. 434–49.

Becher, T. and Trowler, P.R. (2001). *Academic Tribes and Territories*, Buckingham: The Society for Research into Higher Education and Open University Press, 2nd edn.

Burnard, L. (1999). 'Is Humanities Computing an Academic Discipline? or, Why humanities computing matters', Part of 'Is humanities computing an academic discipline?', Interdisciplinary Seminar University of Virginia, http:// www.iath.virginia.edu/hcs/burnard.html.

Burnard, L. (2001). 'Humanities Computing in Oxford: A Retrospective', http://users.ox.ac.uk/~lou/wip/hcu-obit.txt.

Clark, B. (1980). 'Academic Culture', Working Paper number 42, New Haven, CN: Yale University Higher Education Research Group.

de Smedt (2002). 'Some reflections on studies in humanities computing', *Literary and Linguistic Computing*, 17, pp. 89–101.

de Smedt, K., Gardiner, H., Ore, E. et al. (eds) (1999). *Computing in Humanities Education, a European Perspective*, University of Bergen, http://helmer.aksis. uib.no/AcoHum/book.

Dill, D.D. (1992). 'Academic Administration', in B.R. Clark and G. Neave (eds), *The Encyclopedia of Higher Education*, Vol. II, Oxford: Pergamon Press, pp. 1318–29.

Drucker, J., Unsworth, J. and Laue, A. (2002). Final Report for Digital Humanities Curriculum Seminar, Media Studies Program, College of Arts and Science, University of Virginia, http://www.iath.virginia.edu/hcs/dhcs.

Evans, C. (1995). 'Choosing People: Recruitment and Selection as Leverage on Subjects and Disciplines', *Studies in Higher Education*, 20 (3), pp. 253–65.

Fraser, M. (1996). 'A Hypertextual History of Humanities Computing', http://users.ox.ac.uk/~ctitext2/history.

Gilfillan, D. and Musick, J. (2001). 'Wiring the Humanities at the University of Oregon: Experiences from Year 3', Paper at 'The Humanities Computing Curriculum: The Computing Curriculum in the Arts and Humanities', 9–10 November, Malaspina University College, Nanaimo, British Columbia, Canada, http://web. mala.bc.ca/siemensr/HCCurriculum.

Hockey, S. (1999). 'Is There a Computer in this Class?' Part of 'Is Humanities Computing an Academic Discipline?', Interdisciplinary Seminar, University of Virginia, http://www.iath.virginia.edu/hcs/hockey.html.

Hockey, S. (2001). 'Towards a Curriculum for Humanities Computing: Theoretical Goals and Practical Outcomes', Paper at 'The Humanities Computing Curriculum: The Computing Curriculum in the Arts and Humanities', 9–10 November, Malaspina University College, Nanaimo, British Columbia, Canada, http://web.mala. bc.ca/siemensr/HCCurriculum.

Hughes, E.C. (1971). *Is Education A Discipline? In The Sociological Eye: Selected Papers*, Chicago: Aldine.

Jackson, P.W. (1968). *Life In Classrooms*, New York: Holt, Reinhart and Winston.

Kelly, A.V. (1999). *The Curriculum: Theory and Practice*, London: Paul Chapman, 4th edn.

Kymlicka, B.B. (1992). 'The Faculty of Education: An Interpretation of History and Purposes', http://www. oqe.org/doc/kymlicka.pdf (accessed 2 June 2005); (1986) *Literary and Linguistic Computing*, 1.

Margolis, E. (ed.) (2001). *The Hidden Curriculum in Higher Education*, New York: Routledge.

McCarty, W. (1998). 'What is Humanities Computing? Toward a definition of the field', http://www.kcl.ac.uk/humanities/cch/wlm/essays/what.

McCarty, W. (1999a). 'Humanities Computing as Interdiscipline', part of 'Is Humanities Computing an Academic Discipline?', Interdisciplinary Seminar, IATH, University of Virginia, 5 November, http://www.kcl.ac.uk/humanities/cch/wlm/essays/inter.

McCarty, W. (1999b). 'We would know how we know what we know: Responding to the computational transformation of the humanities', for the conference 'The Transformation of Science – Research between Printed Information and the Challenges of Electronic Networks' held by the Max Planck Gesellschaft, Schloss Elmau, 31 May to 2 June, http://www.kcl.ac.uk/ humanities/cch/wlm/essays/know.

McCarty, W. (2002). 'Humanities Computing: Essential problems, experimental practice', *Literary and Linguistic Computing*, 17, pp. 103–25.

McCarty, W. (2003). 'Humanities Computing', Preliminary draft entry for *The Encyclopedia of Library and Information Science*, New York: Dekker.

McCarty, W. (2005a). *Humanities Computing*, London: Palgrave.

McCarty, W. (2005b). 'Tree, Turf, Centre or Archipelago? Poetics of disciplinarity for humanities computing', *Literary and Linguistic Computing*, 20 (4).

McCarty, W. and Kirschenbaum, M. (2003). 'Institutional Models for Humanities Computing', http://www.kcl.ac.uk/humanities/cch/allc/imhc.

McCarty, W. and Short, H. (2002). 'A Roadmap for Humanities Computing', http://www.kcl.ac.uk/humanities/cch/allc/reports/map.

McCarty, W., Burnard, L., Deegan, M., Anderson, J., and Short, H. (1997). 'Root, Trunk, and Branch: Institutional and infrastructural models for humanities computing in the U.K', Panel session at the Joint International Conference of the Association for Computers and the Humanities and the Association for Literary & Linguistic Computing, Queen's University, Kingston, Ontario, Canada 3–7 June.

McGann, J. (1999). 'IATH and Humanities Computing', part of 'Is Humanities Computing an Academic Discipline?', Interdisciplinary Seminar, University of Virginia, http://www.iath.virginia.edu/hcs/mcgann.html.

Monroe, J. (2002). 'Introduction: The Shapes of Fields', in *Writing and Revising the Disciplines*, Ithaca: Cornell University Press, pp. 1–12.

Moulthrop, S. (1999). 'Computing, Humanism, and the Coming Age of Print', part of 'Is Humanities Computing an Academic Discipline?', Interdisciplinary Seminar, University of Virginia, http://www.iath.virginia.edu/hcs/moulthrop.html.

Nerbonne, J. (1999). 'Humanities Computing: A Federation of Disciplines', part of 'Is Humanities Computing an Academic Discipline?', Interdisciplinary Seminar University of Virginia, http://www.iath.virginia.edu/hcs/nerbonne.pdf.

Orlandi, T. (n.d.). 'The Scholarly Environment of Humanities Computing: A Reaction to Willard McCarty's talk on The Computational

Transformation of the Humanities', http://rmcisadu.let.uniroma1. it/~orlandi/mccarty1.html.

Rockwell, G. (1999). 'Is Humanities Computing an Academic Discipline', part of 'Is Humanities Computing an Academic Discipline?', Interdisciplinary Seminar, University of Virginia, http://www.iath. virginia.edu/hcs/rockwell. html.

Rowland, S. (2000). *The Enquiring University Teacher*, Milton Keynes: Society for Research into Higher Education and Open University Press.

Scheffler, I. (1963). 'Is Education a Discipline?', in J. Walton and J.L. Kuethe (eds), *The Discipline of Education*, Madison: University of Wisconsin Press, pp. 47–61.

Schreibman, S., Siemens, R. and Unsworth, J. (eds) (2004). *A Companion to Digital Humanities*, Blackwell Companions to Literature and Culture, Blackwell Publishing.

Siemens, R. (2001). 'The Humanities Computing Curriculum: The Computing Curriculum in the Arts and Humanities', 9–10 November, Malaspina University College, Nanaimo, British Columbia, Canada, http://web.mala.bc.ca/siemensr/HCCurriculum.

Snyder, B.R. (1973). *The Hidden Curriculum*, Cambridge, MA: MIT Press.

Taylor, P.J. (1976). 'An interpretation of the quantification debate in British Geography', *Transactions of the Institute of British Geographers New Series*, 1, pp. 129–42.

Tobias, S. (1997). *The Hidden Curriculum: Faculty-Made Tests in Science*, London: Plenum.

Unsworth, J. (1993). 'Networked Scholarship: The Effects of Advanced Technology on Research in the Humanities', presented at Harvard University, Cambridge, MA, November, http://www3.isrl.uiuc. edu/~unsworth/gateways.html.

Unsworth, J. (1996). 'Digital Research in the Humanities: Community, Collaboration, and Intellectual Technologies', Petrou Lecture, University of Maryland, 24 April, http://www3.isrl.uiuc. edu/~unsworth/petrou.umd.html.

Unsworth, J. (2000). 'What is Humanities Computing and What is Not?' A talk delivered in the Distinguished Speakers Series of the Maryland Institute for Technology in the Humanities at the University of Maryland, College Park, MD, 5 October, http://www.iath.virginia. edu/%7Ejmu2m/mith.00.html.

Unsworth, J. (2002) 'The Emergence of Digital Scholarship: New Models for Librarians, Scholars, and Publishers,' delivered as part of 'The New Scholarship: Scholarship and Libraries in the 21st Century',

Dartmouth College, Hanover, NH, 9 November, http://www3.isrl. uiuc.edu/~unsworth/dartmouth.02.

Unsworth, J. (2003). 'Tool-Time, or "Haven't We Been Here Already?" Ten Years in Humanities Computing', delivered as part of 'Transforming Disciplines: The Humanities and Computer Science', 18 January, Washington, DC, http://www3.isrl. uiuc.edu/~unsworth/ carnegie-ninch.03.html.

Unsworth, J. (2004). 'What is Humanities Computing (and What is Not)?' Texas A&M, as part of the Humanities Informatics Lecture Series, College Station, TX, 10 September, http://www3.isrl. uiuc. edu/~unsworth/texas-hc.html.

Vanhoutte, E. (forthcoming). *Humanities Computing and (Electronic) Textual Editing. History, Theory, Applications, and Implications*, Ph.D. dissertation, Antwerp: University of Antwerp.

Viñao, A. (2002). 'A History of Education in the 20th century: A View from Spain', *Mexican Journal of Educational Research*, 7 (15), pp. 223–56. Available from http://www.comie.org.mx/revista/ PdfsEnglish/Carpeta15/15investTem1Engl.pdf.

Warwick, C. (2004). 'No Such Thing as Humanities Computing? An Analytical History of Digital Resource Creation and Computing in the Humanities', Paper given at ALLC Goteborg University, 11–16 June.

Wenger, E. (1998). *Communities of Practice: Learning, Meaning, and Identity*, Cambridge: Cambridge University Press.

Note from the author:
This paper emerged from an investigation undertaken in 2005 as part of my probationary requirement of my first academic post. We all had to undertake a postgraduate teaching qualification with a dissertation requirement, and I thought I would marry the literature and approaches we were learning about in class with the subject I was teaching in *my* class. It was an interesting foray into educational literature, and made explicit many of the tacit presumptions that existed in the community at the time about its activities. It is interesting to see how the main conclusions of the paper have fared: less than a decade later many Digital Humanities centres and related degree and postgraduate courses are springing up across the world, meaning that – on some level – Digital Humanities is now more accepted, and mainstream. The community has certainly grown, from the figures that are supplied here (for recent figures, see my 'Quantifying Digital Humanities' infographic at http://melissaterras. blogspot.co.uk/2012/01/infographic-quanitifying-digital.html). However, enough questions remain about the focus and scope of the discipline to ensure that I wanted to edit this entire volume! On a personal note, I detect in this paper some of my frustrations at not doing 'enough' computing: my

call to interacting with the computational and engineering sciences still stands, I think. For me, the fertile stomping ground is the place between the humanities and the computational sciences, allowing us to undertake activities which would otherwise be impossible. We should still be aiming to bridge that Computer Science and Humanities divide.

Melissa Terras, November 2012

Tree, Turf, Centre, Archipelago – or Wild Acre? Metaphors and Stories for Humanities Computing[1]

Willard McCarty
King's College London

Willard McCarty (2006). Originally published in *Literary and Linguistic Computing*, 21 (1), pp. 1–13.[2]

Note from the Editors:

In this article McCarty aimed to offer practitioners of humanities computing 'a different professional myth to live by'. New metaphors, stories and in turn myths were needed, he argued, in order to better understand the new demands that humanities computing made of the academy. He begins by examining three well established metaphors: Tree, Turf and Centre and, from the perspective of humanities computing, finds them lacking. In their place he argues for the metaphor 'archipelago', its most salient characteristics being the sense of helpful distancing that it can create and the 'core anthropological event of encounter' that it evokes. Whether in its discussion of the act of mythologizing a discipline or its emphasis on 'cross-cultural encounters' this article broke new ground in terms of defining Humanities Computing. Elsewhere in this volume we will see some manifestations of both of these themes, for example in portrayals of Digital Humanities as being 'Big Tent'. Nevertheless, much research remains to be done from both these perspectives: collaboration may lie at the centre of digital humanities but very little literature exists on the social, intellectual and theoretical aspects of DH collaboration, the aspects that both set it apart and unite it with other disciplines. This article is an important starting point for any such work.

---

[1] For Sinéad O'Sullivan.

[2] This essay was originally delivered as a plenary address at 'Computing Arts 2004', Centre for Literary and Linguistic Computing, University of Newcastle, NSW, Australia, www.newcastle.edu.au/centre/cllc/ca2004. My thanks to the organizer, Professor Hugh Craig, for his many kindnesses and patience, to the anonymous reviewers who stimulated me to improve the first attempt and to John Burrows for advice on the connotations of words. All URLs have been verified as of 29 July 2005.

Abstract

The social acceptability of computing to the humanities is no longer a serious problem, although its role in research is sometimes overlooked or must be kept decorously out of sight. The real problem is that in an academic world largely defined by disciplinary turf-polity, possibilities for it are severely constricted. As was true in the early days of computer science, humanities computing is still likely to be seen, judged and funded not as an integral practice but piecemeal, in the widely differing terms of the disciplines to which it is applied. In this essay, I go after antiquated figures of thought responsible for this blinkered, piecemeal view. Reasoning from the evident importance of geopolitical metaphors to our operative conception of disciplinarity, I look down under, and back in time, for different, less constricting metaphors and draw out of them a different professional myth to live by.

> Through gentle digging one can uncover the old latent configurations, but when it comes to determining the system of discourse on the basis of which we still live, as soon as we are obliged to question the words that still resonate in our ears, that are mingled with those we are trying to speak, then archaeology … is forced to work with hammer blows.
>
> (Michel Foucault, 'On the Ways of Writing History', 1998, p. 293)

> The imposing edifice of society above my head holds no delights for me. It is the foundation of the edifice that interests me. There I am content to labor, crowbar in hand, shoulder to shoulder with intellectuals, idealists, and class-conscious workingmen, getting a solid pry now and again and setting the whole edifice rocking. Some day, when we get a few more hands and crowbars to work, we'll topple it over.
>
> (Jack London, 'What Life Means to Me', in *Revolution and Other Essays*, 1909)

We commonly take fear to be a sign of ignorance, and so doctor it with knowledge. Thus Clifford Geertz begins his attack on anti-relativism by noting that, 'A scholar can hardly be better employed than in destroying a fear' (2000, p. 42). But this much can be said for fear: it is at least a response to something perceived, however imperfectly. Take, for example, the recent fear expressed in the US *Chronicle of Higher Education* by the pseudonymous Ivan Tribble.[3] Of one job candidate who was discovered to have a blog, Professor Tribble writes that because 'the true passion of said blogger's life was [revealed in it to be] not academe at all, but the minutiae of software systems, server hardware, and other tech exotica', he or she could not be trusted: 'we can't afford to have our new hire ditching us to hang

---

[3]　8 July 2005, chronicle.com/jobs/2005/07/2005070801c.htm.

out in computer science after a few weeks on the job.' In the short term, applicants may rightly be worried about professors Tribble, but the scenario this one imagines is so unlikely, we are apt to dismiss it as the ignorant imaginings of an old guard on its way out, and so counsel patience. Indeed, his reaction sounds the tiresomely familiar denial of academic seriousness to one field by another, in particular the dismissal of a hands-on practice by a discourse-centred discipline. The haughty brush-off of 'rude mechanicals' by their presumptive social betters is with us still, it seems.

But there is more to Tribble than that. To paraphrase Bacon, the problem is not that senior colleagues, fearing change 'as children fear to go in the dark', are unable to cope. Rather, what is worth our attention here is the social institution that they are leaving behind for their young-turk successors. From the perspective of computing for the humanities, this institution embodies a problematic way of thinking about knowledge not directly related to the social acceptability of technical work. A confirming sign of something deeper at fault is the digirati's own frustration at a mismatch between emergent possibilities of computing and existing disciplinary structures. (Consider, for example, how computing is currently fitted into academic positions in the humanities, or how the possibilities for research are defined by panels of assessment.[4]) Given this mismatch, Tribble's fear of desertion seems far less irrational, even soberly pragmatic. Who, loving challenges and excited by the possibilities of computing, would not be tempted by escape from a hide-bound, intellectually exhausted department in the humanities to pursue them?[5] Computer science, which together with molecular biology is 'the fastest growing sector of academia' (Mahoney,

---

[4]   For a typical example of a job advertisement, see *Humanist*, 19 (151), lists.village. virginia.edu/lists_archive/Humanist/v19/0150.html. For online databases of jobs, see those listed by Academic360, www.academic360.com; note the semiotics of their structures and search facilities. For funding and assessment structures, see the following schemes: (1) the 'Units of Assessment' for the UK Research Assessment Exercise (RAE 03 2005, pp. 35–6), www.rae.ac.uk/pubs/2005/03; (2) 'Research Subject Coverage' of the UK Arts and Humanities Research Council; (3) the 'Research Fields, Courses and Disciplines Classification' for the Australian Research Council, www.arc.gov.au/htm/RFCD_codes.htm; (4) the 'Standard Research Grants Selection Committees' of the Social Sciences and Humanities Research Council of Canada, www.sshrc.ca/web/about/committees/standard_research_e.asp. Saul Fisher, Director of Fellowship Programs of the American Council of Learned Societies, notes that the approach of the ACLS for funding purposes is to view 'humanities computing as divisible into the traditional humanistic disciplines'. This view is traditional in that it defines the disciplines according to their subject matter, and pragmatic in that it reflects the organizational status quo. Its 'central commitment [is] to humanistic scholarship so defined (as against computing or any of the other natural or formal sciences)'. The principle at play is to 'identify the specifically humanistic disciplines in terms of what humanistic domain they study, not what method (humanistic or otherwise) they employ' (private e-mail, by permission, 7 August 2005).

[5]   For a statement of the problem, see McGann (2005).

2002, p. 27), is hungry for worthy problems and is an increasingly broad church.[6] The field variously known as 'information studies' or 'library and information science' is not far behind, in fact may offer a better home.[7]

Frustration, like fear, is not always merely a sign of an unenlightened or disturbed mind. It can also indicate an unenlightened, disturbing institution.

In this essay, I go after a cause of the darkness in an idea of institutionalized research which blinkers us to a fundamental consequence of computing for the humanities. I begin with George Lakoff's and Mark Johnson's argument for the foundational role of metaphor in how we conceive the world and act in it (1980). I suggest the shaping influence of metaphor on our structures of knowledge, then argue that the inherited imagery which pervades our disciplinary thinking seriously interferes with our ability to understand what scholarly computing demands of us institutionally. I look to imaginations shaped by a particular geography for a better metaphor, then, by expanding that metaphor into a narrative, suggest the beginnings of what might be called a new professional myth. The myth I tell is only one possibility out of many. I make no particular claims for it other than a somewhat improved account of humanities computing's role in the academy. My purpose is much more to exemplify mythologizing.

To paraphrase Lakoff and Johnson, I use 'myth' in this context to mean a story one lives by, and 'myth-making' to denote the process of constructing a recognizable account of what one does. I take the role of such a myth to be not deterministic but analogous to the winds and currents with or against which a sailor navigates, allowing degrees of freedom, giving exercise to cunning intelligence but exerting strong influence on course and speed, and so giving shape to the known world. Similarly, with E.H. Gombrich I take metaphor not to have an allegorical meaning but rather 'qualities that lend themselves to symbolic use' (1971, p. 13). Metaphors as a result accumulate a history of uses to which they have been put, a history that helps us to identify those qualities but does not necessarily adhere to them. As Gombrich notes, 'the temptation to regard all symbols as codes' – as keys to a perennial philosophy, an historical or psychological programme or a hidden agenda – is strong. Questions to be asked are,

---

[6]   For a measure of the expansion of interest within computer science for the humanities, compare 'Computing the Future' (1994) with Mitchell, Inouye and Blumenthal (2003).

[7]   John M. Unsworth (Graduate School of Library and Information Science, Illinois at Urbana-Champaign) points to common ground 'in scholarly communication, in knowledge representation, in access to information, in preservation of the cultural record, and in the organization and analysis of information' (private e-mail, 23 July 2005).

What figures of thought best suit our purpose? What does each do for us? What is its symbolic trajectory?

At issue is how we come up with an empirically adequate story to tell. Here, I will simply assert that having a story is essential, first to make best sense of one's professional life, then to be equipped to explain it to others. The reactions of the old guard tell us this in addition: that a compelling explanation is long overdue.

1 The Constructive Power of Metaphor

Lakoff and Johnson argue that metaphor is not merely an extraordinary flowering of thought or product of mental exuberance but the ground in which our thinking is rooted.[8] Our prejudices condition us to treat metaphor as ornament to plain speech, perhaps useful but ultimately inessential. Mostly, we relegate it to flagrantly imaginative genres, such as poetry. When we dig down into ordinary language, we may notice what we call 'dead' metaphors but, as the label suggests, we are apt to treat them merely as fossils left behind in forming the bedrock of plain speech – historically interesting but dead. What we tend to see as metaphor is thus the obvious, striking, remarkable. Lakoff and Johnson direct our attention back to the supposed fossils, which they show to be tacitly active in shaping our ideas and actions.

'How strange it is', Ian Hacking comments in remarks on disciplinarity, 'that ancient meanings are continued below the level of conscious awareness' (2004). In this essay I do not stop to enquire why they continue, but simply invoke Lakoff and Johnson in order to question a set of metaphors we seem unwittingly to work by – or, more specifically, those in terms of which we are now (mistakenly, I argue) struggling to construct computing's relation to the humanities. My contention is that the tropes and imageries we unquestioningly accept from our immediate disciplinary ancestors are unfit for the purpose and so lead to confusion and misspent effort. To echo Geertz, a scholar can hardly be better employed than in putting such a situation to rights.

In particular, I highlight the general tendency to read metaphors of disciplinarity as if they were essentially factual terms describing an unpleasant but unavoidable academic Realpolitik rather than the figures of thought by which it is created and maintained. This misreading becomes

---

[8]　Lakoff and Johnson (1980). Their argument parallels Northrop Frye's for mythology, constructed with metaphor: 'the traditional view of nature seems right to the extent that man does not live directly in nature like the animals—there are no noble savages of that kind—but within a cultural envelope that conditions his approach to nature' (1990, p. 247).

especially problematic when we attempt to accommodate a genuinely new epistemological practice, such as humanities computing. We encounter difficulties because, as I will argue, it does not fit the academy we erect on top of the old metaphorical infrastructure. Here I intend to direct Foucauldian hammer blows at this infrastructure by going after the first three metaphors listed in my title – 'tree', 'turf' and 'centre' – which are foundational to it. I then develop the fourth metaphor, 'archipelago', as basis for imagining a structure generous enough to accommodate the kind of practice humanities computing has shown itself to be. I conclude by undercutting any claim to canonicity this metaphor may seem to have by suggesting yet another alternative.

I suspect that, if asked in private, most practitioners would liken the work they do to a discipline like history, classics or English literature, to a cross-disciplinary speciality like textual editing or to a technical practice like digital library research. If asked to explain their participation in the multi-disciplinary congregations of humanities computing (for example the Digital Humanities conference[9]), they would explain it by saying that humanities computing is useful to what they do, so they share in this interest, then go back to editing texts, writing histories, designing metalanguages or whatever. I have no quarrel with this sharing of interests. Indeed, it is a source of much that is good about the field. But as an acting out of institutional possibilities, it is radically incomplete. It fails to take direct account of the potent commonalities and synergies that are among the most intellectually and socially beneficial effects of computing. It suggests – here we verge on the problem I intend to address – that these commonalities and synergies are largely invisible to practitioners because of the institutional structures they inhabit.

A slightly better move might seem to be to establish a new discipline. Even if the immediate practical difficulties could be overcome, however, this would still attenuate the benefits by fencing off our subject as the bailiwick of specialists. The behaviour of other disciplines suggests that the agenda of humanities computing would then move away from collegial service and from a wide sharing of interests to intra-professional concerns. The new discipline, as a discipline, would become immediately ethnocentric like the rest, concerned chiefly with itself, with luck and hard work making jobs for a few but with considerably less benefit to most of those who, gathering at the occasional conference or with a technical practitioner, now find themselves at home away from home.[10]

---

[9] This is the conference formerly known as ALLC/ACH or ACH/ALLC; see wwwdigitalhumanities.org under Community.

[10] Note that I am not arguing here for an end to disciplinarity, or for its comprehensive replacement by multi-, inter- or trans-disciplinarity, only that the conventional status does not suit humanities computing.

But if humanities computing is not to be a discipline like the rest, how do we configure it so that it can be seen to exist as a scholarly pursuit, so that it can survive? What metaphors do we use to imagine, build and communicate its institutional form?

2 Conventional Figures of Thought

To answer that question, we need first to examine conventional tropes. As promised, I look at three words common to disciplinary discourse, excavate the metaphorical tenor of each and test it against the realities of practice.

2.1 Tree

One of the commonest ways of describing a subject of enquiry is to call it a 'branch' of learning. This is in many ways an appealingly dynamic, organic and suitable figure: branches grow and subdivide into smaller and smaller segments in complex inter-relationship with their environment. They produce flowers and fruit. Indeed, idealized tree-like structures have for millennia proven useful in diagramming categorizations, interrelationships and their products, for example in the medieval metaphor of the 'tree of knowledge' depicted in Ramón Llull's late thirteenth century encyclopaedic compendium, *Arbor Scientiae*.[11] The tree metaphor 'is very deep in human culture', as Hacking points out (2004), though the use of tree-diagramming is comparatively recent – he suggests a Western Asian origin ca. AD 500.

Nevertheless, as an epistemological metaphor the tree leads us in the wrong direction. There are two problems with it. First, in the time-scale in which we perceive them, trees are more or less static: what you see is all and only what you get, magnificent though it may be. Second, as Peter Burke points out in *A Social History of Knowledge*, the metaphor naturalizes what we now regard as man-made divisions of learning (2000, pp. 86–7). Fundamental innovation, thus made implicitly unnatural, is ruled out, literally denatured. There is no place on the tree for an epistemological activity which both defines its own agenda and interrelates with all the other fields of enquiry. We need to look elsewhere.

---

[11] See, for example, the Wikipedia entry for 'Arbor scientiae', de.wikipedia.org/wiki/Arbor_scientiae. For obvious reasons the image is popular in the subdivision of AI known as Knowledge Representation (KR); see the dust-jacket of Sowa (2000) and pp. 4–5, and cf. 'The Tree of Knowledge Technologies', www.topquadrant.com/tq_tree_of_knowledge.htm. The image illustrates many notions of what knowledge might be, as a search of the Web will reveal. On KR and humanities computing, see McCarty (2005), pp. 30–31.

Since my aim is story-telling, it is worth asking what kind of narrative can result from the *arbor scientiae*. The image itself suggests that the onlooker's job is to behold or contemplate; in the context of computing, the imperative would be to implement. But the contemporary story of knowledge representation (in which the tree represents not Llull's doctrinal truth but commonsense knowledge) suggests that for us this metaphor's story is centrally of the attempt to discover what modern trees of such knowledge (or, in the more dogmatic projects, *the* tree) might be like. In essence, the story is of working toward a perfect mimesis of a totalizing vision such as we are presumed to have commonsensically. Even if the ambition is a good-enough mimesis, the vision remains as singular.

2.2 Turf and Related Figures

In less bureaucratic, more obviously political contexts, areas of learning are defined by the subject matter they command or possess. Here geopolitical metaphors are common, e.g. 'turf', 'domain' and the related 'boundary', 'wall', 'fence' and the like. We speak or think in terms of private property and the means used to defend or acquire it.

'Turf' denotes 'a sod of grass, with the roots and earth adhering', a medieval synecdoche for property, as in the sixteenth century sense of 'sod cut from the turf of an estate ... as a token or symbol of possession' (*OED*). Hence 'turf-warfare'. 'Domain' points back from the possessed to the possessor, originally referring to *quod ad dominum spectat*, i.e. a lord's private property (*OED*). In recent years, the phrase 'knowledge domain' has become popular in computer science and related areas to denote a well-defined territory populated by experts from whom reliable ontologies can supposedly be extracted. Speaking of 'boundaries' or 'walls' similarly leads back to ownership, ruling authority and territorial politics, with defence and aggression on either side.

The chief problem for a new epistemological practice is not the claim to private property. There cannot be, after all, any such private property in ideas, so attempts to possess will always be weak.

Rather the hard problem is with the implications of a finite, well mapped and cultivated world: it allows for no *terra incognita* – nothing to be discovered, only something to be possessed; its divisions are fixed, or changeable only at great cost; and clear distinction between what does and what does not belong requires anxious, intellect-sapping attention. For a conventional discipline, boundaries are problematic because, as William Wulf has said, they mark where our knowledge fails, and so where the real challenges lie (1995, p. 56). They are problematic for humanities computing because, as with the *arbor vitae*, they exclude it. If boundaries denote the law, then disciplinary boundaries define humanities computing as an outlaw – homeless, stateless, gypsy.

Could it be that these territorial metaphors originate in or are cognate with the European geopolitical scene, especially prior to the European Union? Consider, for example, the German mathematician David Hilbert's robust introduction to a lecture delivered in Zurich, Switzerland, in 1917, as the great empires of Europe were coming to a violent end:

> Just as in the life of nations the individual nation can only thrive when all neighbouring nations are in good health; and just as the interest of states demands, not only that order prevail within every individual state, but also that the relationships of the states among them be in good order; so it is in the life of the sciences. In due recognition of this fact the most important bearers of mathematical thought have always evinced great interest in the laws and the structure of the neighbouring sciences; above all for the benefit of mathematics itself they have always cultivated the relations to the neighbouring sciences, especially to the great empires of physics and epistemology. (Ewald, 1996, p. 1107)

Here is a vision of knowledge as fixed and totalizing as the medieval *arbor scientiae*: all domains of enquiry are known, *ordentlich* as the professoriate Hilbert so brilliantly exemplified; what remains are the investigations within them and the negotiations among them. Few would speak thus today, at least not openly but, as Hacking suggests, the continuation of old meanings below the level of conscious awareness should not be underestimated. For example, we continue to talk, in what are derivatively aggressive terms, of breaking down boundaries between fields of learning but, as long as we continue to talk in this way, we give new strength to the boundaries that must be there so that we may continue heroically to break them down.

Again allow me to ask, what kind of a professional myth is promised here for humanities computing? Surely the story cannot be optimal: of existing on the fringes of the established domains, fighting local battles with other peripheral newcomers (such as new media studies) and making alliances as opportunities arise.

2.3 Centre

My next metaphor, a *centre* of learning, is not so much wrong for the purpose as it is incomplete. It is acceptable as a way of describing the place to which scholars come for help or to gather for collaborative work: originally the library, recently also the (humanities) computing centre, now in addition the evolving fusion of both in the digital library. It is capable of great power in Northrop Frye's use of it to denote the potential of a discipline to become 'a centre of all knowledge' by providing 'a structure that can expand into other structures' (1988, p. 10). This is, one suspects, his secular rendition of that ancient formula for God, *centrum ubique, circumferentia nusquam*, 'centre everywhere, circumference nowhere', which de-centres the idea of ultimately localized space by turning it inside out, and so discovering 'a world in a grain of sand'.[12] Thus, also, the idea of a world-wide digital library turns the library (or its local manifestation, the computer screen) into a portal on the docuverse.

Hacking (who has 'dabbled in, and sometimes contributed to, more fields of thought than most people can shake a stick at') portrays much the same conception of a scholarly life: 'applying my discipline in different directions', guided by curiosity, hard work and respect for the learned skills and innate talents of others. 'Who else to go to', he asks, 'but someone who knows more than you do, or can do something better than you can? Not because you are inexpert in your domain, but because you need help from another one' (2004). This is, I suspect, as generous a conception of disciplinary life as one will find. But what do you do if you do not have a long-established domain, if the geopolitical metaphor does not suit?

As I have suggested, the metaphor of a centre, though powerful as the matrix for an individual scholarly life, cannot open out into the kind of story we need. It is little help in imagining how humanities computing (or any other field) might relate socio-intellectually, on a collegial basis, to the intellectual world in which it finds itself.

3 Metaphors of Exploration

Earlier, quoting Gombrich, I referred to the qualities of metaphor 'that lend themselves to symbolic use'. Each of the rejected metaphors contributes some qualities we can use – the tree defines space for movement among its branches; mapped terrain lays out settled ways of life to be visited; the centre paradoxically everywhere transcends locality. To paraphrase Gombrich, making our figures of thought conscious liberates us not just from regarding them as encoded programs but also from their programming. Frustration gives way to clues toward a more generous way of conceiving scholarship.

As an example of one such way, I offer the fourth term in my title, 'archipelago', for its qualities and especially for the stories it evokes of exploration by sea. A specifically European focus to these stories helps

---

[12]   I quote first Alain de Lille (1128–1202) from Alverny (1965, p. 297), then William Blake's 'Auguries of Innocence'.

because it captures the sense of transition from a finite, thoroughly settled and well mapped metaphorical terrain (from which humanities computing needs escape) to an uncertainly distributed group of diverse cultural places with room in which to act out unimagined possibilities.

The word 'archipelago' (It. *arci-* 'chief, principal' + *pélago* 'deep, pool', fr. Gk. *pélagos* 'sea') was perhaps first used in its etymological sense in the later thirteenth century to name the Adriatic, 'principal sea' of Venice, but its chief association was with the Aegean, archetypal place of explorations since Odysseus entered the European imagination. By the early sixteenth century explorers had reapplied 'archipelago' to mean the many islands of that sea, or a group of islands in any sea (*OED* [2]).

As metaphor the first virtue of 'archipelago' is that it necessarily implies a constant if moving perspective on something observed from without, at a distance. It is a sea-going rather than a land-locked term. Its second virtue is that the objects in sight are separated and so separately accessible, each across an ambivalent, liminal margin of ebb and flow. Approach from the sea, to islands or anything like an island,[13] evokes the story of exploration, and with it the core anthropological event of encounter.

Numerous European voyages, from the High Middle Ages on, supply us with a considerable number of individuals motivated by a varying mixture of scholarship, curiosity, mercantilism, piracy and so forth. Marco Polo is an obvious example from the thirteenth century; William Dampier, 'pirate of exquisite mind' from the seventeenth; and from the eighteenth two of James Cook's crew, the naturalists Joseph Banks on the first voyage and Johann Georg Adam Forster on the second.[14] Throughout this period, as well as before and after it, Christian missionaries, such as the Jesuits, explored alongside them. Long before any of these, sea-going merchants and adventurers of the ancient world, such as the Phoenicians, plotted the explorer's life and built sea-going empires.

The scientific curiosity of explorers like Banks and Forster is obviously relevant to the story we need – more so, perhaps, than might seem. Scott Atran has argued, for example, that earlier discoveries such as theirs, bringing large amounts of new evidence to the attention of European naturalists in the Age of Exploration, so challenged received ways of classifying the living world that revolutionary methods had to be invented (1990). Hence the emergence of scientific *alongside* folk taxonomy – not so much replacing the latter as complementing it in realms of experience

---

[13] The word 'island' can apply to land partially surrounded by water or even approached from across water (*OED*).

[14] The quoted phrase is from the title of Preston and Preston (2004). I am indebted to Timothy Mason, Virginia Knight, Reto Speck, Patricia Galloway and others for some of these suggestions (*Humanist*, 19 (136), p. 140.

for which folk-knowledge is insufficient. We have seen the same happen in the physical sciences of the very small and the very large, while the more intuitive schemes for dealing with the world on a human scale remain as useful as ever. Just so: our ability to command far larger amounts of evidence from computers is having or promises to have a similar effect on disciplines across the humanities.[15] Even areas of philosophy are affected.[16] At the same time, the mercantile and religious purposes of early explorers serve us also, as analogues for the practitioner's exchange of intellectual goods and inculcation of best practices among heretofore rarely communicating disciplines.[17]

The academic disciplines are not, however, passive to computing or mere sites for its revolutionary effects. They are also sources of guidance in our attempts to figure out what we are doing. In particular, the explorer's story brings anthropology immediately into play, to identify the crucial elements of this story and give us a hand in reading them. Here we have a precedent in Peter Galison's study of intensively collaborative scientific research, in which he uses the anthropological metaphor of a 'trading zone' to describe situations in which a highly specialized researcher in one discipline takes an established body of techniques from another, more or less as a black box, for his or her own purposes.[18] The trading zone metaphor has much to recommend it: at one stroke it recognizes academic disciplines as cultural entities, and thus invokes the anthropology of cross-cultural encounter; focuses on dialogic discovery; posits interchange rather than exploitation or conquest; and draws attention to the migration of artifacts from their contexts of origin to other, unrelated ones.[19]

Galison focuses on migrant knowledge-objects passed between collaborating specialists, mostly in a single laboratory. In the practice of

---

[15] The clearest example is the work of John Burrows and colleagues in computational stylistics – clear enough to make the case in principle for other disciplines, although the actual effects depend largely on the match between computing and the current agenda of each discipline. See the chapters by Craig and Burrows in Schreibman, Siemens and Unsworth (2004).

[16] See, for example, Hacking (2005).

[17] I am essentially describing here what elsewhere is called the 'methodological commons' of humanities computing; see McCarty (2005, pp. 114–57) and esp. Figure 3.1.

[18] Galison (1997), chapter 9 esp., but also chapter 1 and sections 3.11, 6.7, 6.11, 8.1, 8.5, 8.7.

[19] Here I can only note in passing the importance of the migrant artifact to this audience of purveyors, students and makers of tools. As Galison says, cross-cultural migration involves 'a partial peeling away, an (incomplete) *dis*encumberance of meaning' (1997, p. 436): while the artifact may enter a culture with no knowledge of its original intention and no theory, or a different theory, of its workings, the object continues to work and to be in particular ways. This raises the related questions first of the intentionality of objects independent of our ideas about them, and second how we read these objects.

humanities computing, such objects (chiefly formalized methods rather than developed applications) are likewise exchanged. The difference is that these objects are developed collaboratively, then carried by the practitioner from project to project – in the metaphor, from island to island. Hence, for humanities computing, great emphasis falls on the practitioner's cross-cultural encounters – in the ethnohistorian Greg Dening's happy phrase, crossing 'beaches of the mind' to become an anthropological participant observer in a foreign disciplinary culture (1998, pp. 85–145). Harold Short has sketched out the broad features of the typical encounter between scholar and practitioner, with particular attention to the development of the scholarly problem, and so indicated where close ethnographic attention is needed: on the change in how the object of investigation is understood, the practitioner's role in this change and especially on his or her practice as a form of research.[20]

Frye's *centrum ubique* metaphor is powerfully suggestive of where the last part of this question might go. Usually when specialists are compelled to reach beyond the limits of their disciplines, Lubomír Dolezel points out, they interpret what they find in terms of what they already know. Taking literary critics as his example, he notes the reductive sameness common to their supposed interdisciplinarity:

> While claiming to cultivate interdisciplinarity, they give philosophy, history, and even natural sciences a 'literary' treatment; their complex and diverse problems are reduced to concepts current in contemporary literary writing, such as subject, discourse, narrative, metaphor, semantic indeterminacy, and ambiguity. The universal 'literariness' of knowledge acquisition and representation is then hailed as an interdisciplinary confirmation of epistemological relativism and indeterminism, to which contemporary literati subscribe. (1998, p. 785)

The same might be said of procrustean *applications* of computing, imposed template-like on scholarly problems, as happens when totalizing ambition fastens onto a trendy technology (such as XML encoding). Frye has something very different in mind. Crucially he speaks of *expanding* one epistemic structure into another, not of acting like the proverbial man with the hammer, to whom everything seems a nail.[21]

---

[20]   McCarty (2005, pp. 121–9) transcribes the essence of an interview with Short on this subject.

[21]   The proverb is widely circulated in a number of versions, some attributed to the entrepreneur and statesman Bernard Baruch (1870–1965), thus 'Baruch's Observation'. It is used by the motivational therapist Abraham Maslow (1908–1970), in Maslow (1966, pp. 15f). Abraham Kaplan calls it 'the law of the instrument', points out its inevitability as a consequence of training and recommends 'applications of the greatest possible range of techniques' (1964, pp. 28–9). My thanks to John Lavagnino for this reference.

To see what this expansion might mean for computing, we need to ask what we might take its epistemic structure to be, and how typically this structure is adapted to the structures of target disciplines in the humanities. When, that is, we look at a particular research problem in terms of computing, when we see its domain as computable data, what are we looking *with*, and how does it organize and filter what is known by means of it? How is the problem affected? There are, I think, two answers. The first is indicated by the concluding sentence of Marvin Minsky's Turing Award lecture: 'The computer scientist', he writes, 'is the one who must study [how we learn], because he is the proprietor of the concept of procedure' (1970, p. 214). With computing, that is, we look procedurally. The second answer I take from the opening sentence of David Kirsch's 'When is Information Explicitly Represented?': 'Computation is a process of making *ex*plicit, information that was *im*plicit' (1991, p. 340). With computing, that is, we see what can be explicitly represented.

But these answers are differently treated with the different kinds of computing. By its standard account, computer science is centred on automation itself, as a mathematically described, mechanically implemented abstraction. Its question is (to quote Peter Denning), 'what can be automated?' (1985, p. 16). Furthermore, in the theoretical sense dominant in computer science, the focus of interest is on the abstract process (computation) rather than what we do with physical instantiations of it (computing). In that context Kirsch's 'making explicit' is therefore a matter of how automated inferencing processes can do the work. In contrast, humanities computing uses the procedural view of cultural artifacts dialectically, against the scholar's mechanically unaided understanding of them. It uses the methodical to find the methodical, then asks what is omitted. Its focus is on computing, taken to be the totality of what a scholar does with a computer. Kirsch's 'making *ex*plicit' (e.g. in an XML encoding or a relational database design) is thus the human process of rendering 'information that was *im*plicit' computationally tractable. Employing particular formalized methods, that is, the computing humanist models a scholarly interpretation or purpose but, prior to them, is concerned with the gap between what can be methodized and what cannot.[22]

The practitioner's idea of knowledge gets its opportunity to expand when stock methods, such as just named, prove inadequate to a theoretical design, and recourse must be had back to the question of what is to be methodized. Consider, for example, a densely encoded digital edition of a

---

[22]   The problem of explicit representation is hard, Kirsch notes at the end of his article, 'because we tend to think of explicitness as a local property of a data structure: something that can be ascertained without studying the system in which it is embedded' (1991, p. 363). In humanities computing this 'system' is the computer-using scholar.

complex text. A principal rationale for such work today is the possibility of realizing a de-centred theoretical structure that allows different conceptions of the text to be modelled (cf. McGann, 2001, pp. 53–74). A dense encoding thwarts that ambition in the very process of attempting to realize it, however, by presenting a complexity of detail without the means to control and manipulate it in the time-frame that exploratory modelling demands. Many know well that it becomes simpler to start again with an unencoded text than to puzzle out the implemented conventions, then locate and modify the encoding as the new scheme requires. Relational database technology provides effective tools for controlling the detail, but at the same time it distances the scholar-maker from the word-by-word engagement that literary-critical practice typically demands. In brief, the partial failure of both technologies in attempting to methodize the theory of editions points forward to a new technology – that is, to an expanded structuring of knowledge.

Manfred Thaller has made the general point that in fact all our inherited stock-in-trade applications fail to some degree to match the demands of scholarly practice – hence that fundamental rethinking of formalized methods needs to be done (2001, 2004). This is not a once-off, rather an endless dialectical process of rethinking scholarly tools in interplay with cultural artifacts.

Hence, again, the mythological requirement of humanities computing to pull back from specific encounters so that the greater story which contains and gives identity to the practice may be seen. Hence, again, the usefulness of the anthropology evoked by my metaphor. In his essay, 'Deep Play: Notes on the Balinese Cockfight', Clifford Geertz tells a parallel story. He describes a moment early in his career when he and his wife gained rapport with the village people they had gone to study: the moment when, watching a highly illegal cockfight with the villagers, they were interrupted by a police-raid and in an instant chose to flee with the natives rather than pull rank as Distinguished Visitors (1973, pp. 412–17). Geertz gives no explanation for the crucial choice other than to call the group of watchers and the fighting cocks they watched 'a superorganism in the literal sense'. Perhaps already, as part of that superorganism, the two foreign observers had become also participants, the choice already in effect made. Some time later they left, to bring to others elsewhere the story of it and, with that, wherewithal to expand into the cognitive structure of another culture.

4 Wild Acre

The Australian context for which this essay was originally written gave me an opportune chance to attempt a public response to a question that had been bothering me for some time: where to look for alternatives to the geopolitical structure of academic turf-polity in the European tradition, which as I have tried to show continues severely to constrict possibilities for humanities computing. David Hilbert's robust imperial metaphor, quoted above, first brought the relationship between geopolitics and scholarship to my attention. Almost simultaneously an alternative surfaced in the works of two Australians. The first was Greg Dening's ethno- historiography, developed through studies of South Pacific explorations. Out of this work has come a generous conception of disciplinary poetics, whose aim (to paraphrase him) is to free our discourse on enquiry from any claim or presumption that by our expertise we are directed to seeing disciplines as having one form or another.[23] Then, through Ian Hacking's interest in the stylistics of reasoning, I encountered Alastair Crombie's comparative historical anthropology of scientific thinking in European culture, special for its focus 'on how we find out, not on what we find out'.[24] In the present context, Crombie's work furnished an important example of the perspective gained by the outsider's view – in his case significantly reinforced, as Hacking remarks, 'by the experiences of teaching in Japan, and of crossing parts of Asia and its oceans when visiting his native Australia'.[25] So what if, I thought, we were to view the disciplines as an indeterminate, loosely connected group of cultural sites to be explored – and humanities computing as the explorer? Hence, the archipelago metaphor, awakening memories of the formative period in European cultural history and so allowing indirectly, as Crombie says, 'some appreciation of Europe from that more ancient viewpoint' (1994, p. xii).

But there is another, also ancient, aspect to the Australian imagination that presents yet another alternative to help make my point that finding and trying out stories is where the effort at this stage must go. This second kind of imagination is what the novelist David Malouf, in his Boyer Lectures, calls 'land-dreaming' – the Aboriginal component complementing the 'sea-dreaming' imported by late-comer Europeans (1998). But the connection we need between this land-dreaming and inherited ideas of disciplinarity comes from Dening. In his curiously powerful meditations on a life in

---

[23] See Dening (1996, pp. 35f) on writing history 'concerned with the authenticity of experience rather than the credentials of the observer' and so productive of 'the most generous way to describe a reflective discourse on all the hermeneutic dimensions of histories as cultural artifacts'.

[24] Crombie (1994); Hacking (2002, p. 178).

[25] Hacking (2002, p. 198); cf. Crombie (1994, p. xii).

scholarship, he writes that 'Where once we thought a discipline – history, say, or politics, or even economics – was at the centre of things by having a blinkered view of humanity, now we realize that we are all on the edge of things in a great ring of viewers' (1998, p. 139). Dening, as noted, is best known for his study of sea-dreamers, such as Captain Bligh of the *Bounty* (1992). But here, I take him to be speaking as a land-dreamer, looking from an encircling periphery, 'on the edge of things', into a common but unpossessable and perilous *terra incognita*. This is a typical sense of the island-continent, Malouf assures us. It is found for example in his fellow novelist Tim Winton's meditations on costal life. 'Australians', Winton writes sea-dreamingly, 'are surrounded by ocean and ambushed from behind by desert—a war of mystery on two fronts' (1998, p. 36).

So, to the point: if we imagine scholarship with the help of Dening's metaphor – as encounters with a bounded but inexhaustible antipodean *centrum ubique* – where do we place humanities computing? What does this metaphor do for us?

By way of answering, we need some imaginative purchase on that antipodean centre. A very good means is provided by Malouf's short story 'Jacko's Reach', which shows us the transcendent quality of such a space, both geographically located (and so rich in detail and experience) and *everywhere*. Jacko's Reach is a wild acre amidst suburban normalcy, 'the one area of disorder and difference in a town that prides itself in being typical: that is, just like everywhere else' (2000, p. 95). The Reach is different:

> openly in communication, through the coming and going of native animals and of birds, or through seeds that can travel miles on a current of air, with the wilderness that by fits and starts, in patches here and great swathes of darkness there, still lies like a shadow over even the most settled land, a pocket of the dark unimaginable, that troubles the sleep of citizens by offering a point of re-entry to memories they have no more use for – to unruly and unsettling dreams.

When the story opens, the land is about 'to be cleared and built on'. Plans are for 'a new shopping mall, with a skateboard ramp for young daredevils, two floodlit courts for night tennis and, on the river side, a Heritage Walk laid out with native hybrids'. But, as he says,

> The possibility of building over [Jacko's Reach] was forestalled the moment it got inside us. As a code-word for something so intimate it can never be revealed, an area of experience, even if it is deeply forgotten, where we still move in groups together, and touch, and glow, and spring apart laughing at the electric spark. There has to be some place where that is possible.

> If there is only one wild acre somewhere we will make that the place. If they take it away we will preserve it in our head. If there is no such place we will invent it. That's the way we are. (pp. 99–100)

Indeed, *sub specie aeternitatis*, that is the way *we* are, or can be. And (to renew my question by querying an answer) if we are, and if we place ourselves as scholars in a great ring around that space, where can humanities computing be but in it?

Sea-dreaming is astronomical and meteorological first of all; it is about navigation to and from. Its focus is the explorer – hence the preference given to it here. In contrast land-dreaming looks not up to the stars and to indicators of wind-direction, nor to instruments, maps or charts, but to the land, to the ground. Thus the ethnographic media artist Kim McKenzie, collaborator in a recent book on the Aboriginal Anbarra, 'people of the rivermouth' in Arnhem Land, notes that '[m]ostly ... they wrench the eye from the great flatness of the land to details such as the starred pattern of the seaweed *Jiwurl* or the iridescent flash of *Jorn*, the kingfisher' (Gurrmanamana et al., 2002, p. xii). Jacko's is hardly a great featureless flatness, rather a mere patch of scrubland within the normality of suburbia, but it reaches 'for the wilderness further out that its four and a half acres have always belonged to and which no documents of survey or deeds of ownership or council ordinances have ever had the power to cancel' (p. 99). Like that great flatness, it is a place of small, accidental particularities – 'a little Eiffel Tower off a charm bracelet, or your first cigarette lighter ... [or] something no one had warned you of', a man 'hanging by his belt from a bloodwood' (p. 95). These irreconcilable things, being together in the Reach, tease the mind to attempt reconciliation but simultaneously guarantee its failure, and so point to 'mystery as real as the rough bark of the tree itself'. This mystery, as Malouf tells it, is the existential engine, 'the way we are'.

The archipelago, we saw, foregrounds cross-cultural encounter and exchange, hence gives the social side of computing practice a myth to live by and much learned commentary to inform it. As the interface to the wilderness that Dening's ringed scholarship delimits, Jacko's is contrastingly inward- rather than outward-looking. It emphasizes the stubborn particularity of what is somehow given, which we have the signifying impulse to rationalize. It serves the scholar's struggle to infer coherence from the data – to struggle along the continuum from implicit to explicit – and so, if honesty rules, the transcendence of these data. It supports if not implies a narrative of exploratory contemplation, for which Dening's disciplinary ring of viewers clears an enormous space.

I repeat my questioning answer: in this particular land-dreaming metaphorical frame, where can humanities computing be but in the Reach, as resident spirit of the place – as the place itself? I have suggested that we need to continue to ask, what is it, exactly, that the humanities computing practitioner does? My answer has been to tell a couple of stories, to invite the telling of many more.

References

Alverny, M.T. d' (1965). 'Alain de Lille', in *Textes inédits. Études de philosophie mediévale*, 52, Paris: Librarie Philosophique J. Vrin.

Atran, S. (1990). *Cognitive Foundations of Natural History: Towards an Anthropology of Science*, Cambridge: Cambridge University Press.

Burke, P. (2000). *A Social History of Knowledge from Gutenberg to Diderot*, Cambridge: Polity Press.

'Computing the Future: A Broader Agenda for Computer Science and Engineering' (1994). National Research Council, Washington DC: National Academies Press, books.nap.edu/html/ctf.

Crombie, A.C. (1994). *Styles of Scientific Thinking in the European Tradition. The History of Argument and Explanation especially in the Mathematical and Biomedical Sciences and Arts*, 3 volumes, London: Duckworth.

Dening, G. (1992). *Mr Bligh's Bad Language: Passion, Power and Theatre on the Bounty*, Cambridge: Cambridge University Press.

Dening, G. (1996). 'A Poetic for Histories', in *Performances*, Chicago: University of Chicago Press, pp. 35–63.

Dening, G. (1998). *Readings/Writings*, Melbourne: University of Melbourne Press.

Denning, P.J. (1985). 'What is Computer Science?' *American Scientist*, 73 (1), pp. 16–9.

Dolezel, L. (1998). 'Possible Worlds of Fiction and History', *New Literary History*, 29 (4), pp. 785–809.

Ewald, W. (ed.) (1996). *From Kant to Hilbert: A Source Book in the Foundations of Mathematics*, Vol. II., Oxford: Clarendon Press.

Foucault, M. (1998). 'On the Ways of Writing History', in *Essential Works of Foucault 1954–1984*, Vol. 2, *Aesthetics, Method, and Epistemology*, London: Penguin, pp. 279–95.

Frye, N. (1988). *On Education*, Markham, ON: Fitzhenry & Whiteside.

Frye, N. (1990), *Words with Power: Being a Second Study of 'The Bible and Literature'*, London: Viking.

Galison, P. (1997). *Image & Logic: A Material Culture of Microphysics*, Chicago: University of Chicago Press.

Geertz, C. (1973). 'Deep Play: Notes on the Balinese Cockfight', in *The Interpretation of Cultures: Selected Essays*, London: Fontana Press, pp. 412–42.

Geertz, C. (2000). 'Anti anti-relativism', in *Available Light: Anthropological Reflections on Philosophical Topics*, Princeton: Princeton University Press, pp. 42–67. First published in *American Anthropologist* NS, 86 (2) (1984), pp. 263–78.

Gombrich, E.H. (1971). 'Visual Metaphors of Value in Art', in *Meditations on a Hobby Horse and other Essays on the Theory of Art* (2nd edn), London: Phaidon, pp. 12–29.

Gurrmanamana, F., Hiatt, L., McKenzie, K. with Ngurrabangurraba, B. Meehan, B. and Jones, R. (2002). *People of the Rivermouth: The Joborr Texts of Frank Gurrmanamana*, Canberra: Aboriginal Studies Press, National Museum of Australia, www.nma.gov.au/about_us/publications/people_of_the_rivermouth.

Hacking, I. (2002). '"Style" for Historians and Philosophers', in *Historical Ontology*, Cambridge: Cambridge University Press, pp. 178–200.

Hacking, I. (2004). 'The Complacent Disciplinarian', in *Rethinking Disciplinarity*, www.interdisciplines.org/interdisciplinarity/papers/7.

Hacking, I. (2005). 'The Cartesian Vision Fulfilled: Analogue bodies and digital minds', *Interdisciplinary Science Reviews*, 30 (2), pp. 153–66.

Kaplan, A. (1964). *The Conduct of Inquiry: Methodology for Behavioral Science*, San Francisco: Chandler.

Kirsch, D. (1991). 'When is Information Explicitly Represented?' in P.P. Hanson (ed.), *Information, Language, and Cognition*, Vancouver Studies in Cognitive Science, New York: Oxford University Press, pp. 340–65.

Lakoff, G. and Johnson, M. (1980). *Metaphors We Live By*, Chicago: University of Chicago Press.

Mahoney, M.S. (2002). 'Software as Science – Science as Software', in U. Hashagen, R. Keil-Slawik and A.L. Norberg (eds), *History of Computing: Software Issues*, International Conference on the History of Computing, ICHC 2000, 5–7 April 2000, Heinz Nixdorf MuseumsForum, Paderborn, Germany. Berlin: Springer Verlag, pp. 25–48, www.princeton.edu/ %7Emike/computing.html.

Malouf, D. (1998). 'A Spirit of Play: The making of Australian consciousness', Sydney: ABC Books, for the Australian Broadcasting Corporation. Published online at www.abc.net.au/rn/boyers/index/BoyersChronoIdx.htm#1998.

Malouf, D. (2000. 'Jacko's Reach', in *Dream Stuff*, London: Chatto and Windus, pp. 93–100.

Maslow, A. (1966). *The Psychology of Science: A Reconnaissance*, John Dewey Society, Lectureship Series 8, London: Harper and Row.

McCarty, W. (2005). *Humanities Computing*, Basingstoke: Palgrave.

McGann, J. (2001). *Radiant Textuality: Literature After the World Wide Web*, New York: Palgrave.

McGann, J. (2005). 'Culture and Technology: The way we live now, what is to be done?' *Interdisciplinary Science Reviews*, 30 (2), pp. 179–89.

Minsky, M.L. (1970). 'Form and Content in Computer Science', *Journal of the Association for Computing Machinery*, 17 (2), pp. 197–215.

Mitchell, W.J., Inouye, A.S. and Blumenthal, M.S. (eds) (2003). *Beyond Productivity: Information Technology, Innovation, and Creativity*, Washington DC: National Academies Press, books.nap.edu/html/beyond_productivity.

OED. Oxford English Dictionary.

Preston, D. and Preston, M. (2004). *A Pirate of Exquisite Mind. Explorer, Naturalist, and Buccaneer: The Life of William Dampier*, London: Penguin.

Schreibman, S., Siemens, R. and Unsworth, J. (eds) (2004). *A Companion to Digital Humanities*, Blackwell Companions to Literature and Culture 26, Oxford: Blackwell.

Sowa, J.F. (2000). *Knowledge Representation: Logical, Philosophical, and Computational Foundations*, California: Brooks Cole Publishing.

Thaller, M. (2001). 'Bridging the Gap; Splitting the Bridge? Studying humanities computer science in Cologne', in *Duisburg: Computers – Literature – Philosophy* (CLiP) 2001, www.uni-duisburg.de/FB3/CLiP2001/abstracts/Thaller_en.htm.

Thaller, M. (2004). 'Texts, Databases, Kleio: A Note on the Architecture of Computer Systems for the Humanities', in D. Buzzetti, G. Pancaldi and H. Short (eds), *Augmenting Comprehension: Digital Tools and the History of Ideas*, Proceedings of a conference at Bologna, 22–23 September 2002. London: Office for Humanities Communication, King's College London, pp. 49–76.

Winton, T. (1998). *Land's Edge*, Sydney: Picador.

Wulf, W. A. (1995). *Are we Scientists or Engineers?* ACM Computing Surveys, 27 (1), pp. 55–7.

Note from the author:

I still like this six-year-old essay and would mostly write it again as is if it weren't already written. Since then, however, I've come to think that a conventional carapace is wise for a department of digital humanities to grow and that many conventional features, such as a PhD programme and publishing or otherwise circulating articles and books, are unconditionally good. To echo Milton, the wildness vital to intellectual life is a paradise within us happier far. The archipelago, or as Ian Hacking remarked in a recent lecture, 'islands of knowledge', is a useful way to think about disciplines as a whole. But

Lubomír Dolezel's point about the implicit disciplinization of interdisciplinary perspectives haunts me as increasingly people feel compelled to profess their (to use a term I now abhor for its weaselly qualities) 'interdisciplinarity'. The archipelago they reveal is their meta-island. In 2006 evidently 'humanities computing' and 'digital humanities' existed side by side; since then the latter has won out, alas (I say). But it has also become hot, the next new thing and so on. The 'big tent' metaphor of uncamps and unconferences is everywhere. We continue to metaphorize and, perhaps with that, metamorphose. And so I come to my formative experience of attempting to encode metamorphosis in the mid-1980s, at which time I did not realise how paradigmatic the confrontation of the two really is for our thing. Writing a book about that confrontation now I see that it is the *centrum ubique, circumferentia nusquam*.

Willard McCarty, September 2012

CHAPTER 6

The Gates of Hell: History and Definition of Digital | Humanities | Computing[1]

Edward Vanhoutte
Royal Academy of Dutch Language & Literature

1. A Metaphor

In 1879, Edmund Terquet (1836–1914), the French Secretary of State for Fine Arts, commissioned a monumental door from the sculptor Auguste Rodin (1840–1917). Rodin's door would be used as the entrance to the planned Decorative Arts Museum in Paris. The artist was given three years to complete it, but the museum project started to go wrong, and the state cancelled it in 1889. In the meantime, the door had lost its original setting and function and Rodin, freed from the restrictions of designing a functional piece of art, explored the creative possibilities of the surface and created a sculpture which he would constantly revisit until his death. The sculpture, which is on exhibition at the Rodin Museum in Paris,[2] is unmistakingly a door, with its two leaves, sideparts, and tympanum. And yet, the door doesn't open. There is no opening mechanism and, even if there were one, the more than 200 figures and groups on the door are too entangled and prevent any movement of the leaves. Rodin called his sculpture *La Porte de l'Enfer* or *The Gates of Hell*, since his original inspiration was the then very popular theme of Dante's *La Divina Commedia*.

When I was watching the documentary 'A Season in Hell. Rodin's Gate',[3] it struck me that the story of Rodin's sculpture could be used as a metaphor for the field of Humanities Computing.[4] By 'Humanities

---

[1]   This essay is for Ron Van den Branden: *Sine te...*

[2]   http://www.musee-rodin.fr/fr/collections/sculptures/la-porte-de-lenfer [accessed 12 January 2013].

[3]   http://www.canal-educatif.fr/en/videos/art/2/rodin/gates-of-hell.html [accessed 12 January 2013].

[4]   Throughout this essay, Humanities Computing with capitalization refers to the field and humanities computing without capitalization refers to the activity of computing in and

Computing' I mean the practice of using computing *for* and *in* the humanities[5] from the early 1950s to 2004 when 'Digital Humanities' became the prominent name for the field.

Just as Rodin's 'door', Humanities Computing consisted of two clearly separated leaves with their own history and understanding behind them but, when put together, they became so heavily interlinked that they could not be separated without any loss of meaning. Humanities Computing was neither a traditional humanities nor a computing subject. That's why, in the course of time, the self-reflective question what constitutes and defines Humanities Computing has in itself become a research theme.

However, the main reason why Rodin's *Gates of Hell* is such a good metaphor for Humanities Computing is that it is the creative result of failure. The failure on the part of the French government to build the Decorative Arts Museum in Paris freed Rodin's design from the functional restrictions, and paved the way for an almost exuberant creation. Likewise, Humanities Computing is the creative result of failure on the part of the manufacturers of early computers to produce operational machines in time to be used during the Second World War (or, one can argue, of failure on the part of the allied forces to make the war last longer).

2. Failure

Probably the first mention of the application of computing to the Arts is found in the notes to the translation of Luigi Federico Menabrea's (1809–1896) *Notions sur la machine analytique de Charles Babbage* (1842)[6] – translated in 1943 as *Sketch of the analytical engine invented by Charles Babbage*[7] (Menabrea, 1961 [1843]; Lovelace, 1961 [1843]) by Augusta Ada, Countess of Lovelace (1815–1852).[8] With the poet Lord Byron (1788–1824) as her father and the mathematician Anabella Milbanke (1792–1860) as her mother, Ada Lovelace, as she is more frequently called, may well be considered the personification of the humanities computing educational idea. Meditating upon the possible uses

---

for the humanities.

    [5] By computing *for* the humanities, I mean the instrumental use of computing for the sake of the humanities. By computing *in* the humanities, I mean the meaning-generating activity of Humanities Computing.

    [6] Originally published in the *Bibliothèque Universelle de Genève*, 82 (October 1842).

    [7] These *Notes* were published separately in *Scientific Memoirs, Selections from The Transactions of Foreign Academies and Learned Societies and from Foreign Journals*, edited by Richard Taylor in 1843.

    [8] See Toole (1996 and 1998) for biographical notes and comments on her work.

of Babbage's Analytical Engine[9] for non-numerical purposes, she wrote
that the operating mechanism:

> might act upon other things besides *number*, were objects found whose mutual
> fundamental relations could be expressed by those of the abstract science of
> operations, and which should be also susceptible of adaptations to the action of
> the operating notation and mechanism of the engine. Supposing, for instance,
> that the fundamental relations of pitched sounds in the science of harmony and
> of musical composition were susceptible of such expression and adaptations,
> the engine might compose elaborate and scientific pieces of music of any degree
> of complexity or extent. (Lovelace, 1961 [1843], pp. 248–9)

However, the first computer music wasn't produced before CSIRAC,[10]
Australia's first digital computer, was used to perform the Colonel Bogey
March in 1950 or 1951, and electronic computer music boomed from
1957 onwards with the release of the first program for sound generation,
appropriately called MUSIC.[11] Moreover, the submission of musicologist
papers to the journal *Computers and the Humanities* in the 1960s and
1970s is substantial. But Lovelace was right in her observation that
computing techniques and devices could have their use in non-numerical
applications as well. This was especially realized after the end of the
Second World War.

In 1943 the US military[12] commissioned the building of the ENIAC
(Electronic Numerical Integrator And Computer) to calculate trajectories
of World War II artillery guns, a task that involved repetitive sequences of
operations on complex mathematical data. The two leading architects of
this giant electronic digital calculator were J. Presper Eckert (1919–1995)[13]
and John Mauchly (1907–1980)[14] of the University of Pennsylvania's Moore
School of Electrical Engineering. Before the ENIAC, these operations had
been executed with the use of differential analysers, desk calculators, and
punched-card installations, consisting of several serialized punched-card
machines (Polachek, 1997), a market dominated by IBM at that time.

---

   [9]   Babbage's Analytical Engine was a proposed programmable mechanical calculator
with a planned memory of 1,000 numbers of 50 digits. It used punched cards for the input of
instructions, the input and output of data, and the storage of data and instructions.
   [10]   CSIRAC: Council for Scientific and Industrial Research Automatic Computer.
   [11]   The program was written by Vernon Matthews (b. 1926) at Bell Labs (Doornbusch,
2004 and 2005).
   [12]   More particularly, the Ordnance Department.
   [13]   See Eckstein (1996) for an account of the early life of Eckert, and Wilkes (1995) for
a tribute to his work.
   [14]   See Stern (1980) for a biographical note on Mauchly, and Mauchly (1984) for an
account of his crucial early years of experimenting and research.

When ENIAC was assembled and delivered to the US army in 1946, its development and production time had exceeded the war and its envisioned purpose for warfare had therefore become redundant. The same happened with the EDVAC (Electronic Discrete Variable Automatic Computer), the first binary stored program computer, which was commissioned from the same team in 1944 and which only became fully operational in 1951.

With the end of the Second World War, the urgent need for computing power for warfare purposes disappeared, although the Cold War kept the importance of (classified) computer research programs at the top of the intelligence agenda till the early 1990s. Among the early thinkers on the social function of computing technology was Warren Weaver (1894–1978)[15] who had been involved with ballistics during the war and who had become director of the Natural Sciences Division of the Rockefeller Foundation afterwards. Inspired by pioneering pre-war computing projects and the developments he witnessed during the war, he started to wonder what sort of applications 'this incredibly powerful tool, the electronic computer' (Weaver, 1970, p. 105) could be used for. The warfare computing practices of ballistics and cryptanalysis convinced him that the computer could be used for two peaceful academic applications in particular: one in the Sciences and one in the Humanities, namely mathematics and machine translation respectively (Weaver, 1970, pp. 104–08).

Just as the failure of the Paris museum project freed Rodin from the restrictions of a functional door, the end of the Second World War freed Weaver from seeing the computer only as a warfare tool for ballistics and cryptanalysis.

3. Machine Translation

Machine Translation (MT) is 'the application of computers to the translation of texts from one natural language into another' (Hutchins, 1986, p. 15). The arguments for research into MT are pragmatic and social (people have to read documents and communicate in languages they do not know), academic and political (international cooperation and globalization through the removal of language barriers in order to promote peace and further knowledge in developing countries), military (to find out what the enemy knows), scholarly (to study the basic mechanisms of language and mind and exploit the possibilities and limits of the computer), and economical (to sell a successful product).

---

[15] See Weaver (1970) for his autobiography, and Hutchins (2000b) for a brief biographical note.

The early 1950s saw some experiments with word-for-word translations of scientific abstracts by Richard H. Richens (1918–1984)[16] and Andrew D. Booth (1918–2009)[17] using punched cards (Richens and Booth, 1952).[18] Until then, the problem of automating translation was thought of in mechanical terms solely: the development of a dictionary lookup system in aid of the human translator. Andrew Booth, a crystallographer at Birkbeck College (University of London) was probably the first person to refer to the possible use of electronic computers for Machine Translation. In a memorandum to the Rockefeller Foundation dated 12 February 1948, he wrote:

> A concluding example, of possible application of the electronic computer, is that of translating from one language into another. We have considered this problem in some detail, and it transpires that a machine of the type envisaged could perform this function without any modification in its design. (quoted from Weaver, 1965 [1949], p. 19)

A Rockefeller Research Fellow at the Institute for Advanced Study at Princeton, Booth was reporting to Warren Weaver who, as early as 1946, had had several conversations with Booth on the use of automatic digital computers for mechanical translation from one language into another (Booth and Locke, 1965 [1955], p. 2; Booth, 1980, p. 553; Hutchins, 1986, p. 24). In the course of his fellowship, Booth, together with his assistant Kathleen Britten (b. 1922), who later became his wife, developed a detailed code for storing a dictionary in an automatic digital computer's memory to be retrieved from standard teletype input. This idea dated back from 1946 and realized dictionary translation on an automatic computer (Booth, 1958, pp. 92–9).

It was Booth's work and his own experience as a cryptanalyst during the war that formed the basis for Weaver's memorandum 'Translation' which was issued on 15 July 1949 (Weaver, 1965 [1949]). The *Weaver Memorandum* was circulated amongst twenty or thirty 'students of linguistics, logicians, and mathematicians' (Weaver, 1970, p. 107) and up to 200 scholars (Locke and Booth, 1965 [1955], p. 15) in different fields. It was this memorandum which initiated research projects at different

---

[16] See Sparck Jones (2000) for an overview of Richens' work in MT.

[17] See Booth (1997) and Booth and Booth (2000) for an overview of Booth's work in MT. See Booth (1980) for details on his work in crystallography and the development of early computers and magnetic storage devices. Booth was also the holder of the British patent on the floppy disk.

[18] This paper 'Some methods of mechanized translation' was written in 1948, but not published before 1955 (Sparck Jones, 2000, p. 263). The paper was presented on the first Conference on Mechanical Translation at MIT in June 1952.

universities and generated some early writings on the problems involved with Machine Translation.[19] These problems included ambiguity of words, the semantic function of syntax, and the resolution of word order problems in different languages.

In 1952, eighteen scholars, including Booth as the only non-American delegate, gathered on the first 'international' conference on Machine Translation at MIT, followed by a meeting later that year in London where some forty linguists met during the International Linguistic Congress. A year later, Machine Translation appeared for the first time in a scholarly textbook written by Andrew and Kathleen Booth. In their book *Automatic Digital Calculators* (Booth and Booth, 1953), aimed at a readership of computer scientists, the authors published a chapter on 'Some applications of computing machines' in which Machine Translation was discussed at length.[20] In 1954, a widely publicized demonstration took place at IBM headquarters and involved a carefully selected sample of 49 Russian sentences, a limited vocabulary of 250 Russian words from different fields and their English equivalents, and six rules of syntax. The IBM press release quoted: 'A girl who didn't understand a word of the language of the Soviets punched out the Russian messages on IBM cards. The "brain" dashed off its English translations on an automatic printer at the breakneck speed of two and a half lines per second.'[21] In the same year, the first doctoral dissertation on Machine Translation was presented by Anthony Oettinger (b. 1929) at Harvard University (Oettinger, 1954) and the journal *Mechanical Translation* appeared for the first time.

From 1955 to 1966, the field organized itself in groups working mainly on dictionary, lexicographic, and semantic problems and groups working on syntactic problems; in groups that took an empirical approach (mainly in the UK) and others that took a theoretical approach (mainly in the US); and in groups working towards operational systems in the short term, and groups working toward high quality systems in the long term. These years saw a dozen important conferences, gatherings, and sessions on Machine Translation, and the founding of the Association for Machine Translation and Computational Linguistics (AMTCL) on 13 June 1962. Apart from the US and the UK, research was undertaken in e.g. Bulgaria, Canada, former Czechoslovakia, France, Israel, Japan, the former USSR, and the later independent states.[22]

---

[19]   See the annotated bibliography in Locke and Booth (1965 [1955], pp. 227–36).

[20]   The book was reprinted twice, in 1956 and 1965, and translated into Russian in 1957.

[21]   IBM press release, 8 January 1954, http://www-03.ibm.com/ibm/history/exhibits/701/701_translator.html [accessed 12 January 2013].

[22]   For recollections and overviews of research in these countries, see the different papers in Hutchins (2000a).

Whereas the funding agencies in the US had applauded the importance of Machine Translation to 'the overall intelligence and scientific effort of our nation' in a report compiled by the Committee on Science and Astronautics of the US House of Representatives in June 1960 (Hutchins, 1986, p. 159), six years later the final conclusions of an independent advisory committee installed by request of the funding bodies put an end to the funding of research in Machine Translation in the US. The notorious ALPAC[23] report 'Languages and Machines: Computers in Translation and Linguistics' (ALPAC, 1966) criticized the need, cost, and performance of automatic translations and even suggested that, since English is the dominant language in science, it was more cost efficient to teach heavy users of translated Russian articles Russian than to provide them with a translation service. The final recommendations outlined that funding should be provided for the improvement of translation by developing machine aids for human translators and for Computational Linguistics, which had grown out of Machine Translation. The ALPAC report put the research towards perfect translation to an end and referred its ideal to the realm of utopia.[24] For linguistics in general, and for Computational Linguistics and Humanities Computing in particular, the report put the future research programme on language in a different perspective, or as Victor Yngve put it:

> The future of linguistics is not in philosophy, from which it is emerging, but in standard science, into which it can now move with confidence. This requires that linguistics finally recognize that the true object of study of a scientific linguist is the people that speak and understand and communicate in other ways, and other relevant aspects of the real world. (Yngve, 2000, p. 69)

Roberto Busa (1913–2011) seemed to agree with Yngve when he identified the major problem with research in Machine Translation not as the inadequacy of *computers* to deal with human language, but as *man's* insufficient comprehension of human languages (Busa, 1980, p. 86).

---

[23]   Automatic Language Processing Advisory Committee.

[24]   The ALPAC report caused ten years of neglect of Machine Translation from the scientific world, and more from the funding bodies, and it fostered a general belief with the public that Machine Translation was more fiction than science. A renewed interest in Machine Translation can be observed from the 1980s onwards with a new journal, *Computers and Translation* (1986), which changed its name to *Machine Translation* (1989), and a series of international conferences and summits. In 1989, *Literary and Linguistic Computing* (4 (3)) devoted a special section to Machine Translation containing six papers edited and introduced by Antonio Zampolli.

4. Lexical Text Analysis

Machine Translation was highly involved with the electronic processing of humanities data. Early writings on Machine Translation mention the essential use of concordances, frequency lists, and lemmatization, which were, according to Antonio Zampolli (1937–2003) typical products of Lexical Text Analysis (LTA) (Zampolli, 1989). In this respect, it is not surprising to find an article on 'The Computer in Literary Studies' in a volume devoted to Machine Translation (Booth, 1967).

Collaboration between scholars of Machine Translation and of Lexical Text Analysis in the 1950s and early 1960s has been reported by Michael Levison, who joined Booth's laboratory as a PhD student in 1958. Although Booth's humanities-based work was mainly situated in Machine Translation, there was a strong interest in the application of the computer to other linguistic processes from the mid-1950s onwards (Booth et al., 1958). Programs for the statistical analysis of text, stylometry, and the production of concordances were developed in the early 1960s (Levison, 1962) and in his 1967 article on 'The Computer in Literary Studies' Levison describes the following classes of literary problems in which computers can be used successfully: concordances, glossaries, authorship attribution, stylistic studies, relative chronology, fragment problems with papyri, and even a preliminary form of the digital library described as a tape library (Levison, 1967). A 'steady stream of visitors' who came 'seeking help with literary and linguistic problems' (Lessard and Levison, 1998, p. 262) frequented Booth's laboratory to work on all of these literary problems, and even a couple of geographers turned up with a proposal to investigate the possibility of accounting for 'Polynesian settlement by drift voyaging', using simulation (Lessard and Levison, 1998, p. 262).

Although Booth had left the laboratory before all of these projects came to fruition, it is certainly his inspiration and reputation that brought about the cooperative ventures. Two of Booth's students, Leonard Brandwood and John Cleave, may even have been the first PhD students who applied computers to non-translation language problems in the Humanities. Brandwood worked on the chronology and concordance of Plato's works (Booth et al., 1958, pp. 50–65), and Cleave on the mechanical transcription of Braille (Booth et al., 1958, pp. 97–109).

One of the most important early computing projects which made use of Lexical Text Analysis, however, was Roberto Busa's *Index Thomisticus*, a lemmatized concordance of all the words in the complete works of Thomas Aquinas. Although the first mention of the project was a short project description published in *Speculum* in January 1950 (Busa,

1950),[25] Busa himself dates his original idea of using modern mechanical techniques for the linguistic analysis of written texts between 1941 or 1942 (Busa, 2004b, p. xvi; Busa 2002, p. 49) when he started his PhD research, and 1946 when he completed his dissertation and was looking for a follow-up research project (Busa, 1980, p. 83). The fact is that Busa's dissertation (Busa, 1949) was written without the use of or reference to any computer technology.[26] But in 1951 Busa teamed up with people from IBM in New York to automatically compile a concordance of the poetry of Thomas Aquinas, which was the first example of a word index printed by punched-card machines (Busa, 1951). However, this proof of concept exercise used no computing and no programming. The main innovation was Busa's insight that commercial accounting machines could be used for humanities purposes with good results. The result of the 1951 project offered six scholarly tools: an alphabetical frequency list of the words; a retrograde frequency list of the words; an alphabetical frequency list of words set out under their lemmata; the lemmata; an index of the words; and a KWIC Concordance (Winter, 1999).

For his complete *Index Thomisticus*, Busa calculated that the stack of punchcards would have weighed 500 tonnes, occupying 108 m^3 with a length of 90 m, a depth of 1 m, and a height of 1.20 m. By 1975, when the *Index Thomisticus* was completed and started to appear on 65,000 pages in 56 volumes (Busa, 1974–1980) some 10,631,973 tokens were processed.[27] This processing consisted of inputting, verifying, and interpreting with references and codes which specify the values within the levels of the morphology – the 'internal hypertext' in Busa's terminology (Busa, 2002 and 2004a). The work was done by a team of keypunch operators who were trained in Busa's own training school which ran from 1954 to 1967 (Busa, 1980, p. 85).

Whereas Busa was using keypunch technology in close cooperation with IBM, John W. Ellison completed his *Computerized Concordance to the Revised Standard Version of the Bible* with the computing facilities offered by Remington Rand, namely magnetic tape technology and the UNIVAC I mainframe computer (UNIVersal Automatic Computer)[28] in 1957. The story goes that Busa met Ellison around 1954, congratulated

---

[25] Although this publication is mentioned in Busa's Bibliography published in Busa (2002), it is not clear whether Busa is really the author of the piece, which is written in the third person.

[26] 1949 is used as the symbolic start of computational work in the humanities by several authors. Cf. recently Burdick et al. (2012, p. 123).

[27] Figure according to the project report *Opera quae in indicem thomisticum sunt redacta* (1975, revised 1980), privately made available to me.

[28] The UNIVAC computers were built by the same team which built the ENIAC and EDVAC computers.

him on his computing work, and went back to IBM to transfer the punch cards onto magnetic tape and use computer technology and programming[29] for the publication of his Dead Sea Scrolls project in 1957.[30] For the *Index Thomisticus*, Busa was working on 1,800 tapes, each one 2,400 feet long, and their combined length was 1,500 km (Busa, 2004b, p. xvii).

Ellison dates his original idea of using 'modern mechanical devices' back to 1945 when he realized that distinguished scholars 'having two or three earned doctorates, were essentially counting on their fingers as they studied manuscripts' (Ellison, 1965, p. 64). In 1950, he asked for computing time at the Harvard Computation Laboratory, which was granted in 1951. His proof of concept exercise was the internal collation of 309 manuscripts of the St. Luke gospel, printed against the standard text with a classification of eight kinds of variant readings with the MARK IV computer in 1952 or 1953. This was the first example of a manuscript collation carried out and printed by a computer.

Up to the publication of the infamous ALPAC report in 1966, Computational Linguistics and Lexical Text Analysis were not separated fields, and used statistical analysis for the creation of indexes, concordances, corpora, and dictionaries. But from then onwards, Computational Linguistics embraced the symbolic approach and abandoned statistical analysis which has been at the heart of Humanities Computing.

5. Literary and Linguistic Computing and Computing in/for the Humanities

The history of both Machine Translation and Lexical Text Analysis are closely related to the technological development of computing machinery, program languages, and software and the economic opportunities identified by their manufacturers. In the years following the end of the Second World War, traditional manufacturers and suppliers of analog tabulating equipment changed their core business to digital computing equipment and services, and were prospecting new markets. This is why key players like Remington Rand and IBM teamed up with humanities scholars and funded conferences and projects that explored new applications of computing. One such early conference was held at Yale University in January 1965 under the hesitating title *Computers for the Humanities?*

---

[29] Since FORTRAN was only released in 1975, the programming was still in card management.

[30] Also in 1957, and independently of the work of Busa or Ellison which hadn't appeared yet, Cornell University launched a program for a computer-produced series of concordances, with Stephen M. Parrish as general editor (Parrish, 1962, p. 3).

The cover of the proceedings, published under the same title (Pierson, 1965), shows a silhouette drawing of Rodin's *Le Penseur* (The Thinker) punched like a punched card to indicate the link between computing and the history of ideas. The proceedings contain papers on the history of computing and the use of computers in the Sciences; on computers and words; language and literature; computers and history; computers and the Arts; and a discussion of some possibilities and speculations on future computer projects. This book is probably the earliest volume surveying the early use of computing in the humanities beyond Machine Translation. Two years later, the selected papers from six such conferences sponsored by IBM,[31] which were attended by some 1,200 academics from all over the US in 1964 and 1965, were published under the not so hesitating title *Computers in Humanistic Research. Readings and Perspectives* (Bowles, 1967). The papers in this book deal with computational applications in anthropology, archaeology, history, political sciences, language, literature, and musicology.

In the UK, the Literary and Linguistic Computing Centre (LLCC) at the University of Cambridge was set up with Roy Wisbey (b. 1929) as its first director in 1964. It was also Wisbey who organized the first international conference on the use of the computer in literary and linguistic research which brought together British scholars with participants from Australia, Canada, continental Europe and the US in 1970.[32] In 1972, a second such conference was organized in Edinburgh.[33] The emphasis on literary and linguistic computing was also reflected in the name of the *Association for Literary and Linguistic Computing* (ALLC)[34] which he co-founded in 1973 and chaired from 1973 to 1978. The ALLC published a periodical called *ALLC Bulletin* from 1973 to 1985 and the *ALLC Journal* from 1980 to 1985. In 1986 both publications were replaced by the journal *Literary and Linguistic Computing* (LLC) which in 2005 changed its name to *LLC: The Journal of Digital Scholarship in the Humanities*. The ALLC started to organize a series of biannual conferences on literary and linguistic computing under its own name and the two previous conferences were added to the list.[35] From 1973 onwards, these conferences alternated with an American series of biannual conferences called International

---

[31]   The conferences were held in 1964 and 1965 at Rutgers, Yale, UCLA, the Consortium of Universities in Washington DC, Purdue, and Boston University.

[32]   Proceedings published in Wisbey (1971).

[33]   Proceedings published in Aitken et al. (1973).

[34]   http://www.allc.org [accessed 12 January 2013]. The ALLC was recently rebranded as EADH: The European Association for Digital Humanities.

[35]   This explains why the first two ALLC conferences listed on the EADH website were organized before the founding of the Association.

Conference on Computers in the Humanities (ICCH) in the odd years.[36] The professional association which was founded in the US in 1978 was hence called the Association for Computers and the Humanities (ACH).[37] Twelve years before, its founding president Joseph Raben (b. 1924) had started to edit the journal, *Computers and the Humanities (CHum)* which ran from 1966 to 2004.[38] Whereas the scope in Europe was mainly on literary and linguistic studies of language in literary form, the American conferences, journal and association showed a broader interest in computer-based studies of language in literary and non-literary form. This is reflected in the titles of the proceedings from the conferences held in the 1970s: *The Computer in Literary and Linguistic Research* (Wisbey, 1971); *The Computer and Literary Studies* (Aitken et al., 1973); *The Computer in Literary and Linguistic Studies* (Jones and Churchhouse, 1976); and *Advances in Computer-aided Literary and Linguistic Research* (Ager et al., 1979) in Europe, and *Computers in the Humanities* (Mitchell, 1974) and *Computing in the Humanities* (Lusignan and North, 1977) in North America. From the start, the ICCH conferences also included papers on history, musicology, computer assisted instruction, and creative arts (dance, music, poetry).[39]

The first monographs about computers in the humanities, however, came from the computer industry. In 1971, IBM published a series of application manuals on computing in the Humanities: *Introduction to Computers in the Humanities* (IBM, 1971a); *Literary Data Processing* (IBM, 1971b); and *Computers in Anthropology and Archaeology* (IBM, 1971c). Almost a decade later, and after thirty years of computing in the humanities, supporters on both sides of the Atlantic were treated to two textbooks on the topic which appeared in the same week in January 1980. Susan Hockey's *A Guide to Computer Applications in the Humanities* (Hockey, 1980a) and Robert Oakman's *Computer Methods for Literary Research* (Oakman, 1980)[40] provided the first consistent overviews from

---

[36] With the exception of ALLC conferences in 1985, 1986, 1987, and 1988. From 1989 a joint conference was organized yearly in Europe in the even and in the US or Canada in the odd years. From 1990 to 2005, the conference was called ALLC/ACH or ACH/ALLC depending on the location. With the foundation of ADHO in 2005, the conference was renamed 'Digital Humanities'.

[37] http://www.ach.org [accessed 12 January 2013].

[38] In 1968 another journal was launched: *Computer Studies in the Humanities and Verbal Behaviour*.

[39] In the UK, however, a separate series of conferences on Computer Assisted Teaching in the Humanities (CATH) were organized.

[40] Notice that it's now Hockey who uses 'computers in the Humanities' in the title of her book, and Oakman narrowed it down to 'literary research'.

an academic point of view.[41] Although both books filled an urgent need for a surveying textbook in the field of literary and linguistic computing, they were not explicitly conceived with a didactic point of view. The authors brought together the issues raised in the journal papers, the several collected volumes of conference proceedings, the available project reports, and the scarce manuals for specific programming languages and applications 'from the unifying perspective of one observer' (Oakman, 1980, p. x) and were very much alike.[42] In synthetizing thirty years of research, the books became reference points for further writing on the history in the field. In this respect it's relevant to notice that Hockey identified Busa as the pioneer of humanities computing, whereas Oakman named Ellison.

One of the first mentions of 'humanities computing' to name the activity of computing in and for the humanities was in an article in the second issue of *CHum* about the use of PL/I as a programming language for humanities research in 1966 (Heller and Logemann, 1966).[43] In 1968 Aldo Duro published a survey of 'Humanities Computing Activities in Italy' (Duro, 1968) which suggests that that the term was already well known, though not dominant in the community.[44] Whereas the late 1960s saw the introduction of the term to name the computing activity, the term began to mark the field in the early 1970s, as we can see in Stacey Tanner's report on the ALLC conference of 1974 published in *Dataweek* and reprinted in *ALLC Bulletin* (Tanner, 1975). Tanner reported on Busa's address to the conference by paraphrasing – the term is not used by Busa himself – that he talked about 'the future of humanities computing' and about 'projecting the programs of humanities computing' (Tanner, 1975, p. 54). By the 1980s, the use of the term for the field was widespread, as demonstrated in Busa's retrospective paper 'The Annals of Humanities Computing: The Index Thomisticus' (Busa, 1980) – although neither Hockey (1980a) nor Oakman (1980) use the term to name the field. From the mid-1980s onwards, 'Humanities Computing' started to appear in the

---

41   Although Howard-Hill's *Literary Concordances* (Howard-Hill, 1979) claimed to be 'A Complete Handbook for the Preparation of Manual and Computer Concordances', the book deals very little with computing. It was, however, published a year before Hockey's and Oakman's books. Hockey had finished writing her book in 1978, but the publisher sat on the manuscript for quite a while. She heard about Oakman writing his book when her manuscript was already at the publishers (Susan Hockey, personal communication, 5 June 2005). Oakman completed his manuscript in early 1978 (Oakman, 1984, p. xv) and explicitly mentioned Hockey's book in the revised reprint from 1984.

42   'I think the similarities are due to the fact that there wasn't a lot of material to draw on, only the proceedings of some conferences and *CHum* and the ALLC publications' (Susan Hockey, personal communication, 5 June 2005).

43   With thanks to Willard McCarty for providing me with a copy of this article.

44   The University of Colorado already had an operational Humanities Computing Facility around the same time.

names of North American teaching programmes (Ide, 1987), computing centres (University of Washingon and McMaster University) and facilities (Arizona State University, Duke University and UCLA). Although the use of the name to delimit a distinctive and coherent discipline was a frequent matter of debate (Miall, 1990, p. 3), the publication of two volumes of the *Humanities Computing Yearbook* (Lancashire and McCarty, 1988 and Lancashire, 1991) and five volumes of *Research in Humanities Computing* (1991–1996) established the name after almost two decades of hesitating use.

6. Text Encoding

One of the main problems since the earliest uses of computers and computational techniques in the humanities was the representation of data for input, processing, and output. Computers, as Michael Sperberg-McQueen has reminded us, are binary machines that 'can contain and operate on patterns of electronic charges, but they cannot contain numbers, which are abstract mathematical objects not electronic charges, nor texts, which are complex, abstract cultural and linguistic objects' (Sperberg-McQueen, 1991, p. 34). This is clearly seen in the mechanics of early input devices such as punched cards where a hole at a certain coordinate actually meant a I or 0 (true or false) for the character or numerical represented by this coordinate according to the specific character set of the computer used. Because different computer systems used different character sets with a different number of characters, texts first had to be transcribed into that proprietary character set. All characters, punctuation marks, diacritics, and significant changes of type style had to be encoded with an inadequate budget of characters. This resulted in a complex set of 'flags' for distinguishing upper-case and lower-case letters, for coding accented characters, the start of a new chapter, paragraph, sentence, or word. These 'flags' were also used for adding analytical information to the text such as word classes, morphological, syntactic, and lexical information. Ideally, each project used its own set of conventions consistently throughout. Since this set of conventions was usually designed on the basis of an analysis of the textual material to be transcribed to machine-readable text, another corpus of textual material would possibly need another set of conventions. The design of these sets of conventions was also heavily dependent on the nature and infrastructure of the project, such as the hardware and software.

Although several projects were able to produce meaningful scholarly results with this internally consistent approach, the particular nature of each set of conventions or encoding scheme had lots of disadvantages. Texts prepared in such a proprietary scheme by one project could not readily be used by other projects; software developed for the analysis of such texts could hence not be used outside the project due to an incompatibility of encoding schemes and non-standardization of hardware. However, with the increase in texts being prepared in machine-readable format, the call for an economic use of resources increased as well. Already in 1967, Michael Kay argued in favour of a 'standard code in which any text received from an outside source can be assumed to be' (Kay, 1967, p. 171). Ideally, this code would behave as an exchange format which allowed the users to use their own conventions at output and at input (Kay, 1967, p. 172).

Some sort of standardization of markup for the encoding and analysis of literary texts was reached by the COCOA encoding scheme originally developed for the COCOA program in the 1960s and 1970s (Russell, 1967) but used as an input standard by the Oxford Concordance Program (OCP) in the 1980s (Hockey, 1980b) and by the Textual Analysis Computing Tools (TACT) in the 1990s (Lancashire et al., 1996). For the transcription and encoding of classical Greek texts, the Beta-transcription/encoding system reached some level of standardized use (Berkowitz and Squiter, 1987).

In 1987, a group of thirty-two humanities scholars[45] gathered at Vassar College in Poughkeepsie, New York in a two-day meeting (11 and 12 November 1987) called for by the ACH and convened by Nancy Ide and Michael Sperberg-McQueen. The main topic of the meeting was the question how and whether an encoding standard for machine-readable texts intended for scholarly research should be developed. The conclusions of the meeting were formulated as a set of methodological principles – the so-called 'Poughkeepsie Principles'[46] – for the preparation of text encoding guidelines for literary, linguistic, and historical research (Burnard, 1988, pp. 132–3; Ide and Sperberg-McQueen, 1988, pp. E.6–4, and 1995, p. 6).

For the implementation of these principles the ACH was joined by the ALLC and the Association for Computational Linguistics (ACL).[47] Together they established the Text Encoding Initiative (TEI) whose mission it was to develop workable text encoding guidelines. The TEI very soon came to adopt the Standard Generalized Markup Language (SGML), an ISO standard published in 1986 (Goldfarb, 1990), as the recommended

---

[45]   Amongst the delegates were representatives from the main European text archives and from important North American academic and commercial research centres.

[46]   I am quoting The Poughkeepsie Principles in 'Module 0: Introduction' of TEI by Example, http://www.teibyexample.org on which this section on text encoding is based [accessed 12 January 2013].

[47]   http://www.aclweb.org [accessed 12 January 2013].

encoding format for electronic texts.[48] Michael Sperberg-McQueen was appointed editor-in-chief and Lou Burnard as European editor of the Guidelines.

The first public proposal for the TEI Guidelines was published in July 1990 under the title *Guidelines for the Encoding and Interchange of Machine Readable Texts* with the TEI document number TEI P1 – for Proposal 1 (Sperberg-McQueen and Burnard, 1990). Further development of the TEI Guidelines was done by four Working Committees (Text Documentation, Text Representation, Text Analysis and Interpretation, Metalanguage and Syntax) and a number of specialist Working Groups.[49] The results of that work included substantial amounts of new material and were published chapter by chapter as TEI P2 between March 1992 and the end of 1993 (Sperberg-McQueen and Burnard, 1992–1993).

In 1999, the initial development work was concluded with the publication of a 1,292-page documentation of the definitive guidelines as the *TEI P3 Guidelines for Electronic Text Encoding and Interchange* (Sperberg-McQueen and Burnard, 1999), defining some 439 elements. With this work, the Poughkeepsie Principles were met by providing a framework for the encoding of texts in any natural language, of any date, in any literary genre or text type, without restriction on form or content and treating both continuous materials ('running text') and discontinuous materials such as dictionaries and linguistic corpora.

The advent and the success of the eXtensible Markup Language (XML)[50] as an industry standard replacing SGML from 1999 onwards called for an XML-compatible edition[51] of the Guidelines (Sperberg-McQueen and Burnard, 2002), published in 2002 by the newly formed TEI Consortium.[52]

---

[48]   Initial funding was provided by the US National Endowment for the Humanities, Directorate General XIII of the Commission of the European Communities, the Canadian Social Science and Humanities Research Council, and the Andrew W. Mellon Foundation.

[49]   Amongst which were groups on character sets, textual criticism, hypertext and hypermedia, formulæ, tables, figures, and graphics, language corpora, manuscripts and codicology, verse, drama and performance texts, literary prose, linguistic description, spoken text, literary studies, historical studies, print dictionaries, machine lexica, and terminological data.

[50]   http://www.w3.org/TR/REC-xml [accessed 12 January 2013].

[51]   The XML support was realized by the expression of the TEI Guidelines in XML and the conformation to a TEI conformant XML DTD. The TEI Consortium generated a set of DTD fragments that can be combined together to form either SGML or XML DTDs and thus achieved backwards compatibility with TEI P3 encoded texts. In other words, any document conforming to the TEI P3 SGML DTD was guaranteed to conform to the TEI P4 XML version of it. This 'double awareness' of the TEI P4 is the reason why this version was called an 'XML-compatible edition' rather than an 'XML edition'.

[52]   The TEI Consortium was established in 2000 as a not-for-profit membership organization to sustain and develop the Text Encoding Initiative (TEI), http://www.tei-c.org [accessed 12 January 2013].

With this XML-compatible version of the P4 Guidelines, equal support was provided for XML and SGML applications using the TEI scheme, while ensuring that documents produced to earlier TEI specifications remained usable with the new version.

In 2003 the TEI Consortium asked their membership to convene Special Interest Groups (SIGs) whose aim could be to advise revision of certain chapters of the Guidelines and suggest changes and improvements in view of a new P5 version. With the establishment of the new TEI Council, which superintends the technical work of the TEI Consortium, it became possible to agree on an agenda to enhance and modify the Guidelines more fundamentally, which resulted in a full revision of the Guidelines published as TEI P5 (TEI Consortium, 2007). TEI P5 contains a full XML expression of the TEI Guidelines and introduces new elements, revises content models, and reorganizes elements in a modular class system that facilitates flexible adaptations to users' needs. Contrary to its predecessor, TEI P5 does not offer backwards compatibility with previous versions of the TEI.[53]

7. Back to the Metaphor

Curiously, Rodin's *La Porte de l'Enfer* is called *The Gates of Hell* in English and not the 'Gate' of Hell as the French would suggest. But actually it's a better translation. Not only are there many interpretations possible of Rodin's vision of hell, there is also more than one sculpture with that name. When Rodin failed to enter his sculpture for the 1900 Universal Exposition in Paris, he set up an independent exhibition with the painter Claude Monet (1840–1926). For this exhibition, he created a plaster model[54] of the sculpture from which most figures and groups are deliberately stripped, leaving nothing but undulations in the surface with no clear focal points. By doing this, he moved from narration to expression. Since the bronze door was state property, and was thus unsellable, he regrouped, enlarged, and cast some of the stripped figures and groups as separate, marketable works, such as The Thinker, The Kiss, Fleeting Love, and The Three Shades.[55] Others were reworked in different materials and sizes, such as Crouching Woman. The abstract character of

---

[53]   The TEI Consortium has, however, maintained and corrected errors in the P4 Guidelines for five more years, up to the end of 2012. Since that date, the TEI Consortium has ceased official support for TEI P4, and deprecated it in favour of TEI P5.

[54]   On display at The Rodin Museum, in Meudon.

[55]   By that time, Rodin needed to make a living by selling the individual sculptures.

the plaster representation of the work also created a renewed interest in his work.

Also in this respect, *The Gates of Hell* is an appropriate metaphor for Humanities Computing and Digital Humanities. Over the course of time, Humanities Computing struggled with problems of self-representation and marketing itself as a discipline or a field. Finding a common practice, theoretical principles, methodology, or philosophy across humanities disciplines which employed computational techniques didn't seem to be that straightforward. The doubts about the validity of a distinctive and coherent discipline which were raised in the mid-1980s still remain 'while most of what is called "Humanities Computing" is carried out within specific Humanities subjects' (Miall, 1990, p. 3). As an applied method, Humanities Computing sold itself as an archipelago (McCarty, 2006; Chapter 5 in this volume) of humanities disciplines, as demonstrated in disciplinary organized teaching programmes, chapters in collected volumes, and strands on conferences. The (hi)story of Humanities Computing has long been the (hi)story of specific subjects, such as authorship studies, electronic textual editing, narratology, and multimedia studies or of the use of computing in broader fields such as history, musicology, lexicography, or performing arts.

The isolation of these subjects paved the way for Humanities Computing to rebrand itself with the more non-jargon-like but more abstract term 'Digital Humanities', which generated a new interest in the field, especially from the broader audience. The hermetic activity of humanities computing was replaced by a convenient hipster qualification of the humanities. The real problems of self-representation and definition, however, remained the same.

8. Self-Representation

If we know what it is that we do in Humanities Computing or Digital Humanities, the argument goes, we should be able to communicate about that research for the purpose of identifying our work, gaining acknowledgement and academic kudos, and furthering research through (interdisciplinary) collaboration and the development of advanced strategies and tools. As Melissa Terras warned us in her opening keynote address to Interface 2011, 'we should be careful what view of ourselves we are projecting into the wider academic world' (Terras, 2011a). In her DH2010 closing plenary 'Present, Not Voting: Digital Humanities in the Panopticon' (Terras, 2011b; Chapter 18 in this volume) Terras threw at us how bad we are at representing ourselves as a field and as a community. Towards the end of her lecture, she presented an agenda for the digital identity, impact, and sustainability of the field. Central to this agenda is the development of a definition of the field, the articulation of the field's relevance, success, and impact, the historical knowledge of the field as a discipline, and the preservation of the discipline's heritage.

Willard McCarty agrees with Terras that historical knowledge about and definition of the field are central issues for the awareness and self-representation of the field. 'A genuine history of the digital humanities in its first half-century', McCarty argued recently, 'would greatly help us turn pitiful laments and dull facts into the stimulating questions we should be asking now' (McCarty, 2012). More challenging than writing a historiography of humanities computing based on existing chronologies is the writing of an historical account for which the historian 'would have to locate practitioners' minority concerns within the broad cultural landscape of the time and then describe the complex pattern of confluence and divergence of numerous interrelated developments' (McCarty, 2012).

However, self-representation has long been restricted to the presentation of chronological overviews and surveys of the field. McCarty himself, for example, in explaining the title of his seminal book *Humanities Computing*, writes that it 'names a field of study and practice found both inside and beyond the academy in several parts of the world' (McCarty, 2005, p. 2). As an illustration he refers to a much longer description that is established in his and Matthew Kirschenbaum's 'Institutional Models for Humanities Computing' (McCarty and Kirschenbaum, 2003), a structured list of 'departments, centres, institutes and other institutional forms that variously instantiate humanities computing' (McCarty and Kirschenbaum, 2003, p. 465).[56]

9. Humanities Computing

This reflex to refer to a list of instantiations of what is covered by the name, and thus to provide enumerative descriptions rather than definitions, is typical for attempts to define fields of (scholarly) activities. Etymologically, definition comes from the Latin 'definitio' which literally means demarcation or fencing. A definition therefore formally freezes the meaning of a term and since Humanities Computing as a field of activity was in constant flux, a formal description was therefore impossible. This

---

[56] Apart from the fact that the URL in the book is broken as a result of the ALLC website's redesign, the list has been superseded by the information on digital humanities centres published by Centernet, http://digitalhumanities.org/centernet [accessed 12 January 2013]. See also Dan Cohen's list of digital humanities scholars and centres on Twitter, https://twitter.com/#!/dancohen/digitalhumanities/members [accessed 12 January 2013].

impossibility has thus been bypassed by providing enumerations of these activities, as in chronologies or overviews of the field. In the late 1980s and early 1990s such overviews have been provided, for instance for history and computing (Adman, 1987), for computing in musicology from 1966 to 1991 (Hewlett and Selfridge-Field, 1991), and for publications in *CHum* on statistical analysis of literature between 1966 and 1990 (Potter, 1991). More recently *A Companion to Digital Humanities* (Schreibman et al., 2004) published such surveys of archaeology, art history, classics, history, lexicography, linguistics, literary studies, music, multimedia, performing arts, and philosophy and religion, albeit mainly from an Anglo-American point of view.

More general surveys of developments in Humanities Computing have reflected on the community's activities for a specific purpose and are either addressed to the community itself or intended for a broader audience. In 1987, Susan Hockey briefly discussed the availability of hardware, software, textual data, and courses for the humanist, and the acceptance of computational techniques in the humanities in an assessment of the significant impact that Humanities Computing developments had on teaching (Hockey, 1987).[57] Three years later, Hockey called for a critical appraisal of the activities in the field and she advised a shift of the meta-critical emphasis from methodology to modelling in her conclusion to a chronological survey of the available and emerging tools since the early 1960s (Hockey, 1990). Ian Lancashire used his reflections on the activities in literary and linguistic computing in the period from 1968 to 1988 to develop strategies for the future. As a way of rethinking the purpose of the present by a reflection on the past, he promoted both the transformation of research into teaching, and the study of meaning as an important agenda for the future of Humanities Computing (Lancashire, 1990). As a last example I mention here the report on computers and the humanities published by the European Science Foundation in 1992 (Genet and Zampolli, 1992) which was conceived as an introduction for the research communities and policy makers in the humanities, the social, and natural sciences to the challenges and the potential of the transversal and interdisciplinary characteristics of computer-based humanities research. This book, submitted as a memorandum to the Standing Committee for the Humanities of the ESF, covers the state of the art of computing methods in humanistic research, and presents overviews of journals, institutions,

---

[57] Especially the rapid development of the independently operable 'microcomputers' as opposed to the 'mainframes' and the rapid increase of storage capacity revolutionized the way in which Humanities Computing interacted with teaching in higher education, e.g. with respect to searching through large collections of texts.

and projects in humanities computing, next to critical reflections on the development and future agenda of the field.[58]

Apart from the fact that such endeavours seem to approach Humanities Computing as a semantic primitive, these more or less chronological surveys all honour the implicit premise that historical knowledge about a field provides that field with its definition or at least enables the detection of theoretical, methodological, and philosophical commons which are both formative and indicative to the field under study. They mainly concentrate on performance and, apart from the concluding research agendas, avoid any involvement with predictions. In other words, they don't provide a definition of 'Humanities Computing', only surveys of activities and tools in the field.[59]

One could argue of course that by studying what is being done in the field, we may better understand it (Warwick et al., 2012, p. xiii) and that chronologies provide Humanities Computing with a definition in use or a contextual definition by chronologically reporting on its activities. The problem here is the chronology of the definition. From its definition it follows that a contextual definition may not contain the expression that is defined but must use an equivalent not containing that expression (OED online, definition, 4.c). In recounting the chronology of Humanities Computing, this equivalent is a virtual contraction consisting of all given contextual definitions or descriptions of the activities which are, at the moment of defining, considered as belonging to the field. McCarty's reference to the list of *Institutional Models* at the beginning of his book (2005) thus defines all elements of that list more in terms of Humanities Computing than it defines Humanities Computing in terms of its (alleged) activities.

However, even if a genuine history of the field existed, it would still need to be complemented with methodological awareness, as McCarty argues in *Humanities Computing* (McCarty, 2005). Methodology is at the basis of any transfer of knowledge about computing in the humanities, which is where Terras and McCarty locate the problem for a fruitful debate about the interdisciplinarity of the field. This is, however, not a recent problem, since Raben already pointed out in 1973 that the funding bodies' general ignorance of the methods of computing in the humanities was the greatest hindrance to its development and success: 'In their eyes, the preparation

---

[58] The cited overviews were an attempt to scope out the activities at a time when the field was still surveyable and when networked infrastructure and resources were inexistent.

[59] In these chronologies, it's the chronologist's intuition, not a definition of the field, which determines the scope and focus of the inventory. They argue falsely that pointing at the field provides it with a definition.

of a text seems like secretarial work, but the publication of a book comes within the definition of scholarship' (Raben, 1973, p. 5).

With his book, McCarty has tried to fill in this knowledge vacuum by attempting to 'anatomize the method of humanities computing into four perspectives: analysis, synthesis, context and profession' (McCarty, 2005, p. 6). Analysis and synthesis are the conventional methods of all humanities disciplines, the first of which is the realm of the private scholar, whereas the second is essential to the sociological role of the scholar in the academy and preferably also in the outside world. Since Humanities Computing is *in* the humanities, as McCarty (2005) sufficiently argues, its general method does not differ from those of the conventional humanities disciplines. The computational aspect offers the humanities scholar the opportunity to develop alternative analytical approaches towards the subject matter. The difference between computing *for* the humanities (instrumental) and computing *in* the humanities (methodological) is exactly the lack (in the former case) or the importance (in the latter case) of modelling as the most essential analytical method of the many forms of computing. Whereas the latter is the realm of Humanities Computing, both exist side by side in Digital Humanities.

By modelling, McCarty means the 'heuristic process of constructing and manipulating models'; a model, McCarty takes to be either 'a representation of something for purposes of study' (denotative model) or 'a design for realising something new' (exemplary model) (McCarty, 2003b; 2004, p. 255; 2005, p. 24). The purpose of modelling is never to establish the truth directly, but it 'is to achieve failure so as to raise and point the question of how we know what we know' (McCarty, 1999b), 'what we do not know,' and 'to give us what we do not yet have' (McCarty 2004, p. 255). Humanities Computing shares this methodological characteristic with, for instance, computer science, but reverses the model. Humanities Computing starts from the modelling of 'imperfectly articulated knowledge' (McCarty, 2005, p. 194), and works its way up through further steps of computational modelling till it reaches the stage of a deeper understanding of the world. Computer science, and programming in particular, starts from a real world problem and travels down to its implementation in hardware.[60]

The method shared by the humanities and computer science that Manfred Thaller and Tito Orlandi argued for in their respective defences of a 'Humanistic Computer Science' (Thaller, 2001 and 2006)[61] or

---

[60] See McCarty's 'Stages of modelling' (McCarty, 2005, p. 197).

[61] Thaller is professor of *Historisch-Kulturwissenschaftliche Informationsverarbeitung* which he translates as 'Computer Science for the Humanities' on his website http://www.hki. uni-koeln.de/manfred-thaller-dr-phil-prof [accessed 12 January 2013].

'informatica umanistica' (Orlandi, 2003) and which they jointly define as 'the canon (or set of tools) needed to increase the knowledge agreed to be proper to a particular field' ([Thaller], 1999, p. 25) leads them to a stronger identification with computer science than is currently acknowledged. The formalization of problems through algorithms and data representation by means of imposing structures on the data are identified by Thaller and Orlandi as central methods for computing in the humanities ([Thaller], 1999, p. 27; Thaller, 2001 and 2004; Orlandi, 2002).

This formalization of problems in particular has met with some criticism from text encoding and modelling theory. Since the humanities are not problem-oriented, Lou Burnard argues that their methodologies cannot be formalized. Instead, Burnard puts hermeneutics and text encoding at the centre of Humanities Computing, two methods that are not shared with computing or any other science. Hermeneutics is the study of interpretation that confers value on cultural objects (Burnard, 2001, p. 32). Burnard locates the starting point for the hermeneutic continuum in transcription and editing which are decisive and subjective acts of interpretation. The use of markup for the articulation and documentation of different semiotic systems in text[62] offers the humanities a single formalism that reduces 'the complexity inherent in representing the interconnectedness of all aspects of our hermeneutic analysis, and thus facilitate[s] a polyvalent analysis' (Burnard, 2001, p. 37). Text encoding in this sense is different from the industrial preparation of a text for scholarship but constitutes a new form of scholarship, as Sperberg-McQueen has argued (Sperberg-McQueen, 1991, p. 34), and which McCarty has called 'a kind of epistemological modelling' (McCarty, 2003a). The Text Encoding Initiative (TEI) provides the humanities with dedicated markup models for the articulation and documentation – that is, representation – of different interpretations of and on text, and makes explicit a theory of text in a formalization that is processable by computers. So Burnard does not argue for the formalization of the definition of problems, but for the formalization of texts and their interpretation into processable data structures.[63]

A second form of critique on what Orlandi and Thaller propose as central methods of Humanities Computing can be distilled from modelling theory which accepts a way of representing the full range of knowledge, even beyond what can be told explicitly and precisely (McCarty, 2004, p. 256) and thus beyond what can be formalized in algorithmic expressions. The problematizing purpose of modelling is furthered not only by failure

---

[62] Burnard discusses three interlocking semiotic systems of text: text as image, text as linguistic construct, and text as information structure (Burnard, 2001, p. 33).

[63] e.g. in the proposed formalization of texts in ordered hierarchies of content objects (OHCO-thesis), and the interpretation of meanings of markup.

but also by success, even when this is accidental and inexplicable from what is known at the time of constructing the model. The fluid status of modelling as experimentation away from formalization plays an important role in the perspective on scholarship as a process rather than a product.[64] The exponent of this is the model as tinkertoy[65] which denotes its playful, experimental character. Indeed 'the virtue of the noun "model" is that in computationally based research, in which the work is fundamentally experimental, it defaults to its present participle "modelling" and so to denoting that process' (McCarty, 2003b).

In their contribution to modelling theory for the humanities, Meurig Beynon, Steve Russ, and Willard McCarty pleaded for 'reappraising computing from a perspective in which experience rather than logic plays a privileged role' (Beynon et al., 2006, p. 145). In order to do so, they offered a perspective on computing they named Human Computing and defined as 'a joint collaborative activity in which devices, typically electronic, augment what is the essentially human activity of the making of meaning' (Beynon et al., 2006, p. 145). Instead of the discovery of meaning (heuristics) that Burnard proposed to realize by means of text encoding – an approach which perceives scholarship primarily as a product[66] – they shifted the central concern of computing in the humanities to the making of meaning by means of what they called Empirical Modelling.[67] By the perspective of Human Computing, computation transgresses its conventional functionality of executing algorithms that was introduced by the acceptance of the Turing machine as its primary model and in which the human and the computer are in an alternating relationship to each other. It does so by including the human in the computational activity which they described as the 'continuous engagement and negotiation of the human with the computer through the experience of the construction and behaviour of the computer model' (Beynon et al., 2006, p. 145). In this approach, the algorithmic formalization of problems as the central method of Humanities Computing is replaced by modelling of an empirical kind.

---

[64]   McCarty (1999a), for instance, sees text-encoding, that is, 'rendering phenomena computable by addition of metadata that unambiguously state what it is' as fundamental to the perspective of scholarship as product. He seems to overlook here that the actual text-encoding is a transformative modelling activity which could produce a tinkertoy as well.

[65]   Originally 'Tinkertoy' was a construction toy with which children could build whatever their imagination could dream up and 'learn by exercising what we now think of as "spatial intelligence"', http://www.toyhalloffame.org/toys/tinkertoy [accessed 12 January 2013]. As McCarty (2003b) noted, the term has been subsequently used 'to describe crude (or simply all physical) modelling techniques' (n. 1).

[66]   Cf. McCarty (1999a).

[67]   For more information on Empirical Modelling see the Empirical Modelling website at http://www2.warwick.ac.uk/fac/sci/dcs/research/em and the Empirical Modelling archive at http://www2.warwick.ac.uk/fac/sci/dcs/research/em/projects [accessed 12 January 2013].

This Empirical Modelling is supported by tools that engage with human cognitive processes and that allow for the 'experimental identification of relevant observables associated with some phenomenon and of reliable patterns of dependency and agency among these observables' (Beynon et al., 2006, p. 146). Thus, it resembles the research methods humanities scholars develop in approaching their objects of study in the personal and subjective relationship that is established between them.

Thus far, it seems that modelling in general and data representation or text encoding in particular – at least in their heuristically and epistemologically qualified meaning – are crucial methods in Humanities Computing. As crude methods of practice they are not exclusive, that is identifying methods of Humanities Computing. Therefore it is essential to distinguish text encoding as a scholarly (modelling) practice from the industrial data representation by markup which is in use, for instance, in the publishing industry. Likewise, modelling which is computational by nature should be distinguished from the ancient art of model-building.

As noted earlier, the application of modelling and data representation may be specific to Humanities Computing but they link back to the two general methods of humanities research, that is, analysis and synthesis respectively. With respect to the issue of synthesis, McCarty (2005) discusses scholarly commentary in digital editions as the most promising instantiation of synthesis in the humanities in which a certain degree of data representation, heuristics and modelling are combined into the scholarly reference work *par excellence* (McCarty, 2005, pp. 73–113).[68] Paradoxically, the characteristic which may identify the application of these common methods of humanities research as belonging to the field of Humanities Computing is indeed the computational aspect that we tried to transcend. If McCarty's book *Humanities Computing* is an attempt to provide a theory of Humanities Computing that incorporates this transgression, then it has failed to provide us with a clear, citeable, or formalized articulation of the methods of Humanities Computing which appeals to the problem of self-representation.[69] Curiously, McCarty presents exactly this problem of communication in two points in his preliminary agenda for Humanities Computing that provides the final perspective of the method of the field in his book. Without a clear description of the formal method of Humanities

---

[68] The idealized structure of the commentary form McCarty discusses comprises the following major parts: '(a) a scholarly introduction to the work on which a commentary is offered; (b) an edited text of that work with textual apparatus; (c) the commentary itself, in the form of paragraph-length notes keyed to the text; and (d) the usual table of contents and index' (McCarty, 2005, p. 77).

[69] McCarty's erudite and philosophical idiolect and stylistic fingerprint produces a dense and sometimes enigmatic prosaic style which takes much effort on the part of the reader to apprehend.

Computing, however, the field of activity will never succeed in providing popularized explanations of every activity and project undertaken in Humanities Computing, and in explaining and justifying what it does.

10. Digital Humanities

The same is true for Digital Humanities. The term has definitely but not definitively replaced Humanities Computing as a name for the field. There seems to be a common understanding of the term as referring to humanities research in the digital era, as opposed to traditional humanities research. However, the popularization and socialization of this new name for the field entails the risk of trivialization. The popular qualification 'digital' only relates to the technological (instrumental?) element of computation without using jargon language such as 'computer', 'computing' or 'computational'. This, however, does not solve the field's defining question, and even obscures the problem. Although Humanities Computing was a more hermetic term than Digital Humanities, it had a clearer purview. Humanities Computing relates to the crossroads where informatics and information science met with the humanities and it had a history built on the early domains of Lexical Text Analysis and Machine Translation, as we have seen above. Digital Humanities as a term does not refer to such a specialized activity, but provides a big tent for all digital scholarship in the humanities. The editors of *A Companion to Digital Humanities* who introduced the term abruptly in 2004 as an expansion of what was commonly referred to as Humanities Computing, argue that the field 'redefined itself to embrace the full range of multimedia' (Schreibman et al., 2004, p. xxiii). It still remains the question, however, whether well established disciplines such as Computational Linguistics or Multimedia and Game Studies will want to live under the big tent of Digital Humanities.

Recently Fred Gibbs, the Director of Digital Scholarship at the Roy Rozenzweig Center for History and New Media, introduced his classification of digital humanities definitions by warning that '[i]f there are two things that academia doesn't need, they are another book about Darwin and another blog post about defining the digital humanities' (Gibbs, 2011; Chapter 21 in this volume). Indeed, since Blackwell's *Companion*, a wide range of defining statements about the aims and nature of Digital Humanities (and sometimes why it differs from Humanities Computing) have been voiced.

The current volume harvests such defining contributions from journal articles and blog posts which are informed by roundtable discussions, conference panels, papers and posters, mission statements of digital humanities centres and institutes, facebook walls, and tweets,[70] and demonstrates that defining essays already constitute a genre of their own (Kirschenbaum, 2010, p. 55; Chapter 9 in this volume).[71] Among the recent and most elaborated additions to this genre is a four-part series of essays by Patrik Svensson in *Digital Humanities Quarterly*. In these essays, Svensson attempts to chart and understand the emerging field of Digital Humanities by examining the discursive shift from Humanities Computing to Digital Humanities in the first essay (Svensson, 2009; Chapter 7 in this volume), by exploring the broader landscape of Digital Humanities in the second essay (Svensson, 2010), and by discussing the cyberinfrastructure for the humanities in general and for the Digital Humanities in particular in the third one (Svensson, 2011). In the fourth essay, Svensson presents 'a tentative visionary space for the future of the Digital Humanities' (Svensson, 2012).

Concluding that a broadly conceived Digital Humanities would necessarily include humanities computing with its focus on 'the instrumental, methodological, textual and digitalized' (Svensson, 2009, p. 56) in his first essay, Svensson also acknowledges that 'the epistemic commitments and conventions of a tradition', namely Humanities Computing, 'cannot easily be subsumed in another type of digital humanities' (Svensson, 2010, p. 4). In other words, Digital Humanities is claiming a larger territory (Svensson, 2009, p. 42).[72] Svensson thus argues that both terms are non-synonymous and that the discursive transition from Humanities Computing to Digital Humanities is not just a repackaging but a broadening of scope. He adds that the term is used by the Digital Humanities community as a collective name for activities and structures in between the humanities and information technology (Svensson, 2009, p. 42).

The identification of Humanities Computing as a mainly instrumental application of computation to the text-based humanities is also present in Tara McPherson's typology of Digital Humanities. In her 2008 HUMlab lecture 'Dynamic Vernaculars: Emergent Digital Forms in Contemporary Scholarship', McPherson distinguishes among the Computing Humanities, the Blogging Humanities, and the Multimodal Humanities and sketches a certain interdependency among them. While the Computing Humanities refer to the long-lasting tradition of Humanities Computing with its focus on tools, standards, and interoperability (McPherson, 2008, 0:10:00) and

---

[70] Assembled on the companion website to this volume, http://blogs.ucl.ac.uk/definingdh.

[71] Volumes which gather such essays and discussions have also constituted a genre of their own. Cf. Berry (2012), Gold (2012), Lunenfeld et al. (2012).

[72] The editors of *A Companion to Digital Humanities* argue that the field 'has redefined itself to embrace the full range of multimedia' (Schreibman et al., 2004, p. xxii) with the launch of the name Digital Humanities.

the Blogging Humanities refer to networked peer-to-peer writing, mainly by non-specialist computing humanists, the Multimodal Humanities combine these and investigate the computer as simultaneously a platform, a medium, and a display device. It is in this multimodal scholarship that McPherson sees an agenda for Digital Humanities. We notice the same interdependency in Svensson's analysis where he states that '[t]here are many humanities scholars involved in what may be called digital humanities who have no or little knowledge of humanities computing, and vice versa, many humanities computing representatives who do not engage much with current "new media" studies of matters such as platform studies, transmedia perspectives or database aesthetics' (Svensson, 2009, p. 7).

Defining statements about Digital Humanities as those discussed so far commonly take references to Humanities Computing methodologies and scope as their starting point but hardly come to a definition. According to Rafael Alvarado that is because there is no definition of digital humanities. 'Instead of a definition,' Alvarado argues, 'we have a genealogy, a network of family resemblances among provisional schools of thought, methodological interests, and preferred tools, a history of people who have chosen to call themselves digital humanists and who in the process of trying to define the term are creating that definition' (Alvarado, 2011).

Therefore, Alvarado calls Digital Humanities a *social category*, not an ontological one. He is supported by Matt Kirschenbaum, who defined Digital Humanities in the 2011 Day of Digital Humanities survey as 'a term of tactical convenience' (Taporwiki, 2011). Kirschenbaum in his essay 'What Is Digital Humanities and What's It Doing in English Departments?' (Kirschenbaum, 2010; Chapter 9 in this volume) reminds us that the affirmation of Digital Humanities as the common name for the field was facilitated by the publication of *A Companion to Digital Humanities* in 2004 (Schreibman et al., 2004), the establishment of the Alliance of Digital Humanities Organizations (ADHO)[73] in 2005, the launch of the Digital Humanities Initiative by the NEH in 2006, and the publication of *Digital Humanities Quarterly* from 2007 onwards. Only recently, the Association for Literary and Linguistic Computing joined this movement by changing its name to European Association for Digital Humanities (EADH) in 2013. In a recent essay, Kirschenbaum (2012) insists on the reality of circumstances in which the term is currently used to get things done:

> At a moment when the academy in general and the humanities in particular are the object of massive and wrenching changes, digital humanities emerges as a rare vector for jujitsu, simultaneously serving to position the humanities at the

---

[73]   http://www.digitalhumanities.org [accessed 12 January 2013].

very forefront of certain value-laden agendas—entrepreneurship, openness and public engagement, future-oriented thinking, collaboration, interdisciplinarity, big data, industry tie-ins, and distance or distributed education—while at the same time allowing for various forms of intrainstitutional mobility as new courses are mooted, new colleagues are hired, new resources are allotted, and old resources are reallocated. (Kirschenbaum, 2012)

Not only the current use of the term, but also its origin was a moment of tactical convenience, as we learn from Kirschenbaum's 'What is Digital Humanities' essay. Apparently, Blackwell's editorial and marketing people disliked the title *A Companion to Humanities Computing* and wanted to name the volume *A Companion to Digitized Humanities*. Even the Humanistic Informatics was mentioned to cover the field, but as a compromise and to shift the emphasis away from simple digitization and complicated computing, John Unsworth suggested *A Companion to Digital Humanities* (Kirschenbaum, 2010, pp. 56–7).

11. Conclusion

As stated before, the problem of self-presentation and self-representation remains with Digital Humanities. Willard McCarty, in his concluding chapter of *Humanities Computing*, defines a preliminary agenda for the field which shows kinship with McPherson's Multimodal Humanities. Most of the items in McCarty's agenda can be related or partly related to McPherson's three types and even the big tent idea is implicitly advocated in McCarty's argument for a rapprochement between scholars and practitioners. In fact, McCarty's book demonstrates nicely that Svensson's qualification of Humanities Computing as focused on 'the instrumental, methodological, textual and digitalized' is a reductionist perception. If one book has argued against an overemphasis of the instrumental use of the computer in the humanities and has promoted computing as a meaning-generating activity building on and bringing forth models of the world, it is McCarty's *Humanities Computing*.

The question 'what it is that we are doing in Digital Humanities and how does it relate to the world', is a question which should not be eschewed. Even if it opens a can of worms, or, for the purpose of this essay, the Gates of Hell.

For the moment, we know that Digital Humanities tries to model the world around us through success and failure in order to arrive at a better understanding of what we know and don't know about humankind, their activities, artefacts, and record. And this can maybe serve as a definition of the field.

Bibliography[74]

Adman, P. (1987). 'Computers and History', in S. Rahtz (ed.), *Information Technology in the Humanities: Tools, Techniques and Applications*, Chichester: Ellis Horwood Limited, pp. 92–103.

Ager, D.E., Knowles, F.E. and Smith, J. (eds) (1979). 'Advances in Computer-aided Literary and Linguistic Research'. Proceedings of the Fifth International Symposium on Computers in Literary and Linguistic Research held at the University of Aston in Birmingham, UK, 3–7 April 1978, Aston: AMLC.

Aitken, A.J., Bailey, R.W. and Hamilton-Smith, N. (eds) (1973). *The Computer and Literary Studies*, Edinburgh: Edinburgh University Press.

ALPAC (1966). 'Languages and Machines: Computers in Translation and Linguistics', A report by the Automatic Language Processing Advisory Committee, Division of Behavioral Sciences, National Academy of Sciences, National Research Council, Washington, DC: National Academy of Sciences, National Research Council (Publication 1416), http://www.nap.edu/books/ARC000005/html.

Alvarado, R. (2011). 'The Digital Humanities Situation', *The Transducer*, 11 May, http://transducer.ontoligent.com/?p=717.

Berkowitz, L. and Squiter, K.A. (1987). *Thesaurus Linguae Graecae, Canon of Greek Authors and Works*, New York/Oxford: Oxford University Press.

Berry, D.M. (ed.) (2012). *Understanding Digital Humanities*, London: Palgrave Macmillan.

Beynon, M., Russ, S. and McCarty, W. (2006). 'Human Computing? Modelling with Meaning', *Literary and Linguistic Computing*, 21 (2), pp. 141–57.

Booth, A.D. (1958). 'The History and Recent Progress of Machine Translation', in A.H. Smith (ed.) *Aspects of Translation. Studies in Communication 2*, London: Secker and Warburg, pp. 88–104.

Booth, A.D. (ed.) (1967). *Machine Translation*, Amsterdam: North-Holland Publishing Company.

Booth, A.D. (1980). 'Computers in the University of London, 1945–1962', in N. Metropolis, J. Holett and G-C. Rota (eds), *A History of Computing in the Twentieth Century. A Collection of Essays*, New York, London, etc.: Academic Press, pp. 551–61.

Booth, A.D., Brandwood, L. and Cleave, J.P. (1958). *Mechanical Resolution of Linguistic Problems*, London: Butterworths Scientific Publications.

Booth, A.D. and Booth, K.H.V. (1953). *Automatic Digital Calculators*, London: Butterworth.

---

[74] All URIs accessed on 12 January 2013.

Booth, A.D. and Booth, K.H.V. (2000). 'The beginnings of MT', in W.J. Hutchins (ed.), *Early Years in Machine Translation. Memoirs and Biographies of Pioneers*, Amsterdam/Philadelphia: John Benjamins Publishing Company, pp. 253–61.

Booth, A.D. and Locke, W.N. (1965). 'Historical Introduction', in W.N. Locke and A.D. Booth (eds), *Machine Translation of Languages: Fourteen Essays*, Cambridge, MA: The MIT Press, pp. 1–14. Original publication 1955.

Booth, A.D. (1997). 'Andrew D. Booth, an Autobiographical Sketch', *IEEE Annals of the History of Computing*, 19 (4), pp. 57–63.

Bowles, E.A. (ed.) (1967). *Computers in Humanistic Research: Readings and Perspectives*, London: Prentice Hall.

Burdick, A., Drucker, J., Lunenfeld, P., Pressner, T. and Schnapp, J. (2012). *Digital_Humanities*, Cambridge, MA: MIT Press, http://mitpress.mit.edu/sites/default/files/titles/content/9780262018470_Open_Access_Edition.pdf.

Burnard, L. (1988). 'Report of Workshop on Text Encoding Guidelines', *Literary and Linguistic Computing*, 3, pp. 131–3.

Burnard, L. (2001). 'On the Hermeneutic Implications of Text Encoding', in D. Fiormonte and J. Usher (eds), *New Media and the Humanities: Research and Applications*, Oxford: Humanities Computing Unit, pp. 31–8.

Busa, R. (1949). *La terminologia Tomistica dell'Interiorità: Saggi di metodo per un' interpretazione della metafisica della presenza*, Milano: Fratelli Bocca.

Busa, R. (1950). 'Complete Index Verborum of Works of St. Thomas', *Speculum: A Journal of Medieval Studies*, XXV/1 (January), pp. 424–5.

Busa, R. (1951). *S. Thomae Aquinatis Hymnorum Ritualium Varia Specimina Concordantiarum. Primo saggio di indici di parole automaticamente composti e stampati da macchine IBM a schede perforate*, Milano: Bocca.

Busa, R. (1980). 'The Annals of Humanities Computing: The Index Thomisticus', *Computers and the Humanities*, 14, pp. 83–90.

Busa, R. (2002). *Hermeneutika e kompiuterizar. Pas gjashtëdhjetë vjetësh – L'ermeneutica computerizzata. Sessant'anni dopo – Computerized hermeneutics. Sixty years on*, Tiranë: albin.

Busa, R. (2004a). 'Analysis of scientific and philosophical texts. What differentiates them and what they have in common', in D. Buzzetti, G. Pancaldi and H. Short (eds), *Augmenting Comprehension. Digital Tools and the History of Ideas. Proceedings of a conference at Bologna, 22–23 September 2002*, London: Office for Humanities Publication, pp. 15–17.

Busa, R. (2004b). 'Foreword: Perspectives on the Digital Humanities', in S. Schreibman, R. Siemens, and J. Unsworth (eds), *A Companion to*

Digital Humanities, Malden, MA/Oxford/Carlton, Victoria: Blackwell Publishing, pp. xvi–xxi.

Doornbusch, P. (2004). 'Computer Sound Synthesis in 1951: The Music of CSIRAC', *Computer Music Journal*, 28 (1), pp. 10–25.

Doornbusch, P. (2005). *The Music of CSIRAC, Australia's first computer music*, Altona, Vic.: Common Ground Publishing.

Duro, A. (1968). 'Humanities Computing Activities in Italy', *Computers and the Humanities*, 3 (1) (September), pp. 49–52.

Eckstein, P. (1996). 'J. Presper Eckert', *IEEE Annals of the History of Computing*, 18 (1) (March), pp. 25–44.

Ellison, J.W. (1965). 'Computers and the Testaments', in G.W. Pierson (ed.), 'Computers for the Humanities?' A Record of the Conference Sponsored by Yale University on a Grant from IBM January 22–23, New Haven, Connecticut: Yale University Press, pp. 64–74.

Genet, J.-P. and Zampolli, A. (eds) (1992). *Computers and the Humanities*, Aldershot: Dartmouth/European Science Foundation.

Gibbs, F. (2011). 'Digital Humanities Definitions by Type', http://fredgibbs. net/blog/teaching/digital-humanities-definitions-by-type (Chapter 21 in this volume).

Gold, M.K. (ed.) (2012). *Debates in the Digital Humanities*, Minneapolis: University of Minnesota Press.

Goldfarb, C.E. (1990). *The SGML Handbook*, Oxford: Clarendon Press.

Heller, J. and Logemann, G.W. (1966). 'PL/I: A Programming Language for Humanities Research', *Computers and the Humanities*, 1 (2) (November), pp. 19–27.

Hewlett, W.B. and Selfridge-Field, E. (1991). 'Computing in Musicology', *Computers and the Humanities*, 25 (6), pp. 381–92.

Hockey, S. (1980a). *A Guide to Computer Applications in the Humanities*, London: Duckworth.

Hockey, S. (1980b). *Oxford Concordance Program Users' Manual*, Oxford: Oxford University Computing Service.

Hockey, S. (1987). 'An Historical Perspective', in S. Rahtz (ed.), *Information Technology in the Humanities: Tools, Techniques and Applications*, Chichester: Ellis Horwood Limited, pp. 20–30.

Hockey, S. (1990). 'Tools for Literary and Linguistic Computing: What is there? what is emerging? and what is needed?', in Y. Choueka (ed.), *Computers in Literary and Linguistic Research. Literary and Linguistic Computing 1988*, Proceedings of the Fifteenth International Conference, Jerusalem, 5–9 June 1988, Paris/Genève: Champion Slatkine, pp. 29–35.

Howard-Hill, T.H. (1979). *Literary Concordances: A Complete Handbook to the Preparation of Manual and Computer Concordances*, Oxford: Pergamon Press.

Hutchins, W.J. (1986). *Machine Translation: Past, Present, Future*, Chichester: Ellis Horwood Limited, http://ourworld.compuserve.com/homepages/WJHutchins/PPF-TOC.htm.

Hutchins, W.J. (ed.) (2000a). *Early Years in Machine Translation. Memoirs and Biographies of Pioneers*, Amsterdam/Philadelphia: John Benjamins Publishing Company.

Hutchins, W.J. (2000b). 'Warren Weaver and the launching of MT. Brief biographical note', in W.J. Hutchins (ed.), *Early Years in Machine Translation. Memoirs and Biographies of Pioneers*, Amsterdam/Philadelphia: John Benjamins Publishing Company, pp. 17–20.

IBM (1971a). *Introduction to Computers in the Humanities*, White Plains, New York: IBM.

IBM (1971b). *Literary Data Processing*, White Plains, New York: IBM.

IBM (1971c). *Computers in Anthropology and Archeology*, White Plains, New York: IBM.

Ide, N.M. (1987). 'Computers and the Humanities Courses: Philosophical Base and Approach', in N.M. Ide (ed.), *Special Issue on Teaching Computing to Humanists. Computers and the Humanities*, 21 (4), pp. 209–15.

Ide, N.M. and Sperberg-McQueen, C.M. (1988). 'Development of a Standard for Encoding Literary and Linguistic Materials', Cologne Computer Conference 1988. Uses of the Computer in the Humanities and Social Sciences. Cologne University, 7–10 September 1988, Volume of Abstracts, pp. E.6–3–4.

Ide, N. and Sperberg-McQueen, C.M. (1995). 'The TEI: History, Goals, and Future.' *Computers and the Humanities*, 29/1: 5–15.

Jones, A. and Churchhouse, R.F. (eds) (1976). *The Computer in Literary and Linguistic Studies. (Proceedings of the Third International Symposium)*, Cardiff: The University of Wales Press.

Kay, M. (1967). 'Standards for Encoding Data in a Natural Language', *Computers and the Humanities*, 1 (5), pp. 170–7.

Kirschenbaum, M.G. (2010). 'What Is Digital Humanities and What's It Doing in English Departments?' *ADE Bulletin*, 150, pp. 55–61 (Chapter 9 in this volume).

Kirschenbaum, M.G. (2011). Comment to Alvarado (2011) on http://transducer.ontoligent.com/?p=717.

Kirschenbaum, M.G. (2012). 'Digital Humanities as/is a Tactical Term', in M.K. Gold (ed.), *Debates in the Digital Humanities*, Minneapolis MN: University of Minnesota Press, http://dhdebates.gc.cuny.edu/debates/text/48,

Lancashire I. (1990). 'Back to the Future: Literary and Linguistic Computing 1968–1988.' In Choueka, Yaacov (ed.), *Computers in Literary and Linguistic Research: Literary and Linguistic Computing*,

1988: Proceedings of the Fifteenth International Conference, Jerusalem, 5–9 June 1988, Paris: Champion-Slatkine, pp. 36–47.

Lancashire, I. (ed.) (1991). *The Humanities Computing Yearbook 1989–1990*, Oxford: Clarendon Press.

Lancashire, I. and McCarty W. (eds) (1988). *The Humanities Computing Yearbook 1988*, Oxford: Clarendon Press.

Lancashire, I., Bradley, J., McCarty, W., Stairs, M. and Woolridge, T.R. (1996). *Using TACT with Electronic Texts*, New York: Modern Language Association of America.

Lessard, G. and Levison, M. (1998). 'Introduction: Quo Vadimus?', *Computers and the Humanities*, 31 (4), pp. 261–9.

Levison, M. (1962). 'The Mechanical Analysis of Language', *NPL*, pp. 562–74.

Levison, M. (1967). 'The Computer in Literary Studies', in A.D. Booth (ed.), *Machine Translation*, Amsterdam: North-Holland Publishing Company, pp. 173–94.

Locke, W.N. and Booth, A.D. (eds) (1965). *Machine Translation of Languages. Fourteen Essays*, Cambridge, MA: The MIT Press. Original publication 1955.

Lovelace, A.A., Countess of (1961). 'Notes by the Translator', in P. Morrison and E. Morrison (eds), *Charles Babbage and his Calculating Engines. Selected Writings by Charles Babbage and Others*, New York: Dover Publications, pp. 245–95. Original publication in R. Taylor (ed.), *Scientific Memoirs, Selections from The Transactions of Foreign Academies and Learned Societies and from Foreign Journals*, 1843.

Lunenfeld, P., Burdick A., Drucker, J., Presner, T. and Schnapp, J. (2012). *Digital_Humanities*, Cambridge (MA): The MIT Press.

Lusignan, S. and North, J. (eds) (1977). *Computing in the Humanities*, Waterloo: University of Waterloo Press.

Mauchly, K.R. (1984). 'John Mauchly's Early Years', *Annals of the History of Computing*, 6 (2), pp. 116–38.

McCarty, W. (1999a). 'We would know how we know what we know: Responding to the computational transformation of the humanities', Paper, The Transformation of Science – Research between Printed Information and the Challenges of Electronic Networks, Schloss Elmau, Max Planck Gesellschaft, 31 May to 2 June.

McCarty, W. (1999b). 'Humanities Computing as Interdiscipline', a seminar in the series 'Is Humanities Computing an Academic Discipline?' IATH, University of Virginia, 5 November, http://www.iath.virginia.edu/hcs/mccarty.html.

McCarty, W. (2003a). '"Knowing true things by what their mockeries be": Modelling in the Humanities', *Computing in the Humanities Working*

Papers, A.24, jointly published with *TEXT Technology*, 12 (1), http://www.chass.utoronto.ca/epc/chwp/CHC2003/McCarty2.htm.

McCarty, W. (2003b). 'Epistemic Tinkertoys', Unpublished manuscript.

McCarty, W. (2004). 'Modeling: A Study in Words and Meanings', in S. Schreibman, R. Siemens and J. Unsworth (eds), *A Companion to Digital Humanities*, Malden, MA/Oxford/Carlton, Victoria: Blackwell Publishing, pp. 254–70, http://www.digitalhumanities.org/companion.

McCarty, W. (2005). *Humanities Computing*, London: Palgrave.

McCarty, W. (2006). 'Tree, Turf, Centre, Archipelago – or Wild Acre? Metaphors and Stories for Humanities Computing', *Literary and Linguistic Computing*, 21 (1), pp. 1–13 (Chapter 5 in this volume).

McCarty, W. (2012). 'A Telescope for the mind?' in M.K. Gold (ed.), *Debates in the Digital Humanities*, Minneapolis MN: University of Minnesota Press, http://dhdebates.gc.cuny.edu/debates/text/37.

McCarty, W. and Kirschenbaum, M. (2003). 'Institutional Models for Humanities Computing', *Literary and Linguistic Computing*, 18 (4), pp. 465–89, http://www.allc.org/publications/institutional-models-humanities-computing.

McPherson, T. (2008). 'Dynamic Vernaculars: Emergent Digital Forms in Contemporary Scholarship', Lecture presented to HUMLab Seminar, Umeå University, 4 March, http://stream.humlab.umu.se/index.php?streamName=dynamicVernaculars.

Menabrea, L.F. (1961). 'Sketch of the Analytical Engine Invented by Charles Babbage. Translated by Ada Augusta, Countess of Lovelace', in P. Morrison and E. Morrison (eds), *Charles Babbage and his Calculating Engines. Selected Writings by Charles Babbage and Others*, New York: Dover Publications, pp. 225–45. Original publication, *Bibliothèque Universelle de Genève*, 82 (October 1842); original translation by Ada Augusta, Countess of Lovelace, in R. Taylor (ed.), *Scientific Memoirs, Selections from The Transactions of Foreign Academies and Learned Societies and from Foreign Journals*, 1843.

Miall, D.S. (ed.) (1990). *Humanities and the Computer. New Directions*, Oxford: Clarendon Press.

Mitchell, J.L. (ed.) (1974). *Computers in the Humanities*, Edinburgh: Edinburgh University Press.

Oakman, R.L. (1980). *Computer Methods for Literary Research*, Columbia: University of South Carolina Press.

Oakman, R.L. (1984). *Computer Methods for Literary Research*, 2nd edition, Columbia: University of South Carolina Press.

Oettinger, A.G. (1954). *A Study for the Design of an Automatic Dictionary*, PhD Thesis, Harvard University.

Orlandi, T. (2002). 'Is Humanities Computing a Discipline?' in G. Braungart, P. Gendolla and F. Jannidis (eds), *Jahrbuch für Computerphilologie*, 4, pp. 51–8. Also published in *Jahrbuch für Computerphilologie – online*: http://computerphilologie.uni-muenchen.de/jg02/orlandi.html.

Orlandi, T. (2003). 'Per un curriculum europeo di informatica umanistica', in D. Fiormonte (ed.), *Informatica umanistica dalla ricerca all'insegnamento*, Roma: Bulzoni Editore, pp. 19–25.

Parrish, S.M. (1962). 'Problems in the Making of Computer Concordances', *Studies in Bibliography*, 15, pp. 1–14.

Pierson, G.W. (ed.) (1965). 'Computers for the Humanities?' A Record of the Conference Sponsored by Yale University on a Grant from IBM January 22–23, New Haven, Connecticut: Yale University Press.

Polachek, H. (1997). 'Before the ENIAC', *IEEE Annals of the History of Computing*, April, pp. 25–30.

Potter, R.G. (1991). 'Statistical Analysis of Literature: A Retrospective on Computers and the Humanities, 1966–1990', *Computers and the Humanities*, 25 (6), pp. 401–29.

Raben J. (1973). 'The humanist in the Computer Lab: Thoughts on Technology in the Study of Literature', *Bulletin of the Association for Literary and Linguistic Computing*, 1 (1), pp. 3–9.

Richens, R.H. and Booth, A.D. (1952). 'Some Methods of Mechanized Translation', Presented at the Conference on Mechanical Translation, June, Massachusetts Institute of Technology. [Corrected reprint in: W.N. Locke and A.D. Booth (eds) *Machine Translation of Languages: Fourteen Essays*, Cambridge, Mass.: Technology Press of the Massachusetts Institute of Technology, 1955, pp. 24–46], http://www.mt-archive.info/MIT-1952-Richens.pdf.

Russell, D.B. (1967). *COCOA: A Word Count and Concordance Generator for Atlas*, Chilton: Atlas Computer Laboratory.

Schreibman, S., Siemens, R. and Unsworth, J. (eds) (2004). *A Companion to Digital Humanities*, Malden, MA/Oxford/Carlton, Victoria: Blackwell Publishing, http://www.digitalhumanities.org/companion.

Sparck Jones, K. (2000). 'R.H. Richens. Translation in the nude', in W.J. Hutchins (ed.), *Early Years in Machine Translation. Memoirs and Biographies of Pioneers*, Amsterdam/Philadelphia: John Benjamins Publishing Company, pp. 264–78.

Sperberg-McQueen, C.M. (1991). 'Text in the Electronic Age: Textual Study and Text Encoding with examples from Medieval Texts', *Literary and Linguistic Computing*, 6 (1), pp. 34–46.

Sperberg-McQueen, C.M. and Burnard, L. (eds) (1990). *TEI P1: Guidelines for the Encoding and Interchange of Machine Readable Texts*, Chicago/Oxford: ACH-ALLC-ACL Text Encoding Initiative, http://www.tei-c.org/Vault/Vault-GL.html.

Sperberg-McQueen, C.M. and Burnard, L. (eds) (1992–1993). *TEI P2 Guidelines for the Encoding and Interchange of Machine Readable*

Texts Draft P2 (published serially 1992–1993). Draft Version 2 of April 1993: 19 chapters, http://www.tei-c.org/Vault/Vault-GL.html.

Sperberg-McQueen, C.M. and Burnard, L. (eds) (1994). *Guidelines for Electronic Text Encoding and Interchange. TEI P3*, Oxford, Providence, Charlottesville, Bergen: Text Encoding Initiative.

Sperberg-McQueen, C.M. and Burnard L. (eds) (1999). *Guidelines for Electronic Text Encoding and Interchange. TEI P3. Revised reprint*, Oxford, Providence, Charlottesville, Bergen: Text Encoding Initiative.

Sperberg-McQueen, C.M. and Burnard, L. (eds) (2002). *TEI P4: Guidelines for Electronic Text Encoding and Interchange, XML-compatible edition*. XML conversion by S. Bauman, L. Burnard, S. DeRose and S. Rahtz, Oxford, Providence, Charlottesville, Bergen: Text Encoding Initiative Consortium, http://www.tei-c.org/P4X.

Stern, N. (1980). 'John von Neumann's Influence on Electronic Digital Computing, 1944–1946', *Annals of the History of Computing*, 2 (4), pp. 349–62.

Svensson, P. (2009). 'Humanities Computing as Digital Humanities', *Digital Humanities Quarterly*, 3 (3) (Summer), http://digitalhumanities.org/dhq/vol/3/3/000065/000065.html, (Chapter 7 in this volume)

Svensson, P. (2010). 'The Landscape of Digital Humanities', *Digital Humanities Quarterly*, 4 (1) (Summer), http://digitalhumanities.org/dhq/vol/4/1/000080/000080.html.

Svensson, P. (2011). 'From Optical Fiber To Conceptual Cyberinfrastructure', *Digital Humanities Quarterly*, 5 (1) (Winter), http://digitalhumanities.org/dhq/vol/5/1/000090/000090.html.

Svensson, P. (2012). 'Envisioning the Digital Humanities', *Digital Humanities Quarterly*, 6 (1), http://www.digitalhumanities.org/dhq/vol/6/1/000112/000112.html.

Tanner, S. (1975). 'How to bring the dead language to life (Report on the ALLC International Meeting. 1974)', *Dataweek*, 22 January. Reprinted in *ALLC Bulletin*, 3 (1) (Lent), pp. 52–4.

Taporwiki (2011). 'How do you define Humanities Computing/Digital Humanities?' http://tapor.ualberta.ca/taporwiki/index.php/How_do_you_define_Humanities_Computing_/_Digital_Humanities%3F.

TEI Consortium (eds) (2007). *TEI P5: Guidelines for Electronic Text Encoding and Interchange*. Oxford, Providence, Charlottesville, Nancy: TEI Consortium, http://www.tei-c.org/Guidelines/P5.

Terras, M. (2011a). 'Peering Inside the Big Tent: Digital Humanities and the Crisis of Inclusion', http://melissaterras.blogspot.com/2011/07/peering-inside-big-tent-digital.html.

Terras, M. (2011b). 'Present, not voting: Digital Humanities in the Panopticon', Closing plenary speech, Digital Humanities 2010. *LLC*,

The Journal of Digital Scholarship in the Humanities, 26 (3), pp. 257–69, doi:10.1093/llc/fqr016.

Thaller, M. (1999). 'Defining Humanities Computing Methodology', in K. de Smedt, H. Gardiner, E. Ore, T. Orlandi, H. Short, J. Souillot and W. Vaughan (eds), *Computing in Humanities Education. A European Perspective*, Bergen: University of Bergen, pp. 13–62.

Thaller, M. (2001). 'Bridging the Gap; Splitting the Bridge? Studying Humanities Computer Science in Cologne.' Abstract. CLiP. Computers-Literature-Philosophy, Duisburg.

Thaller, M. (2004). 'Texts, Databases, Kleio. A note on the architecture of computer systems for the humanities', in D. Buzetti, G. Pancaldi and H. Short (eds), *Augmenting Comprehension. Digital Tools and the History of Ideas. Proceedings of a conference at Bologna, 22–23 September 2002*, London: Office for Humanities Communication, pp. 49–76.

Thaller, M. (2006). 'Waiting for the Next Wave: Humanities Computing in 2006', CliP, London: King's College London, 30 June.

Toole, B.A. (1996). 'Ada Byron, Lady Lovelace, an analyst and metaphysician', *IEEE Annals of the History of Computing, 18 (3), pp. 4–12*.

Toole, B.A. (1998). *Ada, The Enchantress of Numbers. A Selection from the Letters of Lord Byron's Daughter and Her Description of the First Computer*, Mill Valley, CA: Strawberry Press.

Warwick, C., Terras, M. and Nyhan, J. (eds) (2012). *Digital Humanities in Practice*, London: Facet Publishing/UCL.

Weaver, W. (1965). 'Translation', in W.N. Locke and A.D. Booth (eds) *Machine Translation of Languages. Fourteen Essays*, Cambridge, MA: The MIT Press, pp. 15–23. Original publication 1949.

Weaver, W. (1970). *Scene of Change. A Lifetime in American Science*, New York: Scribner.

Wilkes, M.V. (1995). 'A Tribute to Presper Eckert', *Communications of the ACM*, 38 (9) (September), pp. 20–2.

Winter, T.N. (1999). 'Roberto Busa, S.J., and the Invention of the Machine-Generated Concordance', *The Classical Bulletin*, 75 (1), pp. 3–20.

Wisbey, R.A. (ed.) (1971). *The Computer in Literary and Linguistic Research. Papers from a Cambridge symposium*, Cambridge: Cambridge University Press.

Yngve, V.H. (2000). 'Early research at M.I.T. In search of adequate theory', in W.J. Hutchins (ed.) *Early Years in Machine Translation. Memoirs and Biographies of Pioneers*, Amsterdam/Philadelphia: John Benjamins Publishing Company, pp. 37–72.

Zampolli, A. (1989). 'Introduction to the Special Section on Machine Translation', *Literary and Linguistic Computing*, 4 (3), pp. 182–4.

SECTION II
Digital Humanities

CHAPTER 7

Humanities Computing as Digital Humanities

Patrik Svensson
Umeå University

Patrik Svensson (2009). Originally published in *Digital Humanities Quarterly*, 3 (3), http://digitalhumanities.org/dhq/vol/3/3/000065/000065.html.

Note from the Editors:

This article focuses on the renaming of Humanities Computing to Digital Humanities and the difficulties this brings given the apparently differing scopes of these domains. Svensson draws on a range of materials to substantiate his argument and analysis, including, inter alia, posts from *Humanist*, conference materials, blogs and institutional websites. He goes on to argue that Humanities Computing is instrumental, methodological and text-based in focus and rarely engages with the digital as an object of study. Given the wide-ranging scope of Digital Humanities, which is indicated to be much broader and more generally aligned with the wide-ranging concerns and content of the traditional Humanities, a tension is seen to arise. He reflects that 'A pertinent question is whether the discursive transition from humanities computing to digital humanities is mainly a matter of repackaging (humanities computing), or whether the new label also indicates an expanded scope, a new focus or a different relation to traditional humanities computing work'. It is therefore interesting to compare this piece with the previous chapters which focus particularly on the scope of Humanities Computing. Svensson followed this article with three companion pieces, all published in *DHQ* and freely available ('The Landscape of Digital Humanities' (2010), 'From Optical Fiber To Conceptual Cyberinfrastructure' (2011) and 'Envisioning the Digital Humanities' (2012) – see Selected Further Reading).

Abstract

This article presents an examination of how digital humanities is currently conceived and described, and examines the discursive shift from humanities computing to digital humanities. It is argued that this renaming of humanities computing to digital humanities carries with it a set of epistemic commitments that are not necessarily compatible with a broad and inclusive notion of the digital humanities. In particular, the author suggests that tensions arise from the instrumental, textual and methodological focus of humanities computing as well as its relative lack of engagement with the "digital" as a study object. This article is the first in a series of four articles attempting to describe and analyze the field of digital humanities and digital humanities as a transformative practice.

Introduction

The humanities are undergoing a set of changes which relate to research practices, funding structures, the role of creative expression, infrastructural basis, reward systems, interdisciplinary sentiment and the emergence of a deeply networked humanities in relation to both knowledge production processes and products. An important aspect of this ongoing transformation of the humanities is humanities scholars' increasing use and exploration of information technology as both a scholastic tool and a cultural object in need of analysis. Currently, there is a cumulative set of experiences, practices and models flourishing in what may be called digital humanities. The research presented here explores the scope and direction of this emerging field as well as the role of humanities computing in this enterprise.

In this article, the first in a four-part series, I explore the discursive shift from humanities computing to what is now being termed the digital humanities, examining how this naming is related to shifts in institutional, disciplinary, and social organization. Materials such as the *Humanist* email list, journals, conference materials, principal texts, professional blogs and institutional websites provide an important empirical basis for the analysis. Academic fields are partly produced, represented, reinforced, changed and negotiated through these modes of discourse. As will be evident from the analysis, the renaming of humanities computing to digital humanities brings with it a set of epistemic commitments that are not necessarily congruent with a broad and inclusive notion of the digital humanities. I suggest that interesting tensions arise from the instrumental, textual and methodological focus of humanities computing as well as its relative lack of engagement with the "digital" as a study object.

In the second article, I explore the broader landscape of the digital humanities through a discussion of digital humanities and digital humanists, associated traditions, personal encounters and, importantly, through a suggested set of paradigmatic modes of engagement between the humanities and information technology: information technology as a tool, an object of study, an exploratory laboratory, an expressive medium and an activist venue.

The third article discusses cyberinfrastructure for the humanities more broadly – and for the digital humanities in particular – in relation to the current discourse of cyberinfrastructure, models of implementation and possible directions. The article also presents a fairly extensive case study of HUMlab – a digital humanities center at Umeå University. Finally, tentative advice as to implementing and strategizing humanities cyberinfrastructure is offered.

In the fourth article, I explore the multiple ways in which the digital humanities have been envisioned and how the digital humanities can often become a laboratory and vehicle for thinking about the state and future of the humanities at large. Some foundational issues, including the role of the humanities and changing knowledge production systems, are discussed and related to the development of the digital humanities. Furthermore, a tentative vision of the digital humanities is presented. This vision is grounded in the article series as a whole as well as in the important collaborative possibilities and challenges that lie ahead of us.

Together these four articles constitute an attempt to outline and critically discuss how the humanities interrelate with information technology in multiple ways, to understand the historical, conceptual, and disciplinary aspects of this interrelation, and to present an expansive model for the digital humanities.

Background

One of the things that has fascinated me for a long time is the range of origins, approaches and traditions associated with different varieties of digital humanities, ranging from textual analysis of medieval texts and establishment of metadata schemes to the production of alternative computer games and artistic readings of nanotechnology. An important rationale for this article series is to facilitate a discussion across various initiatives and disciplines and to make connections. There are many humanities scholars involved in what may be called digital humanities who have no or little knowledge of humanities computing, and vice versa, many humanities computing representatives who do not engage much with current "new media" studies of matters such as platform studies, transmedia perspectives or database aesthetics. Few people will engage in activities across the board, of course, but it is important to have a sense of the growing disciplinary landscape, associated methodological and theoretical positions, and emerging collaborative possibilities. To me, this is an integral part of digital humanities as a project.

There are several good reasons for giving humanities computing the particular attention it receives in this article: its rich heritage, historical and current accomplishments, the sheer number of people involved, and the apparent discursive transition to "digital humanities". Furthermore, any attempt at mapping an emerging field presupposes a discussion of disciplinary territory and ambitions, and humanities computing provides a particularly good starting point as it is relatively established and well defined. And as we will see, many of the issues, considerations and parameters relevant to humanities computing are also relevant to digital humanities more generally.

In the following, we will start out from a particular example of humanities computing as digital humanities and associated epistemic commitments. Some of these commitments are traced in the subsequent historical, institutional and contextual description of humanities computing. We will then move on to look at the renaming of humanities computing to digital humanities, which in turn will lead to a critical discussion of humanities computing with a particular focus on some points of tension between traditional humanities computing and an expansive notion of digital humanities. In conclusion, humanities computing will be briefly juxtaposed with a very different kind of digital humanities tradition.

Setting the Stage

The Call for Proposals for Digital Humanities 2009, the principal humanities computing conference, provides an illustrative example of how the disciplinary territory of digital humanities is being defined in relation to the tradition of humanities computing and how epistemic commitments can be manifested discursively.

Epistemic cultures, as defined by (Knorr Cetina, 1999, p. 1) are "those amalgams of arrangements and mechanisms – bonded through affinity, necessity, and historical coincidence – which, in a given field, make up *how we know what we know*" (original emphasis). We are thus concerned with ways in which knowledge is created, represented and defended. Epistemic cultures are constructed and maintained through, among other things, the epistemic commitments of participating scientists as part of the means by which alignments are made between academic disciplines, the fields of enquiry that they represent, and shared notions about what constitutes valid research (Ratto, 2006). In the following, the epistemic commitments of humanities computing and digital humanities are traced mainly through looking at different modes of discourse. While these modes may have different functions and intended audiences, they collectively add to the analysis.

The Digital Humanities 2009 Call (http://mith.umd.edu//dh09/?page_ id=54) is divided into three parts. The first part provides a broad and relatively open definition of the digital humanities.

> The international Program Committee invites submissions of abstracts of between 750 and 1500 words on any aspect of digital humanities, broadly defined to encompass the common ground between information technology and problems in humanities research and teaching.
>
> As always, we welcome submissions in any area of the humanities, particularly interdisciplinary work. We especially encourage submissions on the current state of the art in digital humanities, and on recent new developments and expected future developments in the field.

The invitation relates to "any aspect of digital humanities" which is loosely defined as the common ground between information technology and problems in humanities research and teaching. Interdisciplinary contributions are particularly encouraged. As expected, the second part provides a higher level of specificity.

Suitable subjects for proposals include, for example,

- text analysis, corpora, corpus linguistics, language processing, language learning
- libraries, archives and the creation, delivery, management and preservation of humanities digital resources
- computer-based research and computing applications in all areas of literary, linguistic, cultural, and historical studies, including electronic literature and interdisciplinary aspects of modern scholarship
- use of computation in such areas as the arts, architecture, music, film, theatre, new media, and other areas reflecting our cultural heritage
- research issues such as: information design and modeling; the cultural impact of the new media; software studies; Human-Computer interaction
- the role of digital humanities in academic curricula
- digital humanities and diversity

Here we are presented with a narrowing down of what was described in the first part. This is common in conference calls as a way of indicating the particular focus of the conference, of course, although it is difficult to discern any clear thematic delimitation in this particular case. We are thus concerned with a fairly broad range of possible topics. However, the ordering and phrasing of these topics suggest a specific tradition or framework, and an associated set of epistemic commitments. For instance, it is not by accident that text analysis comes first and that phrases such as "computer-based research" and "use of computation" are used. Even so it could be argued that much of what is included in a broad notion of digital humanities could be subsumed under these topics, and that particularly the sixth topic – research issues – opens up the scope to areas such as new media studies. But the placement, exact wording (e.g. "the cultural impact of new media") and the broader context may not make these potential conference participants feel targeted unless they already have a relation to the community and humanities computing.

In the third part of the call for proposals follows a much more precise definition of digital humanities and associated topics:

> The range of topics covered by digital humanities can also be consulted in the journal of the associations: Literary and Linguistic Computing (LLC), Oxford University Press.

The journal *Literary and Linguistic Computing* has been a key publication for humanities computing for a long time. However, defining digital humanities through the topics presented in *LLC* clearly excludes many other initiatives and developments in the intersection of the humanities and information technology and suggests a very particular tradition, institutional grounding and epistemic culture.[1] Moreover, this level of narrowing down is clearly not congruent with the description of digital humanities given in the first part of the call, which may be said to be less obviously situated in the tradition of humanities computing and associated epistemic commitments.

History and Paradigm

The partial institutionalization of humanities computing has resulted in academic departments or units, annual conferences, journals, educational programs and a rather strong sense of communal identity. These are all qualities that are typically associated with the establishment of a new

---

[1] For instance, the privileged role of text can be indicated through looking at four recent issues of the journal: *Literary and Linguistic Computing*, 24 (1), special theme: Computing the edition, *Literary and Linguistic Computing*, 23 (4), largely statistical text analysis; *Literary and Linguistic Computing*, 23 (3), largely text analysis apart from one article on scholarly visualization; and *Literary and Linguistic Computing*, 23 (2), largely text analysis, annotation and authorship attribution. See also expanded discussion later in this article.

discipline (cf. Klein, 1996, p. 57). The following excerpt from a description of a 1999 panel organized by the Association for Computers and the Humanities seems to confirm this analysis:

> Empirically, humanities computing is easily recognized as a particular academic domain and community. We have our professional organizations, regular conferences, journals, and a number of centers, departments, and other organizational units. A sense for the substance of the field is also fairly easy to come by: one can examine the proceedings of ACH/ALLC conferences, issues of CHum and JALLC, the discussions on HUMANIST, the contents of many books and anthologies which represent themselves as presenting work in humanities computing, and the academic curricula and research programs at humanities computing centers and departments. From such an exercise one easily gets a rough and ready sense of what we are about, and considerable reassurance, if any is needed, that indeed, there is something which we are about.[2]

Communal identity, of course, is built over time, and history and foundational narratives play an important role in this process. Father Roberto Busa is typically cited as the pioneer of the field of humanities computing, and his work dates back to the late 1940s:

> During the World War II, between 1941 and 1946, I began to look for machines for the automation of the linguistic analysis of written texts. I found them, in 1949, at IBM in New York City. (Busa, 2004, xvi)

In this foundational story, two important epistemic commitments of humanities computing are established: information technology as a tool and written texts as a primary object of study (for linguistic analysis). Commitments such as "computer as instrumental tool" and "text as object" end up helping decide what are legitimate types of questions and study objects for the field, and how work and relevant institutions are organized.

The journal *Computers and the Humanities* was started as early as in 1966 and, interestingly, it seems as if early issues were not as textually oriented as one might have assumed. Early articles include "PL/I: A programming language for humanities research," "Art, art history, and the computer" and "Musicology and the computer in New Orleans" (all from 1966–1967). Thirty years later we find articles such as "The design of the TEI encoding scheme," "Current uses of hypertext in teaching literature," "Neural network applications in stylometry" and "Word frequency distributions and lexical semantics" (all from 1995–1996). In 2005, this

---

2   http://www.ach.org/abstracts/1999/renear-ach.html.

journal was renamed *Language Resources and Evaluation*, and had by this time lost its status as one of the "official" journals for humanities computing. In one of the obituaries, Willard McCarty applauds the first 25 years of the journal and comments on the editors' final statement (which points to the difficulty of maintaining the broad scope of the journal):

> CHum's astonishing denial of a future for humanities computing comes in the same year as the Blackwell's Companion to Digital Humanities ... If anything, the development of CHum since then suggests rather the opposite – a narrowing down from the breadth of humanistic interests, across the full range of disciplines, to a sharp focus on material often closer to computational linguistics than anything else – and often too technical for all but the specialist to read. This narrowing does not reflect the field. (McCarty, 2005b)

In other words, *Computers and the Humanities* was seen as having taken a direction not fully compatible with the epistemic tradition of humanities computing. Indicatively, in a Call for Papers from 1998,[3] there is a special invitation for state-of-the-art surveys, and the only example given is "Current Approaches to Punctuation in Computational Linguistics." Also, this happened at about the same time as the Alliance of Digital Humanities Organizations (ADHO) was formed, and another important reason for the "demise" of *Computers and the Humanities* was that it was strategically, financially and institutionally advantageous to make *Literary and Linguistic Computing* and not *Computers and the Humanities* the principal humanities computing journal.[4] Indeed, these reasons were probably more important than the perceived incompatibility between humanities computing at large and *Computers and the Humanities*. Nevertheless, the result was that for a few years, humanities computing only had one principal journal.

The journal *Literary and Linguistic Computing* has from its inception focused on textual and text-based literary analysis – as you would expect from its title. It was established in 1986 by the Association for Literary and Linguistic Computing (itself established in 1973). This journal has clearly played an important role in establishing the field of humanities computing – not only in offering a publication venue, institutional structure and academic exchange but also in publishing self-reflective articles on the role, organization and future of humanities computing. As we saw earlier, the journal has even been used to define the digital humanities – thus in a sense transferring the epistemic culture of the journal and associated field to the "new" field.

---

[3]　http://cfp.english.upenn.edu/archive/Collections/0047.html.
[4]　See e.g. http://www.ach.org/documents/minutes2003.html.

As important as these printed journals have been for establishing humanities computing as a field, humanities computing representatives were also early adopters of communication technologies such as email lists. The first message on the *Humanist* list was sent on May 13, 1987 by founding editor Willard McCarty, making it one of the first academic email lists to be established. Currently about 1,600 people subscribe to the *Humanist* list[5] which is an email list with consistently high quality, carefully organized threads and an often lively discussion.[6] Although the range of topics is very broad it is fair to say that there is persistent and fundamental interest in textual analysis and related matters. As McCarty himself points out, *Humanist* facilitates an ongoing, low-key and important discussion:

> We're always worrying ourselves about whether humanities computing has made its mark in the world and on the world. It seems to me, however, that quiet change, though harder to detect, is sometimes much better and more powerful in its effects than the noisy, obviously mark-making, position-taking kind. If during these 17 years Humanist has contributed to the world, it has done so very quietly by nature, like conversation, leaving hardly a trace. (McCarty, 2004)

Here it is also rather obvious that "humanities computing" serves as an identifying label and collaborative sentiment for the *Humanist* community. We will soon return to this label (and an ongoing relabeling process) as well as the worry or concern that McCarty mentions but first a brief look at another major institution in this field.

One of the most important venues for humanities computing have been the annual conferences jointly organized by the Association for Literary and Linguistic Computing (ALLC) and the Association for Computers and the Humanities (ACH). Originally these organizations ran their own conference series, but from 1996 they started a joint conference series. From 2008, the Society for Digital Humanities/Société pour l'étude des médias interactifs (SDH/SEMI) became a third organizing association. These three associations are all members of the Alliance of Digital Humanities Organizations. It is quite clear that these conferences predominantly address textual analysis, markup, retrieval systems and related areas. A simple frequency analysis based on titles of papers and sessions from 1996 to 2004 shows us that frequent non-functional words include *text* (56), *electronic* (53), *language* (30), *markup* (28), *encoding*

---

[5]   *Humanist*, 21 (436|) In December 2004, there were about 1,500 subscribers in personal communication with Willard McCarty. The readership thus seems relatively stable.

[6]   There is an archive of the *Humanist* list which makes for interesting reading and historical contextualization: http://www.princeton.edu/~mccarty/humanist.

(27), *TEI* (23), *corpus* (22), *authorship* (18), *XML* (18), *database* (13) and *multimedia* (11). In comparison there is one instance of *game* and two instances of the plural form *games*. This is a rather crude measurement, of course, but it does give us a sense of the overall orientation. A more careful look at the 2005 conference (at University of Victoria, BC) does not seem to contradict this sketch. For instance, the themed sessions that extended more than one program slot were "Authorship Attribution," "Libraries, Archives & Metadata," "Computational Linguistics and Natural Language Processing," "Encoding & Multiculturalism," "Scholarly Projects" and "Visualisation & Modeling." One-slot themed sessions included "Automation," "Text & Technology," "Textual Editing & Analysis," "Interface Design" and "Hypertext".[7] Yet another example is the 2008 Digital Humanities Summer Institute (McCarty et al., 2008). Here the focus is on text encoding, transcription, and corpus text analysis in five out of the eight offerings in the curriculum. The other three sessions take up digitization fundamentals, multimedia and large project planning.

While journals, conferences and academic associations play an important role in creating and maintaining an academic field and community, another important factor is the ways in which a field has been institutionalized. In the case of humanities computing, this has been a long and partly uncertain process, which has clearly shaped the field.

Institutional Models

In organizational terms, humanities computing enterprises have been institutionalized in many different ways. And, of course, institutions develop over time. A useful resource is Willard McCarty's and Matthew Kirschenbaum's "Institutional Models for Humanities Computing" (McCarty and Kirschenbaum, 2003). Here a number of questions or criteria are used to list and categorize humanities computing institutions. The first category incorporates academic units that do research, teaching and collegial service. Also "[s]ome members of these units hold academic appointments either in or primarily associated with humanities computing." Examples include the Centre for Computing in the Humanities, King's College London, and the Institute for Advanced Technology in the Humanities. Even though it is said in the document that "[n]o judgement is expressed or implied as to the worth of the centres under consideration," it could probably be argued that this first category serves as a role model

---

[7] Interestingly, Terras (2006) employs a somewhat similar material in her analysis. As far as I know these are independent analyses. My own material was first presented publicly in 2004.

(based on the way criteria are created and presented, the ordering of the categories and a broader humanities computing context).

Historically, and to some extent contemporarily, it would seem that a prototypical organizational form is a humanities computing unit or center affiliated with a school of liberal arts or humanities. Often such units provide service to the rest of the school and this rather instrumental function has typically been primary. Of course, there might have been development in many other directions over time, but this basic function cannot easily be dismissed. A prominent example would be the Humanities Computing Unit (HCU) at Oxford University whose roots go back to the 1960s and which was closed (or transformed) in 2002. Burnard (2002) describes the final stages of this development:

> At the start of the new millennium, the HCU employed over 20 people, half of them on external grants and contracts valued at over £350,000 annually. With the advent of divisionalization, however, it faced a new challenge and a new environment, in which OUCS, as a centrally-funded service, must take particular care to meet the needs of the whole University, in a way which complements the support activities funded by individual divisions, rather than competing with or supplanting them. Our strategy has been to focus on areas where the HCU's long experience in promoting better usage of IT within one discipline can be generalized. In 2001, we set up a new Learning Technologies Group, to act as a cross-disciplinary advocacy and development focus for the integration of IT into traditional teaching and learning. This new LTG is now one of four key divisions within the new OUCS, additionally responsible for the full range of OUCS training activities.

The status of such academic units, of course, is not normally on the same level as (traditional) departments which tend to be the privileged academic organizational unit. In many cases humanities computing units have been seen as service units with a rather instrumental role and representatives find themselves having to present their field in such a way as to maintain financial support as well as their share of integrity and independence. Frequently, as in the case above, academic units which are seen as having a technological service function are susceptible to different kinds of organizational changes and budget cuts. For instance, the central university administration might question whether the most efficient organizational structure is to have departments and faculties run their own computer support functions or whether it is more efficient to adopt a more centralized model. Also humanities computing units that have several functions might have to cut back on the more research oriented activities because, after all, technical support is more instrumental (and sellable/buyable) and there might not be enough explicit interest from humanities departments to motivate a more research and methodology focused function. There are many examples of changes like these (see Flanders and Unsworth (2002) for some other examples and a further discussion). Several prominent service-based units, including the Humanities Computing Unit at Oxford University and Centre for Computing in the Humanities at University of Toronto, have been closed down (or radically reformed) over time and this vulnerable position is part of the shaping of humanities computing.

While it is fair to say that the present institutional landscape is rather diverse and expansive, it is also important to acknowledge that the ratio of thriving humanities computing environments and initiatives at universities in Europe and the United States is still very low in relation to the whole of the Humanities, something that may or may not be seen as a problem. Taking Sweden as an example, there seems to be only one traditional humanities computing unit in the country (at Gothenburg University) at present. Most of the growth seems to happen in places where there is no or little humanities computing legacy (Blekinge Institute of Technology and Södertörn University College). My own environment, HUMlab at Umeå University, does relate to humanities computing, but also to many other influences, and most of the Ph.D. students, for instance, would probably not see themselves as primarily involved in humanities computing. Most of them do subscribe to the *Humanist*, however.

The Question of Autonomy

A related and much-discussed issue – highly relevant to digital humanities generally and to humanities computing as digital humanities – concerns whether humanities computing should be independent and possibly an academic discipline in its own right or whether it should primarily interrelate with existing humanities departments. This discussion has partly been fueled by the need for academic status to create academic positions and a sense of not wanting or needing to be reliant on traditional and slow-moving departments and disciplines.[8] In fact, these disciplines may not even be considered suitable for dealing with relevant study objects and research issues, or appropriate methodologies:

> To study the effects and consequences of digital technology on our culture, and how we are shaping these technologies according to our cultural needs, we can now begin to see the contours of a separate, autonomous field, where

---

[8] In particular English departments are likely to be targeted. They are part of the heritage and identity of humanities computing as well as the foundational narratives mentioned earlier. Geoffrey Rockwell writes, "A discipline maintains common stories of its founding and a history complete with heroes (Father Busa), monsters (English Departments) and timely achievements (the publication of the TEI P4)" (Rockwell, 2002).

the historical, aesthetic, cultural and discursive aspects of the digitalisation of our society may be examined. That way, the field of Humanistic Informatics may contribute to the goal of the Humanities, which is the advancement of the understanding of human patterns of expression. We cannot leave this new development to existing fields, because they will always privilege their traditional methods, which are based on their own empirical objects.[9] (Aarseth, 1997)

Another argument for not involving all of the Humanities may be that it is not seen as an efficient model. McGann (2001, p. 7) tells us about strategies adopted when the Institute for Advanced Technology in the Humanities (IATH) at University of Virginia was started. Alan Batson, Department of Computer Science at UVA, argued that trying to involve everyone (distribute resources evenly) would be to replicate 30 years of failure; providing IT resources to people who are not interested in them or do not want to explore them does not work.

IATH was founded as a resource for people who had already made a commitment to humanities computing, a commitment defined practically by an actual project with demonstrable scholarly importance (McGann, 2001, p. 9).

The tension between trying to involve as many as possible and making a difference through engaging people who have already shown an interest is basic and recurrent. Naturally, any enterprise of this kind is dependent on the local environment. There is obviously a significant difference between being an autonomous academic unit and a service-based organization. In practice most humanities computing units are probably somewhere in between. Also, the "service" function can, of course, be very complex and should not be trivialized. McCarty talks about "practice" and "practitioners," and such terminology might be more suitable for many of the service-like functions more directly related to the humanities computing enterprise. He stresses the importance of methodological knowledge and says that "[t]he practitioner learns a specific but generalizable method for tackling problems of a certain kind" (McCarty, 2005a, p. 120). This focus on methodology and associated tools is common in humanities computing, and arguably part of the epistemic commitments of the field that fundamentally shape the way humanities computing relates to the rest of the humanities and to other work in the humanities and information technology.

---

[9]   It is representative of Aarseth's position and refreshingly provocative style that his ALLC/ACH 2005 keynote was entitled "Old, new, borrowed, blue? Can the Humanities Contribute to Game Research?"

Approaching the Digital Humanities

As we noted earlier "humanities computing" has been a strong common denotation for much of the work and community described above. In his *Humanities Computing*, Willard McCarty describes the development from "computers and the humanities" via "computing in the humanities" to "humanities computing". He characterizes these three denotations as follows: "when the relationship was desired but largely unrealized" (computers and the humanities), "once entry has been gained" (computing in the humanities) and "confident but enigmatic" (humanities computing) (McCarty, 2005a, p. 3). I have argued elsewhere (Svensson and McCarty, 2003) that juxtaposition (as in the first stage) does not necessarily have to indicate separated entities and that "humanities computing" has an instrumental ring to it. Also, "humanities computing" does not necessarily seem to include many of the approaches and materials that interest many humanities scholars interested in information technology (and computing). Of course, these arguments are related to the ambitions and scope of the field you are trying to denote.

From this point of view, it is interesting to note that humanities computing representatives currently seem to be appropriating the term *digital humanities*. Prominent examples of use of the new identifier include the relabeled ALLC/ACH conference (from 2006 onwards entitled "Digital Humanities"), a new book series called "Topics in Digital Humanities," a new comprehensive website[10] sponsored by the major humanities computing associations, the peer-reviewed journal *Digital Humanities Quarterly*, the massive, edited volume *A Companion to Digital Humanities* (Schreibman et al., 2004) and the recent renaming of the Canadian Consortium for Computers in the Humanities to The Society for Digital Humanities. The denotation has certainly been used before (at University of Virginia among other places), but it seems to be employed more broadly now and in a more official and premeditated fashion. An important indication of the spread of the term and institutionalization of the field can be seen in the establishment of the Office of Digital Humanities by the National Endowment for the Humanities (US) in 2008. A broader analysis of different varieties of digital humanities will be returned to in the second article in this series.

Looking at issues 1–20 of the *Humanist*[11] and instances of *humanities computing* versus *digital humanities*, the following figures emerge: 304/2 (1997–1998), 343/3 (2000–2001), 566/16 (2001–2002), 283/15 (2002–

---

[10]   http://www.digitalhumanities.org.

[11]   The text files were taken from the *Humanist* website apart from issues 2005–2006 and 2006–2007 which were created.

2003), 280/19 (2003–2004), 363/45 (2004–2005), 130/44 (2005–2006) and 110/90 (2006–2007). The first instances of *digital humanities* in issues 11 and 14 (1997–1998 and 2000–2001 respectively) refer to nominal constructions such as *digital humanities object* and *digital humanities environment*. While we should be careful about how to interpret crude quantitative data like these, it is fairly clear that *humanities computing* for a long time was the predominant term and still is frequent, but that we are moving towards an increased use of *digital humanities* (relative to *humanities computing*). The retained and frequent use of the older term points to a discrepancy between the over-the-board institutional renaming of the field described above and the community's use of the term as evidenced in the *Humanist* material.

This discrepancy or co-existence[12] is also evident if you look at Blackwell's *A Companion to Digital Humanities* from 2004 (Schreibman et al., 2004). There are about twice as many instances of *humanities computing* as *digital humanities* (139/68). The internal distribution of the terms is more interesting and can be explored easily using the online version of the companion. For instance, *humanities computing* is predominantly used in the section where the contributors are described, while *digital humanities* is much more common than *humanities computing* in the introduction (called "The Humanities Computing and the Digital Humanities: An Introduction"). These two texts represent very different genres. The Notes on Contributors section is largely a venue for self representation and presentation. The introduction is where the (new) field of digital humanities is being described and advocated (by the editors of the volume). In the history section (12 chapters in total) it is clearly the history of humanities computing that is told (58 instances of *humanities computing* versus 1 instance of *digital humanities*). The section on principles (7 chapters) is primarily humanities computing-focused (23/4) as the main topics are text analysis, encoding, classification and modeling. The final two sections – on applications and production, dissemination, archiving – contain fewer instances of either term. One possible reason may be because these sections are more grounded in actual practice. Also, it is clear that individual preference plays an important role. Again, we are concerned with simple, quantitative measurements, but there is definitely a picture emerging.

---

[12] An interesting example of co-existence can be found in the introduction to *A Companion to Digital Humanities*: "The digital humanities, then, and their interdisciplinary core found in the field of humanities computing, have a long and dynamic history best illustrated by examination of the locations at which specific disciplinary practices intersect with computation."

A pertinent question is whether the discursive transition from humanities computing to digital humanities is mainly a matter of repackaging (humanities computing), or whether the new label also indicates an expanded scope, a new focus or a different relation to traditional humanities computing work. The editors of the book series "Topics in the Digital Humanities" indicate an ongoing change:

> Humanities computing is undergoing a redefinition of basic principles by a continuous influx of new, vibrant, and diverse communities of practitioners within and well beyond the halls of academe. These practitioners recognize the value computers add to their work, that the computer itself remains an instrument subject to continual innovation, and that competition within many disciplines requires scholars to become and remain current with what computers can do. (Siemens, 2005)

The book series announcement as a whole, however, maintains a focus on the computer as a tool and humanities computing methodologies. The epistemic commitment to technology as tool is also clearly evident from "[t]hese practitioners recognize the value computers add to their work."

Unsurprisingly, it is difficult, possibly irrelevant, to pinpoint the meaning of a term in change, but it is nevertheless relevant to look at how such terms are introduced and used by an academic community. It is obvious that the term *digital humanities*, as used by the humanities computing community, often serves as an overarching denotation in book and journal titles, etc., while *humanities computing* is often used in the actual narrative.

The territory of the term is being defined and negotiated by institutional entities such as the journal *Digital Humanities Quarterly*. The following text, which also suggests ongoing change, comes from the very first editorial of *DHQ* in the inaugural issue:

> Digital humanities is by its nature a hybrid domain, crossing disciplinary boundaries and also traditional barriers between theory and practice, technological implementation and scholarly reflection. But over time this field has developed its own orthodoxies, its internal lines of affiliation and collaboration that have become intellectual paths of least resistance. In a world – perhaps scarcely imagined two decades ago – where digital issues and questions are connected with nearly every area of endeavor, we cannot take for granted a position of centrality. On the contrary, we have to work hard even to remain aware of, let alone to master, the numerous relevant domains that might affect our work and ideas. And at the same time, we need to work hard to explain our work and ideas and to make them visible to those outside our community who may find them useful. (Flanders et al., 2007)

This is an inclusive and open definition which also suggests a particular community, associated history, changing boundaries and possibly some fence keeping (imposing a notion of centrality or non-centrality and through identifying "us" and "them"). Although no direct reference is made in the text, it is rather clear that the tradition implicitly referred to is humanities computing. The interest in dialogue indicated in the editorial is clearly important to the development of the whole field. Importantly, for a broad notion of digital humanities and a concerted effort, this dialogue must not only incorporate humanities computing as digital humanities and other varieties of digital humanities, but must also take place across a disciplinary landscape that additionally includes quite a number of initiatives and people that might not primarily classify what they do as *digital humanities*. Indeed, not even everyone associated with the enterprises being subsumed under the label digital humanities might be comfortable with that categorization.

In any case, the new name definitely suggests a broader scope and it is also used in wider circles as a collective name for activities and structures in between the Humanities and information technology.[13] And as we have seen in this analysis, there are many examples of humanities computing as digital humanities claiming a larger territory.

Humanities Computing as Digital Humanities

If humanities computing is to be taken as a more general digital humanities project it seems relevant to carefully consider the scope, implementation and ambition of the paradigm. Also, regardless of this perspective, there are certain characteristics of the paradigm that deserve critical attention and discussion. The four issues presented below touch on some of the disciplinary boundaries and epistemic culture of humanities computing and may possibly challenge some established perceptions of humanities computing. In any case, what follows is not so much a criticism of a paradigm as an exploration of boundaries and possibilities. It should also be added that the points discussed here have a bearing on digital humanities more generally.

First, humanities computing as a whole maintains a very instrumental approach to technology in the Humanities. In her introductory chapter in the volume *Digital Humanities*, Susan Hockey says that this is not the place to define humanities computing, and continues, "[s]uffice it to say

---

[13]   In her short reference to terms for the field (Terras, 2006) seems to regard these and other related terms as more or less equivalent. In this analysis the terms are not seen as synonymous. Rather they have certain traditions and values associated with them.

that we are concerned with the *applications* of computing to research and teaching within the subjects that are loosely defined as 'the humanities,' or in British English, 'the arts'" (Hockey, 2004, p. 3) (italics added). Hockey's description is indicative of a paradigm in which information technology is typically not seen as an object of study, an exploratory laboratory, an expressive medium or an activist venue. Rather, technology has this basic and epistemically grounded role as a tool and much of humanities computing is about using these tools, helping others to use them and, to some extent, developing new tools (and methodologies). Many of these tools, such as concordance programs, have a rather long and distinguished history, and there has not necessarily been a great deal of radical change over time (see McCarty, 1996). It could be argued that the focus of traditional humanities computing is not innovating new tools, but rather using and developing existing ones. Also a fair proportion of the development seems to occur on a structural or metadata level. Examples include text encoding and markup systems. Of course work on this level has fundamental implications for the development and use of tools.

Text encoding is typically seen as a core element of humanities computing. Koenraad de Smedt says that "Text encoding seems to create the foundation for almost any use of computers in the humanities" (de Smedt, 2002, p. 95).[14] Classifications such as the major Text Encoding Initiative (TEI) involve very basic theoretical and methodological challenges (McGann, 2006) and there have also been calls for the development of more innovative tools based on these and other schemas (Rockwell, 2003). Rockwell stresses the importance of moving beyond existing personal tools, making community and server based tools more available, allowing for playful exploration and encouraging critical discussion of tools. Clearly there is a need for such a development, and while there are some exemplary projects there is a need for further development, discussion of best practice and further critical analysis. For instance, it would be interesting to see more integration with web 2.0 thinking and platforms,[15] work in interaction and participatory design as well as methodologies such as rapid prototyping. An interesting current example of methodological innovation is Rockwell's and Sinclair's work on extreme text analysis.[16]

It might also be argued that traditional humanities computing has not primarily been concerned with interface and how things look and feel – the materiality of the tools. Kirschenbaum says that "the digital

---

[14]   Renear (2004) provides a useful overview and history of text encoding.

[15]   While web 2.0 is certainly a buzzword there is no doubt much interesting development in web-based collaborative and social software, handling of micro content, visualization and innovative interfaces. See Alexander (2006) for a useful overview.

[16]   http://tada.mcmaster.ca/Main/WhatIsExtremeTextAnalysis.

humanities have also not yet begun ... to initiate a serious conversation about its relationship to visual design, aesthetics, and, yes, even beauty" (Kirschenbaum, 2004, p. 532). McGann asserts that "[d]igital instruments are only as good as the interfaces by which we think through them" (McGann, 2006, pp. 156–7). There have also been calls for tools with more far-reaching and radical scope than the ones that humanities computing typically provides. Drucker and Nowviskie point out that "[w]e are not only able to use digital instruments to extend humanities research, but to reflect on the methods and premises that shape our approach to knowledge and our understanding of how interpretation is framed" (Drucker and Nowviskie, 2004, p. 432).

Second, it has often been pointed out that what brings humanities computing together is largely a common interest in methods, methodology, tools and technology. This partly follows from an instrumental orientation, of course, and there is no reason to question the methodological commons as a valuable interdisciplinary focus and productive collaborative sentiment. However, this strong methodological focus fundamentally affects the way humanities computing operates and relates to other disciplines. The most serious implication is that a predominantly methodological link to other disciplines may not integrate many of the specific issues that are at the core of these disciplines. It could be argued that this makes it more difficult for humanities computing to reach out more broadly to traditional humanities departments and scholars. While there will always be interest in methods and technology, the actual target group – humanities scholars with an active interest in humanities computing tools and perspectives – must be said to be relatively limited.[17] In an interesting and provocative paper, Juola (2008, p. 83) argues that the emerging discipline of "digital humanities" has been emerging for decades and that there is a perceived neglect on the part of the broader humanities community. While he is appreciative of the work done in humanities computing, he also finds that

> For the past forty years, humanities computing have more or less languished in the background of traditional scholarship. Scholars lack incentive to participate (or even to learn about) the results of humanities computing.

Looking at text analysis, Rockwell points out that "text-analysis tools and the practices of literary computer analysis have not had the anticipated impact on the research community" (Rockwell, 2003, p. 210). Juola's analysis shows that citation scores for humanities computing journals are very low and he also points out that the American Ivy League universities

---

[17] Conversely, the target group may be too large or knowledgeable when the methods or technologies are already in use.

are sparsely represented in humanities computing publications and at humanities computing conferences. It could be argued, however, that the lack of citations is partly due to the fact that humanities scholars who use humanities computing tools might not be inclined to cite the creators of these tools. This is especially true if no written work on associated methodology (or theories) has been employed in the research.

A relevant question, of course, is whether humanities computing wants and needs to reach out to the humanities disciplines.[18] This relates to the earlier discussion of autonomy and discipline or not. There seems, however, to be rather strong support for expanding the territory and for achieving a higher degree of penetration. Furthermore, if the methodology and tools are central to the enterprise it seems counter-intuitive to disassociate yourself from many of the potential users (and co-creators) of the tools. It is evident from his discussion of possible high-profile "killer applications" that Juola shares an interest in the development of a new or evolved kind of tools with Drucker and Nowviskie and others. It could be argued that it would be beneficial to have tools or applications that relate more directly to some of the central discipline-specific challenges of the various humanities disciplines. Such a development would probably lead to somewhat less focus on methodology, a tighter integration of humanities computing and humanities disciplines[19] and possibly more tools and applications with a rich, combined theoretical, experiential and empirical foundation.

Third, humanities computing has a very strong textual focus. Given the history and primary concerns of the field as well as the textual orientation of much of the humanities this is not very surprising. Traditional text is clearly a privileged level of description and analysis. In her analysis of humanities computing, which is partly corpus-based, Terras writes that "Humanities Computing research is predominantly about text" (Terras, 2006, p. 236). While this is true, there has certainly been an increased interest in multimedia and non-textual representation. This interest may, for instance, be manifested in the form of metadata schemes for visual material or, increasingly, the interest in using geographical information systems in humanities computing. Reference is sometimes made to different technologies and methods (3D-modeling, GIS, animation, virtual reality etc.) but these are not necessarily integrated in practice. For instance, Jessop says that "the research potential of working with digital tools for

---

[18]   Commenting on Juola's presentation at DH 2006 in Paris in an informal wiki entry, Geoffrey Rockwell writes, "Why do we have to get buy in from others? Do researchers in established fields feel they need to convert everyone else in the humanities? Do we really need legitimization from others?" (http://tada.mcmaster.ca/view/Main/Dh2006?skin=plain).

[19]   Terras says that "[t]he field may only flourish as an academic subject if it becomes less insular and interacts both with Computer Science and those Humanities scholars who are less willing to accept computing as part of their research tools" (Terras, 2006, p. 243).

handling spatial data has been explored in only very limited contexts"
(Jessop, 2007, p. 4). There are many exceptions and prolific scholars with
a strong commitment to these issues but this cannot be said to be true of
most of humanities computing. There is also a risk that other media are
handled much in the same way as text (e.g. another object type to encode)
or merely subservient to text following a very strong epistemic commitment
to text as object. Here follows a rather text-focused discussion of images in
relation to the history (and future) of humanities computing:

> There are of course many advantages in having access to images of source
> material over the Web, but humanities computing practitioners, having grown
> used to the flexibility offered by searchable text, again tended to regard imaging
> projects as not really their thing, unless, like the Beowulf Project (Kiernan,
> 1991), the images could be manipulated and enhanced in some way. Interesting
> research has been carried out on linking images to text, down to the level of
> the word (Zweig, 1998). When most of this can be done automatically we will
> be in a position to reconceptualize some aspects of manuscript studies. The
> potential of other forms of multimedia is now well recognized, but the use of
> this is only really feasible with high-speed access and the future may well lie in
> a gradual convergence with television. (Hockey, 2004, p. 15)

There is nothing wrong with a textual focus, of course, but it does have
effects on the scope and penetration of humanities computing. The so-
called "visual turn"[20] or research on multimodal representation does not
seem to have had a large impact on humanities computing. One reason is
probably because there is little interaction between these communities and
because it is difficult to conceptualize and develop tools for these kinds of
framework. More generally, there seems to be an increasing interest in non-
textual and mixed media in the Humanities and elsewhere (see for instance
research on remediation, trans- or crossmedia texts, digital art and the
current interest in "mashups"). And, needless to say, most native digital
media are not pure text while humanities computing through focusing on
text in its digitalized and encoded form could be said to privilege a rather
"pure" (if annotated and structured) form of text. It seems that there should
be considerable opportunities in this area for humanities computing – both
for innovative tools and thinking – but also in relation to making a strong
case for the need for considerable cyberinfrastructure in the Humanities.[21]
Furthermore, there is clearly a need for people with expert competence

---

20   Or, for that matter, a "post-visual" turn represented by, for instance, Sterne (2006)
and Witmore (2006).
21   While there seems to be interest in text mining and grid computing for textual analysis
in humanities computing it seems more likely that a broader range of data, visualization
and computing intensive applications will develop in relation to non-textual material (or a
combination of textual and non-textual material).

and interest in structuring, annotating and managing data. It is exciting to see that interest in non-textual representation and analysis seems to be growing in humanities computing. It seems worthwhile to support this development – at least if the vision is an expansive and inclusive humanities computing/digital humanities. Such a development would not have to preclude a retained textual focus, of course.

My fourth and final point relates to data and material used in humanities computing – or, put another way, the objects of study of humanities computing and associated disciplines. McCarty distinguishes between four data types in his discussion of a methodological commons: text, image, number and sound (McCarty 2005a, p. 136). It is characteristic of the model that the source materials and approaches of the disciplines are reduced to these four data types and a "finite (but not fixed) set of tools for manipulating them."[22] This touches on a tendency to subscribe to formal and science-driven models of knowledge production in humanities computing (where text is the principal object of study):

> Applications involving textual sources have taken center stage within the development of humanities computing as defined by its major publications and thus it is inevitable that this essay concentrates on this area. Nor is it the place here to attempt to define *interdisciplinarity*, but by its very nature, humanities computing has had to embrace "the two cultures," to bring the rigor and systematic unambiguous procedural methodologies characteristic of the sciences to address problems within the humanities that had hitherto been most often treated in a serendipitous fashion. (Hockey, 2004).

As we have already seen and as the above quote reinforces, text is a privileged data type in humanities computing. Furthermore it could be argued that humanities computing is mainly interested in digitalized texts (or in some cases, digitalized historical sites etc.) and not material that is natively digital. Born digital material would include computer games, blogs, virtual worlds, social spaces such as MySpace, email collections, websites, surveillance footage, machinima films and digital art. Most of these "objects" are studied and analyzed within different kinds of new media settings and to me this is an interesting in-between zone. Would humanities computing be interested in engaging more with new media scholars? There is certainly a need for well-crafted tools for studying online life and culture. Why does there not seem to be any software for doing comparative analysis and interpretation of computer games,

---

[22] McCarty also adds that these tools are derived from and their application governed by "formal methods". The formalistic aspects of humanities computing will not be discussed in any great detail here.

for instance?[23] How can machinima films be tagged and related to the cultural artefacts they reference? How do we systemize and contextualize email archives?[24] Can social software platforms be adapted to humanities computing needs? Can multimodal and multi-channel communication be tracked, tagged, interrelated and made searchable in any consistent way?

I find the intersection between humanities computing and new media studies intriguing. There is some new media-like work going on in humanities computing but it is relatively marginal and there are few tools available. A more complete and multifaceted engagement might stimulate more theoretical work in humanities computing. Rockwell makes a case for the importance of such an engagement:

> Digital theory should not be left to new media scholars, nor should we expect to get it right so that we can go back to encoding or other humanities disciplines. Theorizing, not a theory, is needed; we need to cultivate reflection, interruption, standing aside and thinking about the digital. We don't need to negotiate a canon or a grand theory, instead I wish for thinking about and through the digital in community. (Rockwell 2004).

Regardless of whether such an engagement involved theory or mainly methods and tools, it seems that there might be mutual gains. Not least would humanities computing be able to draw more on a growing interest in digital culture and the "technological texture" that Don Ihde postulates. A further possible result would be a more robust link to humanities disciplines through also working in a field where there are many current and important research challenges in relation to the digital (e.g. participatory culture, surveillance societies, gender and technology, and emerging art and text forms).[25]

The epistemic commitments of humanities computing are not limited to points discussed above; however these are particularly relevant for

---

[23]   To the best of my knowledge.

[24]   Rockwell and Lancashire do discuss preservation of electronic texts: "The future understanding of our past and understanding of this age of technological change will be incomplete if we do not take steps to preserve one of the most widely used forms of electronic information — the electronic text." (http://tapor.ualberta.ca/Resources/TAIntro).

[25]   The need for a stronger link to the disciplines has been articulated in several different contexts. In an interesting *Humanist* thread (Brennan, 1992; Rabkin and Guthrie, 1992) from 1992, Mark Olsen says (rather provocatively) that "Humanities computing is a hobby largely because there has been a consistent failure among the practitioners of humanities computing to rock the boat; to produce results of sufficient interest, rigor and appeal to attract a following among scholars who "do not" make extensive use of computers." While "rocking the boat" should not be a goal in itself it is true that the kind of development indicated here would probably bring about more discipline-specific and humanities-external interest.

the discussion of humanities computing as digital humanities. A broadly conceived digital humanities would necessarily include the instrumental, methodological, textual and digitalized, but also new study objects, multiple modes of engagement, theoretical issues from the humanities disciplines, the non-textual and the born digital.

Multiple Identities and Risk Taking

Let us briefly contrast humanities computing with a rather different kind of institutional setting and epistemic tradition. Anne Balsamo (2000) writes about the Georgia Institute of Technology in the article "Engineering Cultural Studies: The postdisciplinary adventures of mindplayers, fools, and others". More specifically she relates the story, tensions and context of the program in science, technology, and culture offered in the School of Literature, Communication and Culture (LCC) at Georgia Tech. Partly this is done through the work of cyberpunk science fiction writer Pat Cadigan.

LCC used to be an English Department and was transformed in 1990. Balsamo discusses the different identities that faculty wear and the complex interrelations associated with being a humanities representative at a predominantly technical school. For instance, the institutional position requires LCC faculty to be committed to traditional humanities values, in order not to give engineering schools arguments for reducing or doing away with the humanities requirement. The lack of a stable identity is the result of different roles and an interdisciplinary setting, and it resonates with the lack of stable identity that seems to be such an integral part of humanities computing. The interdisciplinary meetings and setting are important to both enterprises, but they are not without risk:

> Forging these new alliances – with technologists, scientists, and medical educators – offers the possibility of staking a claim on a territory that has been previously off-limits to the nonscientist cultural theorists. As with other political struggles, the project of alliance building is not without its risks and dangers. (Balsamo, 2000, p. 268)

Another similarity is instrumentalistic expectations from the "outside". In the case of an institution such as LCC there are expectations of delivering "high culture" and, presumably, useful knowledge, to engineering students. At the same time there are basic values and critical perspectives that need to be expressed:

> As a feminist scholar, I certainly don't want to abandon the epistemological critique of the construction of scientific knowledge as patriarchal knowledge.

Nor do I want to give up on the pursuit of social justice through scientific and technological means. This becomes another occasion for the practice of identity-switching – this time not simply between the humanist and the critic, but between the teacher and the advocate. Whereas the teacher demands the students engage the philosophical critique of an epistemological worldview and construct their own assessment of the value-laden nature of a particular scientific worldview, the advocate continues to guide them towards careers in science and technology and encourage them to find a way to make a difference. (Balsamo, 2000, p. 271)

Both Balsamo's engaging narrative and the narratives of humanities computing speak about being in between, having multiple identities, lacking a stable identity, and engaging richly but not unproblematically with other disciplines within and without the local setting. There is energy, risk taking and wanting to make a difference in such narratives.

Georgia Tech and traditional humanities computing clearly represent very different approaches to digital humanities. For example, while Balsamo sees information technology as a cultural object in need of exploration and epistemological critique, traditional humanities computing treats technology in a more formal and instrumental way. In the next article in this series, an attempt to lay out a more detailed and comprehensive map of the digital humanities will be made. A number of diverse initiatives and approaches are used as examples, and different modes of engagement with the "digital" are discussed at more length. The story of the digital humanities continues to be complex in terms of the theoretical, practice-based, historical, technical and disciplinary foundations and a fast-changing landscape. It is exactly these qualities that make digital humanities an exciting field to study, and a place full of energy and multiple identities.

Acknowledgements

I draw on interaction with a great many helpful and inspiring scholars, managers, artists, developers and others. I would like to thank Matthew Ratto for his careful reading of drafts and his suggestions and Stephanie Hendrick for her comments and language suggestions. In addition, I have greatly benefited from discussions with Geoffrey Rockwell, Willard McCarty, David Theo Goldberg, Lisa Parks, Katherine Hayles, Christopher Witmore, Erica Robles, Michael Shanks, Jeffrey Schnapp, Anne Balsamo, Tara McPherson and many others.

Works Cited

Aarseth, E. (1997). "The Field of Humanistic Informatics and its Relation to the Humanities," *Human IT*, 4 (97), http://www.hb.se/bhs/ith/4-97/ea.htm.

Alexander, B. (2006). "Web 2.0: A New Wave of Innovation for Teaching and Learning?" *Educause Review*, March/April 2006, http://www.educause.edu/ir/library/pdf/erm0621.pdf.

Balsamo, A. (2000). "Engineering Cultural Studies: The postdisciplinary adventures of mindplayers, fools, and others", in R. Reid and S. Traweek (eds), *Doing Science + Culture*, New York: Routledge, pp. 259–74.

Brennan, E. (1992). "Humanities Computing: Merely a Hobby?" *Humanist*, 17 November, http://www.digitalhumanities.org/humanist/archives/virginia/v06/0358.html.

Burnard, L. (2002). "Humanities Computing in Oxford: A Retrospective", *Humanities Computing*, http://users.ox.ac.uk/~lou/wip/hcu-obit.txt.

Busa, R. (2004). "Foreword", in Schreibman et al. (eds), *A Companion to Digital Humanities*, pp. xvi–xxi.

de Smedt, K. (2002). "Some Reflections on Studies in Humanities Computing", *Journal of Linguistic and Literary Computing*, 17, pp. 89–101.

Drucker, J. and Nowviskie, B. (2004). "Speculative Computing: Aesthetic Provocations in Humanities Computing", in Schreibman et al. (eds), *A Companion to Digital Humanities*, pp. 431–47.

Flanders, J. and Unsworth, J. (2002). "The Evolution of Humanities Computing Centers," *Computers and the Humanities*, 36, pp. 379–80.

Flanders, J., Piez, W. and Terras, M. (2007). 'Welcome to Digital Humanities Quarterly', *Digital Humanities Quarterly*, 1 (1).

Hockey, S. (2004). "History of Humanities Computing", in Schreibman et al. (eds), *A Companion to Digital Humanities*, pp. 1–19.

Jessop, M. (2007). "The Inhibition of Geographical Information in Digital Humanities Scholarship", *Literary and Linguistic Computing*, 20 November.

Juola, P. (2008). "Killer Applications in Digital Humanities", *Literary and Linguistic Computing*, 23 (1), pp. 73–83.

Kiernan, K.S. (1991). "Digital Image Processing and the Beowulf Manuscript", *Literary and Linguistic Computing*, 6, pp. 20–7.

Kirschenbaum, M. (2004). "Interface, Aesthetics, and Usability", in Schreibman et al. (eds), *A Companion to Digital Humanities*, pp. 523–42.

Klein, J.T. (1996). *Crossing Boundaries: Knowledge, Disciplinarities, and Interdisciplinarities*, Charlottesville, VA: University of Virginia Press.

Knorr Cetina, K. (1999). *Epistemic Cultures: How the Sciences Make Knowledge*, Cambridge, MA: Harvard University Press.

Literary and Linguistic Computing, Oxford Journals, 23 (2), June 2008, http://llc.oxfordjournals.org/content/vol23/issue2/index.dtl.

Literary and Linguistic Computing, Oxford Journals, 23 (3), September 2008, http://llc.oxfordjournals.org/content/vol23/issue3/index.dtl.

Literary and Linguistic Computing, Oxford Journals, 23 (4), December 2008, http://llc.oxfordjournals.org/content/vol23/issue4/index.dtl.

Literary and Linguistic Computing, Oxford Journals, 24 (1), April 2009, http://llc.oxfordjournals.org/content/vol24/issue1/index.dtl.

McCarty, W. (1996). "Introduction to Concording and Text-analysis: History, Theory, and Methodology", in S. Hockey and W. McCarty (eds), CETH Summer Seminar, Princeton, NJ: CETH, Section 5.

McCarty, W. (2004). "Happy 17th Birthday", *Humanist*, 10 May, http://www.digitalhumanities.org/humanist/archives/virginia/v18/0000.html.

McCarty, W. (2005a). *Humanities Computing*, New York: Palgrave.

McCarty, W. (2005b). "Computers and the Humanities 1966–2004", *Humanist*, 5 March, http://www.digitalhumanities.org/humanist/archives/virginia/v18/0604.html.

McCarty, W. (2007). "Happy & merry solstitial greetings!", *Humanist*, 21 December, http://www.digitalhumanities.org/humanist/archives/virginia/v21/0434.html

McCarty, W. and Kirschenbaum, M. (2003). "Institutional Models for Humanities Computing", http://www.allc.org/imhc.

McCarty, W., Lutz, C. and Chernyk, M. (2008). "More events: Digital Humanities Summer Institute," *Humanist*, 10 January, http://www.digitalhumanities.org/humanist/archives/virginia/v21/0467.html.

McGann, J. (2001). *Radiant Textuality: Literature After the World Wide Web*, New York: Palgrave Macmillan.

McGann, J. (2004). "Marking Texts of Many Dimensions", in Schreibman et al. (eds), *A Companion to Digital Humanities*, pp. 198–217.

McGann, J. (2006). *The Scholar's Art: Literary Studies in a Managed World*, Chicago: Chicago University Press.

Rabkin, E. and Guthrie, J. (1992). "Newspapers Online", *Humanist*, 17 November, http://www.digitalhumanities.org/humanist/archives/virginia/v06/0363.html.

Ratto, M. (2006). "Epistemic Commitments and Archaeological Representation", in L. Oosterbeek and J. Raposo (eds), *XV Congrès de l'Union Internationale des Sciences Préhistoriques et Protohistoriques. Livre des Résumés*, vol. 1, p. 60, http://www.uispp.ipt.pt/uisppprogfin/livro2.pdf.

Renear, A.H. (2004). "Text Encoding", in Schreibman et al. (eds), *A Companion to Digital Humanities*, pp. 218–39.

Rockwell, G. (2002). "Multimedia, Is It a Discipline? The liberal and servile arts in humanities computing", *Jahrbuch für Computerphilologie*, 4. Paderborn: Mentis Verlag, http://computerphilologie.tu-darmstadt.de/jg02/rockwell.html.

Rockwell, G. (2003). "What Is Text Analysis, Really?" *Literary and Linguistic Computing*, 18 (2).

Rockwell, G. (2004). "Humanities Computing Challenges", Blog entry, 31 August, http://www.philosophi.ca/theoreti/?p=544.

Schreibman, S., Siemens, R. and Unsworth, J. (eds) (2004). *A Companion to Digital Humanities*, Malden, MA: Blackwell.

Siemens, R. (2005). "New book series in humanities computing", *Humanist*, 26 May, http://www.digitalhumanities.org/humanist/archives/virginia/v19/0053.html.

Sterne, J. (2006). "The Historiography of Cyberculture", in D. Silver and A. Massanari (eds), *Critical Cyberculture Studies*, New York: New York University Press.

Svensson, P. and McCarty, W. (2003). "History in Terms", *Humanist*, 21 June, http://www.digitalhumanities.org/humanist/archives/virginia/v17/0107.html.

Terras, M. (2006). "Disciplined: Using Educational Studies to Analyse 'Humanities Computing'", *Literary and Linguistic Computing*, 21 (2).

Witmore, C. (2006). "Vision, Media, Noise, and the Percolation of Time", *Journal of Material Culture*, 11 (3), pp. 267–92.

Zweig, R.W. (1998). "Lessons from the Palestine Post Project", *Literary and Linguistic Computing*, 13, pp. 89–97.

CHAPTER 8

Something Called Digital Humanities

Wendell Piez
University of Illinois

Wendell Piez (2008). Originally published in *Digital Humanities Quarterly*,
2 (1), http://digitalhumanities.org/dhq/vol/2/1/000020/000020.html.

Note from the Editors:
Piez's editorial in an early issue of *Digital Humanities Quarterly* reflects on his
unfolding reaction to an English professor's dismissive reference to 'something
called "digital humanities"'. Digital Humanities is not a mere trend, he argues
– it is the Humanities in the digital age. Indeed, such an interpretation of DH
has the potential to be just as dismissive as that which prompted the article.
Yet, when Piez argues that this entails studying 'digital media and the cultures
and cultural impacts of digital media; ... [and] designing and making them'
and highlights the parallels with the Renaissance that such activities evoke
we are reminded that there is little that is 'mere' about the humanities in the
digital age.

Sometimes I find myself procrastinating by surfing the web. I like to think
this is worthwhile. It's a way of clearing mental space and collecting
energy for work to be done, while looking out and enlarging my world.
Reading short articles and essays works best. It needs to be something I
mainly agree with, but not entirely. There should at least be some insight
or perspective that complicates and challenges my own to a degree, which
I can integrate with some reward and satisfaction. Finding it unnerving to
have my prejudices simply confirmed, at such moments I want to change
my mind to whatever extent it can be changed without being troubled,
which is to say, slightly.

For these purposes, the online edition of *The Nation* is just the thing.
And so one day I found myself reading a lament about the present and
future of academic English departments. William Deresiewicz's 'Professing
Literature in 2008'[1] is ostensibly a review of a new reissue of Gerald
Graff's *Professing Literature*. As such, I found it to be trenchant enough,

---

[1] http://www.thenation.com/issue/march-24-2008.

if not about its subject (which it merely glances at, and I have never read) then about its world (which preoccupies it, and with which, at one time, I was very familiar). It stood out in my mind for two things. There was a tidy analogy: by the author's account, the curricula now offered in English departments are fragmented by fashion and identity politics to such an extent as to reflect nothing so much as efforts, ingenuous or not, to win students by flattery. "If grade schools behaved like this, every subject would be recess, and lunch would consist of chocolate cake." And by way of depicting the symptoms of the problem, there is an interesting summary of how this fragmentation manifests itself in the want ads posted by departments in the annual MLA Job Information List. "Contemporary lit, global lit, ethnic American lit; creative writing, film, eco-criticism – whatever. There are postings here for positions in science fiction, in fantasy literature, in children's literature, even in something called 'digital humanities'."

This got my attention. Fair enough, I thought, I can take it. Unless the analysis is completely wrong and wrong-headed, I can allow that "Digital Humanities" (the name "Humanities Computing" no longer serves in an era when the computer club has become an in-group: the rule of identity politics seems to be that for one's old identity to become fashionable, you need a new name for it) could well be seen by an outsider as yet another canapé served up at the humanistic buffet. Yes, as long as things are being compared to food, Digital Humanities may indeed be the smoked salmon, sour cream, capers and dill of the English Department smorgasbord. I imagine one might well feel jaded by this, especially when it is served from a table at which one has already had more than one's fill in any case. So I found myself sympathetic. And thus Prof Deresiewicz had met the need: he had made me think, but not too hard, and he'd put me in my place about this thing called Digital Humanities. Procrastination had been accomplished, I had been stimulated, and I could turn my attention back to the task at hand.

But as I discovered a couple of days later, something still rankled. And it wasn't the casual put-down of my own discipline, such as it is. I'm fortunate enough to be making a happy living at it outside the academy, so what it is called and whether it is academically respectable are secondary concerns to me. Rather, it was the dismissal of all these fragmentary disciplines and sub-disciplines, not only the computer club. I had the sense that however amused I was by his polemic, my new friend Deresiewicz had missed the point. He characterizes this motley chaos as entropy on the way to death. (We are invited, in an essay that disparages those who would pay attention to their wishes and tastes, to make much of the fact that the number of students opting for an English major is declining.) But from a greater distance, I see something more like a field where native plants and wildflowers are overtaking a tidy lawn. I prefer to imagine that the efforts of departments to broaden their offerings may reflect more than just a rear-guard attempt to market to naïve and self-interested undergraduates but, rather more nobly, an effort to cultivate the most committed and imaginative of younger faculty, while also redressing some very old imbalances, and thus to lead, however clumsily, this most esoteric, inexplicable and vital discipline back to relevance and connection. For all the incomprehensible mix of offerings in media consciousness and post-colonial sensibility and historiographical critique and cultural studiousness, it seems to me they all share a kind of genetic code. Maybe all the work of close reading, of abstracting away from context to study the form itself, and then bringing the all-important context of the reading back to the reading, is actually beginning to work itself into seeing the world at large. If so, this reasoning goes, it isn't simply an arid intellectual exercise: maybe the old-fashioned humanists were right when they claimed that these methods and habits of mind, the practiced powers of an encouraging, engaged but critical and self-critical sensibility, are the only way we have to loosen the truly hard, knotted problems, the ones that are complicated by interests and wet with sticky emotion and identification and self-concern. Keep the faith, I wanted to answer: a time when the humanities seem not only to be forgotten, but to be forgetting themselves, is exactly the time when all of us, from bleeding-heart animal liberationists, to neo-Marxists offended by concentrations of capital, to addled Queer Theorists, to cool and collected, technology-competent Digital Humanists with our grand visions and enthusiasms for acronyms, should be enrolling in one another's courses – or at the very least, reading each other's blogs sympathetically while procrastinating – with the deliberate purpose of reminding ourselves what we have in common.

So I returned to the topic, at least in mind. But I had lost the link. It hadn't been important enough to bookmark, and who could remember where it was from? There was this essay to which I wanted to respond, maybe even write about, somewhere out on the Internet, but nowhere in sight. Fortunately, we have search engines to help with this sort of thing, and in only a few seconds spent between things I should have been doing instead, I had not only the original article, but much more.

So let me pass to a couple of the more incisive responses I came upon (at Margaret Soltan's blog,[2] as returned from a search for "something called digital humanities" in March of 2008):

Back in grad school in history (one of the Ivies), a friend made what struck me as a cogent observation. At this high-end university, where students could be

---

[2] http://www.margaretsoltan.com.

> sure of a comfortable income regardless of undergrad concentration, history was the most popular major, far ahead of English. His explanation was that students who wanted a real sense of the development and dynamics of their own civilization could no longer get that from the English department. It was still possible in history. (Dave Stone3)

This struck home because it was one of the reasons I turned to study English, enrolling in a PhD program after I'd finished an undergraduate degree in Classics (Ancient Greek) at one of these same high-end universities. I don't think the explanation captures the whole of it (more on this below), but it does resonate. Certainly, in my own case, the attraction of the humanities was in their promise of some such sense of something called "Western civilization". Nor was the promise empty. Yet the main difference between my own case and that of my classmates who studied history and then went on to master law or finance is also telling. Ten years was hardly enough to teach me that four years of anything so substantial is nothing more than the barest beginning of it.

Now this does not at all either contradict the thesis, or mitigate the concern expressed in Deresiewicz's review. But it does get closer to the heart of it. Given that four years is all that most students will or can choose to take, and that they are not just teenagers but also free adults, what is the best a university can offer them, and especially those who are lucky or bold enough to approach their schooling with a long view? Maybe, something that touches them, something they find meaningful, and that has enough of the real stuff in it that they can take a taste with them for intellectual engagement, for the satisfaction and usefulness of recognizing the macrocosm in the microcosm. An understanding of why you look close up, and also why you step back and look from a distance. And perhaps most importantly, a willingness to have casual assumptions broken down before they are built up again, with care and deliberation. As an exile from the academy, I can vouch for how inestimably valuable such a cast of mind turns out to be even in less high-brow (though no less cerebral) pursuits than academic scholarship.

Or, as another of my virtual interlocutors has it,

> Let's take "the digital humanities". In even the most traditional conception of an English Department, the development of print literature in successive forms was an absolutely core subject. That's what you studied if you studied Beowulf or Chaucer. It's what you studied if you studied Shakespeare. It's what you studied if you studied Richardson and Fielding. It's what you studied if you studied Dickens. It's what you studied if you studied Joyce. You read closely, did the close work of interpretation, but you also looked at the history of

---

3   http://www.margaretsoltan.com/?p=3682#comment-1484.

the book, of publication, of annotation, of circulation. This is not a fancy new trendy concern. How could you read Beowulf in an English course and not ask about the connection between oral literature and writing? Shakespeare and the connection between Elizabethan theater and writing? Fielding and the development of the novel as a popular form? Dickens and serialization? (Timothy Burke[4])

This takes us much further, quite close to the essence of it. By implication, in Burke's telling, the proper object of Digital Humanities is what one might call "media consciousness" in a digital age, a particular kind of critical attitude analogous to, and indeed continuous with, a more general media consciousness as applied to cultural production in any nation or period. Such an awareness will begin in a study of linguistic and rhetorical forms, but it does not stop there. Yet even this is only half of it. Inasmuch as critique may imply refiguration and reinvention, Digital Humanities has also a reciprocal and complementary project. Not only do we study digital media and the cultures and cultural impacts of digital media; also we are concerned with designing and making them. In this respect (and notwithstanding how many of its initiatives may prove short-lived), Digital Humanities resembles nothing so much as the *humanistic* movement that instigated the European Renaissance, which was concerned not only with the revival of Classical scholarship in its time but also with the development and application of high technology to learning and its dissemination. Scholar-technologists such as Nicolas Jenson and Aldus Manutius designed type faces and scholarly apparatus, founded publishing houses and invented the modern critical edition. In doing so they pioneered the forms of knowledge that academics work within to this day, despite the repeatedly promised revolutions of audio recording, radio, cinema and television. Only now are these foundations being examined again, as digital media begin to offer something like the same intimacy and connection that paper, ink and print media have offered between the peculiar and individual scholar, our subjects of study, and the wider community – an intimacy and connection (this cannot be overstressed) founded in the individual scholar's role as a creator and producer of media, not just a consumer. And yet, when we look at their substance, how digital media are *encoded* (being symbolic constructs arranged to work within algorithmic, machine-mediated processes that are themselves a form of cultural production) and how they encode culture in words, colors, sounds, images, and instrumentation, it is also evident that far from having no more need for literacy, they demand it, fulfill it, extend and raise it to ever higher levels.

---

[4] http://weblogs.swarthmore.edu/burke.

But this will be challenging, even upsetting. And so, a view that sees the proliferation of curricula in academic English departments as a catering to the marketplace, or even a sign of decline, is understandable if those who hold such a view are looking out for their own specialties or interests. Within the academic setting, the zero-sum competition over scarce resources like faculty lines, fellowships, students, publication opportunities, awards and recognition must tend to suggest that any broadening of attention must mean a diffusion; thus, the old order, which had thought things were settled well enough, finds itself embattled. Yet these sub-disciplines, both individually and collectively, can now be flourishing only if they can all draw strength from broader and deeper bases than before. There are more publication venues, more channels for access, more ways of reaching audiences and hearing from them, more opportunities for engagement, dialogue and learning than are offered even in the classroom, lecture or dining hall (medieval institutions) or by monograph or journal article (since the age of print) or conference paper (since the age of mobility). Many of these opportunities, especially opportunities for the creation and maintenance of geographically dispersed communities of interest, are created by networked digital media: mailing lists, blogs, wikis, online publishing projects, digests, courseware, shareware, groupware. But that is not the primary point here. Rather, it is that this great variety could never arise from a zero-sum game, but must reflect positive-sum outcomes among and between participants in communities of knowledge that reach far beyond individual departments. And further, this wider economy of knowledge, curiosity and concern offers fantastic opportunities for more such outcomes, if only supposed rivals or antagonists can find common cause in mutual interest. No, faculty lines are not created out of nothing. Yet neither has intellectual wealth ever been created simply by the blind operation of faculty doing their jobs. It is generated in the combustion of passion and community under the compressive force of discipline. And a department that finds a way, while remaining a community, to include in its offerings a range that reflects the breadth as well as depth of interests of students, fellows and faculty, may discover that all its engagements are strengthened. Within this context, "something called digital humanities" – something so obscure and esoteric that it is almost beneath an English professor's notice – may be more than just another subspecialty (although it is that, for the same reason that not all English professors will be experts in print technology): it also works directly at the ground where this new, larger, more elaborate, more entangled and variegated culture is rooted.

Which brings me back to the intuition that all these avenues, whether area or period studies, genre studies (including science fiction, fantasy, children's literature, romance, the graphic novel or what have you), concentrations of concern such as eco-criticism, political or socio-historical or epistemological critiques, or simply diversions as obscure as they are compelling, as when students and faculty become caught up in the creative possibilities of the new media, nevertheless share something vital, which belies the notion that they must induce an irremediable fragmentation. Indeed, when they are pursued conscientiously, I think what they share is what the humanities have always shared. That may not, it is true, always be what the critics warn the new specialties will deny us, a "shared culture"; but then it is something better. The study of the humanities has always offered two things. Or rather, it has offered one thing and then, like a con artist or a fairy-tale trickster, been ready to switch it under your nose for something you didn't think you wanted, but which turns out to be far more valuable than what you had thought you had put down money for. When you signed up, you had thought you were to be awarded a validating and affirming narrative, some account of origins that would banish your doubts and prove your boundless worth. (Maybe it's for this that the ambitious but complacent scions of the well-to-do turn to major in History, if the English Department no longer offers them a satisfying foundation myth.) But if you are lucky, you are initiated instead into a world view that is not only critical, but tolerant of criticism and therefore capable of vitality, creativity and growth. The self-knowledge you are offered does not raise you and your tribe above humanity, but implicates you in it. Seen in this light, 'Digital Humanities' does not need to be a catchphrase or a cause, unless the cause is the humanities themselves in a digital age.

Note from the author:
This piece, written in 2008, certainly speaks of its moment in one way: the term "digital humanities" is no longer quite so sparkly-shiny as it was then. It now seems just a bit strange (four short years later) to start by asking whether "DH" isn't just another label for just another fashion. (The answer, much more obviously than it then was, is both "yes" and "no".) Yet in other ways the battle lines have not moved at all, and the deeper questions here are still very much at issue. Is this a zero-sum game? Can the digital humanities do well only at the expense of other priorities, including the good old-fashioned study of literature and culture? I've never believed this and I don't think most practitioners of DH do.

The article to which this piece replies locates the digital humanities (in a back-handed way) within the culture wars, as yet another rival claimant to the loyalty of students. This may, indeed, not be all wrong, and yet it remains necessary to rethink the premises of the question. Don't digital technologies also have the potential to reshape the battleground itself?

Wendell Piez, November 2012

CHAPTER 9

What Is Digital Humanities and What's It Doing in English Departments?

Matthew G. Kirschenbaum
University of Maryland

Matthew G. Kirschenbaum (2010). Originally published in *ADE Bulletin*, 150, pp. 55–61.

Note from the Editors:
Such is the multiplicity of 'what is DH' articles that have been published, muses Kirschenbaum, that such essays have already become genre pieces. Here he considers, from a number of perspectives, what DH is and why it is especially prominent in English departments. Beginning with DH's organisations and conferences he then looks at its subject matter and methodological outlook while observing that it can also be categorised as 'a social undertaking'. He also reviews a number of significant developments, which, from our current vantage point, we can identify as having been pivotal in the path towards the subject becoming more mainstream. These include the shift in nomenclature from Humanities Computing to Digital Humanities; major publications such as Blackwell's *Companion to Digital Humanities*; and the founding of the NEH Office of Digital Humanities, among other things. When reading this article it is fascinating to reflect on Rockwell's (1999) article in this volume (Chapter 1) and his frustration with the term Humanities Computing. Is Digital Humanities necessarily a more effective and communicative term? To what extent might this renaming of the discipline have contributed to its development and increasing institutionalisation over the past years? And is the term Digital Humanities here to stay?

People who say that the last battles of the computer revolution in English departments have been fought and won don't know what they're talking about. If our current use of computers in English studies is marked by any common theme at all, it is experimentation at the most basic level. As a profession, we are just learning how to live with computers, just beginning to integrate these machines effectively into writing- and reading-intensive courses, just starting to consider the implications of the multilayered literacy associated with computers.

(Cynthia Selfe, 1988)

What is (or are) the "digital humanities," aka "humanities computing"? It's tempting to say that whoever asks the question has not gone looking very hard for an answer. "What is digital humanities?" essays like this one are already genre pieces. Willard McCarty has been contributing papers on the subject for years (a monograph too). Under the earlier appellation, John Unsworth has advised us "what is humanities computing and what is not." Most recently Patrik Svensson has been publishing a series of well-documented articles on multiple aspects of the topic, including the lexical shift from humanities computing to digital humanities. Moreover, as Cynthia Selfe in an *ADE Bulletin* from 1988 reminds us, computers have been part of our disciplinary lives for well over two decades now. During this time digital humanities has accumulated a robust professional apparatus that is probably more rooted in English than any other departmental home.

The contours of this professional apparatus are easily discoverable. An organization called the Alliance of Digital Humanities Organizations hosts a well-attended annual international conference called Digital Humanities (it grew out of an earlier annual series of conferences, hosted jointly by the Association for Computers and the Humanities and the Association for Literary and Linguistic Computing since 1989). There is Blackwell's *Companion to Digital Humanities*. There is a book series (yes, a book series), topics in the Digital Humanities, from the University of Illinois Press. There is a refereed journal called *Digital Humanities Quarterly*, one of several that serve the field, including a newer publication, *Digital Studies/Le champ numérique*, sponsored by the Canadian Society for Digital Humanities (Société pour l'Étude des Médias Interactifs). The University of Victoria hosts the annual Digital Humanities Summer Institute to train new scholars. Crucially, there are digital humanities centers and institutes (probably at least one hundred worldwide, some of them established for a decade or more with staff numbering in the dozens): these are served by an organization known as CenterNet. There have been digital humanities manifestos (I know of at least two) and FAQs, colloquia and symposia, workshops and special sessions. Not to mention, of course, that a gloss or explanation of digital humanities is implicit in every mission statement, every call for papers and proposals, every strategic plan and curriculum-development document, every hiring request and so forth that invokes the term. Or the countless times the question has been visited on electronic discussion lists, blogs, *Facebook* walls, and *Twitter* feeds, contributing all the flames and exhortations, celebrations and screeds one could wish to read.

We could also, of course, simply Google the question. *Google* takes us to *Wikipedia*, and what we find there is not bad:

> The digital humanities, also known as humanities computing, is a field of study, research, teaching, and invention concerned with the intersection of computing and the disciplines of the humanities. It is methodological by nature and interdisciplinary in scope. It involves investigation, analysis, synthesis and presentation of information in electronic form. It studies how these media affect the disciplines in which they are used, and what these disciplines have to contribute to our knowledge of computing.

As a working definition this serves as well as any I've seen, which is not surprising since a glance at the page's View history tab reveals individuals closely associated with the digital humanities as contributors. At its core, then, digital humanities is more akin to a common methodological outlook than an investment in any one specific set of texts or even technologies. We could attempt to refine this "outlook" quantitatively, using some of the very tools and techniques digital humanities has pioneered. For example, we might use a text-analysis tool named Voyeur developed by Stéfan Sinclair to mine the proceedings from the annual Digital Humanities conference and develop lists of topic frequencies or collocate key terms or visualize the papers' citation networks. We could also choose to explore the question qualitatively, by examining sets of projects from self-identified digital humanities centers. At the University of Maryland, where I serve as an associate director at the Maryland Institute for Technology in the Humanities, we support work from "Shakespeare to Second Life" as we're fond of saying: the Shakespeare Quartos archive, funded by a joint grant program administered by the United Kingdom's JISC and the NEH, makes a searchable digital facsimile of each of the thirty-two extant quarto copies of *Hamlet* available online, while the Preserving Virtual Worlds project, supported by the Library of Congress, has developed and tested standards and best practices for archiving and ensuring future access to computer games, interactive fiction, and virtual communities.

Yet digital humanities is also a social undertaking. It harbors networks of people who have been working together, sharing research, arguing, competing, and collaborating for many years. Key achievements from this community, like the Text Encoding Initiative or the Orlando Project, were mostly finished before the current wave of interest in digital humanities began. Nonetheless, the rapid and remarkable rise of *digital humanities* as a term can be traced to a set of surprisingly specific circumstances. Unsworth, who was the founding director of the Institute for Advanced Technology in the Humanities at the University of Virginia for a decade and is currently Dean of the Graduate School of Library and Information Science at the University of Illinois, has this to relate:

> The real origin of that term [digital humanities] was in conversation with Andrew McNeillie, the original acquiring editor for the Blackwell *Companion to Digital Humanities*. We started talking with him about that book project in 2001, in April, and by the end of November we'd lined up contributors and were discussing the title, for the contract. Ray [Siemens] wanted "a Companion to Humanities Computing" as that was the term commonly used at that point; the editorial and marketing folks at Blackwell wanted "Companion to Digitized Humanities." I suggested "Companion to Digital Humanities" to shift the emphasis away from simple digitization. (Unsworth, 2010)

At about the same time the Blackwell's volume was being put together, the leadership of two scholarly organizations opened discussions about creating an umbrella entity for themselves and eventually other organizations and associations with like interests. As anyone who has ever tried to run a scholarly organization will know, economies of scale are difficult to come by with only a few hundred members and so the thought was to consolidate and share infrastructure and services. The two organizations were the aforementioned Association for Computers in the Humanities and the Association for Literary and Linguistic Computing. The umbrella structure that resulted was called ADHO, or the Alliance of Digital Humanities Organizations. Here is Unsworth again, from the same communication:

> Conversations about merging ACH and ALLC began at Tuebingen, in a bar, in a conversation between Harold Short and me, in July 2002. A couple of months later, I had set a list called "adhoc"—allied digital humanities organizations committee), first message dated August 16, 2002 ... We finally got things off the dime in Sweden, at the 2004 ALLC/ACH, and after waffling some more about names (ICHIO, OHCO, and others) we voted, in April of 2005, to go with ADHO, changing "A" from "Allied" to "Alliance."

By 2005, then, the Blackwell's *Companion* had been published and the Alliance for Digital Humanities Organizations had been established. There's one more key event to relate, and that's the launch, in 2006, of the Digital Humanities Initiative by the NEH, then under the chairmanship of Bruce Cole and with leadership provided by Brett Bobley, a charismatic and imaginative individual who doubles as the agency's CIO. In an e-mail to me, Bobley describes a January 2006 lunch with another NEH staffer at which they were brainstorming ideas for what would become the Digital Humanities Initiative:

At the lunch, I jotted down a bunch of names, including humanities computing, ehumanities, and digital humanities. When I got back to the office, I Googled all three of them and "digital humanities" seemed to be the winner. I liked it for a few reasons: due to ADHO and their annual Digital Humanities conference, the name brought up a lot of relevant hits. I believe I'd also heard from Julia Flanders about the forthcoming *Digital Humanities Quarterly* journal. I also appreciated the fact that it seemed to cast a wider net than "humanities computing" which seemed to imply a form of computing, whereas "digital humanities" implied a form of humanism. I also thought it would be an easier sell to the humanities community to have the emphasis on "humanities." (Bobley, 2010)

In 2008 the Digital Humanities Initiative became the Office of Digital Humanities, the designation of "office" assigning the program (and its budget line) a permanent place within the agency. That *the* major federal granting agency for scholarship in the humanities, taking its cues directly from a small but active and influential group of scholars, had devoted scarce resources to launching a number of new grant opportunities, many of them programmatically innovative in and of themselves, around an endeavor termed "digital humanities" was doubtless the tipping point for the branding of DH, at least in the United States.

These events will, I think, earn a place in histories of the profession alongside other major critical movements like the Birmingham school or Yale deconstruction. In the space of a little more than five years digital humanities had gone from being a term of convenience used by a group of researchers who had already been working together for years to something like a movement. Individual scholars routinely now self-identify as digital humanists, or "DHers." There is an unusually strong sense of community and common purpose, manifested, for example, in events such as the Day of Digital Humanities, organized by a team at the University of Alberta. Its second annual iteration featured over 150 participants (up from around one hundred the first year), who blogged on a shared site about the details of their workday, posted photographs of their offices and screens, and reflected on the nature of their enterprise. Digital Humanities has even been the recipient of its own *Downfall* re-mix, the Internet meme whereby the climactic scene from the HBO film depicting Hitler's final days in the bunker is closed-captioned with, in this instance, a tirade about the pernicious influence of online scholarship.

Digital Humanities was also (you may have heard) big news at the 2009 MLA Annual Convention in Philadelphia. On 28 December, midway through the convention, William Pannapacker, one of the *Chronicle of Higher Education*'s officially appointed bloggers, wrote the following for the online "Brainstorm" section: "amid all the doom and gloom of the 2009 MLA Convention, one field seems to be alive and well: the digital humanities. More than that: among all the contending subfields, the digital humanities seem like the first 'next big thing' in a long time." (It seems fair to say that Pannapacker, who is the author of "Graduate School in the Humanities: Just Don't Go," under the pseudonym Thomas Benton, is not a man easily impressed.) Jennifer Howard, meanwhile, a veteran *Chronicle* reporter who has covered the convention before, noted the "vitality" of digital humanities with its "overflow crowds to too-small conference rooms." There were several dozen panels devoted to the digital humanities at the MLA convention, and one could (and did) easily navigate the three-day convention by moving among them.

Crucially, digital humanities was visible in another way at the conference: the social-networking service *Twitter*. *Twitter* is the love-it-or-hate-it Web 2.0 application often maligned as the final triumph of the attention-deficit generation because it limits its postings to a mere 140 characters—not 140 words, 140 characters. The reason has less to do with attention spans than *Twitter*'s origins in the messaging protocols of mobile devices, but the format encourages brief, conversational posts ("tweets") that also tend to contain a fair measure of flair and wit. Unlike *Facebook*, *Twitter* allows for asymmetrical relationships: you can "follow" someone (or they can follow you) without the relationship being reciprocated. Tweeting has rapidly become an integral part of the conference scene, with a subset of attendees on *Twitter* providing real-time running commentary through a common "tag" (#mla09, for example), which allows everyone who follows it to tune in to the conversation. This phenomenon has some very specific ramifications. Amanda French ran the numbers and concluded that nearly half (48%) of attendees at the Digital Humanities 2009 conference were tweeting the sessions. By contrast, only 3% of MLA convention attendees tweeted— according to French's data, out of about 7,800 attendees at the MLA convention only 256 tweeted. Of these, the vast majority were people already associated with digital humanities through their existing networks of followers. Jennifer Howard, again writing for the *Chronicle*, noted the centrality of *Twitter* to the DH crowd and its impact on scholarly communication, going so far as to include people's *Twitter* identities in her roundup of major stories from the convention. *Inside Higher Ed* also devoted coverage to *Twitter* at the MLA convention, noting that Rosemary G. Feal was using it to connect with individual members of the organization—not surprisingly, many of them DHers. Feal, in fact, kept up a lively stream of tweets throughout the conference, gamely mixing it up with the sometimes irreverent back-channel conversation and, in a scene out of *Small World* had it only been written twenty years later, issued an impromptu invite for her "tweeps" to join the association's elite for nightcaps in the penthouse of one of the convention hotels.

While it's not hard to see why the academic press devoured the story, there's more going on than mere shenanigans. *Twitter*, along with blogs and other online outlets, has inscribed the digital humanities as a network topology, that is to say, lines drawn by aggregates of affinities, formally and functionally manifest in who follows whom, who friends whom, who tweets whom, and who links to what. Digital Humanities has also, I would propose, lately been galvanized by a group of younger (or not so young) graduate students, faculty members (both tenure line and contingent), and other academic professionals who now wield the label "digital humanities" instrumentally amid an increasingly monstrous institutional terrain defined by declining public support for higher education, rising tuitions, shrinking endowments, the proliferation of distance education and the for-profit university, and, underlying it all, the conversion of full-time, tenure-track academic labor to a part-time adjunct workforce. One example is the remarkable tale of Brian Croxall, the recent Emory PhD who went viral online for a period of several weeks during and after the MLA. Croxall had his paper, "The Absent Presence: Today's Faculty," read at the convention in absentia while he simultaneously published it on his blog after finding himself unable to afford to travel to Philadelphia because he hadn't landed any convention interviews. As numerous observers pointed out, Croxall's paper, which was heavily blogged and tweeted and received coverage in both the *Chronicle* and *Inside Higher Ed*, was undoubtedly and by many orders of magnitude the most widely seen and read paper from the 2009 MLA convention. These events were subsequently discussed in a series of cross-postings and conversations that spilled across *Twitter* and the blogosphere for several weeks after the convention ended. Many seemed to feel that the connection to wider academic issues was not incidental or accidental, and that digital humanities, with a culture that values collaboration, openness, nonhierarchical relations, and agility might be an instrument for real resistance or reform.

So what is digital humanities and what is it doing in English departments? The answer to the latter portion of the question is easier. I can think of some half a dozen reasons why English departments have historically been hospitable settings for this kind of work. First, after numeric input, text has been by far the most tractable data type for computers to manipulate. Unlike images, audio, video, and so on, there is a long tradition of text-based data processing that was within the capabilities of even some of the earliest computer systems and that has for decades fed research in fields like stylistics, linguistics, and author attribution studies, all heavily associated with English departments. Second, of course, there is the long association between computers and composition, almost as long and just as rich in its lineage. Third is the pitch-perfect convergence between the intense conversations around editorial theory and method in the 1980s and the widespread means to implement electronic archives and editions very soon after; Jerome McGann is a key figure here, with his work on the *Rossetti Archive*, which he has repeatedly described as a vehicle for applied theory, standing as paradigmatic. Fourth, and at roughly the same time, is a modest but much-promoted belle-lettristic project around hypertext and other forms of electronic literature that continues to this day and is increasingly vibrant and diverse. Fifth is the openness of English departments to cultural studies, where computers and other objects of digital material culture become the centerpiece of analysis. I'm thinking here, for example, of the reader Stuart Hall and others put together around the Sony Walkman, that hipster iPod of old. Finally, today, we see the simultaneous explosion of interest in e-reading and e-book devices like the Kindle, iPad, and Nook and the advent of large-scale text digitization projects, the most significant of course being *Google Books*, with scholars like Franco Moretti taking up data mining and visualization to perform "distance readings" of hundreds, thousands, or even millions of books at a time.

Digital humanities, which began as a term of consensus among a relatively small group of researchers, is now backed on a growing number of campuses by a level of funding, infrastructure, and administrative commitments that would have been unthinkable even a decade ago. Even more recently, I would argue, the network effects of blogs and *Twitter* at a moment when the academy itself is facing massive and often wrenching changes linked both to new technologies and the changing political and economic landscape has led to the construction of "digital humanities" as a free-floating signifier, one that increasingly serves to focus the anxiety and even outrage of individual scholars over their own lack of agency amid the turmoil in their institutions and profession. This is manifested in the intensity of debates around open- access publishing, where faculty members increasingly demand the right to retain ownership of their own scholarship—meaning, their own labor—and disseminate it freely to an audience apart from or parallel with more traditional structures of academic publishing, which in turn are perceived as outgrowths of dysfunctional and outmoded practices surrounding peer review, tenure, and promotion (see Fitzpatrick (2010) on "planned obsolescence").

Whatever else it might be then, the digital humanities today is about a scholarship (and a pedagogy) that is publicly visible in ways to which we are generally unaccustomed, a scholarship and pedagogy that are bound up with infrastructure in ways that are deeper and more explicit than we are generally accustomed to, a scholarship and pedagogy that are collaborative and depend on networks of people and that live an active 24/7 life online. Isn't that something you want in your English department?

Bibliography

Bobley, B. (2010). "What's in a Name: NEH and 'Digital Humanities'," Message to the author, 12 April. E-mail.

"Digital Humanities" (n.d.). *Wikipedia*. Wikimedia (accessed 2 November 2010).

Fitzpatrick, K. (2010). "Planned Obsolescence: Publishing Technology and the Future of the Academy," *ADE Bulletin*, 150, pp. 41–54.

French, A. (2009). "Make '10' Louder; or, The amplification of Scholarly Communication," *Amandafrench.net*, 30 December (accessed 2 August 2010).

Howard, J. (2009). "The MLA Convention in Translation," *Chronicle of Higher Education*, 31 December (accessed 2 August 2010).

McCarty, W. (2005). *Humanities Computing*, New York: Palgrave.

Pannapacker, W. (2009). "The MLA and the Digital Humanities," *Chronicle of Higher Education*, 28 December (accessed 2 August 2010).

Selfe, C. (1988). "Computers in English Departments: The Rhetoric of Technopower," *ADE Bulletin*, 90, pp. 63–67 (accessed 2 August 2010).

Svensson, P. (2009). "Humanities Computing as Digital Humanities," *Digital Humanities Quarterly*, 3 (3) (accessed 2 August 2010).

Svensson, P. (2010). "The Landscape of Digital Humanities," *Digital Humanities Quarterly*, 4 (1) (accessed 2 August 2010).

Unsworth, J. (2002). "What Is Humanities Computing and What Is Not?", in G. Braungart, K. Eibl and F. Jannidis (eds) *Jahrbuch für Computerphilologie*, 4, Paderborn: Mentis Verlag, pp. 71–84.

Unsworth, J. (2010). Message to the author, 5 April. E-mail.

Note from the author:

This short essay was originally written for presentation at the Association of Departments of English Summer Seminar East at the University of Maryland in June 2010, and then revised for publication in the *ADE Bulletin* (No. 150, 2010). Thus it wears its disciplinary bias on its sleeve. But while I would happily acknowledge that there have been other important settings in the story of the development and maturation of digital humanities, including history, linguistics, and composition and rhetoric (when these last are separate programs or departments not subsumed by English), not to mention non-departmental venues such as libraries and academic computing centers, I remain comfortable with the idea that departments of English language and literature were among the key early adopters. (And while much has been made of the "arrival" of DH at #mla09 and #mla11, in fact humanities computing panels have been a staple of the annual MLA convention since the early 1990s, as a scan of past years' programs will confirm.) So this piece, which has enjoyed more than its share of circulation and comment, can perhaps best be taken not as *the* canonical account of what digital humanities is (others in this volume have done the real spadework here), but as an artifact of a particular perspective from someone who witnessed first-hand the emergence of digital humanities from the vantage point of several large departments of English at public research universities in the United States.

Matthew G. Kirschenbaum, November 2012

CHAPTER 10

The Productive Unease of 21st-century Digital Scholarship

Julia Flanders
Brown University

Julia Flanders (2009). Originally published in *Digital Humanities Quarterly*, 3 (3), http://www.digitalhumanities.org/dhq/vol/3/3/000055/000055.html.

Note from the Editors:

Flanders begins by reflecting on the progressive narratives that are often used to diagnose or predict technological developments, for example, Moore's law. From a practical viewpoint Digital Humanities has profited from such technological developments in, for example, hardware and computing power. Notwithstanding this it is argued that the models of Humanities data that the Digital Humanities community makes change not in response to such technical concerns but rather as a result of shifts in emphasis or theory, and from this perspective the Digital Humanities is much closer to traditional understandings of the Humanities. Thus, it is argued that a fundamental tension, or productive unease, exists in Digital Humanities between its 'Digital' and 'Humanities' facets: 'If the rhetoric at the heart of the "digital" side of "digital humanities" is strongly informed by a narrative of technological progress, the "humanities" side has equally strong roots in a humanities sensibility which both resists a cumulative idea of progress (one new thing building on another) and yearns for a progressive agenda (doing better all the time)'. Flanders goes on to discuss three ways that this productive unease is manifested in Digital Humanities research: namely, its analysis of medium, the institutional structures of scholarly communication and the significance of representation in forming models of the world.

Abstract

Despite prevailingly progressive narratives surrounding the impact of digital technology on modern academic culture, the field of digital humanities is characterized at a deeper level by a more critical engagement with technology. This engagement, which I characterize as a kind of "productive unease", is focused around issues of representation, medium, and structures of scholarly communication.

Technological Progressivism

The narratives that surround technology tend, understandably, to be progressive. Moore's law, which states that the complexity and hence the processing power of computer chips is doubling every couple of years, and Kryder's law, which says something similar about disk capacity, have visible and in some cases stunning illustrations in the world around us. We see evidence in products such as palmtop devices that have thousands of times the computing power and storage capacity of ENIAC, the first stored-program electronic computer; personal disk storage is now purchasable almost by the terabyte, and processor speed is now measured by the gigahertz; both of these statements will have dated by the time this article is published. We also see the effects of these developments in processes whose increasing speed produces subtle luxuries that creep into our lives, almost without our taking particular notice: for example, color screens for computers, three-dimensional icons, the clever animation behaviors that are as ubiquitous (and as useful) as small plastic children's toys. Or, more substantively: the fact that you can now store and edit digital video footage on your laptop, or view streaming movies on a device you can put in your pocket. These kinds of change produce easy metrics for success and a correspondingly easy sense of progress.

Digital humanities scholarship to a large degree shares this sense of progress. We see, first of all, simple infrastructural developments that change the social location of computers and bring them into our sphere of activity. The ubiquity of computing resources means that it's no longer remarkable for humanities scholars to work with computers: one doesn't have to get a special account from Central Computing or explain why one needs it; it's not considered quaint or cute or bizarre. Certain efficiencies and conveniences are now commonplace; it has become expected that things scholars want to read or learn will be more or less easily available from anywhere, at any hour, electronically. And there are indirect effects as well: all of these changes produce the conditions for consumer-level products like electronic book readers, hand-held browsing devices, social software like Flickr and YouTube. These products provide extended horizons of usage, and produce a generation of students (and eventually future scholars) for whom computers mean something completely different: for whom they are not a specialized tool but part of the tissue of the world.

The effects of these developments are all around us in the emerging shape of digital scholarly tools and research materials. At a basic level, the increased power of modern computers is almost literally what makes it possible to use them effectively for humanities research. In early computer systems, scarcity of storage space dictated extremely frugal methods of representing characters: because it only uses 7 bits of information to represent each character, ASCII can represent only 128 characters, of which only 95 are actually printable characters. This limited the effective alphabet to upper- and lower-case roman letters, Arabic numerals, and common punctuation marks, with no accented characters or characters from non-roman alphabets. The advent of Unicode in the 1990s is a direct outcome of the increase in storage space, allowing the representation of nearly all human writing systems and freeing digital scholarship on texts from early artificial limitations.

This same comparative abundance of space has also opened up the whole domain of image processing, giving us another information vector to use for research, leading to work in which the graphical meaning of text can be explored alongside its linguistic meaning and allowing us also to explore the interpenetration of image-based and text-based approaches. To appropriate a term Jerome McGann suggested in his opening keynote to the conference at which this paper was originally presented, there is a dialectical process opening up here as well: the mutual pressure of image and text, of alphabetic and figural modes of representing meaning, is now blossoming into an extremely lively field of study.

The rhetoric of abundance which has characterized descriptions of digital resource development for the past decade or more has suggested several significant shifts of emphasis in how we think about the creation of collections and of canons. It is now easier, in some contexts, to digitize an entire library collection than to pick through and choose what should be included and what should not: in other words, storage is cheaper than decision-making. The result is that the rare, the lesser known, the overlooked, the neglected, and the downright excluded are now likely to make their way into digital library collections, even if only by accident. In addition, the design of digital collections now frequently emphasizes precisely the recovery of what has been lost, the exposure of what has been inaccessible. Projects like the Women Writers Project, or Early English Books Online, or any one of countless digital projects now under way at universities across the country, focus on providing access to materials that would otherwise be invisible to researchers. This access proceeds on two fronts: first, by digitizing them so that they can be read without visiting the specific archive where they are held, but also, more importantly, by aggregating them and making them discoverable, by heaping them up into noticeable piles. The result is that minority literatures, non-canonical literary works, and the records of what goes on in (what appeared earlier to be) the odd corners of the universe are all given a new kind of prominence and parity with their more illustrious and familiar cousins.

Invisibly, under the hood (so to speak), increased speed and computing power has also given us tools that finally propel us over the threshold of possibility: humanities novices are becoming able to participate meaningfully in what would formerly have appeared to be impossibly technical projects. Examples include tools for XML text encoding that are good enough, and fast enough, that anyone can learn to use them within ten minutes; or, similarly, tools for image manipulation that put real power in a novice's hands. Even improvements in things like compression algorithms, as Morris Eaves (2009) observes, have a huge impact on the accuracy and effectiveness of digital image representation.

But despite the fact that these are tangible improvements, there is also an important sense in which their progressive momentum is not, ultimately, what is characteristic of the digital humanities as a field. John Unsworth, in an article entitled "What is Humanities Computing and What is Not?" makes a point of noting the difference between using a computer for any of its many practical purposes, and using the computer as a scholarly tool:

> one of the many things you can do with computers is something that I would call humanities computing, in which the computer is used as tool for modeling humanities data and our understanding of it, and that activity is entirely distinct from using the computer when it models the typewriter, or the telephone, or the phonograph, or any of the many other things it can be. (Unsworth, 2002)

Unlike its comparatively recent ability to model the telephone or the phonograph, the computer's role as a tool for modeling humanities data is of long standing—arguably extending back to Father Roberto Busa's 1945 *Index Thomisticus* and certainly including early tools and methods including concordancing, text analysis, and text markup languages. Although our ability to work with these models has without doubt been made easier by the advent of faster, more seamless tools, the complexity and interest of the models themselves has been affected little, if at all. We have only to consider as an example Willard McCarty's remarkable project of modeling mutability in his *Analytical Onomasticon to the Metamorphoses of Ovid*, a project of great complexity and nuance which was undertaken almost entirely through markup and without the aid of any specialized tools for model construction, visualization, or data manipulation. The nature of the models being created in the digital humanities may be changing with time, not as a function of speed or power, but rather as a result of changes in emphasis or theoretical concern.

In this respect, the digital humanities domain reflects the non-progressiveness of the humanities disciplines more generally, and also reveals what may be a fundamental tension at its heart. If the rhetoric at the heart of the "digital" side of "digital humanities" is strongly informed by a narrative of technological progress, the "humanities" side has equally strong roots in a humanities sensibility which both resists a cumulative idea of progress (one new thing building on another) and yearns for a progressive agenda (doing better all the time). The theoretical and methodological shifts that constitute disciplinary change in the humanities, when viewed in retrospect, do not appear clearly progressive in the way that sequences of scientific discoveries do, though they do appear developmental: they are an ongoing attempt to understand human culture, from the changing perspective of the culture itself. But the resilience of fundamental habits and assumptions concerning literary value, scholarly method, and academic standards suggests that the humanities are in fact governed by a self-healing ideology that persists comparatively unchanged.

In charting the intellectual aspirations of the digital humanities, it is tempting to elide the difference between this sense of ongoing debate and the gains in size and speed that come from the technological domain. But the intervention made by digital technology when it truly engages with humanities disciplines is something apart from both the simple progressivism of technology and the canonical resilience of the traditional humanities. In the same article I quoted from earlier, John Unsworth characterized humanities computing as follows:

> [h]umanities computing is a practice of representation, a form of modeling or ... mimicry. It is ... a way of reasoning and a set of ontological commitments, and its representational practice is shaped by the need for efficient computation on the one hand, and for human communication on the other. (Unsworth, 2002)

In other words, it is neither about discovery of new knowledge nor about the solidity of what is already known: it is rather about modeling that knowledge and even in some cases about modeling the modeling process. It is an inquiry into how we know things and how we present them to ourselves for study, realized through a variety of tools which make the consequences of that inquiry palpable. This is why, when humanities practitioners learn a technology like text encoding, they feel both a frisson of recognition of a process that is familiar, that expresses familiar ideas and also the shock of the new: the requirement that one distance oneself from one's own representational strategies and turn them about in one's hands like a complex and alien bauble. As Unsworth puts it further along,

Humanities computing, as a practice of knowledge representation, grapples with this realization that its representations are surrogates in a very self-conscious way, more self-conscious, I would say, than we generally are in the humanities when we "represent" the objects of our attention in essays, books, and lectures. (Unsworth, 2002)

Representational technologies like XML, or databases, or digital visualization tools appear to stand apart from the humanities research activities they support, even while they encapsulate and seek to do justice to the assumptions and methods of those activities. Humanities scholarship has historically understood this separateness as indicating an ancillary role—that of the handmaiden, the good servant/poor master— in which humanities insight masters and subsumes what these technologies can offer. Technology implements what humanities insight projects as a research trajectory. But in fact the relationship is potentially more complex: by expressing "human communication" in the formal language needed for what Unsworth calls "efficient computation," these representational technologies attempt to restate those methods in terms which are not identical to, not embedded in the humanities discourse. They effect a distancing, a translation which, like any translation or transmediation, provides a view into (and requires an understanding of) the deep discursive structures of the original expression.

Unsworth is careful to observe that not all digital humanities activities— in fact, very few—really constitute this kind of intervention, or count as "humanities computing" according to his strict definition. The act of publishing digital content, of making an uncritical digital facsimile of a physical artifact, does not produce this effect of translation or the resulting potential for insight. I would argue that we can recognize humanities computing, in his sense of the term, precisely by a kind of productive unease that results from the encounter and from its product. This unease registers for the humanities scholar as a sense of friction between familiar mental habits and the affordances of the tool, but it is ideally a provocative friction, an irritation that prompts further thought and engagement. In the nature of things—systems and people being imperfect—it might produce a suspicion that the tool in question is maladapted for use in humanities research. In some cases that may be true, and in some cases that may be a self-defensive response which deserves further probing. But where that sense of friction is absent—where a digital object sits blandly and unobjectionably before us, putting up no resistance and posing no questions for us —humanities computing, in the meaningful sense, is also absent. Humanists may learn from the content of such objects, treated as research materials, as they always have. These objects will serve as more or less effective surrogates for their physical originals and may produce efficiencies of access and other practical benefits of one sort or another. But they have no contribution to make to humanities scholarship: they make no intervention, they leave no intellectual mark.

Productive Unease

Where, then, is this unease manifesting itself? and what useful insights and intellectual traction does digital humanities scholarship provide on the central problems of the humanities? Here are three areas where I would argue that interesting critical friction is being produced by work in digital humanities.

1. Digital scholarship is uneasy about the significance of medium

One almost immediate effect of the emergence of digital texts was to instigate a discussion of medium: a discussion which raised the stakes and broadened the scope of the discussion, which had previously been of concern primarily in scholarly editing, in the tradition of D.F. McKenzie. The initial manifestations of this discussion were expressed as anxiety about the unreliability of digital texts, linking this quality to the medium itself rather than to social practices such as peer review. As the Women Writers Project reported in summarizing its 1995 survey of scholars, "anxiety about the accuracy of electronic texts was so acute that some respondents discussed it even in answer to questions on other subjects, and it clearly represented the single largest obstacle to general scholarly use of electronic texts." Early threads in electronic discussion forums such as SEDIT-L also foregrounded this problem of inaccuracy as a kind of worrisome dark side to the "polymorphic, polysemic, protean" qualities attributed to digital texts in more optimistic analyses. The theme attests to an odd sense of self-consciousness about how to make digital texts reliable—in other words, how to transplant a familiar set of social practices into unfamiliar territory, as if this might involve profoundly different processes from those which had been used to produce reliable print texts.

This anxiety looks dated in retrospect, but it has had a salutary effect: it has produced an interest in understanding medium and its role in anchoring our textual perceptions. Digital humanities scholarship now includes an awareness of the representational significance of medium as a fundamental premise. This is not only because the digital medium is seen as a kind of meta-medium in which other media can be modeled or represented (which requires us to think about the special characteristics of those other media, for modeling purposes), but also because the digital medium itself is not representationally uniform. The kinds of sampling and decomposition that seem at first blush like typically "digital" effects are very different from the formalizing properties of text encoding or vector graphics.

The digital humanities world is in fact full of intensive and fruitful debate about representation and medium. Jerome McGann's sustained engagement with the question of how structured text markup may fail or succeed at representing literary texts—his account of the dialectical influence of different representational modes and what we can learn by their insufficiencies—and the responses and research this work has elicited from markup theorists, taken together have provided a great deal of insight into how digital formats represent textual and figural information. And this insight has in turn shed light backwards (as it were) upon the traditional printed scholarly edition.

2. Digital scholarship is uneasy about the institutional structures of scholarly communication

By its emergence through innately cross-disciplinary and cross-organizational (and widely differing) formations, the digital humanities domain has helped to create a critical self-consciousness about the role institutions play in establishing and maintaining cultural habits that affect how humanities research is done. Alan Liu, in a 2003 MLA presentation, asserted that "The humanities should embrace the *poiesis* of IT for alternative ends—first of all at the level of organizational imagination" to "reimagine the protocols of the work of education" (Liu, 2003, p. 6).

> Here I come to what I perceive to be one of the frontiers of IT in the humanities. That is the far territory on which the many, scattered humanities computing programs, centers, projects, and so on that have used IT as a catalyst to reorganize the normal disciplinary work of the humanities evolve from ad hoc organizational experiments into strategic paradigms of interest to the profession as a whole. In general, we must acknowledge, the profession of the humanities has been appallingly unimaginative in regard to the organization of its own labor, simply taking it for granted that its restructuring impulse toward "interdisciplinarity" and "collaboration" can be managed within the same old divisional, college, departmental, committee, and classroom arrangements supplemented by ad hoc interdisciplinary arrangements. (Liu, 2003, p. 7)

Digital humanities projects, practices, and practitioners typically emerge out of working relationships which by their nature raise questions about the politics of work, and occupy a space that is naturally and productively critical of current tenure and reward systems. These systems are still struggling to understand the fundamentally collaborative and interdisciplinary work of digital humanities or the new modes of scholarly communication it is engendering.

Following almost inevitably from this unease about institutional and organizational containers for professional identity is a related concern with published expressions of professional identity and the question of how we evaluate new forms of communication and scholarly work. In effect, digital scholarship reveals a conundrum that has lain at the heart of humanities scholarship for decades: how can we simultaneously encourage paradigm shifts and radical revisions of our modes of analysis, and also know how to evaluate them once we have them before us? Digital scholarship proceeds through collaborations and hybridizations that challenge our notions of discipline—indeed, often that is the desired goal—but evaluation and professional acknowledgement are typically provided through conduits that are slower to adapt and may not necessarily view such a challenge as ipso facto valuable. The MLA's "Guidelines for Evaluating Work with Digital Media in the Modern Languages" acknowledge this difficulty, marking the disciplinary changes that are taking place and the uncertain position that "traditional notions of scholarship" occupy in relation to emerging forms of academic work:

> Digital media have created new opportunities for scholarship, teaching, and service, as well as new venues for research, communication, and academic community. Information technology is an integral part of the intellectual environment for a growing number of humanities faculty members. Moreover, digital media have expanded the scope of textual representation and analysis to include, for example, image and sound. These innovations have considerably broadened the notion of "text" and "textual studies," the traditional purview of modern language departments.
>
> While the use of computers in the modern languages is not a new phenomenon, the popular success of information networks like the World Wide Web, coupled with the proliferation of advanced multimedia tools, has resulted in an outpouring of critical publications, applied scholarship, and curricular innovation. Humanists are not only adopting new technologies but are also actively collaborating with technical experts in fields such as image processing, document encoding, and information science. Academic work in digital media should be evaluated in the light of these rapidly changing institutional and professional contexts, and departments should recognize that some traditional notions of scholarship, teaching, and service are being redefined. (MLA, 2002)

At the same time, the Guidelines suggest that there may be a necessary—and fairly durable—interdisciplinarity in play here, which will always place work of this kind in a procedurally awkward interdepartmental space. In their recommendations they advise tenure and promotion committees to:

> Seek Interdisciplinary Advice. If faculty members have used technology to collaborate with colleagues from other disciplines on the same campus or on different campuses, departments and institutions should seek the assistance of experts in those other disciplines to assess and evaluate such interdisciplinary work. (MLA, 2002)

If the future of digital scholarship may thus be (for some time at least) to remain "other" to the standard disciplinary structures of the academy, however, this should not be taken as a misfortune. The unease that is the theme of this essay is productive in this case precisely because it makes us aware of discipline as both a formative intellectual constraint, and a somewhat arbitrary institutional reality. Acknowledging the arbitrariness is crucial because it reminds us that change is possible and may be necessary. But acknowledging the formative qualities of the constraint is equally crucial, because it reminds us that we cannot simply posit a return to some pre-lapsarian, pre-disciplinary state of unfettered intellectual free play. Digital scholarship works in relation to established disciplines, even as it stands in some degree usefully apart from them.

3. Digital scholarship is uneasy about the significance of representation in forming models of the world

Jerome McGann observed, at the start of the conference for which this cluster of essays was written, that humanistic study is all about representation: it is about decoding, understanding, historicizing, and critiquing the representational modes and artifacts of the past and present, and reflecting on what they tell us about human culture. But while we are good at distancing ourselves critically from the representational forms we encounter in the materials we study, we're surprisingly less so when it comes to the modes we use ourselves. One of the most significant contributions of the digital humanities on modern scholarship is precisely to foreground issues of how we model the sources we study, in such a way that they cannot be sidestepped. Where printed editions allowed us to treat their contents as if no change in medium had taken place, digital editions force us to confront the very same set of issues with far more rigor and clarity. As John Unsworth observes,

> once we begin to express our understanding of, say, a literary text in a language such as XML, a formal grammar that requires us to state the rules according to which we will deploy that grammar in a text or texts, then we find that our

representation of the text is subject to verification – for internal consistency, and especially for consistency with the rules we have stated. (Unsworth, 2002)

The word *verification* stands out here, sounding very cut and dried, threateningly technical, a mental straitjacket, but in fact the key phrase there is "the rules we have stated": it is the act of stating rules that requires the discipline of methodological self-scrutiny. It is in fact precisely the distance, the discomfort even, that digital representations carry vis-à-vis their print counterparts that reminds us that they are models. At first, this distance registers as a loss: digital representations are models "rather than" the real thing, taking the place it should occupy. But as our tools for manipulating digital models improve, the model stops marking loss and takes on a clearer role as a strategic representation, one which deliberately omits and exaggerates and distorts the scale so that we can work with the parts that matter to us.

In effect, digital scholarship embodies an unresolved conflict about scale, human effort, and the nature of digital work. The great bulk of digital research material now available does not look very "scholarly"; with the institutional focus on digital library development and the funneling of digitization money through efforts of this type, there has been a great deal of emphasis on large-scale activities with light informational yield and strong tradeoff of scale against precision, such as Google Books. Traditionally, humanistic scholarship has been focused on high-labor "craft" activities where care and precision matter and, despite the importance of digital libraries, there is thus a kind of mismatch between current digital library approaches and scholarly expectations. Typically, scholars are not involved closely in the development of these resources: they are alienated, in a way, from the technology because they see it as intrinsically not about their craft, intrinsically maladapted to the kinds of thoughts they are accustomed to think.

Alan Liu has observed this shift in the way digital resources are crafted, and noted the politics of the change. In an essay called "Transcendental Data," he charts the emergence of a new aesthetic of the "data pour" in which information is in its most characteristic and powerful state when separated from specific form. The information design of twenty-first-century digital resources draws on precisely this approach: on presentational models that can scale up by orders of magnitude to accommodate the vast and increasing quantities of material. But they do so by decreasing our ability to apprehend the details of individual objects. The challenge information designers now face is how to span that distance, and how to represent the macrocosm so that we don't lose sight of its parts. This is true not only literally, but also intellectually: the question is how scholarly methods can adapt to this shift in scale without losing their grasp on the concrete and beloved quiddity of texts and words and books and artifacts.

The world of social software is way ahead of us, in some ways, in addressing these problems. Although without our critical sensitivity and unease, casual users are experimenting with tools like Flickr and YouTube and del.icio.us, which attempt to represent the texture of the relevant landscape, as imagined by the people living in it: the photographs that matter to people, the web sites they read, the topics they think these things are about. But the scholarly tribe are not so very far behind, or at least they are in the race: efforts like TAPoR, the Text Analysis Developers Alliance, NINES, and MONK are setting their sights on this same problem, trying to see how far the human perceptual mechanisms can be stretched as they try to grasp both the macrocosm and the microcosm and the informational strands that connect the one to the other.

Looking to the Future

All of this unease, as my title has already asserted, is productive: not of forward motion but of that same oscillating, dialectical pulsation that is the scholarly mind at work. Digital tools add a challenge and give us a new set of terms—like a new planet in the system, they change the vectors of all the other things we have in our universe. They will probably change the way humanities research is done. When writing the grant proposals that so often fund digital humanities work, all of the natural rhetoric is progressive—there will be more, and it will be better, and it will open up new ways of thinking. But it is healthy to remember that the most interesting papers and books we read, in any genre, are those that foretell neither doom nor glory, but give us instead an interesting idea about the world to play with. Methods and tools that combine what has been gained in power and scale with a real measure of scholarly effort and engagement can give us such an idea. But the intellectual outcomes will not be judged by their power or speed, but by the same criteria used in humanities scholarship all along: does it make us think? does it make us keep thinking?

Bibliography

Eaves, M. (2009). "Picture Problems: X-Editing Images 1992–2010", *Digital Humanities Quarterly*, 3 (3).
Flanders, J. (1999). "Scholarly Habits and Digital Resources: Observations from a User Survey", Women Writers Project, 1999, http://www.

wwp.brown.edu/research/publications/reports/rwo/rwo_initial_report.
html.

Liu, A. (2003). "The Humanities: A Technical Profession", Panel on "Information Technology and the Profession", Modern Language Association Convention, San Diego, 18 December, http://www.english.ucsb.edu/faculty/ayliu/research/talks/2003MLA/Liu_Talk.pdf.

Liu, A. (2004). "Transcendental Data: Toward A Cultural History and Aesthetics of the New Encoded Discourse", *Critical Inquiry*, 31, pp. 49–84.

MLA (2002) Modern Language Association. "Guidelines for Evaluating Work with Digital Media in the Modern Languages", http://www.mla.org/resources/documents/rep_it/guidelines_evaluation_digital.

Shillingsburg, P. (1993). "Polymorphic, Polysemic, Protean, Reliable Electronic Texts", in G. Bornstein and R.G. Williams (eds) *Palimpsest: Editorial Theory in the Humanities*, Ann Arbor: University of Michigan Press.

Unsworth, J. (2002). "What is Humanities Computing, and What is Not?" in G. Braungart, K. Eibl and F. Jannidis (eds) *Jahrbuch für Computerphilologie*, 4, Paderborn: Mentis Verlag, http://computerphilologie.uni-muenchen.de/jg02/unsworth.html.

Note from the author:

When I wrote this piece, for a conference in 2006, the digital humanities felt to me like a space full of fascinating intellectual problems. My theme of "productive unease" was an attempt to situate those problems within a humanist space of ongoing inquiry, rather than within a narrative of technological improvement: in other words, to sidestep the rhetoric of "better," "faster," "more." I would have characterized the field as importantly motivated by questions about representation and medium, about the ways we produce and consume objects of knowledge. Six years later, the digital humanities has become a field characterized by its attention to institutional and professional structures. My own field of view has expanded so that questions about production and consumption of objects of knowledge are reframed as questions about who "we" are who engage in such activities, and how we construct institutional spaces for such activities. At the 2012 MLA convention in Seattle, this preoccupation with the profession was very much in evidence, in numerous digital humanities sessions addressing topics like peer review, publication practices, professional training and acculturation. And at that same convention, Alan Liu called for us to acknowledge even higher stakes for the digital humanities: to "fundamentally reimagine humanities advocacy" and contribute to a profound restructuring of the relationship between scholarship, its institutional representations, and the commonwealth. Within this larger frame of reference, "unease" is thus a starting point – but only a starting point – in a process of imagining what must be changed.

Julia Flanders, November 2012

Liu, A. (2012). "Where is Cultural Criticism in the Digital Humanities?" in M.K. Gold (ed.) *Debates in Digital Humanities*, University of Minnesota Press, p. 497.

CHAPTER 11

Toward a Conceptual Framework for the Digital Humanities

Paul Rosenbloom
University of Southern California

Paul Rosenbloom (2012). Originally published in *Digital Humanities Quarterly*, 6 (2), http://www.digitalhumanities.org/dhq/vol/6/2/000127/000127.html.

Note from the Editors:

This article contends that there are four 'great scientific domains': Physical, Life, Social, and Computing. It situates Humanities as a subdomain of the Social and situates DH in terms of the Social and Computing domains. A relational architecture that, it is argued, can allow the systematic investigation of overlays between the domains, their disciplines and topics, is presented, as is the Metascience Expression language which can be used for the formal expression of such investigations. This article is set apart from many of the others included in this collection in two ways. Firstly, it seeks to situate, contextualise and contour digital humanities not only from the perspective of computing and/or the humanities but also with regard to the other domains and understandings of methodologies, knowledge and structures from the philosophy of science. Secondly, it proposes and draws on a comprehensive framework in order to analyse not only what DH is but also what it could be. This leads to the observation that Svensson (2010) discusses computing from the perspective of engagement; however, computing as a domain has much broader concerns including 'theoretical results about information and its transformation, algorithms for transforming information, and a wealth of interdisciplinary topics involving interactions with one or more additional domains'. It is argued that the problems and opportunities opened up for DH as a result of the identification of this broader remit of computing remain unexplored.

Abstract

The concept of a great scientific domain broadens what is normally considered to be within the purview of science while identifying four such domains – the physical, life, social and computing sciences – and suggesting that the humanities naturally fit within the sciences as part of an expanded social domain. The relational architecture that has been developed to aid in understanding disciplinary combinations across great scientific domains then guides an exploration of the structure and content of the digital humanities in terms of a space of relationships between computing and the humanities.

Introduction

For roughly a decade (1998–2007) I led new directions activities at the University of Southern California's Information Sciences Institute across the domain of computing and its interactions with engineering, medicine, business, and the arts & sciences. Reflections on this extended multidisciplinary experience have led to the articulation of a new perspective on the nature and structure of computing as a scientific discipline (Rosenbloom, 2004, 2009, 2010, 2012; Denning and Rosenbloom, 2009). In the process has come: a new conception of what a *great scientific domain* is; the realization that computing forms the fourth such domain, with the physical, life, and social sciences comprising the other three domains; the recognition that much of the core content and future of computing is inherently multidisciplinary; the understanding that this multidisciplinarity can be reduced to a small fixed set of across-domain relationships, defining the *relational architecture*; the demonstration that the relational architecture yields a novel organizational framework over computing; and the application of this framework to illuminating some of the connections between computing and other scientific disciplines. It has also suggested several tentative conclusions concerning disciplines outside of computing, such as that mathematics and the humanities can both be considered as part of the scientific enterprise, but that neither amounts to a great scientific domain on its own. Mathematics instead nestles naturally within a broad understanding of the computing domain, while the humanities fit within a comparably broad understanding of the social domain.

The purpose of this article is to further explore these notions with respect to the emerging area of the *digital humanities*, with their focus on the interchange between computing and the humanities. In particular, we will look at the idea that the humanities can be viewed as a part of science – in fact, as part of the social domain – and at the framework that this yields for understanding the space of relationships between computing and the humanities. Such an exploration requires some understanding of computing, the humanities, and the philosophy of science. I am a professional within the first of these, but no more than an interested amateur with respect to the latter two. So there are inherent risks in this enterprise, but the hope is that the utility of its results will overbalance any naiveté exposed in the process.

The Humanities as Social Science

As I have been reflecting on computing, and following the resulting implications where they lead, I have come to accept the notion that any enterprise that *tends to increase our understanding of the world over time* should be considered as essentially scientific, and thus part of science. This is more akin to Lakatos's concept of a *progressive research programme* (Lakatos, 1978) than to Popper's focus on *falsifiability* (Popper, 1959), although not limited by Lakatos's conception of the necessary role of correct predictions in establishing progressiveness. The ability to make correct predictions provides one means of assessing whether the world is better understood over time, but it need not be the only way. For example, development of a simple theory whose scope and predictions are comparable to those of a more complex extant theory may also provide an increase in understanding even without yielding additional correct predictions.

On the flip side, it is important that a scientific enterprise also not tend to increase our misunderstanding over time. Fortune telling and religious prophecy can lead to correct predictions, particularly when ambiguity is combined with generous post-hoc interpretations and rationalizations, but neither has demonstrated any ability to predict better than random guessing. On the whole, they thus can contribute much more to misunderstanding than to understanding despite occasional hits. Such activities are clearly not scientific. But, while the difference is clear here, there can be grey areas where it is difficult to determine whether some activity tends to increase our understanding. Work on a normative *scientific method* attempts to deal with this by prevalidating the approach taken to understanding. As long as the scientific method is used, what comes out of it will be science. The problem, of course, is that much of actual science does not proceed by such a method, and it would be greatly impoverished if it were forced to do so. Moreover, much trivial science follows the method to the letter.

When I read a scientific article, what I care about is learning something new and important that I can be convinced is true (or at least plausible enough to be worth considering further). I am agnostic, at least in principle, concerning what methods were used to invent or discover the new thing, or what methods were used to convince me of their reality, as long as they achieve the desired ends. Great science requires all three of these attributes: novelty, importance and veracity. Good science makes some compromises. To many researchers, all that is important for good science is veracity, and work may be publishable with minuscule quantities of the other two attributes as long as there is sufficient evidence of – or methodology for establishing – truth. In contrast, I often learn more from sufficiently novel and important conjectures – even before there is a great deal of evidence or methodology in their favor – leaving me more comfortable in labeling such papers as good science than traditional small-but-validated results. I don't learn of necessary truth from such articles, but they may still revolutionize my way of thinking about a topic, opening up new possibilities and plausibilities never previously considered. This is a form of increase in understanding more akin to that emphasized by Kuhn in his work on scientific revolutions, and that is absolutely crucial to long-term progress in science (Kuhn, 1962).

This distinction is actually reminiscent of an interchange in Austen's (1818) *Persuasion*, between Anne Elliot and Mr. Elliot, concerning the nature of good company. The former prefers "the company of clever, well-informed people, who have a great deal of conversation," while the latter states that "Good company requires only birth, education, and manners, and with regard to education is not very nice." Mr. Elliot then goes on to state of Anne's notion that "that is not good company; that is the best." What is "best" in both company and science is that which improves understanding, whether based on novel facts or new ways of thinking. The forms are of secondary importance at best.

The scientific method provides a validated approach for developing insights, but it is not the only method, nor necessarily always the most appropriate method. For any particular domain, and any particular problem within that domain, there may be zero, one, or more methods applicable to them. If we define the *strength* of a method for a domain or problem as the degree of veracity it can guarantee for the results it generates, good science should in general be pursued via one from among the strongest applicable methods. Using weaker methods when stronger ones are available can be one of the hallmarks of bad science. We need to be careful though about what is meant by two methods being applicable to the same problem, and thus the circumstances under which a stronger method should necessarily dominate. If two methods can yield the same insights, and one provides more assurance with respect to these insights, then the two are applicable to the same problem and the stronger should be preferred. However, if the problems are nominally the same but the two methods provide different insights about it, then the weaker method may still be of value, and the problems they tackle are in an important sense different.

The potential diversity of appropriate methods, both within and across domains, does suggest a form of *methodological pluralism* in which multiple methods may be necessary to increase our understanding of individual domains, and those methods that are strongest in one domain, or on one problem, may not necessarily be strongest, or even applicable, in other domains or to other problems. Yet this need not, and should not, go anywhere near as far as Feyerabend's *epistemological anarchy*, with its denial of preeminence for any particular methods and its notion that conventional science is just one among many ideologies (Feyerabend, 1975). All else being equal, the strongest among the applicable methods should always be the most appropriate.

Domains can be ranked by the strength of the methods they are able to effectively use, with the physical sciences traditionally able to use stronger methods than the life sciences and the life sciences stronger methods than the social sciences. But this should not be confused with a claim that this hierarchy correlates with the quality of the science pursued within the domain. We have the need to understand all of these domains, and good science is equally possible within each, based on the strongest methods available for them. The methods used within the humanities, although generally even weaker than those standard in the social sciences, can be applied to increase our understanding within their domain, while stronger methods have so far not proven so successful. They thus can potentially serve as the basis for good science. Still, it is worth noting that even good science can be relatively unproductive if the best available methods are insufficient to increase our understanding of it to any significant extent.

The notion that the term "science" is appropriate for all human intellectual endeavors that meet the criterion of tending to increase our understanding over time can, to some extent, be viewed as a return to the original notion of philosophy, or *love of wisdom*, from which modern science descended through the splintering off of natural philosophy. But whether the generic is called philosophy, or science, or even *Wissenschaft* – a German word for science that includes not only those academic disciplines typically labeled as science in English but also other areas of academic study, such as the humanities (Hansson, 2008) – the key point is to consider how our understanding is increased across the full range of subjects of interest, along with the methods best able to increase this understanding.

The notion of a great scientific domain actually goes beyond even this broad notion of understanding, to also include *shaping*. Understanding involves a flow of influence from the domain of interest to a scientist, altering how the scientist views the domain. Shaping is a creative activity that goes in the reverse direction, with influence flowing from the scientist to the domain, resulting in alterations to the domain itself. Shaping may more conventionally be thought of as engineering, but traditional engineering only tends to focus on mathematically oriented shaping of the physical domain. Many other traditional professional activities – such as law, business, education, and medicine – are shaping activities as well, but in the social or life domains. In computing, it can be very difficult to separate understanding from shaping because most of what is to be understood has first been shaped, and in fact created, by people. However, the same kinds of issues will become continually more important in the future of the other domains as we are increasingly able to create and modify physical, life, and social entities at their most basic levels.

Interestingly, the humanities are already very much like computing along this dimension, in that they primarily study human-created artifacts. In Simon's terms, both computing and the humanities are "sciences of the artificial" (Simon, 1969); although even the distinction between natural and artificial is unlikely to remain tenable in any fundamental sense as we increasingly understand people as part of nature rather than as special beings outside of it, and as our increasing power to shape all kinds of entities further blurs the lines between what does and does not involve human intervention. With understanding and shaping being two sides of the same coin, and with them being (increasingly) intertwined across all scientific domains, I have been arguing that the top-level decomposition in science should focus on divisions by subject matter into great scientific domains, rather than on science (understanding) versus engineering (shaping) or artificial versus natural. The latter distinctions can then be appealed to as useful only via second-order within-domain organizational principles.

Broadly, a great scientific domain concerns the *understanding and shaping of the interactions among a coherent, distinctive, and extensive body of structures and processes*. Each such domain is then characterized by its distinctive structures and processes. Structures are things of interest in a scientific domain, while processes actively alter these structures over time. The physical sciences focus on (non-living) matter and energy, and their associated forces. The life sciences focus on living beings and the processes by which they live, die, and reproduce. The social sciences focus on humans, their products, and their cognitive and social processes. The computing sciences focus on information and its transformation. In physics (physical sciences) we might, for example, talk about particles and forces; in cell biology (life sciences), the focus may be on cells plus how they originate, operate, and die; in cognitive psychology (social sciences), the concern might be with the human mind and how it yields intelligent behavior; and in compilers (computing science), the interest may be in programs and how they get translated into executable form.

It is the dynamic richness and vitality of the interactions among an extensive body of structures and processes that leads to great scientific domains. It is also what drives the need for experimentation across much of the sciences. It isn't that science itself inherently requires experimentation, but that complex interactions among structures and processes can severely limit the effectiveness of the analytical methods that can be so useful in less dynamic domains. Mathematics, for example, focuses almost exclusively on structures – equations, theorems, proofs, etc. – and is thus able to make great strides without resorting to experiments. However, its resulting lack of processes and their interactions with structures make it a *static* domain that does not reach the level of a great scientific domain on its own. Because mathematical structures are informational in nature – rather than physical, biological, or social – it makes sense to consider it as part of the great scientific domain of computing, with its broader focus on information (structures) and its transformation (processes). According to this view, mathematics is a part of theoretical computing that uses one of the strongest methods known – proof – in understanding specific types of informational structures. The computing domain as a whole broadens this to cover the understanding and shaping of the full set of dynamic interactions possible among all kinds of informational structures and transformational processes. Altogether, this domain comprises not just computer science and mathematics, but also computer engineering, computational science, informatics, and information theory, science, and technology.

The story for the humanities is analogous to that for mathematics. The humanities are full of structures – books, paintings, statues, etc. – and analyses of such structures, but there is, in general, little process to interact with these structures. There are some limited exceptions to this, such as: disciplines like history for which there is significant ambiguity as to whether they belong to the humanities or the social sciences; and linguistics, whose informational aspect implies an overlap with the domain of computing. However, aside from these multidisciplinary outliers, the predominant lack of processes in the humanities deprives it of the dynamic richness that demands experimentation and enables a great scientific domain.

This essentially static essence of the humanities has been noted before, such as in Janlert (2000) where the artificial (shaped) nature of the humanities is also discussed. The key additional point here is that, where there is process in the humanities, it is principally human activity. When this is combined with the fact that the artifacts studied by the humanities tend themselves to be about people, it ought to be clear why it is natural to consider them as part of the social sciences, when broadly construed as the great scientific domain that deals with (non-biological) human structures and processes. The humanities become a mostly static component of this domain focused on structures that help to reveal the essential human condition, but span both the understanding of such structures and their shaping (i.e., their creation). The close relationship between the humanities and social sciences is already recognized implicitly in universities that combine the two into colleges of humanities and social sciences, and in disciplines such as history that are ambiguous about where they belong, but the suggestion here involves an even tighter coupling, at least conceptually.

The political problem with such a merger is, of course, that stronger methods tend to drive out weaker ones that strive to coexist in the same environment. Even in subdomains where the stronger methods are not applicable, their presence in the same intellectual environment can sap the credibility of the weaker ones. Computer science grew out of mathematics in a number of universities, but had to separate itself, at least in part, to have the freedom to perform experiments, a method that although weaker than proof is essential in studying much of computing. The analytical and critical methods of the humanities are weaker than those used in the more traditional sciences, or even than those used in the rest of the social sciences, but they are presumably particularly attuned to their subdomain of the social sciences, and can thus still be valuable to the extent that they remain among the strongest methods available for increasing our understanding of important aspects of people and their culture. Even acknowledging this political problem, though, shouldn't keep us from an awareness of the true conceptual connection that exists between the humanities and the social sciences, or of the understanding that this connection is possible without diminishing either participant.

A Relational Analysis of the Digital Humanities

The relational architecture provides a means of analyzing scientific topics and disciplines in terms of the great scientific domains they involve and the relationships among these domains that are implicated. It also provides a vehicle for systematically investigating the space of interdisciplinary overlaps that can occur among domains. In this article, the focus is on analyzing the digital humanities in terms of the potential space of overlaps the architecture identifies between computing and the humanities. In computing, architectures often induce languages, and the relational architecture is no exception. The *Metascience Expression (ME) language* was developed to enable concise semi-formal representations of complex, particularly multidisciplinary, scientific disciplines and topics, in service of understanding them both individually and in aggregate. Expressions in ME are provided in the remainder of this discussion in conjunction with explanations in English.

At the top level of the relational architecture, the four great scientific domains are denoted by their initial letters: P(hysical), L(ife), S(ocial), and C(omputing). The discipline of digital humanities then concerns the relationships between two of these domains: the social sciences (S) and the computing sciences (C). If the addition symbol (+) is used to denote that there is some form of relationship between two domains, we can express the digital humanities as S+C. However, we can also introduce a new initial for the H(umanities) – with H understood to be a subdomain of S (H ⊂ S) – to specialize the overall expression more particularly for the digital humanities to H+C.

The relational architecture further partitions the generic notion of across-domain relationships (+) into two general types: *implementation* (/) and *interaction* (↔). Together, these two types of relationships have proven adequate for understanding the multidisciplinary aspects of computing so far investigated, and have even proven useful in illuminating many aspects of computing not traditionally considered multidisciplinary.

An implementation relationship (/) exists between two domains when multiple structures and processes in one domain combine to bring into being elementary structures and processes in the other. The physical domain implements the life domain (L/P) when molecules and their forces combine to yield cells and their processes. Similarly the life domain implements the social domain (S/L) when neurons in the brain combine with each other to implement thoughts in the mind, and the brain joins with the rest of the body to yield human behavior. Sometimes this general form of relationship yields a true or full implementation and at other times only a *simulation*, where some definitional aspects of the implemented domain are missing. For example, a computational simulation of a person – a *virtual human* (S/C) – may look and behave much like a real person, but cannot actually be one (at least as long as biological realization is part of the definition of a person). In other cases, it may be hard to differentiate whether something is real or simulated. Can, for example, the discipline of artificial intelligence produce real intelligence without biological realization or can it merely yield a computational simulation of intelligence? Disagreements continue over this question. Still, whether reality actually results, or merely a simulation is produced, either can be considered generically as an instance of implementation.

The implementation relationship yields multiple flavors of digital humanities. When computing implements the humanities (H/C) we get digital cultural artifacts, such as digital paintings, sculptures in virtual environments, immersive experiences, and digital books. Given the dynamic nature of computing, we can expect an ever-larger fraction of the future of H/C to involve active rather than static artifacts, whether they are thought of as digital plays, videogames, or simply interactive experiences.

Sometimes H/C artifacts are digital reproductions (simulations) of existing non-digital artifacts and at other times they are unique artifacts in their own right. But even a reproduction may itself be a true cultural artifact; a copy of a famous work of art may, for example, be a cultural artifact despite not being the original it appears to be. In addition, all computing artifacts can themselves be viewed as (implementing) cultural artifacts even if there was no such intention when they were constructed. The area of *critical code studies*, for example, views conventional computer programs as cultural artifacts, and applies the humanities' analytical methods to aid in deriving a more complete contextual understanding of them (Marino, 2006). The implementation of the humanities by computing also yields computational linguistics, where computers implement and simulate human language processing.

In the other direction, the largely static nature of the humanities means that it cannot generally yield a full implementation of computing (C/H) – a book or a painting simply cannot compute all by itself – although special classes of dynamic cultural artifacts, such as complex mobiles, could conceivably be made to compute, and thus to provide a full implementation. What a book or a painting can do is provide a depiction or representation of a computer, essentially yielding a limited form of static simulation. In addition, if we extend the notion of the digital humanities from the overlap between computers (i.e., hardware and software) and the humanities, to the overlap between computing (as a great scientific domain) and the humanities, then the representation of information in general by cultural artifacts – which is also denoted as C/H – could be absorbed within the digital humanities. However, a broader appeal to the dynamics of the great scientific domain of the social sciences – within which the humanities exist as a static subdomain – is necessary more generally to fully implement computing. For example, a *Wizard of Oz* experiment involves a person acting as a computer (C/S) in a situation in which a computer is either not available or would be more trouble to program for the situation than it is worth. In such a circumstance, the person is simulating a standard electronic computer – that is, a computer implemented by the physical sciences (C/P) – but simultaneously socially implementing an actual computer (C/S).

Interaction involves a peer relationship between two domains. For example, in human-computer interaction (S↔C), there is a bidirectional flow of information and influence between entities from the social and computing domains. However, the relationship can in general either be bidirectional, as in this example, or unidirectional. Computational sensing, for example, involves flow of information from the physical world to a computer (P→C), while robotic manufacturing involves flow of influence from the computer to the physical world (P←C). In the digital humanities, flow from the humanities to computing represents the automated computational analysis of cultural artifacts (H→C); for example, determining clustering of authors based on their literary styles (Luyckx, Daelemans and Vanhoutte, 2006). It could even be considered to include recent work on machine reading, where computers automatically extract meaning from text (Etzioni, 2007). In the reverse direction, a flow from computing to the humanities represents computational composition (C→H). This is an area still in its infancy, but that already includes, for example, computational composition of simple poems (Manurung, Ritchie and Thompson, 2000), stories (Pérez y Pérez, 2007) and drawings (McCorduck, 1990); and is likely to eventually include novels, plays, movies and interactive experiences.

These two directions of interaction can loosely be considered as representing computational understanding of the humanities (H→C) and computational shaping of the humanities (C→H). In both cases, it is the computing domain that must be the active partner in the interaction because of the static nature of the content of the humanities. However, one way to remove this limitation is to shift the focus from the static structures of the humanities to those active scholars and scientists who study it. In the relational architecture, scientists are typically represented as members of the social domain (i.e., people) who internally represent and simulate part of their domain. For the humanities, this yields H/S. We can then represent the analysis of computing artifacts by humanities scholars, as is for example studied in critical code studies, by C→H/S. However, if the scientist is an expert in the combination of the humanities and computing – denoted as (C↔H)/S – such studies should actually be denoted as C→(C↔H)/S instead. Either way, this is a compound relationship involving both implementation and interaction. It also includes the full social domain, to represent the scientist, in addition to the humanities and computing.

Other complex variants of the digital humanities can also be represented in an analogous manner. For example, human-computer collaboration in understanding the humanities becomes H→H/(C↔S), signifying analysis of the humanities (H→) by a human-computer entity (C↔S) with expertise in the humanities: H/(C↔S). Similarly, more traditional forms of informatics within the humanities – where the computer serves as a tool for use by the scientist rather than as a full scientific partner – become H→(C↔H/S), where the humanities expertise is now limited to the human participant. These relationships can also go in the reverse direction for shaping, or be bidirectional to represent the interplay between understanding and shaping. But either way, they involve two forms of interaction between computing and the humanities: the interaction of computing with the humanities researcher and the interaction of this pair with the humanities subject matter.

Linguistics provides an interesting special case. It is a core topic within the humanities, and obviously has a tight coupling with sister disciplines such as literature, but language is inherently informational and its use is predominantly social. A natural expression for its subject matter would therefore be something like C/S↔C/S – denoting informational interactions among people. If, as discussed earlier, the purview of the digital humanities is expanded to include the full domain of computing – not just computers themselves but information and its transformation – then linguistics as a whole becomes a prime example of this broader notion of the digital humanities; or at least of computational social science, since the expression uses S rather than H.

For comparison, and to help evaluate the relational approach to understanding the structure and scope of the digital humanities, it is informative to juxtapose it with the five major modes of engagement between computing and the humanities discussed by Svensson: "information technology as a tool, as a study object, as an expressive medium, as an experimental laboratory and as an activist venue" (Svensson, 2010). We can ask both whether these five modes fit naturally into the relational architecture and whether the architecture might indicate any significant areas missing from the list (while acknowledging that the list was unlikely to have been intended as comprehensive).

To start, it does turn out that all five modes fit naturally within the architecture, although some yield more complex expressions than others. Computing as a tool used by humanities researchers maps directly onto the informatics example above: H→(C↔H/S). In this mode, the computer helps researchers acquire, manage, and analyze data about cultural artifacts. Computing as an object of study implicitly views it as (implementing) a cultural artifact: H/C. However, if we also want to explicitly represent that such an artifact is being analyzed by a humanities researcher, this expression can be extended to H/C→H/S. Computing as an expressive medium also takes the form H/C because cultural artifacts are being implemented on computers, although here we may want to expand this to H/C←H/S to emphasize the creative shaping aspect that is central to this mode. The difference between the computer as an artifact and the computer as a medium thus reduces to whether the focus is on understanding what already exists as a cultural artifact – even if not initially intended as such an artifact – versus deliberately creating new cultural artifacts. Computing as an experimental laboratory relates back to computing as a tool, and thus to informatics: H→(C↔H/S). However, instead of using computers as one-shot analysis tools, interactive exploratory analysis is supported in this mode. In contrast with traditional experimentation in active domains though, from what I can understand of the description of this mode, it really does seem to be more exploratory analysis than experimentation.

Computing as an activist venue involves a shaping activity, but here the shaping is of society at large rather than merely the scientific domain of the humanities: $S \leftarrow (C \leftrightarrow H/S)$.

Based on the relational architecture, the two most obvious topics missing from the list of five modes of engagement correspond to two simple relationships: C/H and C→H. With respect to the first, the earlier discussion of the static nature of the humanities implies that a full implementation of computing via the humanities is impossible, except for the limited special case of dynamic artifacts. However, cultural artifacts about computing – whether books, movies, or other forms – do fit naturally here, as would all cultural artifacts embodying information if the digital humanities were broadened to the full domain of computing. Any of these possibilities yields a sixth mode of engagement based on implementing or representing information and its transformation. The closest we have seen to C→H among the five modes discussed by Svensson is H/C→H/S, where a humanities researcher studies fragments of computing as cultural artifacts. The simpler expression can be considered as a more abstract characterization of this kind of activity, with the focus narrowed to just the relationship between the two primary domains involved. However, this simple expression can also denote computing actively shaping the humanities, harking back to automated composition – authoring, painting, etc. – by computers. As discussed earlier, this is an area still in its infancy, yet it is one that could grow to become a major component of the digital humanities.

As a final comment on the digital humanities it is worth noting that while Svensson's list is cast in terms of engagement with information technology – i.e., the more applied tool-building aspect of computing – computing as a great scientific domain is much more than just a set of tools. It is also theoretical results about information and its transformation, algorithms for transforming information, and a wealth of interdisciplinary topics involving interactions with one or more additional domains, from artificial intelligence (S/C) and robotics (L/(P↔C)) to automated construction (C→P), brain computer interfaces (L↔C), quantum and biological computers (C/P and C/L), online social networks (S↔C)* – where the star (*) represents interactions among arbitrary numbers of human-computer pairs – and the simulation, or possibly even implementation, of everything (Δ/C, where Δ denotes all domains). The set of possibilities opened up for the digital humanities by this broader perspective on computing, and in particular by domain combinations that go beyond H and C to include more complex relationships with additional domains, has yet to be tapped. We have seen a few examples already where it has been useful to bring in the full social domain (S), but it is not hard to conceive of further such topics, such as collaborative human-computer composition: (S↔C)→H.

Combination with the physical domain leads to possibilities such as the computational analysis of both the content and physical embodiment – i.e., implementation by the physical domain – of cultural artifacts such as books, paintings and sculptures, yielding the expression H/P→C, or H/P→S/C if the analysis occurs via artificial intelligence. The relational architecture cannot all by itself identify where the interesting points are in this larger space, but it does provide a systematic structure over the space, while also guiding us towards an initial population of this structure.

Conclusion

The focus of this article has been on using the concept of a great scientific domain to understand the humanities as a subdomain of the social sciences, without diminishing either in the process, and then exploring the nature and structure of the digital humanities via the space of possible multidisciplinary relationships afforded by the relational architecture between the humanities and computing. The result is hopefully a better understanding of both the humanities and computing, and in particular of their overlap in the context of the digital humanities.

Bibliography

Austen, J. (1818). *Persuasion*, London: John Murray.

Denning, P.J. and Rosenbloom, P.S. (2009). "Computing: The fourth great domain of science", *Communications of the ACM*, 52, pp. 27–9.

Etzioni, O., Banko, M. and Cafarella, M.J. (2007). "Machine reading", in Proceedings of the AAAI Spring Symposium on Machine Reading.

Feyerabend, P. (1975). *Against Method: Outline of an Anarchistic Theory of Knowledge*, London: New Left Books.

Hansson, S.O. (2008). "Science and Pseudo-Science", in E.N. Zalta (ed.) *The Stanford Encyclopedia of Philosophy*, Stanford, CA: The Metaphysics Research Lab, Center for the Study of Language and Information at Stanford University, http://plato.stanford.edu/archives/fall2008/entries/pseudo-science.

Kuhn, T.S. (1962). *The Structure of Scientific Revolutions*, Chicago: University of Chicago Press.

Lakatos, I. (1978). "Science and Pseudoscience", in J. Worrall and G. Currie (eds) *The Methodology of Scientific Research Programmes: Philosophical Papers Volume 1*, Cambridge: Cambridge University Press.

Luyckx, K., Daelemans, W. and Vanhoutte, E. (2006). "Stylogenetics: Clustering-based stylistic analysis of literary corpora", in Proceedings of LREC–2006: The 5th International Language Resources and Evaluation Conference, Workshop Towards Computational Models of Literary Analysis.

Manurung, H., Ritchie, G. and Thompson, H. (2000). "Towards a Computational Model of Poetry Generation", in Proceedings of AISB Symposium on Creative and Cultural Aspects and Applications of AI and Cognitive Science, Birmingham, April, pp. 79–86.

Marino, M. (2006). "Critical Code Studies", *electronic book review*, 4 December, http://www.electronicbookreview.com/thread/electro poetics/codology.

McCorduck, P. (1990) *Aaron's Code: Meta-Art, Artificial Intelligence and the Work of Harold Cohen*, New York: W. H. Freeman and Co.

Pérez y Pérez, R. (2007). "Employing Emotions to Drive Plot Generation in a Computer-Based Storyteller", *Cognitive Systems Research*, 8 (2), pp. 89–109.

Popper, K. (1959). *The Logic of Scientific Discovery*, London: Routledge.

Rosenbloom, P.S. (2004). "A New Framework for Computer Science and Engineering", *Computer*, 37 (11), pp. 31–6.

Rosenbloom, P.S. (2009). "The Great Scientific Domains and Society: A Metascience Perspective from the Domain of Computing", *The International Journal of Science in Society*, 1 (1), pp. 133–44.

Rosenbloom, P.S. (2010). "Computing and Computation", *ACM Ubiquity*.

Rosenbloom, P.S. (2012). *On Computing: The Fourth Great Scientific Domain*. Cambridge, MA: MIT Press.

Simon, H. (1969). *The Sciences of the Artificial*, Cambridge, MA: MIT Press.

Svensson, P. (2010). "The Landscape of Digital Humanities", *Digital Humanities Quarterly*, 4 (1).

SECTION III
From the Blogosphere

Note from the Editors:
Recently, discussions about the nature and definition of digital humanities have moved online, with many posts featured on websites, blogs and social media. Here we present a selection of commonly cited blog posts which show the range and breadth of discussions happening on personal blogs from those working within the digital humanities community. Other core online material not featured here is listed in the 'Selected Further Reading' section.

CHAPTER 12

Digital Humanities is a Spectrum, or "We're All Digital Humanists Now"

Lincoln Mullen
Brandeis University

Originally posted on 29 April 2010 at http://lincolnmullen.com/blog/digital-humanities-is-a-spectrum.

Digital humanities is a spectrum. To put it another way, all humanities scholars use digital practices and concepts to one degree or another, even those who do not identify as digital humanists. Working as a digital humanist is *not* one side of a binary, the other side of which is working as a traditional scholar.

Consider a few examples: one historian keeps notes and transcribed documents in MS Word documents so that they can be searched. A literary scholar uses a print-on-demand machine to get a physical copy of a book or newspaper scanned by Google. A medievalist in the US uses a library or archive website to read a document that would otherwise require a trip to Europe. A professor making assignments for a class posts readings to Blackboard. A graduate student in a hurry uses Amazon's "Look Inside" feature to verify a footnote. A history department circulates papers for a workshop via e-mail.

These examples are all done by scholars every day. The examples are unremarkable: using these methods does not imply that the scholar works in the digital humanities. They are unremarkable, though, because they are ubiquitous.

Moving from these practices to the digital humanities is a difference of degree, not of kind. It's only one step from searching Word documents to using Zotero (http://zotero.org), and from there it is only a few more steps to text mining (http://en.wikipedia.org/wiki/Text_mining). A scholar who uses online digital collections is that much closer to curating an online collection, perhaps using Omeka.net (http://omeka.net). A professor who can post readings to Blackboard can create a course website using WordPress (http://wordpress.org). Circulating papers for comment via e-mail might be a second cousin to posting your manuscript online for comment (http://mediacommons.futureofthebook.org/mcpress/plannedobsolescence), but the two types of review are related.

My argument that all scholars now use digital practices to some degree is not to miss how the digital humanities fundamentally transform scholarship. I'm simply arguing that we're already being transformed—all of us.

Defining digital humanities as a spectrum might help resolve one of the contradictions I see in discussion of the digital humanities. On the one hand, these discussions often lament the barriers between digital scholars and traditional scholars, with worries about how new scholarship can be recognized as valid and how digital humanists can be tenured. I do not want to minimize these concerns at all; they are some of the pressing problems of the digital humanities. But the solution to these problems is not a rhetoric of binary. I think the answer will come from what is, on the other hand, digital humanities' ethos of inclusion. It's the ethos that says, I'm a coder and you're not, so let me teach you (http://thatcamp.org/2010/who-wants-to-be-a-hacker), or let me build the tools you need (http://oneweekonetool.org). It's the ethos that says texts and tools should be available for all and that publicly funded research and instruction should be publicly accessible.

This concept of a spectrum can turn the ethos of inclusion into a tool of persuasion. Does someone question whether digital humanities work counts as scholarship? Demonstrate how the work advances or refines techniques implicit in more traditional scholarship. Does a scholar doubt the value of identifying as a digital humanist? Point out how that scholar is already using digital methods and concepts.

In other words: we're all digital humanists now. Persuading other scholars of that is a way to spread what is best in the ethos of digital humanities.

CHAPTER 13

Who's In and Who's Out

Stephen Ramsay
University of Nebraska-Lincoln

Originally published on 8 January 2011 at http://stephenramsay.us/
text/2011/01/08/whos-in-and-whos-out.html.

*[I'm pleased to offer a transcript of my pithy, underdeveloped position
paper at the "History and Future of Digital Humanities" panel at the 2011
MLA. The panel, which was organized and expertly chaired by Kathleen
Fitzpatrick from Pomona, included Alan Liu from UC Santa Barbara, Tara
McPherson from USC, Kathy Harris from San José State, Beth Nowviskie
(in absentia) from the University of Virginia, and Brett Bobley from the
NEH. Beth Nowviskie's important (not to mention hilarious) intervention
is online,[1] as are Alan Liu's remarks on the role of cultural criticism in
digital humanities[2] and Kathy Harris's on teaching (and learning) in digital
humanities.[3]]*

Kathleen has asked that we spend exactly three minutes giving our thoughts
on this subject, and I like that a lot. With only three minutes, there's no
way you can get your point across while at the same time defining your
terms, allowing for alternative viewpoints, or making obsequious noises
about the prior work of your esteemed colleagues. Really, you can't do
much of anything except piss off half the people in the room. As I said, I
like it a lot. Here goes:

"Digital Humanities" sounds for all the world like a revolutionary
attitude – *digital* humanities, as opposed to old-school analogue
humanities. As such, it has most recently tended to welcome anyone and
anything exemplifying a certain wired fervor. Nowadays, the term can
mean anything from media studies to electronic art, from data mining to
edutech, from scholarly editing to anarchic blogging, while inviting code
junkies, digital artists, standards wonks, transhumanists, game theorists,

---

[1] http://nowviskie.org/2011/mambo-italiano.
[2] http://liu.english.ucsb.edu/where-is-cultural-criticism-in-the-digital-humanities.
[3] https://docs.google.com/document/d/1Mitic3yJJ4U-36eTGsijqGVfdfLIKmIOmd
3xl7O_yjk/edit?hl=en.

free culture advocates, archivists, librarians, and edupunks under its capacious canvas.

Over the last year or so, I've heard lots of discussions – both on and offline – about who's in and who's out. For the most part, people agree that having a blog does not make you a digital humanist. But beyond that, things are a bit fuzzy. Do you have to know how to code? Does it have to be about text? Can you be a digital humanist if you've never been to a THATCamp?

"No, no, no," we all say. But we go further, and say that it doesn't really matter. Everyone is included. It's all about community and comity, collaboration and cooperation.

But this, of course, is complete nonsense. Community and collaboration are undoubtedly signs of the spirit, but to say that disciplinary definition doesn't really matter is to eschew the hard reality of life in the modern academy. Digital Humanities is not some airy Lyceum. It is a series of concrete instantiations involving money, students, funding agencies, big schools, little schools, programs, curricula, old guards, new guards, gatekeepers, and prestige. It might be more than these things, but it cannot not be these things.

Do you have to know how to code? I'm a tenured professor of digital humanities and I say "yes". So if you come to my program, you're going to have to learn to do that eventually. Does it have to be about text? If you go to, say, the University of Alberta, I suspect the answer might be "no" – a reflection, again, of the faculty, many of whom have been in the field for a long time. But what if Duke or Yale were to offer a degree in Digital Humanities and they said "no" to code and "yes" to text? Or "no" to building and "yes" to theorizing? Or decided that Digital Humanities is what we used to call New Media Studies (which is the precise condition, as far as I can tell, at Dartmouth)? You might need to know how to code in order to be competitive for relevant grants with the ODH, NSF, or Mellon. Maybe that means Yale's DH ambitions will never get off the ground. Or maybe Yale is powerful enough to redefine the mission of those institutions with respect to the humanities. Most institutions, for the record, are not.

Now, I've been in this game long enough to understand a few things about how disciplines develop. First, they really can destroy themselves through overprecise definition. That has already happened in Classics, and Philosophy may be next. You can also successfully create a polyglot discipline without schism (the average psych department successfully incorporates the tell-me-about-your-childhood psychologists and the slicing-open-rat-brains psychologists). You can also have a schism and have it not result in bloodshed (computational linguistics, a community now mostly separate from linguistics, comes to mind). But no discipline can survive without actively engaging with disciplinary questions. Not because there are definitive answers. Least of all because it's important to alienate people. But simply because without those questions, we cede the answers to institutions eager to oblige people who are paying attention.

Personally, I think Digital Humanities is about building things. I'm willing to entertain highly expansive definitions of what it means to build something. I also think the discipline includes and should include people who theorize about building, people who design so that others might build, and those who supervise building (the coding question is, for me, a canard, insofar as many people build without knowing how to program). I'd even include people who are working to rebuild systems like our present, irretrievably broken system of scholarly publishing. But if you are not making anything, you are not – in my less-than-three-minute opinion – a digital humanist. You might be something else that is good and worthy – maybe you're a scholar of new media, or maybe a game theorist, or maybe a classicist with a blog (the latter being a very good thing indeed) – but if you aren't building, you are not engaged in the "methodologization" of the humanities, which, to me, is the hallmark of the discipline that was already decades old when I came to it.

Am I right about this? With less than three minutes, of course not. But ask yourself this: Does having an opinion like this move us forward or backward? Is this a good fight or a bad one? Or is it better to let the whole thing emerge as it will? I say that the institutional structures in which we work have already decided in favor of having this discussion, and that we can have it while still retaining our well-earned reputation for collaboration, cooperation, and good will.

[Update: Boy, did this get me in trouble. But I made it all better (well, sort of) with "On Building".]

CHAPTER 14

On Building

Stephen Ramsay
University of Nebraska-Lincoln

Originally published on 11 January 2011 at http://stephenramsay.us/text/2011/01/11/on-building.html.

I've said a few controversial things over the course of my career, and it seems to me that, if you are so honored as to have other people talking about what you said, you should probably sit back and let people respond without trying to defend yourself against every countercharge.

But I'm worried that my late remarks at MLA 11 [see chapter 13 in this volume] are touching a nerve in a way that is not provocative (in the good sense), but blithely exclusionary. The particular remarks are as follows:

"Do you have to know how to code? I'm a tenured professor of Digital Humanities and I say 'yes'."

"Personally, I think Digital Humanities is about building things. ... If you are not making anything, you are not ... a digital humanist."

I suppose I could say that both of those quotes are taken out of context, but given that all quotes are by nature taken out of context, it doesn't seem exactly fair to protest. But just stating things like this (as I soon discovered) really does touch upon a number of anxieties both in DH and among those who bid participation. I don't know if I can alleviate that anxiety. I'm not even sure that I want to, insofar as some anxieties can be oddly productive. But there's a lot more to be said here.

I've had the pleasure of talking with lots and lots of people in Digital Humanities from among a wide range of disciplines. And I've been having that conversation since the mid-nineties. I've discovered that there are lots of things that distinguish an historian from, say, a literary critic or a philosopher, and there are a lot of differences between 1995 and 2011. But to me, there's always been a profound – and profoundly exciting and enabling – commonality to everyone who finds their way to DH. And that commonality, I think, involves moving from reading and critiquing to building and making.

As humanists, we are inclined to read maps (to pick one example) as texts, as instruments of cultural desire, as visualizations of imperial ideology, as records of the emergence of national identity, and so forth. This is all very good. In fact, I would say it's at the root of what it means to engage in humanistic inquiry. Almost everyone in Digital Humanities was taught to do this and loves to do this. But *making* a map (with a GIS system, say) is an entirely different experience. DH-ers insist – again and again – that this process of creation yields insights that are difficult to acquire otherwise. It's the thing I've been hearing for as I long as I've been in this. People who *mark up* texts say it, as do those who *build* software, *hack* social networks, *create* visualizations, and pursue the dozens of other forms of haptic engagement that bring DH-ers to the same table. Building is, for us, a new kind of hermeneutic – one that is quite a bit more radical than taking the traditional methods of humanistic inquiry and applying them to digital objects. Media studies, game studies, critical code studies, and various other disciplines have brought wonderful new things to humanistic study, but I will say (at my peril) that none of these represent as radical a shift as the move from reading to making.

This partially explains why we have so long been accused of being "undertheorized". At its most sneering, this is a charge of willful exogamy: we're not quoting the usual people when we speak. But there's frankly some truth to it. As Geoffrey Rockwell wisely noted (http://www.philosophi.ca/pmwiki.php/Main/InclusionInTheDigitalHumanities):

> [DH] is undertheorized the way any craft field that developed to share knowledge that can't be adequately captured in discourse is. It is undertheorized the way carpentry or computer science are. To new researchers who have struggled to master the baroque discourses associated with the postmodern theoretical turn there appears to be something naive and secretive about the digital humanities when it mindlessly ignores the rich emerging field of new media theory. It shouldn't be so. We should be able to be clear about the importance of project management and thing knowledge – the tacit knowledge of fabrication and its cultures – even if the very nature of that poiesis (knowledge of making) itself cannot easily (and shouldn't have to) be put into words. We should be able to welcome theoretical perspectives without fear of being swallowed in postmodernisms that are exclusive as our craft knowledge.

Now that this scrappy band of naive gear-heads are becoming the "cool kids," (https://chronicle.com/blogs/brainstorm/pannapacker-at-mla-digital-humanities-triumphant/30915) an anxiety that has also been around for a long time re-emerges with new vigor: Do I have to know how to X?

Most readers of this blog know that I have devoted my life as a teacher to teaching other humanists how to code. I do that for the exact same reason that others devote their lives to the study of Shakespeare or the

American Civil War: because it's fascinating and soul charging. Like any passionate enthusiast – indeed, like any teacher worth their salt – I'm inclined to say that everyone should do as I do. But really, that's as far is it goes. Learn to code because it's fun and because it will change the way you look at the world. Then notice that we could substitute any other subject for "learn to code" in that sentence.

"Build," though, casts a wider net (and is, I think, a more useful candidate for X above). All the *technai* of Digital Humanities – data mining, xml encoding, text analysis, GIS, Web design, visualization, programming, tool design, database design, etc. – involve building; only a few of them require *programming*, per se. Only a radical subset of the DH community knows how to code; nearly all are engaged in building something. "Procedural literacy" has been suggested as a substitute, and I like that term. Still, I think some of the people who use it are trying to answer the question, "How much tech do I need to know to do cultural studies?" not "What is distinctive about DH?"

In the panel that set this off, Alan Liu tried to describe himself as not being a builder, but those of us with long memories know better. Because truly, we can date Alan's entry into the field (literally, as well as spiritually) to a very precise moment: namely, the day he started building Voice of the Shuttle (http://vos.ucsb.edu). Being a man of great range, he has gone on to do other very brilliant things (most significantly, in media studies), but I doubt very much if he'd be associated with DH at all had he not found his way to shop class with the rest of us bumbling hackers in the early nineties. He's one of many crossover acts in DH, and those of us with less talent are surely more honored by the association. One of the reasons the DH community is so fond of Alan is because we feel like he gets it/us. He can talk all he wants about being a *bricoleur*, but we can see the grease under his fingernails. That is true of every "big name" I can think of in DH. Every single one.

Now, some of my closest friends in the community bailed about five paragraphs ago, because they're sick to the teeth of this endless meta-discussion that another crossover DH-er once described as the "DH whine." They're especially tired of the "who's in who's out" discussion and, being generous folks, they're much more inclined to say that anyone can join. I feel their pain. And anyone *can* join (the "cool kids" metaphor, honestly, makes me worry about my career). If I had been less prone to provocation, I might have found a way to put things more positively. But in the end, I feel obliged to say that there *is* something different about DH, and that it's okay to say what that something is, even if to do so is indirectly to say that some are doing it and some are not.

CHAPTER 15

Inclusion in the Digital Humanities

Geoffrey Rockwell
University of Alberta, Canada

This short essay started as a working essay.[1] It has been edited for this collection.

We have finally become what we warned people about.
Ever since the *Chronicle of Higher Education* story[2] about the emergence of the digital humanities at the MLA there have been grumblings and reflections about who is included or not in the fold. Some of the places where this discussion has gathered are:

- Stéfan Sinclair posted a blog essay, "Some Thoughts on the Digital Humanities Conference"[3] in February 2010 about rejections from the DH conference and how that should be interpreted (don't feel rejected).
- John Unsworth in his "The State of Digital Humanities" at DHSI[4] talked about discussions in the blogosphere about exclusion. This led to a discussion about why people feel excluded.
- Susan Brown gave a keynote at the DHSI on "What do scholars want? Of Collaboratories, Gender, and DH Evangelism"[5] that dealt with gender and inclusion – how women are poorly represented in many of the powerful bodies of the field. She made the point that "On the one hand DH is extremely inviting to women and yet there is a preponderance of men in the field or senior men." (This is from my Conference Report so it is a paraphrase of her comments.[6])
- The Day of Digital Humanities project[7] gathered a wealth of information about what digital humanists say they do and definitions of the digital humanities[8] from the participants.

---

[1] At http://www.philosophi.ca/pmwiki.php/Main/InclusionInTheDigitalHumanities.
[2] http://chronicle.com/blogPost/The-MLAthe-Digital/19468.
[3] http://www.stefansinclair.name/dh2010.
[4] http://www3.isrl.illinois.edu/%7Eunsworth.
[5] http://www.uoguelph.ca/phdlts/faculty/brown.html.
[6] http://www.philosophi.ca/pmwiki.php/Main/DigitalHumanitiesSummerInstitute 2010.
[7] http://tapor.ualberta.ca/taporwiki/index.php/Day_in_the_Life_of_the_Digital_Humanities.
[8] http://tapor.ualberta.ca/taporwiki/index.php/How_do_you_define_Humanities_Computing_/_Digital_Humanities%3F.

- There was a discussion on *Humanist* around whether a graduate student organized conference at Yale was a "watershed event" as Ed Ayers is reported to have summed up the conference. (*Humanist* Discussion Group, Vol. 23, no. 647). Willard McCarty's report to *Humanist*[9] celebrated the independent interest of graduate students who organized the conference. "Quite independently of the work us older ones have done for so long, these students see the possibilities now visible and question them as befits the humanities."

Having wandered in the wilderness that was humanities computing since the late 1980s I find it ironic to be part of something that is suddenly "popular" or perceived to be exclusive when for so many years we shared a rhetoric of exclusion. Our biggest problem for years was getting anyone to come to meetings, especially graduate students. We traded stories about the lack of respect from the established disciplines and how we had sacrificed traditional careers to pursue computing. How many times were we warned not to do computing or not to put it on our CV if we wanted to be taken seriously as humanists? We were inclusive because we were passionate and wanted company. We were probably even a bit desperate. Now the shoe is on the other foot and the field is perceived by some to be excluding people. We are at a point of disciplinary evolution that calls for reflection, grace, and a renewed commitment to inclusion. Above all we need to critically review our history and our narrative of exclusion and inclusion lest it blind us to needs of the next generation. Here are some thoughts on the subject:

Jobs. As John Unsworth pointed out in his talk, this is partly about jobs. There are a lot more jobs per capita now in the digital humanities than in traditional fields. This is in part because of all the semi-academic and para-academic jobs in libraries, digital humanities centres, computing observatories and instructional technology centres. The issue of inclusion comes up in part because people want to know how to prepare for such jobs and digital humanities careers.

The temptation is to draw a line and specify particular skills (as in TEI encoding) as essential to getting into the field. Specific skills are, of course, found in particular job ads depending on the skills needed, but it would be a mistake to scale up the needs for a particular job to the field as a whole. It would be a mistake to limit the field to one particular technology given how fluid the field is. It would be a shame for us to fixate on a particular

---

[9]   http://www.philosophi.ca/pmwiki.php/Main/McCarty?action=edit.

technology (and skill with that technology) rather than a more general ability to think about and adapt information technology as it changes.[10]

That said, many of the jobs that make the digital humanities desirable do require real technical expertise and often expertise with text encoding (which means an understanding of the collective wisdom gathered by the TEI.) The applied nature of these jobs will generally exclude those that have a strong critical understanding of information technology but little experience with implementation in computing environments.

Theory. The digital humanities, in part because of the need for practitioners with extensive skills, tends to look undertheorized, and it is. It is undertheorized the way any craft field that developed to share knowledge that can't be adequately captured in discourse is. It is undertheorized the way carpentry or computer science are. To new researchers who have struggled to master the baroque discourses associated with the postmodern theoretical turn there appears to be something naive and secretive about the digital humanities when it mindlessly ignores the rich emerging field of new media theory. It shouldn't be so. We should be able to be clear about the importance of project management and thing knowledge – the tacit knowledge of fabrication and its cultures – even if the very nature of that *poesis* (knowledge of making) itself cannot easily (and shouldn't have to) be put into words.[11] We should be able to welcome theoretical perspectives without fear of being swallowed in postmodernisms that are as exclusive as our craft knowledge. We should be able to explain that there is real knowledge in the making and that that knowledge can be acquired by anyone genuinely interested. Such explanations might go some way to helping people develop a portfolio of projects that prepare them for the jobs they feel excluded from.

Put another way, there is nothing wrong in valuing thing knowledge as long as we also recognize the value of theoretical critique. My guess is that there is a residual fear in the digital humanities of theory, both because many digital humanists fled theory for application and because poor theory can be totalizing in a way we fear will delegitimize all the makings we struggled with in that "gotcha" sort of way. Fear of theory can lead to

---

[10]   You can see my answer to a question on *Humanist* about what skills are recommended at *Humanist* Discussion Group, Vol. 23 no. 758.

[11]   For more on thing knowledge see D. Baird (2004). *Thing Knowledge: A Philosophy of Scientific Instruments*, Berkley: University of California Press. On page xvii he writes polemically, "In the literary theater, lacking any arsenal of techniques to understand and advance instrumentation, textual analysis will have free play, while in the instrumental and technological theatre humanists will be relegated to the sidelines, carping at the ethical, social and – following the Heideggarian line of criticism – metaphysical problems of modern science and technology."

an excluding that uses institutional mechanisms to cordon off those that might ask awkward questions. We have all witnessed brutal theory wars and know colleagues left behind, but that doesn't mean that we should push all critique and theory out for fear of recapitulating a past. For that matter theory has itself matured in ways that provide insight into thing knowledge and the sociology of labs. Can there not be reciprocal respect of theorists and practitioners that leads to forms of thinking through that weave theories in as another form of thing that is also made?

Disciplinary Violence. In a paper I gave years ago at the University of Victoria I asked, in the spirit of Giambattista Vico, what crime we were committing in order to form a new discipline. Vico, in his *New Science*, looks at the birth of institutions and suggests that all institutions are born in a crime or violation of other institutions.[12] Romulus commits the crime of killing Remus for stepping over the virtual walls of the city he is founding. What are the violations of humanities computing in its emergence and how will they come back to haunt us?

Of course, founders never think of their foundational work as a violence. They tend to think of the founding of an institution like a new discipline as a heroic escape from the limitations and violations of the parent disciplines. Romulus wasn't committing a crime so much as defending the walls of a new city, at least from the perspective of the founding of that city. In humanities computing we used to grouse about English, History and Philosophy and how we weren't understood by them. The perception that we are victims can then authorize a callousness or exclusion even when we are no longer in any real sense excluded. This is the irony – the discipline of the refused continues to think of itself as victimized and in so doing treats others in the ways it was formed to escape. The refugees become the disciplinarians. How can we avoid such false disciplinarity?

One of the sites of this stress in the digital humanities has been the inclusion of those alternative academics without faculty jobs. Since the beginning, many of those contributing to the digital humanities were not tenure-track faculty, but programmers, librarians, computing support staff, graphic designers and so on. The character of the digital humanities as a community came in part from the provision of a safe and inclusive space where having a faculty position (or not) made no difference. This is one of the differences that made the community and it is tied to the emphasis on development and implementation over theory (because so many participants were in charge of just that – making things work for the faculty who theorized.) We don't want to lose this aspect of our traditional

---

[12]   G. Vico (1968). *The New Science of Giambattista Vico*, Ithaca, N.Y.: Cornell University Press.

inclusivity just because in the North American university there is a caste system that generally excludes students, staff and librarians from full participation as the other that has to be disciplined. That, in my mind, is one of the important differences between the digital humanities and neighboring fields like communication studies or computational linguistics, though they probably have their para-academics. We are committed to practicing collaborative research across the lines of disciplines and job category. Communication studies and linguistics are fine fields with their own forms of diversity, but they don't tend to be inclusive in the ways humanities computing has been inclusive.

In short, I believe that we need a site where computing staff, librarians, students and faculty who are interested in the applications of computing can meet and learn from each other. It would be a shame if the digital humanities ceases to be such a site in order to accommodate other forms of difference. In particular, I think we need to be careful to not delegitimize the non-textual forms of making knowledge important to those who implement and maintain information systems. This is the danger of theory and perspectives that value theoretical discourse over practice. The ideal would be to develop a space where the theoretical and the pragmatic can inform each other without participants needing to excel at both.

To return to jobs – the emphasis on the pragmatic and the ongoing participation of the alternative academics is intimately tied to the very success of the field in employment because most of the jobs advertised are not for faculty, but for alternative academics able to straddle the academic and the applied. Our success is, I believe, tied to this form of inclusion.

None of this should blind us to the forms of exclusion and the limitations of the field. In particular I think we suffer from being a field in which an old boys (and a few women) network formed because there are few formal ways that people can train.[13] The only way in seems to be informal apprenticeship in projects with senior people that then conveys inclusiveness. If you can't get on a project and train with those already "in" then you can have a hard time demonstrating requisite skill. One reason we are trapped now with only informal entry venues is that there are very few graduate programs and training opportunities for people interested with which they can circumvent the vicious circle of not being a digital humanist until you apprentice and not being able to apprentice until you are a digital humanist. This is, to some extent, due to the youth of the discipline, but it is also due to the understandable desire to resist becoming a rigid discipline with all the walls of departments, formal programs, and

---

[13]   I have also been convinced by colleagues in Europe that we are an anglo-centric field that is not really interested in what happens in other languages, but that is for another essay and others like Domenico Fiormonte have written on it (in English).

canonical skills. Further, the first generations of digital humanists, most of whom did not enter the field through formal avenues (how many of us have degrees in humanities computing?) are probably blind to the need for documented and open entry avenues. After all, if we risked our careers wandering in the wilderness, why shouldn't others? If we learned to learn on our own and in the face of disciplinary rejection, why shouldn't others? If our character was formed in the oedipal violence of work crossing walls, why shouldn't we ask others to leap over buildings?

We thus find ourselves in the ironic situation that the very frontier character that we thought was inclusive and character-forming is now excluding those without access to the apprenticeship opportunities we had. We find ourselves trying to develop formal programs that prepare new researchers and alternative academics where we have no experience with formal avenues (let alone respect for formal disciplinary avenues). We compound the problem by trading in "war stories" that emphasize our independence and the glory frontier days while forgetting the luck, generosity, and forms of training we did receive. We would like to believe that we were special when, at least in my case, I was just lucky to get a job in a computing centre. Our stories are just that – stories we told ourselves in the cold to keep warm through frontier community spirit. They are not the measured critical history of the field we should aspire to.

Beyond Stories. But I'm not worried about the stories so much as the problem of interdisciplinarity mentioned above. This is an issue we have discussed before (and will probably discuss again if one side doesn't drive out the other.) It is the issue of maintaining the digital humanities as a commons while still providing open and inclusive ways into the commons. It is the problem of defining the community so that it is inclusive without being so undefined as to be meaningless. It is the problem of encouraging and supporting expertise without fixing skills as barriers.

I used to argue for disciplinarity at the expense of maintaining a commons. I used to think we should stop worrying about what the other disciplines thought about us; stop thinking of ourselves as a servile (as opposed to liberal) art that must support the application of computing to whatever problems come from our betters in the humanities. The advantage of choosing disciplinarity is that we can build formal ways in; we could develop graduate programs, skills training and a common discourse that provides people with open and negotiable guides to participation. (We could also set our own standards for tenure and promotion.) If some level of programming is desirable we can create courses to introduce humanities students to coding and code studies rather than asking them to figure it out on their own (as we think we did.)

Now I am no longer confident that we want to take the route of forming a discipline with all its attendant institutions. We may want many of the institutions, but I am increasingly swayed by Willard McCarty's vision of interdisciplinarity as worked out in *Humanities Computing* (New York: Palgrave, 2005). Is there some way to maintain both the permeability of an interdisciplinary commons where the perspectives of different disciplines are welcome in the commons while encouraging appropriate skills and rigour? Can we have it both ways – have both the commons and well articulated onramps?

One model is the relationship between statistics as a discipline and all the other disciplines that apply it from sociology to social work. We could maintain "humanities computing" as a designation for the study of methods that contributes to the commons and "digital humanities" for the broader and more inclusive commons of application. I believe this was the idea when people like John Unsworth introduced "digital humanities" as a more inclusive term so as to designate the breadth of activities by humanists using technology that don't necessarily come to our conferences or care about analytical tools as long as they work when they need them. Such a model would recognize that for application to work we need both specialists in the application of computing AND those bringing new problems in.

Above all I am convinced that the answers don't lie in what we have been, but in what we could be. I am encouraged by the whole unconference movement, especially the THATcamp model.[14] These unconferences provide a different model of inclusion than that of experts (the in-crowd) lecturing (or training) the undigitized. They are chaotic, but when they work they allow a democratic sharing of gifts, including the unexpected gifts that are excluded by conferences. The spirit of unconferences is driven by new researchers bringing ideas and new techniques and creating a new "we" of community. At the unconferences I have participated in I get to be the student again, learning to embroider fabric with electronics or hack an interactive out of electronic trash. They create community without the traditional gatekeeping of the established – a more open and flexible commons that isn't defined by what an old guard thinks should be included. In such oedipal events there can be a violence to the accumulated and expected expertise valued by those long in the tooth of discipline but that tension is what it takes to renew a field and keep it open. May we have the grace to welcome the exuberance of passion of the next generation (as long as they don't make us do theory).

---

[14]   THATcamp stands for The Humanities And Technology camp. See http://thatcamp. org.

CHAPTER 16

The Digital Humanities is not about Building, it's about Sharing

Mark Sample
George Mason University

Originally posted on 25 May 2011 at http://www.samplereality.com/2011/05/25/the-digital-humanities-is-not-about-building-its-about-sharing.

Every scholarly community has its disagreements, its tensions, its divides. One tension in the digital humanities that has received considerable attention is between those who *build* digital tools and media and those who *study* traditional humanities questions using digital tools and media. Variously framed as do vs. think, practice vs. theory, or hack vs. yack, this divide has been most strongly (and provocatively) formulated by Stephen Ramsay. At the 2011 annual Modern Language Association convention in Los Angeles, Ramsay declared, "If you are not making anything, you are not ... a digital humanist".[1]

I'm going to step around Ramsay's argument here (though I recommend reading the thoughtful discussion that ensued on Ramsay's blog). I mention Ramsay simply as an illustrative example of the various tensions within the digital humanities. There are others too: teaching vs. research,[2] universities vs. liberal arts colleges, centers vs. networks,[3] and so on. I see the presence of so many divides—which are better labeled as *perspectives*—as a sign that there are many stakeholders in the digital humanities, which is a good thing. We're all in this together, even when we're not.[4]

I've always believed that these various divides, which often arise from institutional contexts and professional demands generally beyond our control, are a distracting sideshow to the true power of the digital

---

[1]   http://lenz.unl.edu/papers/2011/01/08/whos-in-and-whos-out.html.

[2]   http://triproftri.wordpress.com/2011/05/14/acceptance-of-pedagogy-dh-mla 2012.

[3]   http://www.samplereality.com/2010/03/26/on-the-death-of-the-digital-humanities-center.

[4]   http://lincolnmullen.com/2010/04/29/digital-humanities-is-a-spectrum-or-were-all-digital-humanists-now.

humanities, which has nothing to do with *production* of either tools or research. The heart of the digital humanities is not the production of knowledge; it's the *reproduction* of knowledge. I've stated this belief many ways,[5] but perhaps most concisely on Twitter:

> DH shouldn't only be about the production of knowledge. It's about challenging the ways that knowledge is represented and shared (October 6, 2010 6:51 am via Twitter for iPad@samplereality, Mark Sample)

The promise of the digital is not in the way it allows us to ask new questions because of digital tools or because of new methodologies made possible by those tools. The promise is in the way the digital reshapes the representation, sharing, and discussion of knowledge. We are no longer bound by the physical demands of printed books and paper journals, no longer constrained by production costs and distribution friction, no longer hampered by a top-down and unsustainable business model. And we should no longer be content to make our work public achingly slowly along ingrained routes, authors and readers alike delayed by innumerable gateways limiting knowledge production and sharing.

I was riffing on these ideas yesterday on Twitter, asking, for example, what's to stop a handful of scholars from starting their own academic press?[6] It would publish epub books and, when backwards compatibility is required, print-on-demand books.[7] Or what about, I wondered, using Amazon Kindle Singles as a model for academic publishing. Imagine stand-alone journal articles, without the clunky apparatus of the journal surrounding it. If you're insistent that any new publishing venture be backed by an imprimatur more substantial than my "handful of scholars," then how about a digital humanities center creating its own publishing unit?

It's with all these possibilities swirling in my mind that I've been thinking about the MLA's creation of an Office of Scholarly Communication,[8] led by Kathleen Fitzpatrick. I want to suggest that this move may in the future stand out as a pivotal moment in the history of the digital humanities. It's not simply that the MLA is embracing the digital humanities and seriously considering how to leverage technology to advance scholarship. It's that Kathleen Fitzpatrick is heading this office. One of the founders of MediaCommons[9] and a strong advocate for open review and experimental

---

[5] http://www.samplereality.com/2010/03/06/loud-crowded-and-out-of-control-a-new-model-for-scholarly-publishing.

[6] https://twitter.com/samplereality/statuses/73048411082997761.

[7] https://twitter.com/kfitz/status/73054050156949504.

[8] http://www.mla.org/news_from_mla/news_topic&topic=303.

[9] http://mediacommons.futureofthebook.org.

publishing,[10] Fitzpatrick will bring vision, daring, and experience to the MLA's Office of Scholarly Communication.

I have no idea what to expect from the MLA, but I don't think high expectations are unwarranted. I can imagine greater support of peer-to-peer review as a replacement of blind review. I can imagine greater emphasis placed upon digital projects as tenurable scholarship. I can imagine the breadth of fields published by the MLA expanding. These are all fairly predictable outcomes, which might have eventually happened whether or not there was a new Office of Scholarly Communication at the MLA.

But I can also imagine less predictable outcomes. More experimental, more peculiar.[11] Equally as valuable though—even more so—than typical monographs or essays. I can imagine scholarly wikis produced as companion pieces to printed books. I can imagine digital-only MLA books taking advantage of the native capabilities of e-readers, incorporating videos, songs, dynamic maps. I can imagine MLA Singles, one-off pieces of downloadable scholarship following the Kindle Singles model. I can imagine mobile publishing, using smartphones and GPS. I can imagine a 5,000-tweet conference backchannel edited into the official proceedings of the conference backchannel.

There are no limits. And to every person who objects, *But, wait, what about legitimacy/tenure/cost/labor/& etc.*, I say, you are missing the point. Now is not the time to hem in our own possibilities. Now is not the time to base the future on the past. Now is not the time to be complacent, hesitant, or entrenched in the present.

William Gibson has famously said that "the future is already here, it's just not very evenly distributed." With the digital humanities we have the opportunity to distribute that future more evenly. We have the opportunity to distribute knowledge more fairly, and in greater forms. The "builders" will build and the "thinkers" will think, but all of us, no matter where we fall on this false divide, we all need to share. Because we can.

---

[10]   http://mediacommons.futureofthebook.org/mcpress/plannedobsolescence.
[11]   http://terpconnect.umd.edu/~mruppel/MLA2010_homepage.htm.

CHAPTER 17

I'm Chris, Where Am I Wrong?

Chris Forster
Syracuse University

This was originally published on 8 September 2010 at http://hastac.org/
blogs/cforster/im-chris-where-am-i-wrong, and edited for this volume.

Preparatory to anything else, I have to thank Bethany Nowviskie[1] of
the Scholars' Lab at the University of Virginia. The Scholars' Lab, and
the wonderful people there, provide a consistently exciting intellectual
community.

And now to introduce myself.

Or maybe not. In introducing yourself, you inevitably assume
the coherence of your categories and treat them as though they were
meaningful and self-evident. Even if you are able to avoid the worst perils
of the genre (the bragging, the narcissism, the faux humility), the genre
of the self-introduction (the professional autobiography in a paragraph
or less) still seems too static, too much a self-report, to really engage an
interesting response.

So rather than introduce myself, let me try introducing you. Well, maybe
that is too clever a way of putting it. (Didn't I say these introductions
are a dreadful genre?) What I'd like to do is locate myself by trying to
simply answer the question, what is the "digital humanities"? In trying
to introduce the perspective from which I am speaking, the gaps in my
perspective and the assumptions I am making (both consciously and
inadvertently) will, I hope, be more obvious—more open to discussion
and conversation.

This is another equally well-trod genre: the "What is the digital
humanities?" (a paltry five google results) or "What are the digital
humanities?" (127,000 results). Claire Ross, in her introductory post
alludes to the seemingly interminable and inevitable question of defining
the digital humanities.[2] I think the best single thing to read on the broad
question of "what are the digital humanities?" is Patrik Svensson's recent

---

[1] http://www.scholarslab.org.
[2] http://hastac.org/blogs/claire-ross/me-museums-and-digital-humanities-hopefully-
not-needle-hastac.

"The Landscape of Digital Humanities"[3]; in addressing this question here (a question so basic, I've heard some express frustration that we're still hung up on it), I'm just continuing repeating some of what has already been said.[4]

Well-trod or not, this basic question nevertheless continues to elicit some disagreement. In his blog post, Tanner Higgin suggests that the valuable, and frequently heard, talk of "collaboration" in the "digital humanities" "often becomes an uncritical stand-in for an empty politics of access and equity."[5] From Higgin's point of view, important issues of cultural politics are insufficiently addressed in DH, leading him to make this recommendation: "I would like THATCamp and all of DH to expand and clarify what it is we do and to embrace a vigorous politics of inclusion and provocation." Two requests: clarify what we do (who? me?); and, in the future, do it in a more politically inclusive and provocative way.

The substance of Higgin's post merits consideration. But I want to contrast it with the very short comment it elicited from Craig Bellamy:[6] "Thanks for your post but I am not sure I understand how you are using the term 'Digital Humanities'. You actually don't need to use the term at all." And then, somewhat cryptically, the comment recommends, "Read this entry about Roberto Busa"[7] (I assume this comment is gesturing to what I'll list as 1 below). This degree of disagreement seems interesting.

I find something similar when speaking to my colleagues and peers (or at least those of them who I don't regularly bump into at the Scholars' Lab). When I say I am interested in the "digital humanities" they are always very polite. That is the thing "where you use computers." ("That's funny, though; I don't *see* an Apple logo on your laptop...")

The confusion is traceable, I think, to the capaciousness of the term "digital humanities" (itself, no doubt, a function of that strange term the "humanities"; maybe that's the problem); this capaciousness is celebrated in the Digital Humanities 2011 conference theme: "Big Tent Digital Humanities".[8] This definition, from Kathleen Fitzpatrick[9] has been repeated elsewhere;[10] Fitzpatrick defines the digital humanities as:

---

3   http://digitalhumanities.org/dhq/vol/4/1/000080/000080.html.

4   http://hastac.org/forums/hastac-scholars-discussions/future-digital-humanities.

5   http://www.tannerhiggin.com/cultural-politics-critique-and-the-digital-humanities.

6   http://www.craigbellamy.net.

7   http://en.wikipedia.org/wiki/Roberto_Busa.

8   http://www.digitalmedievalist.org/news/2010/09/02/cfp-digital-humanities-2011-conference.

9   http://chronicle.com/blogs/profhacker/reporting-from-the-digital-humanities-2010-conference/25473.

10   http://blogs.nitle.org/2010/08/31/nitle-launches-digital-humanities-initiative.

a nexus of fields within which scholars use computing technologies to investigate the kinds of questions that are traditional to the humanities, or, as is more true of my own work, who ask traditional kinds of humanities-oriented questions about computing technologies.

There isn't anything there I'd disagree with. But I'm not sure it would help my colleagues really understand what DH folks do. So, were I forced to try to explain exactly what is going on under that big tent, based on the glimpses I've had, I might split the circus into these four rings. (Recall, my point in offering this division is as much to reveal where I stand, how things look from where I am, rather than to offer a genuine taxonomy.)

1. **Direct, Practical Uses of Computational Methods for Research:** Here are your dyed-in-the-wool "humanities computing" projects. Things like (one of my favorite subjects) statistically grounded, computer-enabled authorship study, text mining, etc. I think I'll have something to say about this sort of work (which I've done—enthusiastically) and the unfortunate antagonism which has emerged between it and more "theoretically" grounded humanities (on the division between theory, or "ideology" and methodology, see Tom Scheinfeldt's post on ideology vs. methodology[11]), about which I hope to say something in the future too). Another vein here, no doubt would be folks associated with TEI markup, and the question of how to best represent texts digitally, or (another of my favorites) text visualization.

2. **Media Studies folks studying "New" Media:** I think this is the position which Tanner Higgin, in the post I linked to above, is coming from. I take his points there to be reasonable and his method to be recognizable to any academic in the humanities: political critique. But it is his object of study (in that post at least) which is "digital" rather than, say, his method. (There is no sense of Scheinfeldt's "sunset for ideology" in Higgin's post, for example).

3. **Using Technology in the Classroom:** The concern for how various technologies change pedagogy has been written about by Brian Croxall.[12] And it isn't coincidental that Brian's very next post is about the state of adjunct teachers.[13] Concern with pedagogy brings

---

[11]   http://www.foundhistory.org/2008/03/13/sunset-for-ideology-sunrise-for-methodology.

[12]   Here among other places: http://www.briancroxall.net/2010/07/06/whither-technology-in-the-graduate-english-seminar.

[13]   http://www.briancroxall.net/2010/08/16/adjuncts-the-glenn-beck-ification-of-cultural-commentary.

with it the political situation of teachers. And anyone interested in pedagogy comes up against the complicated politics of the relationship between teaching and research within university culture. (By calling it "complicated," *à la* a Facebook update, I get to just walk away, right?)

4. **The way new technology is reshaping research and the profession:** Here I am thinking of Kathleen Fitzpatrick's work on academic publishing[14] as well as Bethany Nowviskie's posts on alternative academic career paths.[15] Here the "digital" in the digital humanities is not a method so much as an event happening to the humanities, something humanistic scholarship is undergoing, and which opens up new avenues even as it presents certain challenges.

These borders are hardly absolute, and there is plenty of room for permeability between them. Cutting a chicken, though, requires knowing where the joints are. And this is how I would cut up that thing, neither truly flesh nor fowl, that is the "digital humanities."

So, I'm Chris. I'm happy to be a HASTAC scholar this year. Where am I wrong? What I have left out? I'm here to learn.

---

14   http://mediacommons.futureofthebook.org/mcpress/plannedobsolescence.
15   http://nowviskie.org/2010/alt-ac.

CHAPTER 18

Peering Inside the Big Tent

Melissa Terras
University College London

Originally posted on 26 July 2011 at http://melissaterras.blogspot.
co.uk/2011/07/peering-inside-big-tent-digital.html.

(This is an overview of what I hoped – or planned – to say for my
plenary talk at Interface 2011, 27 July 2011, UCL London (http://www.
interface2011.org.uk). I'm not a fan of reading from the script, so may
have deviated, hesitated, repeated, and elided on the day).

I'm delighted to be here at Interface 2011, and to be partaking – and
mixing – with the Digital Humanities community. The title of my talk
refers to a few things. Firstly, I've not actually done any Digital Humanities
for over a year: I've been peering at DH from afar, due to being at home
doing voluntary work with my own circus troupe (aka "maternity leave").
It is amazing, though, how much you can glean from the twitters, blogs,
and email lists whilst up all hours with the bairns, so whilst I have not been
hands on, I've been closely following the doings and goings on of those
who have actively been Digital Humanitiesing.

Secondly, "The big tent" was – of course – the theme of DH 2011,[1]
which I was unable to attend and am frankly jealous of anyone who did. I
was peering at it from afar, and this issue of "Big Tent Digital Humanities"
seems to have galvanised discussion in the field about the changing nature
of the discipline. I thought it a useful perspective, and definition, to explore
(without criticising anyone who organised DH2011).

And finally, "Peering inside the big tent" alludes to the fact that Interface
is primarily a conference for graduate students working between the fields
of humanities and technology: so many, if not all, of those attending,
although still backstage at the moment, aim to be performing front of
house in an employed position in the academic circus sooner rather than
later. I hope what I say is, then, of use to those nearing the end of graduate
studies in DH.

---

[1] https://dh2011.stanford.edu.

But I want to start with something decidedly non digital. Pre-digital, even. I studied Art History in my undergraduate days, and was thinking of what a career in the humanities meant to students then. It started with the slide test, where we learnt and memorised hundreds of paintings, and were expected to be able to mobilise knowledge about them expertly. (Note – In the lecture I undertake a slide test of Degas' *Miss La La at the Cirque Fernando*, 1879, National Gallery, London: a painting of a circus performer holding herself up by her teeth, hanging from the ceiling.) We would study 35mm slides, cramped round a slide cabinet perhaps five students deep, for hours, and back this up through print publications and gallery visits. If you caught the bug, you might do your undergraduate dissertation on, say, Degas and his circus paintings. You may then do an MA dissertation on the Impressionists and their circus paintings. If you were good enough, and fortunate to gain funding, you might do your PhD dissertation on the use of perspective in Degas' circus paintings, and what this "means" for modern art. Eventually, after stiff competition, you may get a post teaching modern (used in the broadest sense) art, and your research would become highly specialised in perspective in Impressionist paintings of performance. After years of hard graft you'd own this area, and write in this area, and have found and read every book and article on this area, and publish the elusive monograph in this area. You may have even travelled widely to see every painting in this area in the flesh, not to mention visiting many archives and libraries. It would take years to even piece together all the information you needed to become an expert in the field.

Let's contrast that to today's information environment. You are not sure of the exact painting you are interested in and, rather than remember it, a quick google of "degas circus painting" leads you to the Wikipedia page of *Miss La La*.[2] You can find a link to it at the National Gallery, London, where you can zoom in in so much more detail that you could ever see in a 35mm slide, or even up close when visiting the gallery.[3] You can see where this fits in to the pantheon of Degas' – and the Impressionists' – oeuvre by looking up the complete works of all Impressionist paintings, online.[4] The complete works of Edgar Degas shows you every single known study for *Miss La La*,[5] and you can see high definition images of a pastel study for the painting on the Tate website.[6] You can look up historical newspaper archives to see if there was anything written about the painting or artist in

---

[2]   http://en.wikipedia.org/wiki/Miss_La_La_at_the_Cirque_Fernando.
[3]   http://www.nationalgallery.org.uk/paintings/hilaire-germain-edgar-degas-miss-la-la-at-the-cirque-fernando.
[4]   http://www.impressionistsgallery.co.uk.
[5]   http://www.edgar-degas.org.
[6]   http://www.tate.org.uk/servlet/ViewWork?workid=3697.

the past,[7] find relevant journal articles that refer to the painting from the comfort of your own laptop,[8] and see if it had been mentioned particularly in any book published since the painting was painted.[9] You could even wander up to the painting virtually using the Google Art Project (well, you will be able to once the NG expand their coverage of Google Art beyond the couple of galleries that have been digitised via street view technology.[10] You can see others' views and visits of the artwork by a simple Flickr search (which is something art historians love, in particular for looking at alternative views of sculptures held in museums, beyond the official viewpoint in the print catalogues.[11] If you are in the Gallery, and want more information about a painting, you can simply take a picture on your phone, and search Google with that image, or use Google goggles[12] to tell you more about it. (I am aware that I am mentioning Google frequently: a) I am "not-working" from home and therefore unable to easily access other institutional resources, and b) they do provide an easy suite of tools to use in the first instance, even if there are shortcomings and limitations.) You can do a reverse image search using Tin Eye to see who else is talking about that image/artwork.[13] If you have the access, and resources, you could use advanced imaging techniques to study both the creation and the current condition of the artwork, for conservation purposes and beyond.[14] You could use computational methods to analyse the angles and perspectives of the human figure in Degas' artworks. You could virtually recreate the Cirque Fernando in 3D to investigate the artist's perspective of *Miss La La*. If you didn't know how to do any of this, you could ask twitter for some pointers, and within minutes someone in the DH community would have responded. Post a question on DH answers, and within 24 hours you would have the best advice on how to study perspective in modern art, using computational methods.[15]

What part of this is Digital Humanities? Is it the act of googling the painting? Using the zoom on the NG website? Using the complete works of Edgar Degas, Google Art Project, JStor, Flickr or even Wikipedia? Is

---

[7] http://news.google.com/newspapers?id=v0cqAAAAIBAJ&sjid=OE8EAAAAIBAJ&pg=
³763,5521007&dq=degas&hl=en.

[8] http://www.jstor.org/pss/25067359.

[9] http://www.google.com/search?tbm=bks&tbo=1&q=%22miss+la+la%22&btnG=Search+Books.

[10] http://www.googleartproject.com/museums/nationalgallery.

[11] http://www.flickr.com/search/?q=degas%20national%20gallery%20london.

[12] http://www.google.com/mobile/goggles.

[13] http://www.tineye.com/search/b888c0105666e52edc2e685db558b403014c8eef.

[14] http://www.nap.edu/openbook.php?record_id=11413&page=120.

[15] http://digitalhumanities.org/answers/topic/computational-analysis-of-perspective-in-paintingsart.

DH the creation of the online resources? The digitisation of books and journals? Is DH the use of tools to study how the painting was created? Composed? Curated? Is DH the study of the use of these tools by users to study art? Is DH the development of techniques and algorithms to analyse the painting? Is DH the means to ask the wider community advice? Is DH the infrastructure which allows the advice to be detailed and delivered to even more scholars? Is DH the use of electronic images of art in powerpoint slides discussing DH? And who is the Digital Humanist? The creator of digital resources? The writer of algorithms? The user of programs? The person who analyses the action of the user? And should academia take any of this seriously?

What is Digital Humanities? And what is Digital Humanities for? To paraphrase Larkin, Ah, solving that question brings the doctors of philosophy in their long coats running over the fields. There is a lot written about this (it's not the place here to give a history of the definition of DH, but emergent scholars could do worse than make themselves familiar with a lot of the arguments). It's something to do with the Humanities, and digital technologies, but what exactly we are slow – and even reluctant – to pinpoint. The latest definition, "Big Tent Digital Humanities", deliberately obfuscates the focus of the field. Roll up, roll up! Everything is Digital Humanities! Everyone is a digital humanist!

The concept of a "big tent" to demarcate a group of individuals is a pragmatic and flexible description usually used to give strength in numbers, permitting a broad spectrum of views or approaches across the constituency. The term has been around for a long time, actually originating from religious American groups in the nineteenth century (see also "broad church") rather than the circus background the name implies. It is most commonly applied to political coalitions that have a wide spread of backgrounds, approaches, and beliefs. In some respect it is well suited to Digital Humanities – what are the "Humanities" if not a "big tent" of scholars interested in the human condition and human society? What are the "Digital Humanities" if not a broad spectrum of academic approaches, loosely bound together with a shared interest in technology and humanistic research, in all its guises?

In many regards, "Big Tent Digital Humanities" is a nice concept. It is true that the DH community is considerably more open, approachable, welcoming, and willing to embrace new approaches than many traditional areas of humanities academia. Big Tent DH, then, is an ecumenical approach, whilst giving the freedom for individual scholars to explore their own interests, wherever in the research and teaching spectrum they lie. And why would anyone want to limit the constituency of DH? Surely as technology becomes more and more pervasive in society, finding humanities scholars who do not use any aspect of digital technology in their research will become rarer. As recent blog postings have discussed,[16] anyone who has the interest to do so can tinker with DH, and DH is one of the easiest disciplines to go DIY in. Big Tent DH provides a shared core of like-minded scholars who are exploring digital frontiers to undertake work in the humanities, and welcomes those interested in engaging and learning further about the application of potentially transformative technologies.

But. Just as political parties who are too "big tent" can be criticised for adopting populist policies without any clear remit, stance or goal, "Big Tent Digital Humanities" has its issues when you look at the detail. It is all very well saying that DH is open and welcoming and encourages participation – but despite open platforms such as DH answers, and the DIY approach, it is still a very rich, very western academic field with a limited number of job openings for the growing number of humanities PhDs that are being produced that have some digital element to them. Let's be honest: most people undertaking graduate research who want to continue doing research when their studies are finished would like to be paid for it and make it their livelihood, rather than go the DIY, in your own time after the day job, route. I don't want to dwell on the numbers of PhDs that go onto have academic posts – as far as I'm concerned PhD students should have done their homework on that before undertaking a PhD, and there have always been limited openings. It's probably true that DH, at the moment, still has more career openings than other, singular humanities subjects. We also have an increasingly popular "#alt-ac" trajectory, where individuals can go on to rewarding alternative academic careers that are not tenure track (what is the alternative to #alt-ac? #ten-trac-ac?) However, despite all this, there will be a lot of folk left peering into the big tent, without ever gaining full access to any paid employment in DH. Institutional support means access to computational infrastructure, journals, money for equipment, conference travel, paid sabbaticals to write up research, payment which enables you to subscribe to journals and scholarly societies, etc. We should be careful with our descriptions of how open DH actually is, and the resources required to participate in DH research and development, for those without institutional backing. Personally, I don't like the associations that come with the "Big Tent" label: it paints DH as a transitory spectacle with all the connotations that come with the circus. Branding is important, and (given the experience we in DH have had in trying to be taken seriously by our traditional humanities colleagues) suggesting the field is best described using a big top metaphor, although it may be a bit of fun, is worrying. You don't see many string theorists describing themselves as "Big Tent Particle Physicists"! we should be careful what view of ourselves we are projecting into the wider

---

16   http://www.trevorowens.org/2011/07/the-digital-humanities-as-the-diy-humanities.

academic world. Our acceptance, even our current fashionable status, has been hard won: and what goes up must come down. Is there really no better way to describe the strengths and objectives of our community?

In lots of ways, though, getting hung up about the term "Big Tent Digital Humanities" is a red herring. Like London buses, there will be another theory – or three – about Digital Humanities along in a minute. However, it is an acceptance that the field is changing, and growing. And therein lies the "crisis" in my title. The field can only continue to expand, as more and more people engage with the technology that allows them to undertake academic tasks, and who are we to ring-fence the academic field that lets people discuss this and learn more? Who are we to limit participation in the field to those with paid full-time jobs? But if everyone is a Digital Humanist, then no one is really a Digital Humanist. The field does not exist if it is all pervasive, too widely spread, or ill defined.

As DH expands we run into issues chasing funding (there will always be limited resources, which are now competed for by larger and larger groups of scholars). But perhaps the sticking point that we all most keenly feel, when applied to our own research, is the effect the expansion of DH has on peer review – the essential sifting mechanism around which a discipline functions. There were many vocal complaints on twitter about reviews for papers submitted to DH2011. In some cases, including papers that I was co-author on, the returned reviews varied from high score to dismally low scores – with the comments from the low scorers making it clear that the reviewers did not have the foggiest what the research was about. There is no mechanism to appeal this – and one low score can mean a paper is rejected. The acceptance onto conference programmes can spell the difference between attending and not attending conferences, or being published or not being published, and so, in the longer term, career progression. The problem of the Big Tent, or the Broad Church, is that the experience and knowledge of individuals is so loosely bound that "peers" can often have little real insight into the relevance or applicability of a given specific research topic (which, by its nature, should be specialised). As the community around the DH conference expands, this will become an ongoing problem. If everyone is DH, if the field is all encompassing, how can we trust the peer reviews (good or bad) that come from within the community? Does "Big Tent Digital Humanities" mean that DH peer review is broken?

I think there are other, more useful things to concentrate on when defining DH than the "big tent" idea. Going back to the pre-digital versus digital scenario given at the start of the lecture: I believe DH has been poor in articulating the changes the digital information environment and its related tools have wrought to humanities scholarship, and the changes and potential that this means for individual scholars. The roles and positions

I find myself filling are not those I would have associated with a singular academic career in the pre-digital environment, nor do the publishing avenues of our research chime with the traditional views of the academy (although what did I know then of how academia worked?). Partaking in DH and building a career around its framework means that I have enjoyed researching in many fields: classics, archaeology, history, archival studies, computer gaming, high performance computing, image processing ... but unlike the scholars of "old" (all of 15 years ago) I'm very aware I do not own a specialised field, or have a specific research remit, or have the will, means or opportunities to churn out the monographs. DH has allowed me to be jack of all trades, master of none – is this what the Big Tent really means? It is something I have occasionally struggled with, as it would be nice to lay claim to a research area and become noted for work in that area alone. Many digital outputs will never be found on library shelves. Many of the senior scholars in DH, though, have "portfolio" research careers, keeping up to date with developments in technology and applying them variously in different disciplines in ways that would not make tenure in the pre-digital world. Behind the scenes at the Big Tent there are people building interesting, diverse skillsets, and it would be useful at some stage to acknowledge the changing academic role and remit as personified by DH scholars, as well as saying "we're all DH now".

The irony is, of course, that the way for young scholars to gain full entry to the Big Tent (whether in #alt-ac or tenure track posts) is still through the specialised focus of PhD research. (Although there are plenty of established scholars in DH without doctorates, even the most perfunctory of positions now usually dictates that applicants hold a PhD in a relevant area.) Like an individual circus performer, the individual scholar must become the expert in their chosen, niche area, and hone their own skill and approach. However, if there is one piece of advice I can give to those embarking on an academic career, it is to look around the Big Tent, and to see what skills are most needed, asked for, and employable, and to make sure that these are also part of your skillset. For example, I have no research interest in textual encoding and markup, but I make sure that I follow the gist of what is going on with the technology, and would be able to teach it. XML and TEI are such a core part of any DH teaching programme that it would be remiss not to have experience in this area. Make sure you know the basics of Internet Technologies, Databases, and even GIS. Experiment with programming, at least just to see what it is about. You may not believe it at the moment, but graduate students have the luxury of time to pick up and learn new skills beyond your immediate research. Use whatever training courses your institutions offers wisely, while you have the opportunity. Once you hit employed life, the time and opportunity to develop your skills in such a wide manner becomes severely rationed.

Make sure you are visible in Social Media circles (show that you are actively peering in, before applying for positions). Engage with others doing different DH research: use the Big Tent as a way to network with people, whilst seeing what new technologies are being appropriated within DH. Make sure you make yourself ready for employment: a cursory glance at employment adverts for DH will show that those with job openings are asking for a lot. I wonder if the spread of topics and skills demonstrated in the Big Tent constituency mean we are almost asking too much from individual applicants at the very start of their careers: you want to join the circus? Show us you know how it all works!

My second piece of advice would be – read "Alternative Academic Careers for Humanities Scholars" (edited by Bethany Nowviskie[17]). Understand the arena you want to be employed in, and the various approaches there can be there to getting jobs there.

My final piece of advice is – learn to touch type. If you are planning to be a professional Digital Humanist, there is a whole lot of silicon-face time to be spent. Invest in your future by learning how to engage with the digital in the fastest and most efficient way possible (at the moment).

And then I should probably wish you all good luck out there, but I'm going to end with the painting of *Miss La La at the Cirque Fernando*. It's the analysis of such an object, and the potential for digital techniques and technologies to aid us in understanding different perspectives of the human condition that drives Digital Humanities. But it is also about tenacity, and application, and hard work, and expertise. There's not much "luck" in the skill demonstrated by Miss La La in this painting: its sheer, hard won, strength and agility. Despite all the "Roll up! Roll up!" talk and advertising, the wonder comes down to whether or not she can actually apply herself, and undertake the task. It's the same for Digital Humanists: despite the changing definitions and perspectives that surround our field, the value and usefulness of our skills are demonstrated through what we actually do, the research we undertake, the tools we build, the people we teach, the literature we write.

I am looking forward to actually doing Digital Humanities again. It is in the doing that we can explore what the changing information environment means for the humanities, and scholars in the humanities. We can argue the limits and boundaries of our constituency, and the list of essential skills that make up DH, over and over. But as digital technologies become increasingly pervasive, the work and skills of Digital Humanists become increasingly important. We are holding on tight to our place in academia – by our teeth, if needs be.

---

[17] http://mediacommons.futureofthebook.org/alt-ac.

CHAPTER 19

ADHO, On Love and Money

Bethany Nowviskie
University of Virginia

An earlier version was published as "DH Wonks, Step This Way" on 19 September 2011 at http://nowviskie.org.

Here's a word meant for the small audience of people who care about the inner workings of digital humanities professional societies. DH wonks, step this way.

The Association for Computers and the Humanities (ACH) was established in 1978 and is the primary US-based association for practitioners of humanities computing. I am its president, and a steering committee member of the umbrella group it helped to found in 2005. This is the Alliance of Digital Humanities Organizations (ADHO), consisting of five international societies: ACH, ALLC (the Association for Literary and Linguistic Computing), CSDH-SCHN (the Canadian Society for Digital Humanities/Société Canadienne des Humanités Numériques), centerNet (an international consortium of digital humanities labs and centers), and aaDH (the Australasian Association for Digital Humanities). Shortly, a sixth organization will join us: JADH, the new Japanese Association for Digital Humanities.

I've been a member of ACH for much longer than I've been active in its leadership or involved in ADHO—so my encounters with its budget sheets and expenditure records are recent enough to make me conscious of how opaque its doings must seem to the larger DH world it aims to serve. I hope to share some information here to help members and potential members understand how these organizations fit together, and what—particularly from the ACH point of view—we're up to, in an era of great expansion (and not a small amount of navel-gazing) for the digital humanities.

I write this post as an individual member of the ADHO organizations— seeking clarity (like you, maybe) on what it means to join a radically interdisciplinary professional association, how ACH works with its international partners, and (most of all) where exactly my membership fees go. Needless to say, this is not the official word from ACH or ADHO. It's just me, wanting to codify what I keep finding myself trying to express in 140-character tweets to questions online! It's also an offer to solicit fresh ideas and help them get heard.

The joint ADHO financial model—which strengthens our work and helps to coordinate and maximize the value of DH initiatives internationally—makes the last of that series of questions ("where does my money go?") a little more complicated than it might be for other smallish professional societies. But it's important to ACH that we answer it, because we're a community-driven organization, supported by volunteer effort and membership fees. Our most important activities seek to cultivate and strengthen the digital humanities through our advocacy work and support of presentation and conversation venues, publications of various sorts, awards, and events. We are also known for focusing a great deal of energy and material support on people new to the field— through mentorship activities (including networking events and our long-standing mentor-matching program), subsidies to training workshops such as DHSI (the Digital Humanities Summer Institute) and to unconferences, contributions to allied initiatives (like *4Humanities*), and the hosting of a variety of sites for dialogue and problem-solving. A lot of this runs on love, but it also takes money.

ACH and ADHO finances work like this:

The primary monetary transaction between individual members and the ADHO organizations is handled by Oxford University Press, publisher of our sole commercial journal: *LLC: The Journal of Digital Scholarship in the Humanities*. Individual subscribers to *LLC* are asked to indicate a primary affiliation with ACH or another association. They are also given the option to join all of the ADHO societies at once—therefore becoming eligible to vote in elections and receive communications or other specialized membership benefits from each group—by increasing their base payment. For instance, at the time of this writing, to move from an ACH-only membership to a joint ADHO membership, your fee will increase by US$14–25, depending on your status. The present rate for ACH-only student or senior citizen members is US$69/year (soon to be drastically reduced!), while regular members pay US$139.

The cost for an individual ADHO membership is kept in balance with significant registration discounts offered to members for the annual Digital Humanities conference, held each year in different regions of the world. This means that, if you plan to attend DH, it is cheaper to join an ADHO organization than to pay the non-member's price.

Currently, 70% of the total profits from *LLC* are returned to ADHO. These form almost 100% of our income, not including considerable in-kind contributions made by our all-volunteer councils and committees. (I am not certain how the other groups handle this, but ACH does not subsidize travel or other costs incurred by its officers and executive council members in conducting the organization's business.) The arrangement with OUP allows us to take in more than members' fees; we add institutional or library subscription fees for *LLC* to the overall funding picture for ADHO, greatly increasing our financial stability. In fact, institutional subscriptions to *LLC* are far and away the largest revenue stream for the ADHO orgs, though we are conscious that this is not an expanding market.

ADHO is governed by a steering committee representing all its constituent organizations, and this committee authorizes disbursements to each according to an established (partly geographical) formula—after taking off a "top slice" of the income to cover operations that ADHO funds jointly. Disbursements to individual societies, like ACH, are meant to allow us the independence to serve our distinct (but increasingly shared) constituencies and to undertake local projects. Meanwhile, the ADHO top slice funds: web hosting and infrastructure; training and conference attendance bursaries that make it possible for new people to get engaged in our work; support given to standards bodies; awards like the Fortier, Busa, and Zampolli prizes; a small subvention for local hosts of the annual DH conference; and costs related to our other publications. In other words, ADHO organizations are just as solidly imbricated with the academic publishing industry as all of our peer professional societies—with the possible difference that we throw the profits from our one closed journal to a host of *open access* publications and resources.

A desire to broaden in scope and serve a larger community motivated *Literary and Linguistic Computing*'s adoption, several years ago, of the "*LLC*" moniker and its new, more general subtitle. (Apparently the wholesale changing of journal names—with their historical associations, ISSNs, and institutional subscribers' lists—is a sticky affair.) I often hear concern that a perceived focus on text-based digital humanities limits *LLC*'s penetration into that larger community. *LLC*'s focus is evolving rapidly, but for many this remains a valid concern.

Unlike many similarly-sized professional organizations, however, ACH sponsors more than a single journal. We are aware that our members come from many different disciplinary perspectives and have just as many needs and requirements for their publication venues. In some DH professions, traditional print journals published by respected presses and participating in established citation ranking systems are critical (career-making or -breaking) publication venues. To others, newer and more interactive online publication venues are key. Different segments of the international DH community have differing relationships to open access publication. Sharp disciplinary focus is more and less important in different corners of DH.

To that end, ACH and its partner organizations in ADHO also sponsor:

- two peer-reviewed online, open access journals: *DHQ: Digital Humanities Quarterly* and *Digital Studies/Le champ numérique*;
- ongoing open access to two seminal edited collections, published by Blackwell's: *A Companion to Digital Humanities* and *A Companion to Digital Literary Studies*;
- and two book series: *Digital Research in the Arts and Humanities*, published by Ashgate, and *Topics in the Digital Humanities*, published by Illinois University Press.

These come in addition to less formal communications venues. Among others, we offer:

- the Humanist listserv (a long-standing "online seminar on humanities computing and the digital humanities");
- *DH Answers: Digital Humanities Questions and Answers* (the open Q&A forum for all things DH, mentioned above);
- *DH Commons*, for finding project collaborators;
- the annual *Day of Digital Humanities* ethnography project;
- ADHO's informational website;
- and the websites of our constituent organizations, including whatever blogs, news-feeds, or initiatives they might individually host there—such as ACH's 16-year catalog of digital humanities-related sessions at the annual MLA Convention, and our ongoing effort to create a searchable database of all presentations at DH and ACH/ALLC conferences dating back to the 1980s.

This is a big list of publication and communications initiatives, and it is growing all the time.

What's my point? Although we often say that membership is "by subscription to *LLC*," what we really should say is that copies of *LLC* are one of the benefits of your membership in the ADHO associations. That our other publications are overwhelmingly open access does not mean that they are free. Neither are ACH's other services and initiatives—and our colleagues at the other ADHO orgs do similar good work with their slices of the pie. At the risk of sounding like a public radio fund drive, your membership dollars (or pounds or euros) make these things possible.

We must get better at communicating with our members—at bringing in new ideas and clarifying the broad range of activities we undertake. I think ACH has made great strides in the past few years. We've rolled out a new website and newsletter, undertaken a grassroots agenda-setting exercise, redoubled our efforts at mentoring, created *DH Answers*, and become much more active as an advocacy group, lobbying government agencies and offering expert testimony on issues important to our constituents and the future of the humanities. ACH has taken valid and helpful criticism to heart—such as that offered by Melissa Terras in her 2010 DH conference plenary talk, and frequently from our members via social media. I believe our ADHO partners have as well.

I hope this small and rough explanation—of how our membership model works and what we do with members' fees—is a further step in the right direction.

SECTION IV
Voices from the Community

CHAPTER 20

Selected Definitions from the Day of Digital Humanities: 2009–2012

Introduction

In 2003 Willard McCarty asked 'What is Humanities Computing? This, for the humanities, is a question not to be answered but continually to be explored and refined' (p. 1233). Since 2009 the Day of Digital Humanities project has offered the DH community a platform to explore exactly that, en masse and on a yearly basis. The project was conceived as 'a social publication project that began with reflection on what we do as we do it' (Rockwell et al., 2012). In addition to blogging about their day every year participants are invited to answer the question 'What is Digital Humanities?' The wealth of definitions that has been proposed is remarkable both in form and content: they range from the pithy to the bombastic, from the poetical to the enigmatic and from the disruptive to the expositional. In tone a symphony of moods is also conjured, which portray the digital humanities as variously revolutionary, conventional, problematic or even non-existent.

Discussing the nature of the discipline of history Donnchadh Ó Corráin wrote that 'Different authors bring varied interpretations and understandings to the work. No effort has been made to edit out these differences of opinion and interpretation. Historians differ for many genuine reasons, and students must learn that' (Multitext, n.d). In relation to digital humanities we believe this to be equally true. The definitions selected and included below have been chosen to expose the differing and sometimes contradictory views that exist on the nature of DH; we make no attempt to imply that one view is more correct than another, nor do we believe this to be the case. Below you will find definitions that argue that DH is or is not about, among other things, making, tinkering, doing, building, destroying, dreaming, theorising and/or philosophising. In order to do DH some hold the use of computers essential; for others the framework DH might offer to understand the use of computers in the Humanities, and to rethink traditional uses of tools and technologies in general, is what sets it apart. For some DH is about small-scale, bespoke projects such as scholarly editions; for others it is about huge quantities of data and corresponding infrastructures that offer a kind of Humanities that is otherwise impossible. For some emerging technologies such as social media are vital aspects of it; others view it as primarily addressing more traditional objects of study such as text and image. Others believe its essence is not to be found in what it does but in the ways that it does it, for example, in the kinds of interdisciplinary and trans-Institutional collaborations that it is built on and its stance on copyright and sharing of information. Some believe it is the future of the traditional humanities; others argue that it is no different from them or that it will ultimately be absorbed back into them. Some would rather not define digital humanities while others believe that no stable definition is possible.

We follow these selected definitions with Fred Gibbs' blog post 'Digital Humanities Definitions by Type' as he attempts to elucidate the different themes which emerge from the community as individuals define what Digital Humanities means to them. Together, this selection and classification demonstrate the range of thought regarding what Digital Humanities should or can be: and the fact that there is no overall definition which everyone subscribes to.

Bibliography

McCarty, W. (2003). 'Humanities Computing', in *Encyclopedia of Library and Information Science*, New York: Marcel Dekker, p. 1224–35.
Multitext project (n.d.). http://multitext.ucc.ie.
Rockwell, G., Organisciak, P., Meredith-Lobay, M., Ranaweera, K., Ruecker, S. and Nyhan, J. (2012). 'The Design of an International Social Media Event: A Day in the Life of the Digital Humanities', *Digital Humanities Quarterly*, 6 (2).

Day of Digital Humanities Definitions: 2009

I often say that humanities computing involves three distinct research areas. First, some researchers apply computing to research questions in the humanities. These might be questions they've always pursued but can now pursue faster or at a larger scale, or they may be questions that could not be addressed satisfactorily at all without computers. Second, some researchers take computing as an object of study using humanities methods. Examples include cyberculture and posthumanism. Third, some researchers take a generative approach, creating new online materials or tools for subsequent study and use. Most of my own work is in this third area.   Stan Ruecker, University of Alberta, USA

Digital Humanities is a misnomer: there nothing to essentially distinguish it from the disciplines of Arts and Letters as practised for centuries. Just as scientists who utilise grid-computing are not 'digital scientists' but still 'scientists', and fiction authors who publish in hypertext are not 'digital novelists', those working in Arts and Letters who use and generate digital materials and digital tools remain 'humanists'.

Matthew Steven Carlos, Europäische Universität für Interdisziplinäre Studien, Switzerland

Digital humanities attempts to bring humanistic inquiry and the artifacts of human experience into useful dialogue with digital technology. It is, at once, a practical and a philosophical endeavor: a matter of building and of theorizing the built. Practitioners are as likely to be adept at Java as they are post-structuralism; as drawn to the iPhone as they are to Moby Dick; as committed to a kind of optimistic futurism as they are deeply skeptical of a posthuman condition. Digital humanities is also one of most exciting fields in the humanities today, with a burgeoning community of enthusiasts ranging from undergraduate students to senior scholars.

Stephen Ramsay, University of Nebraska-Lincoln, USA

Digital Humanities: the creation and preservation of extensible digital archives to document, and tools to interact with, material culture.

Robert Whalen, Northern Michigan University, USA

The best way I've found to describe what Digital Humanities is, in first place to myself, is using a quote from Thomas Pynchon's Crying of Lot 49: 'You know what a miracle is ... another world's intrusion into this one'.   Federico Meschini, De Montfort University, UK

Day of Digital Humanities Definitions: 2010

Just as man is, according to Nietzsche, 'the animal whose type is not yet determined' ('das noch nicht festgestellte Tier'), digital humanities are those kind of humanities that are as yet undefined. We cannot yet gauge the full impact of digital corpora on the future of scholarly research. We can only speculate what the effects will be of the increasingly digital nature of scholarly publishing. We do not yet grasp the consequences of applying computational methods to 'traditional' disciplines such as History, Literature, and Theatre Studies. My digital humanities are fundamentally a playground for experimentation.

Thomas Crombez, University of Antwerp, Belgium

Modelling and recording traditional humanities data sets in such a way that they can be read by both humans and machines.

Steven Hayes, University of Sydney, Australia

Using digital media to explore, create, analyse and decode meanings in cultural products, current affairs and social life.

Alex Sevigny, McMaster University, Canada

I prefer the term Humanities Computing as I think 'Digital' is reductive to the Computing Science portion of the term. My definition for that term is: Any project which combines computing problems with humanities methods, humanities problems with computing methods, or the creation of new objects of study that are somewhere on that continuum.

Matthew Bouchard, Canada

I think Digital Humanities is a kind of 'fast-acting glue' that allows scholars with different academic backgrounds to collaborate instantly.

Mitsuyuki Inaba, Ritsumeikan University, Japan

For me, 'digital humanities' is 'humanities amid the digital capabilities we have'. Most of my programming and scripting is less about consciously defining new digital paradigms for humanities research and much more about 'eradicating the boring and repetitive research tasks, making my life easier thereby'.   Tara L. Andrews, University of Oxford, UK

I think 'Digital Humanities' is a vague and ambiguous term; in fact, I think it causes a fair amount of confusion both inside and outside of the academy. DH is an umbrella term that, depending on who you are talking to, covers a huge territory: everything from applied text analysis and corpus stylistics to the more esoteric and theoretical realms of video game criticism.   Matthew Jockers, Stanford University, USA

There's no way to divide humanities from its digital basis just as there was no way of separating the humanities from their previous (still alive) analog medium, paper. We live, write, read, learn, work, digitally, and we create, deliver and use every content digitally as well.

Joaquín Rodríguez, EOI (School of Industrial Organization), Spain

Day of Digital Humanities Definitions: 2011

I think digital humanities is an unfortunate neologism, largely because the humanities itself is a problematic term. The biggest problem is that the tent isn't big enough! I have participated in a number of DH events and they are strikingly similar to things like Science Online. With that said, DH is at its best when it embraces the digital not simply as a means to the traditional ends of scholarship, but when it transforms the nature of what humanists do. The digital allows for scholars, librarians, archivists and curators to engage much more directly with each other and the public. Further, it allows them not simply to write for each other, but to build things for everyone.   Trevor Owens, Library of Congress, USA

Digital Humanities: A riddle the humanist has to tackle now if he wants to be a contemporary of his own time. — See also: Computer; Conundrum; Humanités numériques.   Aurélien Berra, Université Paris-Ouest, France

I understand DH as the iterative design and application of digital research and teaching tools to meet the real-world needs of living, breathing humans. This could include students (I'll be working on a pilot digital writing assessment study that day) or cultural stakeholders (I'll also be working on a long-term project involving the design of a digital archive for cultural stakeholders).   Jim Ridolfo, University of Cincinnati, USA

The Digital Humanities is not just technology people and not just traditional humanistic scholars. It should include anyone interested in digital pedagogy and scholarship with a humanistic ethic. They might work under the hood, behind the technological screen or out front on the stage making it possible to collect and analyze the changing relationships of all agents involved in determining the human condition in the 21st century.
                              Dickie Selfe, Ohio State University, USA

[S]omething borrowed, something new...   Brad Brace, Japan

A term of tactical convenience.
                 Matthew Kirschenbaum, University of Maryland, USA

Digital Humanities is the informed and intentional use of digital objects and practices to create and study in the humanities, broadly defined. In that sense, it is a specialization that cuts across disciplinary boundaries to the work of digital humanists in other disciplines. It is also the insistence that the humanities comes to understand the implications of its assumption that only print technologies exist, and it is the insistence that the humanities learns that no technology is invisible, natural, or inevitable, and that someday all humanists will be digital. A few will specialize in print, chirographic or oral-culture humanities.
                 Sharon Cogdill, St. Cloud State University, USA

Humanity (and not just the humanities) mediated through the largest extant body politic. A global vehicle (and personal prosthetic) for containing what it is to be human and humanist—within and without the academy.

Robert Long, University of Oregon, USA

The Digital Humanities are awesome! We're seeing increased cross-pollination between fields like writing and science, literature and computers, history and engineering. Plus, there are so many new interactive tools that allow us to (re)discover ideas in a new way!

Kim Lacey, Wayne State University, USA

I think digital humanities, like social media, is an idea that will increasingly become invisible as new methods and platforms move from being widely used to being ubiquitous. For now, digital humanities defines the overlap between humanities research and digital tools. But the humanities are the study of cultural life, and our cultural life will soon be inextricably bound up with digital media.   Ed Finn, Stanford University, USA

Where the English department surrenders to the Media Arts department under the conditions that they remain in charge of what storytelling means in the 21st century. Hehe. Just kidding. The merging of Literature, Media Arts and other schools of storytelling and criticism into an emergent network that benefits from history but lacks the downside and fixed ideas of entrenched interests be it in the classroom, the boardroom or copyright office. This is an attempt to cast a wider net to include social media and the democratization of media production into the literary cannon complete with thoughtful and insightful analysis and scholarly study and reportage. Literature department walls become osmotic membranes and connecting tissue between liberal arts scholarship in academia, art, technology and social media content producers. DH is a conceptual location where good ideas, best practices and innovation is encouraged. Transdisciplinarity is the new DH norm. DH is a network aggregate university. While individual universities are slow to change, the networked body consisting of DH individuals from many different universities can combine to evolve an educational ecosystem that thrives on change, embraces technology, plurality and open doors, while benefitting from the support of traditional educational organization.

DC Spensley, San Jose State University, USA

I wouldn't dare! I'm interested in how the definition is evolving. I'm more interested in the variety of methods employed in the digital humanities.

And I'm most interested in the results and interpretation of research and scholarship in the digital humanities.

Jon Christensen, Stanford University, Bill Lane Center
for the American West, USA

Day of Digital Humanities Definitions: 2012

Digital Humanities as a whole is something I am extremely reluctant to define, because any definition will inevitably cause controversy. However, I have not heard any dispute over my work being part of digital humanities, and that work involves computationally analyzing data sets from the field of Slavic linguistics, and de-siloing scholarship in that same field through a collaboratively authored academic wiki.   Quinn Dombrowski

Digital Humanities means, to me, more now than it did back in 2009 when I first did the Day of DH. DH offers a set of tools to pose humanistic inquiry, but it doesn't necessarily offer definitive answers to those questions. Instead it celebrates and records a process of intellectual pursuit that is then distributed and disseminated to the Humanities community and abroad. Engaging in Digital Humanities is also an ethos: collaboration, building knowledge, sharing projects, screwing around. I apply this to my scholarship as well as my teaching. If my work is better, more complex, because of Digital Humanities, so too will my students' work benefit from the tools, state of mind, and ethos.   Katherine D. Harris

Digital Humanities are the first step towards Future Humanities.   Davor

For me, digital humanities is thinking through making, as well as writing. More specifically, it's currently about thinking critically about the impact of digitality on scholarly practice in addition to applying digital techniques to the concerns of the humanities.   Mia

Taking people to bits.   Graeme Earl

Humanities.   Martin Holmes

It's what 'we' do.   Simon Mahony

Cross-disciplinary projects coined by a new generation of humanists as model users, who are asking and creating novel applications and solutions from and with more geeky and technical disciplines, with excellent innovative outcomes, connecting contemporary and fashionable technology with scientific research.

Mona Hess

DH is what critical theory is or was—an opportunity to ask new questions, try new methods, engage in new conversations.

ssenier

Not sure!

Lorna Richardson

What sets Digital Humanities apart, for me, is its genuine interdisciplinarity, its permanent emergence, and its open communication.   Christof Schöch

I'm a committed DH Big Tenter, and believe (at least at this point in our history) that we can find room in the field for almost anyone who self-identifies as a DHer. That said, for me personally, DH is either 1) any digital approach to humanistic objects, or, 2) any humanistic approach to digital objects.

Glen Worthey

The great opportunity to burn down academic walls.   Enrica Salvatori

I don't! I just do it.

Nick Mirzoeff

It's beyond interdisciplinary—it's a new ecosystem that includes scholars, librarians, archivists, computer scientists, graphic designers, administrators, students, teachers, granting agencies (public and private), and anyone else interested in promoting humanistic ways of experiencing digital media (or digital ways of experiencing the humanities).

Edward Whitley

I define Digital Humanities as the re-figuring of computing, a historically positivist field, in order to pose and answer the more speculative questions typical of the humanities. Of late I have been considering the difference between Digital Humanities (which seems to centre on humanities inquiry) and humanities computing (which focuses on the intersection of humanities with computer as a material object).

Constance Crompton

Qualitative queries, quantified.

Michael Ullyot

Digital Humanities is more than a methodology.

James O'Sullivan

1. n. a field of study, research and teaching focused on the intersection of computing and disciplines in the humanities. It involves the investigation, analysis, synthesis and presentation of information in electronic form. 2. v. thinking in multimodal ways, not necessarily involving digital or

electronic technologies. 3. adj. increasing access changes representation; a description of an intensity of reading as in 'a DH reading'.   Craig Saper

While I endorse all the work done under the rubric of Digital Humanities, I am actually not a fan of the term. I feel that the term is used to define a political move within academia that is focused on the privileging of certain technologies and technological approaches over the greater epistemological questions that define the humanities and its constituent disciplines. As someone who has to work with people who may be wary of digital technology in their teaching, research, and publishing practice, I find that insinuating that 'digital humanities' is in some way essentially different from general humanities alienates the unfamiliar and more deeply entrenches the already conservative. I believe that an approach that considers the incorporation of these technologies as part of a continuum in the ongoing impact of technology on academic work that predates the digital and not as a political paradigmatic shift better reminds us that scholarship is centrally focused on the answering of questions about the unknown with whatever tools are at our disposal. The digital shouldn't really matter in the name and we should think about incorporating this approach to scholarship across all work and not a subset of research. The work is good and important, the term I find more problematic and rarely if ever use to define my work or the work we do at my institution.

Kimon Keramidas

CHAPTER 21

Digital Humanities Definitions by Type

Fred Gibbs
George Mason University

This post was originally published at http://fredgibbs.net/digital-humanities-definitions-by-type/

If there are two things that academia doesn't need, they are another book about Darwin and another blog post about defining the digital humanities. But it's always right around this time of year that I find myself preparing for my digital history course and being pulled down the contemplative rabbit hole about how to describe the nature of the digital humanities to a new and varied audience. But rather than create my own definition, I wanted one cobbled together from everyone else.

There have been some very good digital humanities definition pieces recently (those by Rafael Alvarado[1] and Matt Kirschenbaum[2] spring to mind). But many of the longer ones, as smart and provocative as they are, often muddy the introductory waters more than clarify them. Sometimes that's precisely their point, but I'm always on the lookout for a reductionist, well-precipitated overview mixture for my class (and for myself, when I get confused) that can be progressively dissolved into a more homogenous solution. I wanted a list of acceptable DH definitions that was as simple as possible—but no simpler—from the community itself. Even better, I wanted a shortlist of *types of definitions* that sketch out the contours of the field.

For this kind of exercise, there's no better resource than the TAPoR wiki on "How do you Define Humanities Computing/Digital Humanities?"[3] (which presents pithy definitions from ~170 people, who for one reason or another were compelled (thankfully) to offer their own take on the nature of digital humanities or humanities computing. The format surely encouraged sound bites rather than nuanced formulations, but the quick

---

[1] http://transducer.ontoligent.com/?p=717.

[2] http://mkirschenbaum.files.wordpress.com/2011/03/ade-final.pdf.

[3] http://tapor.ualberta.ca/taporwiki/index.php/How_do_you_define_Humanities_Computing_/_Digital_Humanities%3F.

take still reveals the sentiment of the community—perhaps better than longer essays would have. What follows is my categorization of the responses from 2011. I raced through these at the end of #clioF11(tues)'s first meeting, so I post them here mostly as a reference for my whiplashed students. But I'd love to know if anyone else finds it useful.

At first glance, it appeared that the fascinating but disparate variety of responses more closely resembled an unruly pile of pick-up sticks than any useful guide to the DH community. After a bit more perusing, however, I found that the definitions could be cleanly sorted into a relatively small number of categories. Needless to say, my scheme is neither the only possible grouping, nor necessarily the best. But I found mutually exclusive sorting to be simple and easy, perhaps an indicator that I wasn't being too arbitrary or forceful. Surprisingly few definitions landed on the boundaries between categories. In those cases I filed them under what I took to be the predominant sentiment. A handful of responses that did not seem to really say anything (besides explicit refusals to offer a definition) were left uncategorized (my working label was "what?").

Due to a few tricky category decisions, categorical gray areas (though I tried to minimize possible overlap), and arithmetic failure, the numbers themselves are meaningless as precise counts. But I think that they are rather suggestive and illustrative as to how the wiki contributors see the field. What's most interesting is how the relatively few categories themselves grew organically from the responses—with what I consider very little invention on my part.

The Categories (and some observations)

55 – variation on "the application of technology to humanities work"
22 – working with digital media or a digital environment
15 – minimize the difference between DH and humanities
12 – umbrella or blanket nature of DH label; issues that humanists now face
12 – using digital AND studying digital
12 – refusals to define the term
10 – method AND community
9 – digitization/archives
9 – studying the digital

The most popular response—the application of technology to humanities work—was unsurprising to say the least. It is perhaps worth noting that phrases like "application of technology to humanities work" were about three times as common as those like "intersection of technology and the humanities". Either way, I still can't shake off a vague unease about defining

DH in such broad technology terms (the umbrella responses described below focused less on technology per se), and I think it raises important questions about the nature of how much technology (given its pervasive nature) needs to explicitly figure into the digital humanities. As other respondents hinted: isn't everyone using technology in the humanities these days? And increasingly so? Perhaps it's *innovative* use that's important (as Doug Reside suggests), but isn't innovation always required in scholarly pursuits? Or maybe we just need to be technologically innovative with regard to the analog humanities? But does a technology emphasis detract from the humanistic value of our work, and shift the focus to research methodologies rather than results?

Reluctance to foreground research (dare I say computing?) over communication and workflows perhaps led some respondents to emphasize the use of digital media, or publishing and collaborating in new media environments. Though responses took the nature of "the digital" as crucial to DH, ranging widely across the spheres of publishing and networking within humanistic scholarship. Obviously there is a fine (if extant) line between using new media and using technology. But I think the responses—in both spirit and language—warrant separate categories between using technology and using digital media, even if that difference can be considered one of emphasis rather than of kind.

The next cluster of four categories, most explicitly the (usually glib) refusals, foreground the difficulty in crafting any kind of definition. Others responded more thoroughly, and more helpfully, but refused to differentiate digital humanities from the humanities at large. This is a valid point, but to hold this position is to suggest that DHers don't have any different kind of concerns (methodological, theoretical, practical, professional) than anyone else in the humanities. This doesn't seem to be true right now. Truer to the status quo, in my opinion, were the several responses in that same category that emphasized the (ideally) fleeting nature of any difference between the digital humanities and the humanities—that is, digital humanities as the future of the humanities; different in some ways now, but not fundamentally so. Or, perhaps digital humanities is simply akin to new media in that its core characteristics ride the wave of technological change.

The responses I have labeled as umbrella- or blanket-like, I think are some of the most helpful because they pursued a discriminatory inclusivity—a middle ground between open arms and gate-keeping—that embraced the variety of issues that digital humanists like to talk about (in addition to new research methods and digital media of the other categories) like copyright, access to information, curation and use of digital resources, publishing, and so on, without making it inordinately difficult to think of something that *wasn't* included under the DH tent.

A solid group of responses must be located at the intersection of using the digital and studying the digital. In a way, this group overlaps with the "applying technology" group, but are singled out here for the insistence that studying the effects of the digital is just as important as using it. These two efforts might well be two shows under the same DH tent with different performers and audiences. Whether this is mutually beneficial or distracting remains an open question, I think.

Not surprisingly, community and methodology tended to get mentioned together; I wouldn't characterize any definition as pointing to one without the other. But it isn't just methods that make the community, either: respondents rightly and broadly construed "methods" as ranging over various aspects of research, teaching, and broader communication, all the while embracing the variety of methodological approaches that their colleagues take. To me, this suggests that the community has some autonomous existence outside of methodological similarities.

Responses that foregrounded digitization or studying the digital (without consideration for the effect on humanities scholarship itself) thankfully received the fewest nods. At least as formulated on the wiki, these definitions were the most restrictive, and in many ways fundamentally contrary to the general sentiment of the community about what kinds of efforts really characterize the digital humanities. This is not to say that digitization efforts and the corresponding challenges are not to be included as part of the digital humanities (they are!), but that a useful definition must be more inclusive.

Some Representative (usually short) Examples of the Categories

Some variation of "the application of technology to the humanities"

The intersection of humanities and computer technologies. (Lorna Richardson, UCL, UK)

Digital humanities is the intersection of work in the humanities (research, teaching, writing) with technology (tools, networks, interactions), when the practitioner is consciously exploring a humanistic subject and a technological method, at the same time. (Elli Mylonas, Brown University, USA)

Digital Humanities are the application and the use of computing technologies for the research, teaching and investigation in the disciplines of the humanities. (Ali Albarran, Universidad Nacional Autónoma de México, Mexico)

Five responses included in the above category emphasized computing
Using computational tools to do the work of the humanities. (John Unsworth, University of Illinois, USA)

The theorizing, developing and application of/on computational techniques to humanities subjects. (Edward Vanhoutte, Centre for Scholarly Editing and Document Studies/Royal Academy of Dutch Language and Literature, Belgium)

Use of digital media/medium/environment

Anything a Humanities scholar does that is mediated digitally, especially when such mediation opens discussion beyond a small circle of academic specialists. (David Wacks, University of Oregon, USA)

The performance of humanities related activities in, through and with digital media. (Christopher Long, Penn State University, USA)

For me, but this is very specific, Digital Humanities is to interconnect humanities researchers, software developers and infrastructure providers in order to contribute to the research and the research possibilities in this discipline. (Douwe Zeldenrust, Meertens Institute (Royal Netherlands Academy of Arts and Sciences), The Netherlands)

Emphasis on its umbrella or blanket nature

I think of digital humanities as an umbrella term that covers a wide variety of digital work in the humanities: development of multimedia pedagogies and scholarship, designing & building tools, human computer interaction, designing & building archives, etc. DH is interdisciplinary; by necessity it breaks down boundaries between disciplines at the local (e.g., English and history) and global (e.g., humanities and computer sciences) levels. (Kathie Gossett, Old Dominion Univ, USA)

We use "digital humanities" as an umbrella term for a number of different activities that surround technology and humanities scholarship. Under the digital humanities rubric, I would include topics like open access to materials, intellectual property rights, tool development, digital libraries, data mining, born-digital preservation, multimedia publication, visualization, GIS, digital reconstruction, study of the impact of technology on numerous fields, technology for teaching and learning, sustainability models, and many others. (Brett Bobley, NEH, USA)

Refusals

With extreme reluctance. (Lou Burnard, UK)

I hate this question, and I don't have an answer for it. Neither, it seems, does a large portion of the people who might be called Digital Humanists. I'll leave it at that. (Justin Tonra, University of Virginia, USA)

Studying the digital

An area of study that focuses on the digital in our daily lives—how we study, think, and interact. (Pollyanna Macchiano, USA)

Digital Humanities is the acknowledgement that human creativity is, for the moment, deeply entangled with our technological tools and networks. The media extensions cannot be separated from our reality. (Anastasia Salter, University of Baltimore, USA)

Explicitly using digital AND studying digital

I am currently using a short definition, which is that Digital Humanities is a combination of using computer technologies to study human cultures and studying the effect of computer technologies on human cultures. (Scott Kleinman, California State University, Northridge, USA)

I see 'Digital Humanities' as an umbrella term for two different but related developments: 1) Humanities Computing (the specialist use of computing technology to undertake Humanities research) and 2) the implications for the Humanities of the social revolution created by ubiquitous computing and online access. Since the late noughties the latter seems to have become the driving force in DH with responsibility for much of the 'boom' in public interest and funding. (Leif Isaksen, University of Southampton, UK)

Method AND Community

It is both a methodology and a community. (Jason Farman, University of Maryland, College Park, USA)

Somewhere between a toolset and a mindset, to do DH is to confront the assumptions and implications of the long analog history of the word. (Matthew Fisher, UCLA, USA)

The digital humanities is a name claimed by a community of those interested in digital methodologies and/or content in the humanities. (Rebecca Davis, National Institute for Technology in Liberal Education, USA)

Minimal difference between DH and humanities

We don't distinguish digital sociology or digital astronomy, so why digital humanities? Just because computers are involved doesn't mean the basic nature of the subject area is any different than it has been traditionally. (Philip R. "Pib" Burns, Northwestern University, USA)

Digital Humanities is, increasingly, just Humanities—as far as I'm concerned. New tools lead to new methodologies, new perspectives, and new questions that all humanists should be aware of and concerned with. (Benjamin Albritton, Stanford University, USA)

Humanities gone digital and vice versa. (Anna Caprarelli, università degli studi della Tuscia (Viterbo), Italy)

Five included in the above category emphasized the fleeting nature of any present difference

A name that marks a moment of transition; the current name for humanities inquiry driven by or dependent on computers or digitally born objects of study; a temporary epithet for what will eventually be called merely Humanities. (Mark/Marino, University of Southern California, USA)

Digital Humanities is what humanities will be in the future. It is public, dialogical, collaborative and made of collectives. It allows for remixing and re-imagining how we think and analyze traditional forms of knowledge creation, knowledge sharing and knowledge storage. (Jade E. Davis, University of North Carolina at Chapel Hill, USA)

Focus on digitization and archives

Digital libraries are a great example of an outcome of Digital Humanities. The interaction and combination of the new digital era with history, librarianship, literature, etc. gives a wider frame for researchers of all different branches to work in. Now the full texts of important writers are just a click away! (Ines Jerele, National and University Library, Slovenia, Slovenia)

Developing tools and workflows to create comprehensive, interoperable, and innovative digital resources. (Jennifer Stertzer, Papers of George Washington, University of Virginia, USA)

So What?

The categories here are hardly surprising. More interesting, to me at least, was that one needs only a handful of categories to cleanly parse so many formulations; and these categories deliberately highlighted rather subtle differences in definitions.

Even if attempts at constructing (and reading) definitions grow tired, periodically taking the pulse of the DH community seems worthwhile in that it reflects both recent and future developments in how the field is being shaped by those who consider themselves its practitioners. Scholarly legitimacy, for which DH work seems to be continually reaching, requires some disciplinary boundaries, at least for now. Without it, people who will make important judgments and decisions about our scholarship, funding, and jobs cannot properly evaluate our proposed or completed work (hence Matt Kirschenbaum's apt definition of DH as a "term of tactical convenience"). Feeling out boundaries is not always fun. I admit that I vacillate between wanting to draw some disciplinary lines in the sand, to pee on some research hydrants, and to simply throw up my hands in the face of an utterly pointless and futile debate.

The relatively few categories suggest some important questions: Are all of the definitions and their crucial qualities (community, communication, methodology, digitization, etc.) worth equal emphasis? Are some more representative of "the field" as it is or as it should be? Perhaps the DH label has gotten enough traction within the broader community that the more pressing question is: what should NOT be included within the big tent of the digital humanities? That's the subject for a different essay, of course.

Although I haven't attempted a comparison to 2010, my sense from the definitions (especially with the many references to digital media and studying the digital) was that the field seems to be sending out tendrils in all directions, and in particular moving away from its original Humanities Computing roots. I couldn't make a cruder measure, but I found it interesting that "computing" appears about 30 times among 170 total responses in 2011, and about 40 times among 70 total responses in 2010.

In the End

I must tip my cap to Eric Forcier, whose reply adroitly eschews disciplinary rigor in favor of admirably capturing the spirit of the DH community—especially in painting DH as an ephemeral, seemingly idiosyncratic curiosity that either attracts or repels people, and often changes them fundamentally:

When I first applied to this grad program, my understanding of what DH was all about was crystalline in its purity. Not so today. My idea of DH is that it's sort of like a highway oil slick on a sunny day. When you look at the slick, depending on the angle, you might get a psychedelic kaleidoscope of reflected colours; if you're lucky you might spot your reflection in it; then again, all you might see is darkness. And if you feel compelled to step in it, don't be surprised if you slip. Those stains will not come out. (Eric Forcier, University of Alberta, Canada)

SECTION V
Further Materials

CHAPTER 22

Selected Further Reading

Note from the Editors:
A range of other material not chosen for this volume has been published regarding Digital Humanities: here we present a select list of reading matter which is useful when considering the breadth and scope of the field, including journal papers, articles, blog posts and manifestos. This list will be regularly updated with a range of other materials at http://blogs.ucl.ac.uk/defningdh.

Books

Bartscherer, T. and Coover, R. (eds) (2011). *Switching Codes: Thinking Through New Technology in the Humanities and the Arts*, Chicago: University of Chicago Press.
Berry, D.M. (ed.) (2012). *Understanding Digital Humanities*, Basingstoke: Palgrave Macmillan.
Cameron, F. and Kenderdine, S. (2007). *Theorizing Digital Cultural Heritage: A Critical Discourse*, Cambridge MA: MIT Press.
Cohen, D.J. and Rosenzweig, R. (2005). *Digital History: A guide to gathering, preserving and presenting the past on the web*, Philadelphia: University of Pennsylvania. Available online at http://chnm.gmu.edu/digitalhistory.
Deegan, M. and McCarty, W. (eds) (2012). *Collaborative Research in the Digital Humanities*, London: Ashgate.
Hockey, S. (2000). *Electronic Texts in the Humanities: Principles and Practice*, Oxford: Oxford University Press.
Gold, M.K. (ed.) (2012). *Debates in the Digital Humanities*, Minneapolis: University of Minnesota Press.
Greengrass, M. and Hughes, L. (2008). *The Virtual Representation of the Past*, London: Ashgate.
Hayles, N.K. (2012). *How We Think: Digital Media and Contemporary Technogenesis*, Chicago: University of Chicago Press.
McCarty, W. (2005). *Humanities Computing*, Basingstoke and New York: Palgrave Macmillan.
McCarty, W. (2010). *Text and Genre in Reconstruction: Effects of digitalization on ideas, behaviours, products and institutions*, Cambridge: OpenBook Publishers, http://www.openbookpublishers.com/reader/64.

Schnapp, J., Drucker, J., Burdick, A. and Lunenfeld, P. (2012). *Digital_ Humanities*, Cambridge MA: MIT Press. Available from http://lab. softwarestudies.com/2012/11/digitalhumanities-book-is-out.html.

Schreibman, S. and Siemens, R. (eds) (2008). *A Companion to Digital Literary Studies*, Blackwell Companions to Literature and Culture. Available online at http://www.digitalhumanities.org/companionDLS.

Schreibman, S., Siemens, R. and Unsworth, J. (eds) (2007). *A Companion to Digital Humanities*, Blackwell Companions to Literature and Culture. Available online at http://www.digitalhumanities.org/companion.

Ramsay, S. (2012). *Reading Machines: Toward an Algorithmic Criticism*, Chicago: University of Illinois Press.

Vandendorpe, C. (2009). *From Papyrus to Hypertext: Toward the Universal Digital Library*, 1st ed., Chicago: University of Illinois Press.

Warwick, C., Terras, M. and Nyhan, J. (eds) (2012). *Digital Humanities in Practice*, London: Facet.

Journals and Academic Papers

Borgman, C. (2009). 'The Digital Future is Now: A Call to Action for the Humanities', *DHQ*, 3 (4), http://www.digitalhumanities.org/dhq/vol/3/4/000077/000077.html.

de Smedt, K. (2002). 'Some Reflections on Studies in Humanities Computing', *Literary and Linguistic Computing*, 17 (1), pp. 89–101.

Hockey, S. (2004). 'The History of Humanities Computing,' in S. Schreibman et al. (eds.), *A Companion to Digital Humanities*, pp. 3–19.

Liu, A. (2009). 'Digital Humanities and Academic Change', *English Language Notes*, 47 (1), pp. 17–35.

Liu, A. (2011). 'Where is Cultural Criticism in the Digital Humanities?' Original full text of paper presented at the panel on 'The History and Future of the Digital Humanities', Modern Language Association convention, Los Angeles, 7 January, http://liu.english.ucsb.edu/where-is-cultural-criticism-in-the-digital-humanities.

McCarty, W. (1998). 'What is Humanities Computing? Towards a Definition of the Field', http://staff.cch.kcl.ac.uk/~wmccarty/essays/McCarty,%20What%20is%20humanities%20computing.pdf.

McCarty, W. (1999). 'Humanities Computing as Interdiscipline', a seminar in the series 'Is Humanities Computing an Academic Discipline?', IATH, University of Virginia, http://www.iath.virginia.edu/hcs/mccarty.html.

McCarty, W. (2002). 'Humanities Computing: Essential Problems, Experimental Practice', *Literary and Linguistic Computing*, 17 (1), pp. 103–125.

McGann, J. (2005). 'Culture and Technology: The way we live now, what is to be done?', *Interdisciplinary Science Reviews*, 30 (2), pp. 179–188.

Orlandi, T. (2002). 'Is Humanities Computing a Discipline?' in G. Braungart, K. Eibl and F. Jannidis (eds), *Jahrbuch für Computerphilologie*, 4, Paderborn: Mentis Verlag, pp. 51–8.

Short, H. (2006). 'The Role of Humanities Computing: Experiences and Challenges', *Literary and Linguistic Computing*, 21 (1), pp. 15–27.

Smith, M.N. (2005). 'Democratizing Knowledge', *Humanities*, September/October, 26 (5).

Svensson, P. (2010). 'The Landscape of Digital Humanities', *DHQ*, 4 (1), http://digitalhumanities.org/dhq/vol/4/1/000080/000080.html.

Svensson, P. (2011). 'From Optical Fiber To Conceptual Cyberinfrastructure', *DHQ*, 5 (1), http://digitalhumanities.org/dhq/vol/5/1/000090/000090.html.

Svensson, P. (2012). 'Envisioning the Digital Humanities', *DHQ*, 6 (1), http://digitalhumanities.org/dhq/vol/6/1/000112/000112.html.

Unsworth, J. (1997). 'Documenting the Reinvention of Text. The Importance of Failure', *Journal of Electronic Publishing*, 3 (2).

Unsworth, J. (2000). 'Scholarly Primitives: What methods do humanities researchers have in common, and how might our tools reflect this?' Part of a symposium on 'Humanities Computing: Formal methods, experimental practice', sponsored by King's College, London, 13 May, http://www.iath.virginia.edu/~jmu2m/Kings.5-00/primitives.html.

Blog Posts and Online Material

Alvarado, R. (2011). 'The Digital Humanities Situation', *The Transducer*, 11 May, http://transducer.ontoligent.com/?p=717.

Bogost, I. (2011). 'Beyond the Elbow-Patched Playground, Part 1: The Humanities in Public,' Ian Bogost – videogame theory, criticism, design, 23 August, http://www.bogost.com/blog/beyond_the_elbow-patched_playg.shtml.

Bogost, I. (2011). 'Beyond the Elbow-Patched Playground, Part 2: The Digital Humanities', Ian Bogost – videogame theory, criticism, design, 25 August, http://www.bogost.com/blog/beyond_the_elbow-patched_playg_1.shtml.

Cohen, P. (2010). 'Humanities 2.0 Series', *New York Times*, http://topics.nytimes.com/top/features/books/series/humanities_20/index.html.

Fitzpatrick, K. (2011). 'The Humanities, Done Digitally', *Chronicle of Higher Education*, 8 May, http://chronicle.com/article/The-Humanities-Done-Digitally/127382.

Mattern, S. (2010). 'Trying to Wrap My Head Around Digital Humanities', Words in Space blog, http://www.wordsinspace.net/wordpress/2010/06/23/trying-to-wrap-my-head-around-the-digital-humanities-part-i.

Owens, T. (2010). 'The Digital Humanities as the DIY Humanities', http://www.trevorowens.org/2011/07/the-digital-humanities-as-the-diy-humanities.

Pannapacker, W. (2009). 'The MLA and the Digital Humanities', *Chronicle of Higher Education*, Brainstorm Blog, 28 December, http://chronicle.com/blogPost/The-MLAthe-Digital/19468.

Pannapacker, W. (2011). '"Big Tent Digital Humanities", A View from the Edge, Part 1', *Chronicle of Higher Education*, 31 July, http://chronicle.com/article/Big-Tent-Digital-Humanities/128434.

Pannapacker, W. (2011) '"Big Tent Digital Humanities," A View from the Edge, Part 2', http://chronicle.com/article/Big-Tent-Digital-Humanities-a/129036.

Scheinfeldt, T. (2010). 'Where's the Beef? Does Digital Humanities Have to Answer Questions?', http://www.foundhistory.org/2010/05/12/wheres-the-beef-does-digital-humanities-have-to-answer-questions.

Scheinfeldt, T. (2010). 'Why Digital Humanities is "Nice"', http://www.foundhistory.org/2010/05/26/why-digital-humanities-is-%E2%80%9Cnice%E2%80%9D.

Smith, K. (2009). Q&A with Brett Bobley, Director of the NEH's Office of Digital Humanities (ODH), HASTAC, http://hastac.org/node/1934.

Sullivan, J. (2012). 'What makes Digital Humanities Digital?', http://publish.ucc.ie/boolean/2012/00/OSullivan/19/en.

Turkel, W.J. (2008). 'A Few Arguments for Humanistic Fabrication', *Digital History Hacks: Methodology for the Infinite Archive* (2005–08), 21 November, http://digitalhistoryhacks.blogspot.co.uk/2008/11/few-arguments-for-humanistic.html.

Manifestos

Bloomsburg University Students (2010). 'Bloomsburg U. Undergraduate "Manifesto" on Digital Humanities', http://humanistica.ualberta.ca/bloomsburg-u-undergraduate-manifesto-on-digital-humanities.

Davidson, C.N. and Goldberg, D.T. (2004). 'A Manifesto for the Humanities in a Technological Age', http://chronicle.com/article/A-Manifesto-for-the-Humanities/17844.

Presner, T. (UCLA) and Schnapp, J. (2009). 'Digital Humanities Manifesto', http://www.humanitiesblast.com/manifesto/Manifesto_V2.pdf.

CHAPTER 23

Questions for Discussion

We present here a range of questions which can be used to begin a class discussion on the issues raised when trying to define Digital Humanities (DH).

1. Having read these works defining Digital Humanities, how would *you* define DH?
2. What is Digital Humanities and what is not?
3. How old is DH? Is there a difference between Humanities Computing and Digital Humanities?
4. How effective is the name Digital Humanities? Would you change it if you could?
5. What are the hallmarks of Digital Humanities research? What kinds of topics and sources does DH address?
6. Which skills and knowledge must a DHer have? Which are useful but not essential?
7. Digital Humanities opens new possibilities for the Humanities: discuss using examples.
8. Is Digital Humanities revolutionary?
9. Is Digital Humanities traditional?
10. Can Digital Humanities help us to see the old in the new as much as the new in the old?
11. A computer is just a tool: discuss.
12. Why is collaboration so important in Digital Humanities projects?
13. What is interdisciplinarity? Has this term become a hollow buzzword?
14. Do we expect digital projects to be of a higher standard than more traditional humanities projects such as books?
15. What is your favourite Digital Humanities tool or resource? Why?
16. Describe the Digital Humanities research question that interests you most.
17. When everyone uses digital techniques in research, will Digital Humanities become obsolete?
18. What relationship do the learned societies – such as the Alliance of Digital Humanities Organisations – have to the definition of the discipline? Is this important?
19. Why does Defining Digital Humanities matter?
20. Do other disciplines worry about defining themselves in the way that Digital Humanities does?

Index